Bruce W. Longenecker (Ph.D.
University of Durham) is a lecturer of New
Testament Studies at St. Mary's College,
University of St. Andrews, Scotland. He
is the author or editor of eight books
including *The Lost Letters of Pergamum*
(2003), *Luke, Paul and the Graeco-Roman
World* (2002), *Narrative Dynamics in Paul*
(2002), *The Triumph of Abraham's God*
(1998), *2 Esdras* (1995), and *Eschatology
and the Covenant* (1991).

BAYLOR UNIVERSITY PRESS
Waco, Texas

Rhetoric at the Boundaries

Rhetoric at the Boundaries

The Art and Theology of the New Testament Chain-Link Transitions

BRUCE W. LONGENECKER

Baylor University Press
Waco, Texas USA

Cover Design: Joan Osth

Library of Congress Cataloging-in-Publication Data

Longenecker, Bruce W.
  Rhetoric at the boundaries : the art and theology of New Testament chain-link
transitions / Bruce W. Longenecker.
    p. cm.
  Includes bibliographical references and index.
  ISBN 1-932792-24-4 (hardcover : alk. paper)
  1. Bible. N.T.--Criticism, interpretation, etc. I. Title.

BS2341.52.L66 2005
225.6'6--dc22
                              2005012758

Printed in the United States of America on acid-free paper

For Fiona

Contents

Preface

The roots of this research project go back to the early 1990s when I first started teaching in Durham England. While preparing for a course on John, I came across a few sentences about chain-link construction in John 12 in Charles Talbert's book *Reading John* (London: SPCK, 1992, pp. 179–80). The construction was intriguing and I lodged it in the back of my mind as something to consider further in relation to other passages of the New Testament. In the mid-1990s while teaching at Cambridge, I first started putting ideas down on paper. But it wasn't until a one-year research period was afforded to me in 2002–2003 by the Alexander von Humboldt Stiftung in Germany that I was able to explore the subject to the extent that it deserves, and to that renowned institution I express my thanks for its generosity.

During my time in Germany, Professors Martin Hengel and Herman Lichtenberger of Tübingen expressed keen interest in my research. At that same time, Dr. David Hester contributed significantly to the development of my ideas in his weekly examinations of my progress over coffee in some of Tübingen's quaint cafés, while Chrissy Hester managed their family. The research was aided by discussions with friends passing through Tübingen: Dr. Rick Beaton, Dr. Markus Bockmuehl, Dr. Mark Elliott, Dr. Darrell Hannah, Dr. David Horrell, Dr. David Kupp, Dr. John Proctor, Dr. Dan Wallace. To these scholars and friends I am deeply appreciative of their interaction and encouragement.

Upon returning to my academic post with the University of St. Andrews, I benefited greatly from bi-weekly discussions of the project with St. Andrews Ph.D. candidates who committed themselves to reading the text chapter by chapter and commenting on it: Gary Colledge, Kate Donahoe, Mark Gignilliat, Mickey Klink, Darian Lockett, Al

Lukaszewski, Matt Marohl, and Carl Mosser. Seeing how the text was being read by early readers has helped me to improve it for later readers. And Dr. Nathan MacDonald, a former student who is now a colleague, has on two occasions pointed me to Old Testament data that I would not otherwise have known and that supports my thesis. So my thanks obviously go to all of these colleagues for their efforts and insights.

Along the way, chapters of this book were presented at a variety of seminars and conferences: the New Testament Seminar of the University of Cambridge, the Institut zur Erforschung des Urchristentums at the University of Tübingen, the Greco-Roman World of the New Testament seminar of Studiorum Novi Testamenti Societas (SNTS), and the British New Testament Conference. Engagement with colleagues in these contexts has considerably spurred me on to consider issues in new depth and dimension, so I am much in their debt.

My appreciation must also be extended to the anonymous readers of the manuscript for Baylor University Press, whose suggestions have improved the finished product. And the same is true for the executive editor of Baylor University Press, Dr. Carey C. Newman, whose understanding of the worlds of academia and publishing is simply second to none. My appreciation also goes to Diane Smith of Baylor University Press, whose oversight of this book's production was impeccable, and to Kate Donahoe and Mickey Klink who kindly prepared the indexes.

I would be remiss not to salute the members of my growing little family: Callum, our thriving son, full of fun and mischief, whose attention to detail (at least when it comes to having fun or listening to music) is an object lesson to this aspiring academic; to Torrin, a gift of new life, being just three days old as I write this (12 April 2004); and especially to my wife Fiona, whose energy and support simply know no bounds. This book is dedicated to her, as a tribute to our continuing friendship and love.

CHAPTER I

Introduction

§1.1   Tracing the Explanation of a New Testament Issue

A plethora of structural patterns can be observed within New Testament texts. One of those patterns has consistently baffled New Testament interpreters. This itself is somewhat curious since the pattern (1) appears in a number of New Testament books and (2) usually occurs more than once in any given book. These two simple observations might well have caused interpreters to consider whether in fact the pattern would have been easily recognisable to those who wrote and first heard these texts. For the most part, however, interpreters have failed to pursue issues of this sort.

Curiosity on this score increases in view of two terse but suggestive references to this structural pattern in the works of Graeco-Roman

1

rhetoricians, who commended the pattern to those interested in effective presentation of their ideas. Curiosity mounts even further in view of claims by interpreters of the Old Testament that the same pattern appears in the Hebrew Scriptures with some frequency, suggesting that the pattern had currency much earlier than the Graeco-Roman world of the New Testament. In fact, the pattern seems to be rooted in the oral patterning of the ancient world in general, rather than simply being a phenomenon of the Graeco-Roman world in particular.

Data of this kind have consistently been overlooked by New Testament interpreters. When New Testament passages animated by this particular structural pattern are revisited against this backdrop, they are not to be seen as involving problematical structural anomalies. Instead they are shown to be important structural landmarks, full of interpretative potential that has remained untapped and unexplored thus far in the guild of New Testament scholarship.

This, in a nutshell, comprises the interests of the study that follows. The particular structure that will be the focus of attention is a transitional feature, outlined briefly in §1.3 below. Initially, however, it is appropriate to highlight more generally the structural significance of transitions in relation to the interpretation of texts.

§1.2   Transitions as Key Rhetorical Components

With the recent proliferation of methodological disciplines in biblical study, the examination of structural relationships in biblical texts has proved to be an important enterprise within various interpretative approaches. According to some practitioners of discourse analysis[1] and rhetorical analysis,[2] for instance, the discovery of textual structure aids interpretation by outlining textual cohesion and persuasive development, or by revealing a text's artistic and aesthetic qualities. Repeatedly, structural analyses have brought home the crucial interplay between the formal features of a text and the interpretation of its content.

In this regard, one of the most important structural features is the transition marker. A well-constructed transition oils the machinery of rhetorical persuasion, indicating that a new line of thought is beginning

[1] E.g., L. P. Louw, "Discourse Analysis and the Greek New Testament," *Bible Translator* 24 (1973): 108–18; E. A. Nida, *Componential Analysis of Meaning* (The Hague: Mouton, 1975); P. Cotterell and M. Turner, *Linguistics and Biblical Interpretation* (London: SPCK, 1989), 230–56.

[2] E.g., J. Dewey, *Markan Public Debate: Literary Technique, Concentric Structure, and Theology in Mark 2:1–3:6* (Chico: Scholars Press, 1980); D. A. Black, "The Pauline Love Command: Structure, Style, and Ethics in Romans 12:9–21," *Filologia Neotestamentaria* 1 (1989): 3–21.

and occasionally giving some indication as to the content of the new topic and how it relates to what has gone previously. Transitional units often play a critical role in the process of interpreting a text. For instance, in his work on the structure of Hebrews, George Guthrie notes: "One of the most neglected topics in discussions on the structure of Hebrews is the author's use of various transition techniques."[3] In an accompanying footnote Guthrie adds: "This neglect, perhaps more than any other factor, accounts for the tremendous diversity in current outlines of Hebrews." In Guthrie's view, then, undervaluing the import of textual transitions has the potential of skewing one's broader understanding of a text's flow. This coheres with George Kennedy's first rule of thumb when interpreting the New Testament through rhetorical criticism: the first step in textual analysis is the determination of rhetorical units, which are marked out as such within the text.[4] Transitions at text-unit boundaries play a role in identifying precisely those rhetorical units.

Where text units meet, one can expect to find a transition from one to the other. This, at least, is the case for the most literary of texts, and it is usually the case for those that would aspire to be among that number.[5] As Philip Tite notes, "[t]he transitional elements of a document are ... elements of ancient rhetoric. That is, rhetoric, as a form of persuasive argumentation, seriously took the transitional flow of the discourse into consideration."[6]

The rhetoricians' marked interest in transitions should not be surprising. In helping to demarcate different rhetorical units within an orator's speech or the different text units within a literary work, transitions play a fundamental communicative role. Whereas the anonymous rhetorical handbook *Rhetorica ad Herennium* (ca. 85 BCE) speaks of there being five parts to rhetoric (invention, arrangement, style, delivery, and memory), the ancient rhetoricians seemed to think of transitional effectiveness as falling most naturally within the category of style. So, the rhetoricians spoke of the need to win over an audience by enhancing the

[3] G. H. Guthrie, *The Structure of Hebrews: A Text Linguistic Analysis* (Leiden: Brill, 1994), 57.

[4] G. A. Kennedy, *New Testament Interpretation through Rhetorical Criticism* (Chapel Hill: University of North Carolina Press, 1984).

[5] Contra R. A. Horsley (*Hearing the Whole Story: The Politics of Plot in Mark's Gospel* [Louisville: Westminster John Knox , 2001], p. 68), the simple markers "and" (καί), "and immediately" (καὶ εὐθύς) or "and again" (καὶ πάλιν) that characterise so many transitions in the Markan Gospel would probably not have overly impressed the ancient rhetors whose works are extant and for whom transitions were of critical importance.

[6] P. L. Tite, *Compositional Transitions in 1 Peter: An Analysis of the Letter-Opening* (London: International Scholars, 1997), 23.

"affective" component of communication. In this regard, Quintilian (95 CE) spoke of the need to charm and delight one's audience by one's style, so that they might surrender themselves to the case that is being made (*Inst.* 9.4.129). It is important for our purposes to note that Quintilian speaks about the affective function of style precisely when discussing a particular *transitional* construction, suggesting that transitions have a part to play in the charming and delighting of one's audience through stylistic means.

If transitions can be considered a subset within the category of rhetorical *style*, they also are related to other categories within the rhetorical taxonomy of *Rhetorica ad Herennium*. So, impressive transitions help to endear one's audience to one's case by assisting (1) in the demarcation of the *arrangement* of one's presentation, (2) in the ease of its *delivery*, and (3) in the ease of its retention by an audience (i.e., *memory*). Since transitions play a key role in these rhetorical parts in predominantly oral/aural contexts, it is crucial that their place and function within a speech or text is recognised if those presentations are to be properly appreciated.

§1.3   *The Focus of This Study: Chain-Link Transitions*

It has been suggested above that transitional markers fall especially well (but not exclusively) within the category of rhetorical style. It is important, then, to heed Stanley Porter's advice about the need to relate a text's stylistic features to its substance:

> [M]any studies of style (or ornamentation) have treated the individual [stylistic] elements in isolation and often as merely ornamental, in other words, as individual literary features that contribute little to the substance or content of a passage, but are included only for aesthetic value. . . . [But] so far as the ancients were concerned, stylistic matters were not simply for decorative value but were part of the way in which substance was conveyed. . . . More must be done to treat the stylistic features, not in isolation but in terms of their coordinated use within an entire passage, or even an entire book.[7]

Furthermore, the question that A. H. Snyman asks of stylistic devices in general can be applied specifically to transitional devices within texts: "In what way do these devices promote the communication of [the author's] message and how do they contribute to the impact and appeal of his argumentations?"[8]

---

[7] S. E. Porter, "The Theoretical Justification for Application of Rhetorical Categories to Pauline Epistolary Literature," in *Rhetorica and the New Testament* (ed. S. E. Porter and T. H. Olbricht; Sheffield: Sheffield Academic, 1993), 100–22, esp. 116-17.

[8] A. H. Snyman, "Style and Meaning in Romans 8:31-39," *Neot* 18 (1984): 94.

In the chapters that follow, issues of this sort will be pursued in relation to one of the many transitional methods evident within ancient
texts. Described by the first-century rhetorician Quintilian and the second-century rhetorician Lucian of Samosata, this technique involves the
overlapping of material at a text-unit boundary in order to facilitate a
transition. This interlocking transition technique (whose form and function are discussed in chapters 2–4 below) is likened by Lucian to the
manner in which a chain is constructed, with its individual links overlapping in order to form a connected and continuous whole. This study
most frequently makes use of Lucian's analogy in its nomenclature, referring to "chain-link transition," "chain-link interlock," "chain-link construction" or simply "chain link" when studying a New Testament
passage in which this feature occurs. Occasionally I will refer to it as
"text-unit interlock" or simply "interlock."

To date, no one has engaged in an in-depth study of the appearance
and significance of this transitional feature within New Testament texts
(not to mention texts of antiquity in general). So for instance, in his 1961
book on Lucian of Samosata and the New Testament,[9] Hans Dieter Betz
concerned himself with the religio-historical and paraenetic parallels
between Lucian and selected New Testament texts (as his subtitle
announced) without interesting himself in the rhetorical features that
Lucian prescribed. Similarly, in his 1993 book comparing features of
Quintilian and Luke, Robert Morgenthaler's attention focussed on features other than text-unit interlock.[10] The most indepth study of chain-
link interlock in the New Testament is a twelve-page study of Acts
carried out in the mid-70s by Jacques Dupont.[11] As will be shown in
§10.2, however, 40 percent of Dupont's findings are skewed, and the 60
percent that have merit still fail to do justice to all occurrences of chain-
link construction within Acts. Occasionally text-unit interlock is
discussed in a paragraph or sentence pertaining to a particular passage.[12]
Almost as frequently, however, scholars find chain-link interlock in

[9] H. D. Betz, *Lukian von Samosata und das neue Testament: religionsgeschichtliche
und paränetische Parallellen* (Berlin: Akademie-Verlag, 1961).

[10] R. Morgenthaler, *Lukas und Quintilian: Rhetorik als Erzählkunst* (Zürich:
Gotthelf, 1993).

[11] J. Dupont, "La question du plan des Actes des Apôtres à la Lumière d'un
Texte de Lucien de Samosate," *NTS* 21 (1974–75): 220–31; repr. in *Nouvelles
Études sur les Actes des Apôtres* (Paris: Éditions du Cerf, 1984), 24–36.

[12] Cf. C. H. Talbert, *Reading John: A Literary and Theological Commentary on
the Fourth Gospel and the Johannine Epistles* (New York: Crossroad, 1992), 179–80;
F. Ó Fearghail, *The Introduction to Luke-Acts: A Study of the Role of Lk 1,1–4,44 in
the Composition of Luke's Two-Volume Work* (Rome: Editrice Pontificio Instituto
Biblico, 1991), 77 n. 197.

passages where interlock is not in fact apparent.[13] My aims in this project, then, are (1) to give clarity to the form, character, and function of chain-link interlock, (2) to cite instances of its occurrence within selected Pauline, Johannine, and Lukan texts, and (3) to study the consequent structural, theological, and/or historical aspects that arise from such occurrences within New Testament texts.

§1.4   The Contribution of This Study: Structure, Theology, History

It is hoped that the contribution of this book does not lie simply in the fact that a study of this topic has never been undertaken in any significant depth previously. Instead, the primary contribution lies in the broader implications that arise in relation to the identification of fifteen cases of chain-link interlock in the New Testament. In particular, as noted in the third aim above, the implications converge particularly in relation to three primary areas of interest: structure, theology, and history.

With regard to *structural significance*, it will be shown that several New Testament passages that have frequently been thought to involve structural clutter and disorder are in fact text-book cases of first-class style being animated by chain-link construction. The consequences of this are at least two-fold. First, the New Testament authors have not lost control of their arguments, as is commonly suggested by scholars in some of the passages studied here. An ancient rhetor who lost control of the structure of his argument proved himself to be a second-rate rhetor, thereby undermining the effectiveness of his own argument. For instance, with regard to Paul's letter to the Roman Christians, interpreters frequently either intimate or explicitly suggest that Paul has lost control of his argumentative structure at various places in the presentation. Rarely do those same interpreters entertain the consequent implication of this assessment—that structural deficiencies of this sort would have been perceived as damaging Paul's credentials as someone who deserves his audience's attention. It will be demonstrated in chapter 6 below that three of those instances of an apparently defective structure actually involve chain-link construction (§6.2, §6.3, and §6.4). Consequently, since the passages themselves are not structurally defective, neither can these instances be interpreted as instances in which Paul lost control of his presentation.

Second, the recognition of chain-link interlock within certain passages offers interpreters a viable alternative to the oft-times extreme views concerning the compositional history of some New Testament

---

[13] E.g., R. J. Dillon, "The Spirit as Taskmaster and Troublemaker in Romans 8," *CBQ* 60 (1999): 682–702, esp. 701.

texts. For instance, all too often perceived structural "anomalies" have been attributed to the interfering influence of later redactors or scribes who introduced irregularities into the original author's text. Most famously, R. H. Charles noted structural oddities in the book of Revelation and attributed them to the work of an "unintelligent" and "shallow-brained" redactor who suffered from "hopeless mental confusion" and was "profoundly stupid and ignorant."[14] I. T. Beckwith, a contemporary of Charles, differed from him in attributing such passages to the text's main author, but thought that the text itself revealed the rather "irregular" mind of its author.[15] What such views usually demonstrate, however, is simply the ignorance of scholars concerning the existence and function of non-linear chain-link interlock. This will be demonstrated in relation to passages from both the book of Revelation (§7.1–§7.3) and Paul's letter to the Christians in Rome (§6.2, §6.4).

Moreover, it will be shown that the author of the Acts of the Apostles (i.e., "Luke") made fourfold use of chain-link interlock throughout its twenty-eight chapters. On the likelihood that those four transitions signal the start of major text-units, a relatively unique proposal regarding the structure of the Acts of the Apostles will be advanced (esp. §10.2 in relation to §9.1–§9.4). Similarly, in relation to the book of Revelation, it will be shown that chain-link transitions hold together the central narrative concerning the eschatological outworking of God (§7.6, §7.7, and §7.8), thereby enhancing the impression of structural and narrative coherence.

With regard to *theological significance*, it will be shown that chain-link interlock frequently plays a key role in an author's attempt to demarcate his theological itinerary and pathways. For instance, chain-link interlock offered the author(s) of the Johannine Gospel the opportunity to assemble a collection of primary themes in a condensed fashion at main structural junctions in that Gospel (§8.1–§8.9). Through the technique of chain-link interlock, prime structural ground draws to itself key Johannine themes in crystallised fashion, providing the interpretative lens through which to view the major text-units on either side of the interlock. In this manner, the principal chain-link interlock of the Johannine Gospel functions virtually as a condensed miniature of that Gospel. As will be shown in §8.4, it also serves to preclude certain literary and theological readings, while enhancing others.

In chapter 7, it will be seen that the book of Revelation incorporates chain-link construction in a manner that "democratises" the promul-

---

[14] R. H. Charles, *A Critical and Exegetical Commentary on the Revelation of St. John* (2 vols.; Edinburgh: T&T Clark, 1920), 1:l and 1:xviii respectively.
[15] I. T. Beckwith, *The Apocalypse of John* (New York: MacMillan, 1919), 771.

gation of apocalyptic mysteries among the "common" people of God (§7.3, §7.5, and §7.8). In this way, the book of Revelation includes an implicit criticism of a popular tradition in which apocalyptic mysteries are thought to be unhelpful to those uninitiated into the group of the select few among whom such mysteries are properly handled and understood. For the author of the book of Revelation, knowledge of the intricate mysteries of God is relevant to the ordinary person of faith, whose life is to be impacted by the revelation of those mysteries. This point is accentuated by means of the formation of a new genre, with the book of Revelation embodying a generic hybrid (i.e., an apocalyptic epistle) that is created by means of the author's use of chain-link interlock.

A similar connection between a text's structure and its author's theological commitments will be evident in Luke's structuring of Acts by means of chain-link interlock. From that structure emerges a theology intent on bolstering confidence in the God whose power Luke depicts as promoting the inevitable advance of the Christian movement (§10.3). The same construction also undergirds Luke's theology of scriptural fulfilment and promotes his confidence in the reliability of Jesus. So, too, while the identity of the "I" who speaks in Romans 7 has been extensively debated, it will be shown that Paul's use of chain-link construction in that chapter assists in the definition of this central character in Paul's theological presentation (§6.2).

With regard to *historical significance*, it will be shown that recognising the position of chain-link interlock in the narrative of Acts casts fresh light on the thorny issues surrounding the attempt to reconstruct the life of Paul (§10.4). Moreover, in relation to the Johannine Gospel it will be shown that its two chain-link interlocks have undergone contrasting fates in the process of the Gospel's own compositional history (§8.8).

This foreshadowing of things to come in the chapters that follow already illustrates one important feature with regard to chain-link interlock: ancient authors made use of it in a variety of ways towards a variety of ends. Although an overlapping structure consistently lies behind all of the examples analysed below, and although a common purpose unites all of them (i.e., to signal a transition from one text-unit to the next), that interlocked structure itself performs a diverse number of further functions in the various contexts in which it appears. The texts studied here offer little indication that their authors employed chain-link interlock in a mindless, "cookie-cutter" fashion simply as a transitional indicator (although it certainly played that role). Instead, those authors regularly took the occasion to infuse chain-link interlock, an otherwise basic transitional phenomenon, with notable interpretative significance.

§1.5   The Triangulation of Evidence

In view of the paucity of studies given to the study of chain-link inter-lock, a double duty is placed upon this project. That is, it needs to demonstrate both (1) the existence of chain-link construction in the ancient world, and (2) how an awareness of that construction can assist in the interpretation of texts. With regard to demonstrating the exis-tence of chain-link in the ancient world, this project is not reliant on one arena of evidence but on three: (1) first- and second-century Graeco-Roman rhetoricians (assembled in chapter 2); (2) sources antecedent to or contemporary with the New Testament (assembled in chapter 5); and (3) the New Testament itself (assembled in chapters 6–10). The evidential basis for this study, then, involves a triangulation of evidence from three different arenas. This process of triangulation affords chain-link construction better credentials than, say, chiastic con-struction or diatribe, since neither chiasm nor diatribe have a foothold in the rhetorical handbooks prior to the fourth century CE (when chiasm first appears), despite their currency in literary texts prior to that date (these issues are considered in §2.1 below). Consequently chain-link construction will be shown to have support from three triangulated evi-dential databases that reinforce each other in demonstrating not only that chain-link construction was a viable transitional feature in the ancient world but also that an awareness of chain-link construction is an important interpretative tool that has for too long been left out of the toolbag of New Testament interpreters.

§1.6   The Character of This Study: Further Matters

The survey of texts that appears in the following chapters is not intended to be an exhaustive study of all the relevant New Testament texts in which chain-link interlock appears. I have been led to the fifteen exam-ples by way of my own interests and experience of study over the past few years, while the outline of this project has been developing. So, while the book of Revelation and the Johannine Gospel are analysed below (§7.1–§7.8, and §8.1–§8.9 respectively), the Johannine epistles are not. Neither are the synoptic Gospels considered here (except for the end of the Lukan Gospel). The Book of Acts is studied intensively in chapters 9 and 10. Although Paul's letter to the Romans is part of the analysis (§6.2–§6.6), the rest of the Pauline corpus has not been a part of this study, except for one instance in 1 Corinthians (§6.1). The Petrine corpus is not considered, nor is Jude or Hebrews, although Guthrie's structural analysis suggests the presence of a kind of chain-link construction in at least one place within Hebrews.[16]

The following chapters are, to a certain extent, self-standing and can be read independently of the others, and perhaps in any order. Having familiarised themselves with the form, character, and function of chain-link interlock in chapters 2–4, readers interested in the use of this technique in the Johannine Gospel, for instance, may want to consult chapter 8 thereafter, while those interested in the use of this construction in Luke-Acts may want to consult chapters 9–10. It should be pointed out, however, that chapters 6 and 7 offer nine New Testament examples in relatively quick succession (from Paul and Revelation) and demonstrate the way in which cognisance of chain-link interlock would have avoided interpretative pitfalls in the history of New Testament scholarship. For that reason, these two chapters offer accessible entry points into the study of chain-link interlock prior to the more complex argumentation of chapters 8, 9, and 10. Chapter 5 is another accessible entry point into the subject, providing examples of the appearance of chain-link construction in a spattering of ancient texts beyond the New Testament. The final section of chapter 5 (§5.10) reviews the findings and their relevance for the chapters that follow.

Throughout this book, wherever reference to a previous argument is made, the section heading is clearly marked for ease of reference (e.g., "§4.1"). The New Testament translation used here is the New Revised Standard Version (NRSV), except in a few instances where I have preferred to translate the passage alternatively. Those cases are noted. Moreover, wherever quotations of primary or secondary literature appear in the main body of the text in languages other than English (i.e., Greek, Hebrew, Latin, German, French), in most cases I have tried to ensure that (1) a translation can be found nearby, (2) the quotation's content is obvious from my comments surrounding it, or (3) the gist of my argument is clear even without the supporting quotation.

With these matters in view, the first point of evidential triangulation can now be surveyed: the references to transitional interlock in the Graeco-Roman rhetoricians.

---

[16] Guthrie, *The Structure of Hebrews*, 108–9, where Hebrews 2:5-9 is discussed under the descriptor "the woven intermediary transition," which in our terms would simply be a complex chain-link transition.

CHAPTER 2

The Rhetoricians'
Recommendations

§2.1   Evidence from Lucian of Samosata and Quintilian

§2.2   Modelling Chain-Link Interlock

The first of this project's triangulation points is the evidence of Graeco-Roman rhetoricians of the first two centuries CE. Both the first-century rhetorician Quintilian and the second-century rhetorician Lucian of Samosata seem to be aware of the form, function, and utility of chain-link interlock, as demonstrated below.

§2.1   Evidence from Lucian of Samosata and Quintilian

In his book *How to Write History*, Lucian of Samosata (ca. 125–80 CE) instructs his audience about the manner in which historical narrative is to be constructed to ensure its rhetorical effectiveness. In the course of his presentation Lucian gives the following advice concerning the relationship between text units (§55):[1]

[1] The translation is by H. W. Fowler and F. G. Fowler, *The Works of Lucian* (Oxford: Clarendon Press, 1905), 2:133. See also K. Kilburn (*Lucian* [Loeb Classical Library; Cambridge, MA: Harvard University Press, 1968], 6:67) who provides a less free, but also less clear, translation.

R. Morgenthaler (*Lukas und Quintilian: Rhetorik als Erzählkunst* [Zürich: Gotthelf Verlag, 1993], 171) offers the following German translation: "Der Autor

11

[T]hough all parts must be independently perfected, when the first is complete the second will be brought into essential connection with it, and attached like one link of a chain to another; there must be no possibility of separating them; no mere bundle of parallel threads; the first is not simply to be next to the second, but part of it, their extremities intermingling.

καὶ τὸ πρῶτον ἐξεργασάμενος ἐπάξει τὸ δεύτερον ἐχόμενον αὐτοῦ καὶ ἀλύσεως τρόπον συνηρμοσμένον ὡς μὴ διακεκόφθαι μηδὲ διηγήσεις πολλὰς εἶναι ἀλλήλαις παρακειμένας, ἀλλ᾽ ἀεὶ τῷ πρώτῳ τὸ δεύτερον μὴ γειτνιᾶν μόνον, ἀλλὰ καὶ κοινωνεῖν καὶ ἀνακεκρᾶσθαι κατὰ τὰ ἄκρα.

Although the English translation is somewhat free, it nonetheless captures Lucian's meaning well. In Lucian's view, units of narrative material are not merely to sit side-by-side in a linear, boxed fashion, but should be joined inextricably by weaving them together in non-linear fashion through a chain-link interlock. Each textual unit is to overlap with its neighbour and intermingle with it, or more precisely, "to mix across the boundaries' (ἀνακεκρᾶσθαι κατὰ τὰ ἄκρα; i.e., the shared text-unit boundary). In this way a rhetor's presentation can exemplify what Lucian calls the "virtues proper to narrative" (ταῖς τῆς διηγήσεως ἀρεταῖς), ensuring that a narrative progresses "smoothly, evenly, and consistently, free from humps and hollows" (λείως τε καὶ ὁμαλῶς προϊοῦσα καὶ αὐτὴ ὁμοίως ὥστε μὴ προὔχειν μηδὲ κοιλαίνεσθαι).[2]

It is not wholly clear what Lucian meant to convey by the "chain-link" imagery that he uses. Perhaps his point is that the boundary between two text units should be free from tectonic compression and bunching on the one hand (i.e., "humps") and from tectonic spread and separation on the other hand (i.e., "hollows"). Avoiding these two situations, the rhetor should ensure that text-unit boundaries are marked out by an overlap of material. In contrast to transitional constructions that resemble tectonic fault-lines of one kind or another (i.e., "humps and hollows"), the transitional construction preferred by Lucian is likened to

---

wird zunächst alles einzelne getrennt und in sich abgerundet ausarbeiten. Hat er dann den ersten Teil abgeschlossen, so fügt er den zweiten daran; dieser soll sich so anschliessen und anpassen wie ein Kettenglied an das andere, so dass das Ganze nicht abgehackt in viele nebeneinanderstehende Einzelerzählungen zerfällt."

[2] The translation here is Kilburn's (*Lucian*, 67). Note that in *How to Write History* 55, Lucian is not simply talking about the transition from a narrative's prologue to the narrative proper. Having advised that that transition should be "gentle and easy," he then turns to the nature of the narrative in general. In order to prevent it from being "simply a long narrative," it needs to be adorned with "the virtues proper to narrative," and it is at this point that he discusses the chain-link transition.

the construction of a chain (ἀλύσεως) in which text units do not simply sit next to each other but "have fellowship" (κοινωνεῖν) with each other at their transition points by means of the overlapping of their subject matter. Lucian proposed that, in so doing, a rhetor achieves "clarity . . . by the interweaving of subjects" (τὸ σαφὲς . . . τῇ συμτεριπλοκῇ τῶν πραγμάτων).[3]

Lucian, writing *How to Write History* between 166–168 CE, is not the first to discuss the usefulness and importance of this kind of transition. Quintilian lays out rhetorical suggestions for the effective narration of events in a manner that coincides wholly with Lucian's description of chain-link construction. According to Quintilian's *Institutio oratoria* 9.4.129 (95 CE), one's oration should be marked out by

> a certain continuity of motion and connection of style. All its members are to be closely linked together, while the fluidity of its style gives it great variety of movement; we may compare its motion to that of people who link hands to steady their steps, and lend each other mutual support.[4]

> Historia non tam finitos numeros quam orbem quendam contextumque desiderat. Namque omnia eius membra connexa sunt et, quoniam lubrica est, hac atque illac fluit, ut homines, qui manibus invicem apprehensis gradum firmant, continent et continentur.

The specific analogy used by Quintilian is different from Lucian's analogy of overlapping links in a chain, but it amounts to precisely the same thing. The overlapping involved as people hold hands conforms exactly to Lucian's analogy of chain links. In Quintilian's view, the

---

[3] Lucian may well have practised this method of linking parts of narrative together when he comes to the close of Book 2 of his "A True Story" (*Verae Historiae* §47). In Books 1 and 2 he recounted what had (purportedly!) happened to him on a wild and eventful journey up to the point when he reached "the other world." Book 2 then closes in this way: "What happened in the other world I shall tell you in the succeeding books." Unfortunately Book 3 was either never written or, more likely, has been lost, so there is no way to confirm that a retrospective gesture is made at the beginning of that envisaged book. It is very unlikely, however, to have begun simply "I went. . . ." It was much more likely to have begun with a retrospective glance at the narrative of Books 1 and 2.

[4] The fairly free translation, with slight adjustment, is by H. E. Butler, *Quintilian* (Loeb Classical Library; Cambridge, MA: Harvard University, 1986), 3:579–81. Morgenthaler (*Lukas und Quintilian*, 65) offers the following German translation of 9.4.129: "wie eine Art von Rundung und Dichte der Wortfügung. Denn alle ihre Glieder sind verknüpft, und da sie sich auf unsicherem Boden bewegt, schwankt ihr Erzählfluss hin und her, wie Menschen, die dadurch, dass sich sich gegenseitig bei der Hand halten, sicherer gehen, einanderer halten und gehalten werden."

support afforded to people when they link their hands together is comparable to the support afforded to a narrative when its parts overlap.[5]

According to Quintilian, this transition technique does not simply
lend support to a narrative by ensuring that its otherwise independent
parts are intricately interconnected. The technique of transitional interlock also enhances the effectiveness of the rhetor's presentation by means
of endearing the rhetor's audience to himself. Quintilian is convinced
that a rhetor must ensure that his audience is captivated by his style in
order consequently to be won over by his argument.[6] The task of the orator is, he says, to ensure that one's audience "has not merely got a grasp
of the matter, but has been charmed by our style, has surrendered himself
to the pleader and is ready to be led wither we will, by the delight which
he experiences (. . . *non solum rem tenet, sed etiam captus est oratione et se
credit actori et voluptate iam ducitur*)." Significantly, Quintilian's example of
a rhetor endearing his audience to his argument by means of a charming
and captivating style is offered in the context of his discussion of the need
to link rhetorical units together by overlapping their content at transition
points. Evidently he envisaged an interlocked transition to be one of the
"decorous" and "pleasing" techniques whereby a rhetor demonstrates his
stylistic excellence and sophistication.

Quintilian seems to practice his own advice regarding the connection
of independent rhetorical parts in his discourse. Thus, towards the end of
Institutio oratoria 9, where he first introduces Book 10 before concluding
Book 9, he writes as follows (9.4.146):

> [M]y final book [i.e., Book 10] will explain the nature of the difference
> between our language and that of Greece. But I must bring this book

---

[5] In their advocacy of overlapping material at text-unit boundaries, Quintilian
and Lucian maintain a view that possibly runs against the grain of that of
Anaximenes of Lampsacus, the author of the "Rhetoric to Alexander," mistakenly
attributed to Aristotle. In chapter 31 of that work, Anaximenes advocates arrang-
ing the facts "whether it be narrative, or report, or explanation, or anticipation,
separately and distinctly (each with its own substantial, definite, bodily shape)
after the proœmium. This will be done by recounting the facts nakedly, each by
itself, from beginning to end, without including or mixing up anything else in the
treatment of them" (E. M. Cope, *An Introduction to Aristotle's* Rhetoric [New
York: Georg Olms Verlag, 1970], 444–45).

[6] Elsewhere Quintilian decries the "voluptuous and affected style" of some of
his contemporary orators, whose purpose is only "to charm the ears of the uned-
ucated minority" (Inst. 10.1.43). Similarly he complains that they all too frequently "want every passage, every sentence to strike the ear by an impressive
close. In fact, they think it is a disgrace, nay, almost a crime, to pause to breathe
except at the end of a passage that is designed to call forth applause" (*Inst.*
8.5.13–14). Cf. *Inst.* 5.13.42.

[i.e., Book 9] to a conclusion without more delay, since it has already exceeded the limits designed for it. To sum up then. . . .

Sed quae sit differentia nostri Graecique sermonis, explicabit summus liber. Compositio (nam finem imponere egresso destinatum modum volumini festino). . . .

In this way, the closure of Book 9 first makes an anticipatory gesture to Book 10, then includes a retrospective summary of the contents of Book 9. Here, then, is an example of the transitional practice that Quintilian had encouraged just a few verses earlier, and a practice that conforms precisely to the "overlapping" that Lucian would encourage a century later in relation to chain-link transitions.

There are strong indicators, then, that Lucian's transitional technique has precedent within the rhetorical schools of the first century. It is important to note in this regard that neither Lucian nor Quintilian gives any indication that this technique for transitional clarity and artistry is original to himself. In each case, the technique is mentioned without much clarification or elaboration. This suggests that it must have been a recognised practice, and perhaps a common one, in the ancient world. Had it been otherwise, certainly Lucian and/or Quintilian would have offered readers further discussion of the technique to assist them in assimilating the practice.[7] Presumably, then, one need not look far to find examples of chain-link construction in the writings of antiquity.

This evidence is enough to merit the exploration of ancient texts for occurrences of chain-link interlock. Although the evidence provided by ancient rhetoricians on the matter of chain-link interlock is not extensive, that evidence nonetheless exists and, if I have interpreted it correctly, is suggestive of a broad currency for chain-link interlock in the ancient world. Consequently, it would be foolhardy to ignore that

---

[7] Rhetoricians were not inventors of rhetorical strategies. Instead, they observed good and bad rhetorical practice and compiled anthologies based on their observations. Cf. C. J. Classen ("St. Paul's Epistles and Ancient Greek and Roman Rhetoric," in *Rhetoric and the New Testament: Essays from the 1992 Heidelberg Conference* (ed. S. E. Porter and T. H. Olbricht; Sheffield: Sheffield Academic Press, 1993], 265–91, esp. 290–91): "[O]ne should not forget that the occurrence of rhetorical figures does not allow the inference that an author employed them because he was familiar with a theory. For they recommended themselves in practice long before any theory was developed (Quintilian 2.17.5–9), and they are found in authors who were never exposed to any theory in any form." Cf. also J. T. Reed, "Using Ancient Rhetorical Categories to Interpret Paul's Letters: A Question of Genre," in *Rhetoric and the New Testament* (ed. S.E. Porter and T.H. Olbricht; Sheffield: Sheffield Academic Pres, 1993), 292–324, esp. 299. In §4.6, I will root these practices largely in the orality of the ancient world.

evidence or to put it on hold until such time as a stronger evidential basis might somehow be assembled. Scholars studying ancient rhetorical features have found themselves in similar situations in relation to other stylistic and structural features without necessarily resorting to an agnostic or pessimistic attitude towards them. For instance, despite the fairly frequent occurrence of diatribe in a wide variety of ancient philosophical texts, neither the progymnasmata nor the Graeco-Roman rhetorical handbooks discuss diatribe in their endorsements of good rhetorical practice.[8] The same is the case with regard to chiastic structures. So David Aune notes that "[w]hile chiasm (at least micro-chiasmus) is certainly an observable rhetorical feature of ancient texts, it is a feature neither conceptualized nor discussed by rhetorical theorists, until the 4th cent. CE, when it is mentioned by Ps.-Hermogenes."[9]

It would be trite to suggest that, as a result of this evidence (or lack thereof prior to the fourth century), studies of chiasm must be restricted to works of the fourth century and afterwards. While studies of chiasm may frequently become slaves to the subjective interests of modern interpreters, much good work has nonetheless been done on pre-fourth century texts to illustrate Aune's point that chiasm "is certainly an observable rhetorical feature of ancient texts," despite the fact that it goes unmentioned in the progymnasmata and other works of ancient rhetoricians.[10] The disparity between chiasm's solid foothold in pre-fourth-century texts and its first appearance in rhetorical discussion might be explained by the observation of A. B. Lord:

> There is a tendency for us in the European tradition to forget how extensive and how basic our literary heritage from the world of orality has been, and there is a corresponding tendency to believe that the world of literacy invented some of the characteristics of literature, which in reality originated in oral literature. Among them is a sense of

[8] See, for instance, the discussion by D. E. Aune, *The Westminster Dictionary of New Testament and Early Christian Literature and Rhetoric* (Louisville: Westminster John Knox Press, 2003), 127–29.

[9] Aune, *The Westminster Dictionary*, 94. There he cites G. A. Kennedy, *New Testament Interpretation through Rhetorical Criticism* (Chapel Hill: University of North Carolina Press, 1984), 28–29; and I. H. Thomson, *Chiasmus in the Pauline Letters* (Sheffield: Sheffield Academic Press, 1995), 14–15.

[10] On the progynmasmata, see G. A. Kennedy, *Progymnasmata: Greek Textbooks of Prose Composition and Rhetoric* (Leiden: Brill, 2003). Although the progymnasmata have much to say about the placement and division of material within a presentation, discussion of transition techniques is virtually absent. On the chreia, see *The Progymnasmata* (vol. 1 of *The Chreia and Ancient Rhetoric*; ed. R. F. Hock and E. N. O'Neill. Atlanta: Scholars Press, 1986); *Classroom Exercises* (vol. 2 of *The Chreia and Ancient Rhetoric*; ed. Hock and O'Neill. Atlanta: Society of Biblical Literature, 2002).

form and structure . . . and many devices, later termed "rhetorical" and
attributed to schools, which actually were created in the crucible of the
oral world.[11]

It will be argued below that chain-link interlock is itself a feature
whose utility is pronounced in contexts of oral communication.
Moreover, if chiasm and diatribe have no foothold in the writings of
Graeco-Roman rhetoricians but are nonetheless evident in ancient texts,
chain-link interlock does seem to have a foothold within the writings of
two Graeco-Roman rhetoricians, each of whom deals with it in a fashion
suggesting its wider currency. Of course, a broader evidential base for
chain-link interlock within rhetorical texts would be preferable, but the
absence of that breadth should not result in a moratorium on literary
probes in search of the existence and function of chain-link interlock in
ancient texts. In fact, in the absence of that broader evidential base, the
proof of the pudding must simply be in the eating. That is, the notion
that Lucian and Quintilian are "conceptualizing" (to use Aune's term)
chain-link interlock as an established practice of the ancient world must
be tested against a database of ancient examples in order to see whether
that notion makes viable inroads in the interpretation of texts. In fact, as
will be shown in succeeding chapters, ignoring this data has led to grace-
less and awkward interpretations of a number of passages in the New
Testament, itself a literary corpus from the Graeco-Roman world.

The classicist Francis Cornford made much the same procedural
observation as long ago as 1914:

> Many literary critics seem to think that an hypothesis about obscure
> and remote questions of history can be refuted by a simple demand for
> the production of more evidence than in fact exists. The demand is as
> easy to make as it is impossible to satisfy. But the true test of an
> hypothesis, if it cannot be shown to conflict with known truths, is the
> number of facts that it correlates and explains.[12]

The "true test" of Lucian and Quintilian's brief discussions of structural
overlap is not to be delayed until such time as further corroboration is
unearthed in lost documents of the Graeco-Roman rhetoricians. Instead,
the true test of chain-link interlock must lie precisely in "the number of
facts that it correlates and explains." As will be shown in the chapters that
follow, an awareness of chain-link interlock as a transition technique of
the ancient world may lead interpreters of New Testament texts to avoid
the pitfalls of standard interpretations in some cases and, in other cases,

---

[11] A. B. Lord, "Words Heard and Words Seen," in *Oral Tradition and Literacy:
Changing Visions of the World* (ed. R. A. Whitaker and E. R. Sienart; Durhab:
Natal University, 1986), 13.

[12] F. M. Cornford, *The Origin of Attic Comedy* (London: Arnold, 1914), 191.

may lead to a greater appreciation of the literary and theological concerns of New Testament authors.

§2.2   *Modelling Chain-Link Interlock*

The interlocked transition described by Quintilian and Lucian is best illustrated by means of an A-b-a-B pattern, with upper-case letters representing the major portion of a text unit and lower-case letters representing the overlap that is sandwiched on the boundaries of the text units. In this structure, text units are linked through the staggering of a "back-and-forth" arrangement of ideas where the text units meet, thereby interlocking the larger units. This A-b-a-B pattern conforms precisely to the structure of a chain, as in Lucian's analogy, with overlap occurring in the interlocking links of a chain. A cross section of two chain links (below) illustrates the point, with the A-b-a-B structure emerging from the cross-line:

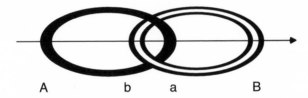

A   b   a   B

This interpretation of the transition likened by Lucian to a chain link also conforms to the transition technique likened by Quintilian to the linking of hands between two people. Instead of text-unit A simply coming to an abrupt end and being immediately followed by text-unit B, text-unit A gives way to a brief signalling of material B, followed by a resumption of material A, and finally a full commencement of text-unit B.

As will be shown in the chapters below, this structure sometimes appears in a "balanced" structure, with the boundary between the text units (indicated here by the forward slash "/") falling halfway between the transitional elements: A-b/a-B.[13] In this pattern the overlap and interweaving is, in a sense, bidirectional. But it also appears in "unbalanced" structures, with the text-unit boundary falling to one side of the transition (e.g., A-b-a/B), or in complex structures, with the intertwining occurring in multiple fashion. For instance, as will be shown, the seam at

---

[13] Cf. also the interpretation of the same by J. Dupont ("La question du plan des Actes des Apôtres à la Lumière d'un Texte de Lucien de Samosate," in *Nouvelles Études sur Les Actes des Apôtres* [Paris: Éditions du Cerf, 1984], 29): "le signe du passage d'une partie à une autre doit donc être cherché, non dans un interruption de la narration, mais au finale d'un développement doit annoncer et amorcer l'étape suivante, et celle-ci doit commencer en revenant sur ce qui a déjà été raconté."

the boundary between Luke's Gospel and the Acts of the Apostles exhibits something of an A-b-a/a-B pattern. In this, text-unit A (Luke's Gospel) includes a transition that first signals text-unit B (identified as "b") and then concludes its own material briefly (identified as "a"), with text-unit B commencing with a gesture towards text-unit A prior to beginning its own material (discussed in §9.1 and §10.1 below). Sometimes the pattern elongates even further into a A-b-a-b/B pattern, as is the case for Revelation 22:6-9 (discussed in §7.1–§7.4). On one occasion, we will consider the possibility of a multiple chain-link construction (cf. Acts 8:1-3, discussed in §9.3, §10.2, and §10.3). This construction is much harder to diagram, but its structural function is clear enough. At the point of its closure, text-unit A includes overlapped material that introduces not only one ensuing block of material but two or more. The construction seems to be quite rare, but evidently one of our New Testament authors considered it to hold attraction at a complex transitional junction. In all of these patterns, the text-unit boundary intertwines two text units that have, in a sense, ragged edges at the point of their intersection.

It needs to be emphasised that chain-link construction is marked out exclusively by the overlapping of material (via content repetition or a gesture of some kind) at the boundary of two text units, not simply by the crossing of the text-unit boundary by material without an interlock being formed. So for instance, while the pattern A/a-B involves the crossing of material "a" over the text-unit boundary, this transition (discussed in §3.6 below) is not a chain-link construction since it does not involve the overlap of material. The crossing of the text-unit boundary alone does not result in chain-link construction; that construction results when material from two text units overlaps in one way or another (i.e., balanced or unbalanced).

Ancient rhetoricians are not the only analysts of structure to notice the usefulness of overlapping text units at transition points. In 1974 the literary structuralist Robert Polzin highlighted the way that narratives frequently overlap at the point where two narrative sequences meet: "one sequence may still be in progress when another is instituted."[14] He diagrams the point in the following manner:

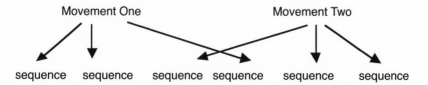

Movement One		Movement Two	

sequence   sequence   sequence   sequence   sequence   sequence

[14] R. Polzin, "The Framework of the Book of Job," *Interpretation* 28 (1974): 182–200, esp. 191.

Here is the precise pattern of transition noted by the ancient rhetoricians nearly two millennia earlier, with "movement one" and "movement two" acting as two links of a chain that overlap at their shared boundary.

Six further features of chain-link interlock will be noted in chapter 4. But before giving consideration to them, it is necessary to differentiate chain-link interlock from other techniques involving repetition, fore-shadowing, staggering, and the linking of textual material in ancient texts. This will ensure that the form of chain-link interlock is firmly established before exploring other aspects of its character and its execution in ancient texts. The task of comparing and contrasting chain-link interlock with closely related compositional techniques is carried out in the next chapter.

CHAPTER 3

Chain-Link Interlock among Other Ancient Rhetorical Devices

In chapter 2 it was suggested that the chain-link structure that both Lucian and Quintilian commended should be understood as a transition appearing at the boundary between two text units. In its structure, text-unit A gives way to a brief signalling of text-unit B, followed by a resumption of material from text-unit A and the proper commencement of text-unit B. In its purest forms, then, chain-link construction follows an A-b-a-B pattern in which a clear overlap of material is evident at the point of transition, conforming to the construction of chain linkage.

In this chapter, this structural pattern is analysed in relation to eight other compositional techniques that are evident in ancient texts and that have some relationship to chain-link interlock. This process of

comparison and differentiation will help to ensure that the form, function and character of chain-link interlock is firmly in place prior to the
textual probes of later chapters.

§3.1   Inter-Unit versus Intra-Unit

Lucian and Quintilian indicate that chain-link interlock is an "inter-unit"
feature, in that it connects two distinct text units. They give no indication
that chain-link interlock performs an "intra-unit" function, in which a
single independent text unit is internally structured. This differentiates
the "inter-textual" chain-link construction from the "intra-textual" *inclusio*, for instance, in which a single text unit is marked out at both its
beginning and its end by a repeated textual feature.[1] For instance,
Romans 5:1-11 exemplifies a text unit defined as such by the appearance
of an intra-textual *inclusio*, with the phrase "through our Lord Jesus
Christ" appearing at both 5:1 and 5:11.[2] In this fashion, *inclusio* functions
as "internal framing,"[3] supporting a single text-unit at its extremities.
And in this way chain-link interlock differs from such intra-unit structuring devices. Rather than marking out a single text unit and differentiating
that unit from its surrounding context, chain-link construction plays a
role in linking two distinct text units, its role being inter-textual rather
than intra-textual.[4]

   This also differentiates chain-link construction from *inclusio*'s more
elaborate cousin, *chiasm*, which involves concentric patterning and
inverted parallelism. One text commonly thought to be animated by an

---

[1] L. L. Neeley ("A Discourse Analysis of Hebrews," in *Occasional Papers in
Translation and Textlinguistics* 3–4 [1987]: 1–146) refers to this structure as "sandwich structures."

[2] Analysis of *inclusio* in New Testament texts is extensive. For an exemplary
study, see G. H. Guthrie, *The Structure of Hebrews: A Text Linguistic Analysis*
(Leiden: Brill, 1994), 76–89.

[3] The term is so used by K. Stanley (*The Shield of Homer: Narrative Structure
in the* Iliad [Princeton: Princeton University Press, 1993], 7), when discussing
"inclusive ring-composition" or *inclusio* in Homer's *Odyssey*.

[4] Cf. J. A. Sanders ("Intertextuality and Canon," in *On the Way to Nineveh:
Studies in Honor of George M. Landes* [ed. S. L. Cook and S. C. Winter; Atlanta:
Scholars Press, 1999], 316–33, esp. 316): "The term 'intertextuality' is currently
used in three basic but distinct senses: the interrelation of blocks of text (large or
small) in close proximity; the function of older literature cited or in some way
alluded to in later literature; and the interrelationship of text and readers." Clearly
I have used the term here in the first sense. According to V. K. Robbins (*The
Tapestry of Early Christian Discourse: Rhetoric, Society and Ideology* [London:
Routledge, 1996], 33), the "current terminology of 'intertextuality' collapses three
arenas of analysis and interpretation together in a manner that is confusing."

intra-textual chiasm is the Johannine prologue (1:1-18), outlined below according to a chiastic structure:[5]

A (1-2)		The Word with God in eternity
	B (3-5)	The Word as source of created life
	C (6-8)	The witness of John the Baptist
	D (9-11)	Logos incarnate rejected in Israel and the world
	E (12-13)	Divine "sonship" through Logos
	D (14)	Logos incarnate indwelling the covenant people
	C (15)	The witness of John the Baptist
	B (16-17)	Incarnate Logos as source of life and truth
A (18)		The Son in the Father

According to a common view, this single text unit (John 1:1-18) is internally organised according to the technique of chiastic structuring, giving the passage an internal unity and a coherent distinctiveness. By contrast, Lucian and Quintilian consider chain-link construction to be an inter-textual device in which two separate textual units are associated and coupled. Whereas *inclusio* and chiasm are intra-textual devices that provide a structural basis for distinct textual units, chain-link interlock is an inter-textual transitional device that conjoins separate units.[6]

§3.2 Foreshadowing

If chain-link interlock connects two distinct text units by means of over-lapping material at the transition point, it serves a larger structural role than simple foreshadowing. Foreshadowing might be involved in the "b" elements of chain-link construction (A-b-a-B), with text-unit B being anticipated by the "b" material prior to it. But the appearance of fore-shadowing alone does not make for a chain-link transition.[7] For instance,

---

[5] The following is taken from J. W. Pryor, *John: Evangelist of the Covenant People* (London: Darton, Longman & Todd, 1992), 9–10. For a similar exercise, see C. H. Talbert, *Reading John: A Literary and Theological Commentary on the Fourth Gospel and the Johannine Epistles* (New York: Crossroads, 1992), 66. For occurrences of chiasm in the Hebrew Bible, see especially W. G. E. Watson, *Traditional Techniques in Classical Hebrew Verse* (Sheffield: Sheffield Academic Press, 1994), 313–91.

[6] An exception to this rule is found in the multiple chain-link structure that Luke assembles at 8:1b-3 in relation to the text unit that follows in 8:4–12:25. In that text unit, a series of subunits are linked to the preceding text unit, thereby affording the subunits a structural cohesion. But this is the result of multiple chain-linking; it is not a feature of chain-link construction in and of itself.

[7] Thus Luke 24:49 is not simply an example of prolepsis/foreshadowing with regard to Acts 2, as D. Marguerat claims (*The First Christian Historian: Writing the*

in Mark 3:9 Jesus instructs his disciples "to have a boat ready for him
because of the crowd, lest they should crush him." This foreshadows
Jesus' action in Mark 4:1, in which he gets into a boat to teach the "very
large crowd that had gathered about him." Although Mark 3:9 foreshadows Mark 4:1, it does not act as part of a transition marker to a later unit.
The two verses are separated by thirty-six verses and have no strong
structural relationship. Clearly, simple literary foreshadowing is to be
differentiated from structural chain-link. While foreshadowing may play
a part in chain-link constructions, it often appears outside the parameters
of chain-link construction.

§3.3   Alternation

The chain-link A-b-a-B pattern needs to be distinguished from two other
types of staggering techniques in which a pendulum effect is evident, neither of which functions as a transitional technique: (1) alternating parallelism, and (2) section alternation.

Alternating parallelism is evident in a variety of ancient Jewish texts.[8]
This pattern operates at the micro-level of texts, tending to involve short
passages of four lines in which the first and third lines correspond, as do
the second and fourth. This pattern can be diagrammed in the following
way: a-b-a-b. Frequently in this construction the second "a-b" sequence
simply repeats the first "a-b" sequence using slightly different terminology, as in Isaiah 29:4:

> Then deep from the earth you shall speak, [a]
>   from the low in the dust your words shall come; [b]
> Your voice shall come from the ground like the voice of a ghost, [a]
>   and your speech shall whisper out of the dust. [b]

"*Acts of the Apostles*" [Cambridge: Cambridge University Press, 2002], 50 n. 19),
but of chain-link construction, as will be shown below (§9.1).

[8] See, for instance, J. T. Willis, "Alternating (ABA'B') Parallelism in the Old
Testament Psalms and Prophetic Literature," in *Directions in Biblical Hebrew
Poetry* (ed. E. R. Follis; Sheffield: JSOT Press, 1987), 49–76; Watson, *Traditional
Techniques*, 252; A. Berlin, "Shared Rhetorical Features in Biblical and Sumerian
Literature," *Journal of the Ancient Near Eastern Society of Columbia University* 10
(1978): 35–42, esp. 39–42.

N. M. Bronznick ("'Metathetic Parallelism'–An Unrecognized Subtype of
Synonymous Parallelism," *Hebrew Annual Review* 3 [1979]: 25–39) argues for the
existence of an a-b[1]/a[1]-b construction at various places in the Old Testament,
involving the transposition of corresponding objects or predicates. He finds this
in the following cases: Isa 17:5; 22:3; 29:3; 29:5; 49:25; 54:14; 55:5; Amos 6:11;
8:12; Psa 25:14; 35:7; 50:19; 90:9; 105:18; Prov 18:15; Job 13:25; 30:17; 38:30;
Mic 2:1.

But frequently the second "a-b" sequence also advances a new idea while maintaining the structural pattern of the first. This is evident in Deuteronomy 32:21:[9]

> They made me jealous with what is no god, [a]
>   provoked me with their idols. [b]
> So I will make them jealous with what is no people, [a]
>   provoke them with a foolish nation. [b]

There is development in this verse, with the first half being the cause of an action and the second half being the result. But in each half an "a-b" pattern is evident, being built primarily on the two verbs "to make jealous" (קנא) and "to provoke" (כעס). The same a-b-a-b pattern appears in alternating parallelisms throughout the Hebrew Bible, including the following three examples:

> Hosea 5:3:
>   I know Ephraim, [a]
>   and Israel is not hidden from me; [b]
>   for now, O Ephraim, you have played the whore; [a]
>   and Israel is defiled. [b]

> Isaiah 11:3b-4a:
>   He shall not judge by what his eyes sees, [a]
>   or decide by what his ears hear; [b]
>   but with righteousness he shall judge the poor, [a]
>   and decide with equity for the meek of the earth. [b]

> Proverbs 10:6-7:
>   Blessings are on the head of the righteous, [a]
>   but the mouth of the wicked conceals violence. [b]
>   The memory of the righteous is a blessing, [a]
>   but the name of the wicked will rot. [b]

Occasionally an alternating parallelism is extended past the simple four-line structure of these passages. While keeping a fourfold a-b-a-b pattern, Psalm 24:7-10 extends the parallelism beyond four lines, doubling its length to eight lines:

> Lift up your heads, O gates! and be lifted up, O ancient doors!
> that the King of glory may come in. [a]
>   Who is the King of glory?
>   The Lord, strong and mighty, the Lord, mighty in battle. [b]
> Lift up your heads, O gates! and be lifted up, O ancient doors!
> that the King of glory may come in. [a]

---

[9] As noted by E. L. Greenstein, "How Does Parallelism Mean?," in *A Sense of Text: The Art of Language in the Study of Biblical Literature* (Winona Lake: Eisenbrauns, 1983), 62 n. 54.

Who is this King of glory?
The Lord of hosts, he is the King of glory. [b]

In other passages, the alternation in the parallelism extends past four occurrences, such as in Isaiah 62:4 where a sixfold alternating parallelism appears (with "you" comprising the components of "a" and "your land" the components of "b"):

You [לך] shall no more be termed Forsaken, [a]
　and your land [ארצך] shall no more be termed Desolate; [b]
but you [לך] shall be called "My delight is in her," [a]
　and your land [ארצך] "Married"; [b]
for Yahweh delights in you [בך], [a]
　and your land [ארצך] shall be married. [b]

Isaiah 65:13b–14b extends the pattern further, incorporating an eight-fold alternating parallelism (with "my servants" [אבדי] comprising the components of "a" and "you" [אתם] comprising the components of "b"):

Behold, my servants shall eat, [a]
　but you shall be hungry; [b]
behold, my servants shall drink, [a]
　but you shall be thirsty; [b]
behold, my servants shall rejoice, [a]
　but you shall be put to shame; [b]
behold my servants shall sing for gladness of heart, [a]
　but you shall cry out for pain of heart. [b]

These patterns of alternating parallelism are only one example of the attraction of the pendulum effect in the ancient world. The alternating of sections is also commonly attested in classical Hellenistic storytelling and literature, where the alternation involves a much greater extent of text than in the alternating parallelism noted above.[10] Whereas the a-b-a-b pattern of alternating parallelism operates at a micro-level of the text, the A-B-A-B pattern is a macro-level construction, in which large text units are placed side by side in alternating repetition. Prime examples are provided by Homer and Herodotus. In Book 6 of his *Iliad*, Homer depicts a battle between the Greeks and the Trojans in which his focus shifts from one group to the other in alternating fashion. So the movements of the Greeks take pride of place in §5–72, followed by the Trojan efforts in §73–118, then the focus reverts to the Greeks in §119–236, after which it shifts to the Trojans in §237–529.[11]

---

[10] See, for instance, B. L. Hijmans, Jr., *Inlaboratus et Facilis: Aspects of Structure in Some Letters of Seneca* (Leiden: Brill, 1976), 131–51; G. W. Most, *The Measures of Praise: Structure and Function in Pindar's Second Pythian and Seventh Nemean Odes* (Göttingen: Vandenhoeck & Ruprecht, 1985), 44–45.

[11] See esp. Stanley, *The Shield of Homer*, 88–89. For another example from

A more extensive pattern of section alternation is provided by the fifth-century BCE historian Herodotus. In Book 8 of his *Histories*, Herodotus is interested in depicting the battle of Salamis in which the forces of Greece and Persia met. This appears in §83–96, roughly the middle of Book 8. On either side of this centrepiece Herodotus recounts the relevant histories of the Greeks and the Persians in a pendulum swing in which the focus of attention alternates thirteen times between the Greeks and the Persians:[12]

§1–22	Greek History
§23–39	Persian History
§40–65	Greek History
§66–69	Persian History
§70–82	Greek History
§97–107	Persian History
§108–12	Greek History
§113–20	Persian History
§121–25	Greek History
§126–30	Persian History
§131–32	Greek History
§133–36	Persian History
§140–44	Greek History

Examples of this kind resonate with Albert Lord's observation regarding the process of composition in aural/oral cultures, in which "composers think in terms of blocks and series of blocks of traditions."[13] A non-literary example of the same is the so-called "Françoise Vase," on which the painter Kleitias depicts a story with intersecting episodes drawn from the lives of Achilles and his father Peleus in a vertical A-B-A-B pattern.[14]

Homer's *Odyssey*, see J. H. Gaisser, "A Structural Analysis of the Digressions in the *Iliad* and the *Odyssey*," *HSCP* 73 (1969): 1–43, esp. 21.

[12] In this analysis, I am indebted to H. Wood, *The Histories of Herodotus: An Analysis of Formal Structure* (The Hague: Mouton, 1972), 171–73, whose analysis is more detailed than is prudent to reproduce here.

[13] A. Lord, "The Gospels and Oral Traditional Literature," in *The Relationships Among the Gospels* (ed. W. O. Walker; San Antonio: Trinity University Press, 1978), 59.

[14] See A. Stewart, "Stesichoros and the Françoise Vase," in *Ancient Greek Art and Iconography* (ed. W. G. Moon; Madison: University of Wisconsin Press, 1983), 53–74. The Gospel of John makes use of this pendulum effect when recounting the story of Jesus' encounter with the woman of Samaria in John 4: the woman and Jesus (4:3-26), the disciples and Jesus (4:27), the woman and Jesus (4:31-38), the disciples and Jesus (4:29-42). The same pendulum effect is evident in the narrative of Jesus' arrest in John 18: Jesus is arrested (18:12-14), Jesus is

These examples of both micro-level alternating parallelism and macro-level section alternation illustrate two things in comparison and contrast to chain-link construction: (1) neither pattern lends itself to a transitional purpose, unlike chain-link interlock; and (2) the back-and-forth pattern that characterises chain-link interlock was a commonly attested phenomenon in the ancient world (a point that would receive even further confirmation through a broader selection of examples).

§3.4 Climax and Catchword Associations

On occasion scholars have wrongly confused chain-link construction with the technique of "climax" (κλῖμαξ) or "ascent" (*ascensus*, also *gradatio*; sometimes also called "step parallelism" or "terrace patterning"). For instance, R. J. Dillon wrongly identifies Romans 8:30 as an example of "chain-linked inferences," while David Aune rightly notes Romans 8:29-30 to be an example of "climax" or "ladder" construction.[15] In those verses, Paul writes: "For those whom he foreknew he also predestined . . . and those whom he predestined he also called; and those whom he called he also justified; and those whom he justified he also glorified" (οὓς προέγνω, καὶ προώρισεν . . . οὓς δὲ προώρισεν, τούτους καὶ ἐκάλεσεν, καὶ οὓς ἐκάλεσεν, τούτους καὶ ἐδικαίωσεν, οὓς δὲ ἐδικαίωσεν, τούτους καί ἐδόξασεν). Paul showed some fondness for this kind of construction in his letter to the Christians in Rome, using it on two other occasions: 5:3-5 and 10:14-15. In Romans 5:3-5 he writes: "knowing that suffering produces endurance, and endurance produces character, and character produces hope, and hope does not dissappoint us" (εἰδότες ὅτι ἡ θλῖψις ὑπομονὴν κατεργάζεται, ἡ δὲ ὑπομονη δοκιμήν, ἡ δὲ δοκιμὴ ἐλπίδα, ἡ δὲ ἐλπὶς οὐ καταισχύνει). In 10:14-15 he writes: "But how are they to call upon him in whom they have not believed? And how are they to believe in him of whom they have never heard? And how are they to hear without a preacher? And how can [some] preach unless the are sent?" (πῶς οὖν ἐπικαλέσωνται εἰς ὃν οὐκ ἐπίστευσαν; πῶς γὰρ πιστεύσωσιν οὗ οὐκ ἤκουσαν; πῶς δὲ ἀκούσωσιν χωρὶς κηρύσσοντος; πῶς δὲ κηρύξωσιν ἐὰν μὴ ἀποσταλῶσιν;).

Most famously, John 1:1-5 demonstrates the same structure (although this is far more clear in the Greek than is evident in any smooth English translation):[16]

---

denied by Peter (18:15-18), Jesus is questioned by the high priest (18:19-24), Jesus is denied by Peter (18:25-27), Jesus is questioned by Pilate (18:28-40).

[15] R. J. Dillon, "The Spirit as Taskmaster and Troublemaker in Romans 8," *CBQ* 60 (1999): 682–702, esp. 701; D. E. Aune, *The Westminster Dictionary of New Testament and Early Christian Literature and Rhetoric* (Louisville: Westminster John Knox Press, 2003), 102.

[16] John 1:2 and 1:3b have been omitted; the latter appears to be a secondary

ἐν ἀρχῇ ἦν ὁ λόγος,
καὶ ὁ λόγος ἦν πρὸς τὸν θεόν,
καὶ θεὸς ἦν ὁ λόγος.
πάντα δι᾽ αὐτοῦ ἐγένετο.
ὁ γέγονεν ἐν αὐτῷ ζωὴ ἦν,
καὶ ἡ ζωὴ ἦν τὸ φῶς τῶν ἀνθρώπων·
καὶ τὸ φῶς ἐν τῇ σκοτίᾳ φαίνει,
καὶ ἡ σκοτία αὐτὸ οὐ κατέλαβεν.

In the beginning was the <u>Word</u>,
And the <u>Word</u> was with <u>God</u>,
And <u>divine</u> was the Word.
Through him everything <u>was made</u>,
What <u>was made</u> in him was <u>life</u>,
And (that) <u>life</u> was the <u>light</u> of humanity,
And the <u>light</u> shines in the <u>darkness</u>,
And the <u>darkness</u> has not overcome it.

But these are not cases of chain-link construction, at least in the view of the ancient rhetoricians, who identify them as instances of "climax," the ordering of thought through sequential phrases in which the last word of one phrase starts the following phrase that builds on its predecessor. Word repetition of this sort can be diagrammed in the following manner: a/ab/bc/cd (with small-case letters indicating the absence of macro-level text units). What this kind of construction shares with chain-link interlock is the hand-off effect, whereby an audience is guided through the material as smoothly and effectively as possible. But climax construction differs from chain-link construction in at least two important respects. First, it operates at micro-levels within a text's structure, whereas chain-link interlock operates at more major structural levels (medial- and macro-levels). Second, while individual phrases share common material at their beginning or end, they exhibit no overlap of material, as in A-b-a-B constructions.

---

redactional insertion (see J. Painter, *The Quest for the Messiah: The History, Literature and Theology of the Johannine Community* [Edinburgh: T&T Clark, 1991], 109), and the former a redactional repetition of John 1:1. G. Mlakuzhyil (*The Christocentric Literary Structure of the Fourth Gospel* [Rome: Editrice Pontificio Instituto Biblico, 1987], 106) suggests that John 1:1-5 is characterised by a series of hook-words, but ancient rhetoricians spoke of it as "climax," in distinction from hook-word linkage (which normally operates at text-unit boundaries). Examples of climax from antiquity appear in R. Volkmann, *Die Rhetorik der Griechen un Römer in systematischer Übersicht* (1885; repr. Hildesheim: Georg Olms, 1963), 474–75, where it is defined as such: "das Schlusswort eines Komma oder Kolon [bildet] das Anfangswort des nächsten." Cf. also G. O. Rowe, "Style," in *Handbook of Classical Rhetoric in the Hellenistic Period (330 B.C.–A.D. 400)* (ed. S. E. Porter; Leiden: Brill, 1997), 121–57, esp. 130.

The same features differentiate chain-link interlock from catchword associations. In his commentary on James, Martin Dibelius discusses this catchword linkage extensively,[17] believing that it is a common technique in paraenetic material, in which different topics are loosely connected by means of a word that then triggers reflections on a slightly related topic. So, for instance, the use of the word "trial/test" (πειρασμόν) in 1:12 leads the author to offer advice in 1:13 on "testing" (πειράζειν). The use of "religious" (θρησκός) in 1:26 causes the author to reflect on "religion" (θρησκεία) in 1:27. Mention of being "judged" (κρίνεσθαι) in 2:12 leads the author to consider "judgement" (κρίσις) in 2:13. Mention of "peaceable" (εἰρηνική) and "fruits" (καρπῶν) in 3:17 results in the author reflecting on "peace" (εἰρήνην) and "harvest" (καρπός) in 3:18.

If Dibelius is right in his identification of these connections, then although catchword associations frequently appear when an author makes a shift in thought, they are not necessarily used as transitional devices from one text unit to another. In none of the examples given here do the catchwords link distinct text units, even if they link discursive shifts. Catchword associations of this kind do not play a transitional function between text units, which is the role that Lucian and Quintilian attribute to chain-link interlock. Moreover, Dibelius identifies catchword associations as "external" to the subject matter, by which he means "not necessarily organic within the material itself." That is, in catchword associations "one saying is attached to another simply because a word or cognate of the same stem appears in both sayings."[18] Whether Dibelius is right in finding a virtually ad hoc arrangement of material within James is highly disputed,[19] but his depiction of catchword links as lacking in coherent order is itself a world away from Lucian's discussion of chain-link interlock, in which textual units are not to be conceived of as "mere bundle[s] of parallel threads; the first is not simply to be next to the second, but part of it, their extremities intermingling."[20]

§3.5 Anticipatory Transitions

Keyword repetition of the kind noted in §3.4 above often operates at a more significant structural level than in climax, and in a manner that has close relation to chain-link interlock. Frequently in ancient literature a keyword, a key theme or phrase, or a temporal marker of some sort will be used at the conclusion of one text unit in order to anticipate and intro-

---

[17] M. Dibelius, *James* (Philadelphia: Fortress, 1976), 6–11.

[18] Dibelius, *James*, 6–7.

[19] See, for instance, the discussion in R. J. Bauckham, *James* (London: Routledge, 1999), 61–62.

[20] *How to Write History*, 55.

duce the theme of the next text unit. The structure is best diagrammed as
A-b/B, with "b" providing an anticipatory springboard from the first text
unit to the second.

Plutarch makes use of this transition technique in his *How to Tell a
Flatterer from a Friend* (hereafter, *Adulator*, from his *Moralia*). Whereas
chapters 6–11 of that work are dedicated to differentiating the flatterer
and the friend, the reader is prepared for this in the final stage of chapter
5 (51D), where Plutarch writes: "And since the flatterer uses resem-
blances to deceive and to wrap about him, it is our task to use the differences (ταῖς διαφοραῖς) in order to unwrap him and lay him bare."[21] The
term "differences" does not appear in the relatively brief chapter 6, making its first appearance in chapter 7 (52A),[22] but chapters 6–11 are all
dedicated to elaborating the theme of the differences that distinguish the
flatterer from the friend. The same form of transition appears at the end
of *Adulator* chapter 11 (55D and 55E), where the mention of commenda-
tion/praise (ἔπαινος) introduces chapters 12–16, which are bound
together by the theme of the flatterer's praise.

The same transition is found frequently in certain New Testament
texts, especially in Hebrews. Three of the clearest examples are:

(1) At the end of 1:1-4 the author makes mention of "the
angels" (τῶν ἀγγέλων), a keyword which is expanded on in
the next text unit (1:5–2:18).

(2) The figure of Melchizedek, although having been mentioned in 5:6 and 5:10, remains a murky figure until his significance is clarified in detail in Hebrews 7, following the
mention of him in the last verse of Hebrews 6 (6:20).

(3) Hebrews 11 discusses the meaning of "faith" (πίστις), after
the same word is introduced in the last two verses of
Hebrews 10 (πίστεως, 10:38-39).[23] In these cases, the clos-

[21] The translation used here is that of F. C. Babbitt, *Plutarch's* Moralia (Loeb
Classical Library; London: William Heinemann; Cambridge, MA: Harvard
University Press, 1969).

[22] διάφορη and διοπρισμός (and their cognates) also appear in chapters 9
(53C), 10 (54D), and 11 (54E).

[23] Guthrie (*Structure of Hebrews*, 96–102) illustrates the importance of keyword transitions in Hebrews. In his review of Guthrie's work (*NovT* 43 [2001]:
182–88, esp. 183), S. H. Levinsohn is critical of Guthrie's results, arguing that
keyword transition must involve the placement of the keyword at the very end of
the first unit. In this criticism Levinsohn is far too wooden. One might compare,
for instance, the linkage between Mark 12:38-40 and 12:41-44. The former
introduces the teachers of the law as those who devour widows' houses (12:40);
the latter gives a portrait of a widow in the temple in contrast to the rich in the

ing part of one section sets the stage for the following section by mention of thematic keywords or concepts that are given explicit attention in the ensuing section.[24]

Paul employs the same frequently in Romans. In 3:19-20, for instance (concluding not only 3:9-20 but also the whole of 1:18-3:20), the word νόμος makes a fourfold appearance and serves as one of the threads for his discussion throughout 3:21-31, where it appears seven times (3:21 [2x], 27 [2x], 28, 30, 31). Similarly, the close of the unit in 8:14-17 (or even 8:1-17) introduces two concepts, suffering and glory, which provide the context for Paul's reflections in 8:18-30 on Christian existence in the run-up to God's final salvific activity; the theme of suffering sets this homily in motion (8:18) and that of glory concludes it (8:30).

This form of structural transition is identified in this study as the "anticipatory transition."[25] Anticipatory linkages vary with regard to their extent, perhaps comprising a word, a phrase, a half sentence, a full sentence or more. In transitions of this kind, a key theme or, in narrative, a temporal indicator is embedded at the closure of one unit in order to

---

temple. The two text units follow on sequentially from each other, the link being χήρα ("widow"), although this is not last word in the sentence of 12:40.

A comparable difference of opinion with regard to chiastic structuring is evident in the respective work of D. J. Clark ("Criteria for Identifying Chiasm," *Linguistica Biblica* 5 [1975]: 63–72) and I. H. Thomson (*Chiasmus in the Pauline Letters* [Sheffield: Sheffield Academic Press, 1995]). Thomson maintains that chiastic correspondence must involve repetition of exact words or phrases, not simply themes, unlike Clark. In my view, W. Brouwer (*The Literary Development of John 13–17: A Chiastic Reading* [Atlanta: Society of Biblical Literature, 2000], 36–37) rightly sides with Clark.

[24] The same construction is found in a less-studied fashion elsewhere in Hebrews. In 7:28, for example, the word τετελειωμένον appears, whose meaning is elaborated throughout 8:1ff. without the word itself reappearing in that discussion. Similarly in 9:28 Christ's high priestly service is said to be εἰς σωτηρίαν, a claim developed throughout 10:1ff., although again without focusing specifically on the term σωτηρία.

[25] This transition technique is identified as "the linked keyword" by H. van Dyke Parunak ("Transitional Techniques in the Bible," *JBL* 102 [1983]: 525–48, esp. 532).

[26] As is the case for most transitions studied here, anticipatory transitions frequently appear in musical form as well as literary texts. One example will be offered here from a song on one of the best albums of one of the most influential musicians of the twentieth century. In his touching song "Treat Her Gently (Lonely Old People)" from the 1975 album *Venus and Mars*, Paul McCartney interlaces two musical pieces in an alternating A-B-A-B format ("Treat Her Gently" being A material, "Lonely Old People" being B material). The A material is composed in 4/4 timing, and the B material in 3/4 timing. However, the

prepare for and introduce a new textual unit that follows.[26] In this regard, the anticipatory transition (A-b/B) resembles one half of the chain-link transition (A-b-a-B). But it also differs from the chain-link transition in that, while material from text-unit B crosses over the text-unit boundary, there is no overlap of material itself.

§3.6   Retrospective Transitions

The inverse form of linkage to that of the anticipatory transition is what will be called here the "retrospective transition." In this construction, either an important word/theme from one unit or, in narrative, a retrospective temporal marker appears at the start of text-unit B, forming an A/a-B pattern.

In the New Testament, this transitional structure can be illustrated repeatedly from Paul's letter to the Romans. In Romans 5:1, for instance, Paul begins a new section (5:1-11) by reminding his audience of the theme of the earlier unit ("having been justified by faith," δικαιωθέντες οὖν ἐκ πίστεως).[27] The same structural transition appears in 12:1. There the phrase "through the mercies of God" (διὰ τῶν οἰκτιρμῶν τοῦ θεοῦ) recalls the *Leitmotif* of mercy/grace that underlies earlier chapters of Romans (cf. ἐλεέω in 11:30-32). Similarly, in 14:13 a section concerned with Christian mutual edification begins by summing up the emphasis of the previous section (i.e., "let us no longer pass judgement"). Finally, in 15:7 the charge "welcome one another" (προσλαμβάνεσθε ἀλλήλους) recapitulates the theme of the whole of 14:1-15:6 (cf. 14:1) before shifting to a christological reflection on Christ's "welcome" of Christians ("Christ received you," ὁ Χριστὸς προσελάβετο ὑμᾶς) in 15:7-13. In each of these five cases from Romans, the initial phrase of one text unit

---

last measure of the A units in each case shifts into the 3/4 timing that characterises the B units, and the last measure of the first B unit shifts into the 4/4 timing that characterises the A units. In this way, each of the first three musical units makes a gesture to the musical unit that follows it, functioning as an anticipatory transition.

[27] For other links between Romans 5:1-11 and the previous chapters of Romans, see S. J. Gathercole, *Where is Boasting? Early Jewish Soteriology and Paul's Response in Romans 1–5* (Grand Rapids: Eerdmans, 2002), 252–55. There he also makes the case that 5:1-11 is not the start of a new text unit (i.e., Rom 5–8) but the conclusion of a preceding unit (i.e., Rom 1–4). But his case is made only by overlooking important evidence that runs contrary to it (e.g., the phrase "through Jesus Christ our Lord" [and its variants] runs as a concluding thread throughout the various sections of Romans 5–8 [5:1, 11, 21; 6:23; 7:25; 8:39]) and by failing to recognise that the backwards links that appear especially in 5:1-2 fall at precisely the point where retrospective transitions are expected to fall—that is, at the start of a new text unit.

sums up one of the main points of the preceding text unit before a new or independent line of thought is developed, in an A/a-B format.[28]

In discursive texts such as Romans, retrospective material usually consists of key words or themes (cf. the same for anticipatory transitions, as in Hebrews). In narratives, however, this kind of transition frequently consists not of key themes but of temporal markers. Accordingly, the beginning of one text unit makes a backward gesture to the preceding unit by means of a temporal marker that takes its cues from the preceding unit in one way or another.

For instance, various books of Herodotus' *Histories* begin with short temporal gestures to the book that preceded them. So, whereas the death of Cyrus appears towards the end of Book 1 (§214, with Book 1 ending at §216), Book 2 begins "After the death of Cyrus" (τελευτησαυτος δὲ Κύρου). With this very brief temporal gesture back to the previous book, Herodotus develops the next episode in his narrative.

In New Testament narratives, the same format is widely evident. The Matthean Gospel, for instance, makes repeated use of this form of transition, with new action building on action from the previous text unit. (In some cases, the "retrospective" aspect is merely implicit in the connective phrase.) So in the following examples we find short temporal connectives reaching backwards from one text unit to its predecessor prior to the commencement of new material:

"Now when they had departed . . ." (ἀναχωρησάντων δὲ αὐτῶν, 2:13);
"Seeing the crowds . . ." (ἰδὼν δὲ τοὺς ὄχλους, 5:1);
"After he came down from the mountain . . ." (καταβάντος δὲ αὐτοῦ ἀπὸ τοῦ ὄρους, 8:1);
"While he was saying these things to them . . ." (ταῦτα αὐτοῦ λαλοῦντος αὐτοῖς, 9:18);
"As they were going away . . ." (αὐτῶν δὲ ἐξερχομένων, 9:32);
"While he was still speaking to the crowds . . ." (ἔτι αὐτοῦ λαλοῦντος τοῖς ὄχλοις, 12:46);
"That same day . . ." (ἐν τῇ ἡμέρᾳ ἐκείνῃ, 13:1);
"When Jesus heard [this] . . ." (ἀκούσας δὲ ὁ Ἰησοῦς, 14:13);
"When they had crossed over . . ." (καὶ διαπεράσαντες, 14:34);
"And after six days . . ." (καὶ μεθ' ἡμέρας ἕξ, 17:1);
"While the Pharisees were gathered together . . ." (συνηγμένων δὲ τῶν Φαρισαίων, 22:41);
"As they were eating . . ." (ἐσθιόντων δὲ αὐτῶν, 26:26);
"While he was still speaking . . ." (καὶ ἔτι αὐτοῦ λαλοῦντος, 26:47);
"While they were going . . ." (πορευομένων δὲ αὐτῶν, 28:11).

[28] The Apocalypse of Abraham (probably a first-century CE text) makes much use of this transition. See discussion of this book in §5.9.

Each of these temporal connectives is marked out by a backward glance towards a previous text unit at the start of a new text unit.[29]

Like the anticipatory transition, the retrospective transition can vary in its extent and explicitness. The Matthean examples cited above, for instance, sometimes comprise as little as one, two, or three words.[30] Contrast Josephus who, while making regular use of retrospective transitions, does so normally in extended fashion. So at the beginning of his *Antiquities* (8.1.1), Josephus writes:

> Concerning David and his prowess and the many benefits which he conferred upon his countrymen and how, after successfully conducting many wars and battles, he died at an advanced age, we have written in the preceding book. Now when his son Solomon. . . .

> περὶ μὲν οὖν Δαυίδου καὶ τῆς ἀρετῆς αὐτοῦ καὶ ὅσων ἀγαθῶν αἴτιος γενόμενος τοῖς ὁμοφύλοις πολέμους τε καὶ μάχας ὅσας κατορθώσας γηραιὸς ἐτελεύτησεν, ἐν τῇ πρὸ ταύτης βίβλῳ δεδηλώκαμεν. Σολομῶνος δὲ τοῦ παιδὸς αὐτοῦ. . . .

Here Josephus employs a retrospective transition by means of a long extended sentence regarding David's career before moving to his new subject, the reign of Solomon.

As will be shown below, the retrospective transition, with its backward glance at a transitional boundary, serves as one of the constitutive elements in the construction of a chain-link transition. Nonetheless, chain-link interlock itself is much different from the retrospective transition on the crucial matter of the overlap of material. While the retrospective transition involves material crossing of text-unit boundaries (as in chain-link interlock), it does not involve the overlap of material that characterizes chain-link interlock.

§3.7 Transitio

Slightly more elaborate than the anticipatory and retrospective transitions (although much like them) is what the anonymously written book of technical rhetoric, *Rhetorica ad Herennium* (ca. 85 BCE), lists simply as *transitio*, a term that will be used in this project. This transition is

---

[29] Matthew famously uses the phrase "When Jesus had finished these sayings . . ." (and its variants) to bring text units to a close, with the phrase sometimes appearing at the end of major text units (e.g., 7:28; 13:53) and sometimes at the start of the following text unit (e.g., 11:1; 19:1; 26:1).

[30] An exceptionally long version (for Matthew) of this kind of transition appears in 22:34: "But when the Pharisees heard that he had silenced the Sadducees . . ." (οἱ δὲ Φαρισαῖοι ἀκούσαντες ὅτι ἐφίμωσεν τοὺς Σαδδουκαίους . . .).

described as a figure of thought that "briefly recalls what has been said, and likewise briefly sets forth what is to follow next" (4.26.35).[31]

Transitio can appear in two forms, depending on which side of the text-unit boundary it appears. It frequently appears at the start of a text unit and consists of an author laying out what he hopes to achieve in the paragraphs that follow after having surveyed what he has already achieved. This transition is used by Quintilian at the beginning of his third book of *Instituto oratoria*. There he offers a retrospective overview of Book 2 and an anticipatory overview of Book 3 (3.1.1):[32]

> In Book Two, I discussed what rhetoric was and what was its end; to the best of my ability, that it was an art, that it was useful, and that it was a virtue, and I defined its material as every subject on which it was obliged to speak. I shall now expound its origins, its component elements, and how we should discover and handle each constituent.

> Quoniam in libro secundo quaesitum est quid esset rhetorice et quis finis eius, artem quoque esse eam et utilem et virtutem, ut vires nostrae tulerunt, ostendimus, materiamque ei res omnes de quibus dicere oporteret subiecimus: iam hinc unde coeperit, quibus constet, quo quaeque in ea modo invenienda atque tractanda sint exequar.

In this case the pattern A/a-b-B emerges.[33]

Transitio can also appear at the end of one text unit in order to introduce the next. This happens, for instance, in *Against Apion* 1.58–59 where, after stating the issues that were covered in the text unit of 1.6–57, Josephus then states what he will accomplish in the text unit that follows (cf. also 2.145–50), an abbreviated form of which appears below.

> Having now, I think, sufficiently shown that. . . , I propose, in the first place, to reply briefly . . . I shall then proceed to cite . . ., and to show. . . .

> ἱκανῶς δὲ φανερόν, ὡς οἶμαι, πεποιηκὼς ὅτι . . . βούλομαι μικρὰ πρότερον διαλεχθῆναι . . . εἶτα δὲ . . . παρέξω . . . καὶ᾽ . . . ἀποδείξω. . . .

---

[31] Cf. D. F. Watson, *Invention, Arrangement and Style: Rhetorical Criticism of Jude and 2 Peter* (Atlanta: Scholars Press, 1988), 202.

[32] The translation is by D. A. Russell, *Quintilian, The Orator's Education*, vol. 2, *Books 3–5* (London: Harvard University Press, 2001), 9.

[33] So, too, in the opening paragraph of his *Against Apion* (1.1–5), Josephus both reminds his reader of the argument of *Jewish Antiquities* (the text to which *Against Apion* was intended to supplement), and he also lays out his outline of the ensuing argument which then commences. On the relationship of these two texts, see especially P. Spilsbury, "*Contra Apionem* and *Antiquitates Judaicae*: Points of Contact," in *Josephus'* Contra Apionem: *Studies in Its Character and Context* (ed. L. H. Feldman and J. R. Levison; Leiden: Brill, 1996), 348–68.

In this case the pattern A-a-b/B emerges, with 1:58-59 functioning as the a-b transition.

These instances of *transitio* bear some relationship to chain-link construction, in that both *transitio* and chain-link constructions involve material crossing the text-unit boundary in some form or other. Moreover, the retrospective and prospective aspect of *transitio* can also be favourably compared to chain-link interlock. Nonetheless, as with the very similar anticipatory and retrospective transitions, what differentiates *transitio* from chain-link interlock is the crucial feature mentioned by both Lucian and Quintilian: the overlap of material. On this score, *transitio* and chain-link go their separate ways. Although *transitio* brings text units A and B "into essential connection" with each other, there is no indication that they have been "attached like one link of a chain to another" (here using Lucian's description of chain-link interlock). While *transitio* is a close kin to the chain-link transition on the matter of material from one text unit crossing the text-unit boundary in order to assist with a transition, it differs from chain-link interlock since no overlap of material is evident. While Josephus does, in fact, use chain-link interlock at major textual seams in other places of his work (see §5.4), these two instances of *transitio* evidence a different construction, in which the overlap of which Lucian and Quintilian speak is not apparent.

§3.8   The Bridge Paragraph

Whereas the chain-link interlock appears at the meeting point of two text units, the bridge paragraph does as well, with material from both text units A and B meeting within a self-contained paragraph that serves as the springboard from A to B. The pattern of a bridge paragraph is as follows: A/a+b/B. In this pattern, the "a+b" feature that characterises the transitional material represents the inseparable intertwining and enfolding of themes belonging to text-units A and B. By contrast, the "a-b" feature that characterises the transitional material of *transitio* represents the distinct and self-contained summaries of topics A and B that appear in sequence.

An example of the bridge paragraph might be Hebrews 4:14-16.[34] These verses conclude the text-unit Hebrews 3:1-4:16 as well as

---

[34] Guthrie (*Structure of Hebrews*, 102–3) speaks of it as a transition consisting of "overlapping constituents," and my use of this passage as an example of a bridge paragraph builds on his case. Guthrie (*Structure of Hebrews*, 103–4) argues that the same construction marks out Hebrews 10:19-25, which both closes the previous section and opens the final portion of the book. Cf. his *Hebrews* (Grand Rapids: Zondervan, 1998), 39–40 (cf. 173–74 and 340–41), where an outline of Hebrews is offered in which 4:14-16 and 10:19-25 are highlighted and identified as "overlap" material.

introduce the next text unit, Hebrews 4:14-10:18. As transitional verses, they continue the exhortatory application of the preceding text-unit, with the author continuing to make use of the hortatory subjunctive ("let us . . ."; 4:14, 16) that he had employed twice in 4:1 and 4:11, and which is nowhere to be seen in Hebrews 5. Similarly, the identification of "Jesus" as "high priest" in 4:14-15 reiterates the same identification made in 3:1, and mention of "confession" (ὁμολογία) in 4:14 recalls the same again made in 3:1, so that the content of 3:1 and 4:14-16 form an *inclusio* bracketing 3:1-4:16. Yet as transitional verses, 4:14-16 also sets the stage for 5:1-10:18, with its reference to Jesus as (1) "Son of God" and "high priest" who (2) "has passed through the heavens." That is, in 4:14-16 the author establishes the foundation for the two scenarios laid out in 5:1–10:18: (1) the appointment of the Son of God as high priest (5:1–7:28), and (2) this high priest's superior offering in the heavenly temple (8:1–10:18). These verses, then, which represent an "a+b" transition in the pattern A/a+b/B, have strong claim to being a transitional pivot point from one text unit to the other by means of the intermingling of text-unit themes.

A second example might come from the second chapter of the Johannine Gospel. Scholars continue to debate whether the "Wedding of Cana in Galilee" (2:1-11) is best associated with the material preceding or following it. Many think of John 2–4 as the "Cana cycle," with Jesus' two Cana miracles forming an *inclusio* around this unit (2:1-11; 4:43-54). But others think that Jesus' wedding miracle, the first of the Johannine "signs," is the final part of an unfolding text-unit consisting of triptych made up of 1:19-34, 1:35-51 and 2:1-11. Running throughout the triptych are temporal indicators that can be interpreted in any number of ways, but which unify the three sections: τῇ ἐπαύριον ("on the next day") appears in 1:29, 35, and 43, and τῇ ἡμέρᾳ τῇ τρίτῃ (variously translated) appears in 2:1, after which temporal indicators of this sort disappear until 4:43.

In the light of these two structural alternatives in relation to John 2:1-11, George Mlakuzhyil writes that John 2:1-11 "both concludes the introduction to the Fourth Gospel . . . and introduces the first part of the Gospel (Jn 2–12) and its first section (Jn 2–4)."[35] Since this important paragraph can be seen as performing a structural function in relation to

---

[35] Mlakuzhyil, *The Christocentric Literary Structure*, 106, defended on pp. 144–47 and 152–54. Cf. J. Ashton, "Narrative Criticism," in *Studying John: Approaches to the Fourth Gospel* (Oxford: Clarendon Press, 1994), 141–65, esp. 152. John 2:1-11 is studied in depth for its structural placement in Ashton's *Understanding the Fourth Gospel* (London: Clarendon Press, 1991), 266–91.

the material that both precedes and follows it, it qualifies as a transitional bridge paragraph.[36]

A third example is also telling, not least since it has been a point of significant structural discussion. Romans 9:30-33 is a passage in which elements from the prior verses (9:25-29) and following verses (10:1ff.) can be discerned. For this reason, scholars continue to debate how these four verses are structured in relation to the verses around them. For many, they are the concluding verses to the previous section, while for others they are the opening verses of a new section.[37]

Those who take 9:30-33 to be the start of a section that continues into Romans 10 emphasise the following points in particular:[38]

(1) The phrase "What shall we then say?" (τί ουν ἐροῦμεν) of 9:30 has already been used on five earlier occasions to introduce a new text unit (4:1; 6:1; 7:7; 8:31; 9:14). That the phrase is used here indicates that Paul is again introducing a new text unit, rather than concluding an earlier one.

(2) The quotation from Isaiah 28:16/8:14, while building on the scriptural catena in 9:25-29, is a development of thought from that catena and actually points forward, with Isaiah 28:16 being repeated again in Romans 10:11 and serving to bind the last verses of Romans 9 with the first half of Romans 10.

(3) Although Paul frequently uses vocatives to signal text-unit transitions, his vocative "brothers [and sisters]" (ἀδελφοί) in 10:1 is not necessarily to be taken as a text-unit introductory marker, as its appearance elsewhere demonstrates (e.g., Rom 1:13; 7:4; 8:12; 1 Cor 1:11; 7:24, 29).

---

[36] For other examples of bridge paragraphs in John, see Mlakuzhyil, *The Christocentric Literary Structure*, 103–6. For an example in Mark (8:22-26), see R. A. Horsley, *Hearing the Whole Story: The Politics of Plot in Mark's Gospel* (Louisville: Westminster John Knox Press, 2001), 14–15, 70–71; W. Shiner, *Proclaiming the Gospel: First-Century Performance of Mark* (Harrisburg: Trinity Press International, 2003), 116–17.

[37] E. Käsemann (*An die Römer* [trans. G. W. Bromiley; 4th ed.; Tübingen: J.C.B. Mohr (Paul Siebeck), 1980], 266–88) takes 9:30–10:21 to be a single macro-unit consisting of four micro-units, so that 10:1 can function as "der neuen Einleitung" without 9:30-33 being considered "als Abschluß zu 26-29" (269).

[38] The first four points are articulated, for instance, by J. D. G. Dunn, *Romans* (Dallas: Word Books, 1988), 2:579.

(4) At 9:30-33 Paul reintroduces the main terms and concepts that drove his earlier consideration of righteousness and faith, elaborating them here as reminders of his earlier analysis—something he would do at the start of a section rather than the conclusion of one (or so it is claimed).

(5) The material in 9:30-33 repeatedly shows itself to have the same interests as that in 10:1-4. Both paragraphs discuss Israel's error/stumble; both have a high concentration of the word "righteousness" (δικαιοσύνη); both include contrasts of faith and works (9:30) or God's righteousness and "their own" righteousness (10:3); and the key phrase "the one who believes" appears in both (cf. 9:33 and 10:4).

Conversely, those who take 9:30-33 to be the conclusion of a previous section (with 10:1 acting as the start of a new text-unit) emphasise the following points in particular:[39]

(1) The vocative "brothers [and sisters]" (ἀδελφοί) in 10:1 must be an introductory marker.[40] It appears in a context where Paul expresses his affection for his fellow Jews, with similar expressions of affection appearing at the beginning of text units (i.e., 9:1-5; 11:1). So 9:30-33 is the concluding paragraph of a preceding text unit.

(2) Romans 9:30-33 is marked out by a diatribe style in which an initial question introduces the theological point to be considered in the same paragraph. Diatribe marks out all the previous sections in Romans 9 (cf. 9:14, 19; the initial question of 9:6 is implied), but does not continue on into Romans 10. So the question of 9:30 shares in this diatribe style that characterises Romans 9, not Romans 10.

(3) The four sections of theological discourse in Romans 9 (i.e. 6-13, 14-18, 19-29, 30-33) each conclude with a quotation from scripture (i.e., 13, 18, 25-29, 33), whereas the use of Scripture "functions differently" in Romans 10.[41] So not only do the four sections begin with the same diatribe style,

---

[39] These three points are articulated in J. Lambrecht, "The Caesura between Romans 9:30-3 and 10:1," *NTS* 45 (1999): 141–47. Lambrecht makes five points in defence of this interpretation, the first three being the strongest.

[40] See, for instance, F. Siegert, *Argumentation bei Paulus gezeigt an Röm 9–11* (Tübingen: Mohr Siebeck, 1985), 116; J. L. White, *The Form and Function of the Body of the Greek Letter: A Study of the Letter-Body in the Non-Literary Papyri and in Paul the Apostle* (Missoula: University of Montana Press, 1972), 66.

[41] Lambrecht, "The Caesura," 144.

they also end in the same manner, allowing Scripture to have the final word.

This is not the place to adjudicate this debate. In light of the ancient rhetorician's respect for the intermingling of material as a means of making a transition, the debate itself might be somewhat anachronistic, driven by the modern scholarly concern for precision and clarity in a manner that might not be appropriate in every case when applied to ancient literature. As will be shown in the following chapters, similar debates regarding text-unit differentiation frequently arise in relation to passages in which chain-link transitions appear, since the overlapping that both Lucian and Quintilian applaud as literary adornment often appears awkward, confusing, and second-rate to many modern interpreters. So, too, the intermingling of text-unit themes in 9:30-33 causes havoc if the text is assessed in relation to an "either/or" structural grid. A few scholars have seen this point. So Ulrich Wilckens, claiming that 9:30-33 is related to both 9:25-29 and 10:1ff., writes:[42]

> Da also dieser Abschnitt formal das Voranstehende abschließt und zugleich inhaltlich das folgende einleitet, wird man ihn nicht exklusiv zu dem einen oder andern ziehen dürfen. Seine Funktion ist, beim Abschluß des ersten Gedankens das Thema des nächsten einzuführen.

M.-J. Lagrange came to a similar conclusion, finding 9:30-33 primarily to be "une conclusion à tirer" and "le mot de la fin pour la péricope précédente," while at the same time beginning "un nouvel aspect de la question, la responsabilité d'Israël."[43]

It is possible to argue that Romans 9:30-33 (along with the other bridge paragraphs from Hebrews and John noted above) is, in fact, comprised of a chain-link transition. In this case, text-unit A is seen to appear up to 9:29 and text-unit B is seen to start at 10:1, with the overlap occurring in the intermingled material of 9:30-33. The intermingling of thematic "fingers" across the text-unit boundary might qualify this passage as comprising a text-unit overlap (not least since the descriptions of chain-link transition offered by Lucian and Quintilian are relatively brief). But if so, it should be considered one particular type of the chain-link transition (say, type B), and a type to be differentiated from that being studied in this project (say, type A), in which the overlap of material can be demarcated according to a "balanced" (i.e., A-b/a-B) or "unbalanced" (i.e., A-b-a/B and A-b-a/a-B) or "multiple" form (as discussed in

---

[42] U. Wilckens, *Der Brief an die Römer* (Neukirchen-Vluyn: Neukirchener Verlag, 1980), 2:211.

[43] M.-J. Lagrange, *Saint Paul Épitre aux Romains* (6th ed.; Paris: Gabalda, 1950), 489.

§2.2 above). That is, in subtype A the overlap emerges by means of a relatively distinct demarcation of "a" and "b" material; in subtype B, however, the overlap comes about through the intermingling of material in a manner that makes the "a" and "b" material virtually impossible to demarcate. In view of this difference, I find it unlikely that type B is, in fact, a chain-link construction, and I consider it preferential to identify the transition exemplified in Romans 9:30-33 as a transitional bridge paragraph (A/a+b/B) rather than an independent type of chain-link interlock. The distinction between bridge paragraphs and chain-link interlock needs to be kept intact, since bridge paragraphs usually contain no clear and significant overlap of material, despite the intermingling of material in them. This is evident, for instance, from Acts 15:36–16:5, which will be considered in §9.6.

The bridge paragraph is the last of the rhetorical devices that can be productively compared with and contrasted to chain-link interlock. Prior to consideration of specific examples of transitional interlock, however, further aspects of chain-link anatomy need to be considered, as outlined in the following chapter.

CHAPTER 4

The Anatomy of Chain-Link
Interlock

In chapter 3, the following four points were demonstrated:

(1) Chain-link construction is an inter-textual phenomenon involving the linkage of two independent text units, rather than being an intra-textual phenomenon by which a single text unit is structured (as in chiastic structuring).

(2) In its anticipatory function, chain-link interlock involves an element of foreshadowing, but it is not reducible to foreshadowing since it serves a transitional role that simple foreshadowing does not serve and since it includes a retrospective aspect at the point of transitional overlap.

(3) In its back-and-forth pattern (A-b-a-B), chain-link construction is well at home in the ancient world in which the
alternating of material was a common technique in a variety
of forms.

(4) The crossing of material over the text-unit boundary, while
intrinsic to chain-link interlock, is shared with a number of
other transition techniques, including anticipatory transitions (A-b/B), retrospective transitions (A/a-B), *transitio*
(A/a-b-B or A/a-b/B), and the bridge paragraph (A/a+b/B).
What differentiates chain-link construction from these
other techniques is precisely the overlap of material in distinct fashion that Lucian specifically mentions and
Quintilian highlights in his analogy of handholding.

Following from these four points of summary, a further six observations
regarding the character and function of chain-link construction are regis-
tered in the paragraphs below. These observations derive from and
develop the observations of previous chapters, and are sometimes cor-
roborated here by the findings of later chapters.

§4.1   The Ingredients of Chain-Link Interlock

Although chain-link interlock is distinctive from other transitions with
regard to the overlapping of material, it is in essence a composite of two
other common transitions. That is, it comprises a simple doubling up of
anticipatory and retrospective transitions (§3.5 and §3.6). The first half
of the anticipatory transitions (i.e., "A-b") is coupled with the second half
of the retrospective transitions (i.e. "a-B"), forming an independent but
clearly recognisable transition, the chain-link transition (i.e. A-b-a-B). In
the same fashion that *inclusio*, if repeated more than once, regenerates
itself as chiasm (cf. §3.1), so too the union of anticipatory and retrospective transitions results in the formation of the chain-link interlock.

The fact that chain-link interlock is comprised of other forms of transition is evident in Dyke Parunak's study of transitional structures. He
uses the phrase "balanced linked keyword"[1] when describing passages

---

[1] H. van Dyke Parunak, "Transitional Techniques in the Bible," *JBL* 102
(1983): 532. In the same article Parunak also itemises another A-b-a-B transition
technique that he refers to as an 'inverted hinge" (541), the only difference being
that the inverted hinge involves a self-contained text-unit between A and B (i.e.,
A/b-a/B). The same A-b-a-B technique is discussed as "interlocking crossover
points" by I. M. Kikawada ("The Shape of Genesis 11.1-9," in *Rhetorical
Criticism: Essays in Honor of James Muilenberg* [ed. J. J. Jackson and M. Kessler;
Pittsburgh: Pickwick Press, 1974], 18–32) and as "inverted intermediary transi-

animated by what is here called "chain-link construction" (A-b-a-B). The adjective "balanced" is significant. Parunak discusses the "linked keyword" construction in relation to the following patterns: A/a-B and A-b/B. By the addition of the adjective "balanced" to the phrase "linked keyword" Parunak indicates precisely the point being made here. That is, when the "A-b" and the "a-B" of Parunak's "linked keywords" are assembled together, they form what he terms the "balanced linked keyword", or, in our terminology, the chain-link transition. While Parunak did not have a distinct terminology to discuss chain-link construction, he recognised that particular construction to be a combination of two readily recognisable transition techniques.

So, too, George Guthrie stumbles upon the overlap structure of chain-link construction in his discussion of "hook key words." According to Guthrie, the keyword "hook" is formed in one of three ways: "either by (1) a characteristic term used in the second unit and introduced in the conclusion to the first unit, (2) a characteristic term used in the first unit and used in the introduction of the next, or (3) a combination of the two." Guthrie's description of the third form (i.e., the combination of the first two forms) approximates the chain-link structure that is of interest in this project. Although the three forms are related, by grouping them together Guthrie missed the chance to distinguish the all-important characteristic of material overlap that distinguishes the third form from the first and second.

So chain-link construction is, at least in theory, not some complicated transition created out of nothing and unrelated to any of the readily recognisable transitions that existed in the ancient world. Instead, it is simply the combination of two of the most common transitions acting simultaneously.

§4.2   Articulated and Unarticulated Forms of Chain-Link Interlock

Just as anticipatory and retrospective transitions can be "articulated" or "unarticulated" transitions, so too can chain-link transitions. With regard to articulated transitions, Josephus has already provided us with several examples in transitions where he explicitly states that a transition is being made. This was seen, for instance, in his retrospective transition of *Antiquities* 8.1.1: "We have already treated . . . in the foregoing book." An articulated transition was also evident in Josephus's *transitio* in *Against Apion* 1.58–59. There Josephus gives an explicit indication that a transition is taking place: "Having now, I think, sufficiently shown that. . . ." We have also seen this articulated feature in Quintilian's own chain-link

---

tion" by G. H. Guthrie (*The Structure of Hebrews: A Text Linguistic Analysis* [Leiden: Brill, 1994], 107).

transition of *Institutio oratoria* 9.4.146: "[M]y final book will explain the nature of the difference between our language and that of Greece. But I must bring this book to a conclusion without more delay, since it has already exceeded the limits designed for it. To sum up then. . . ."

But anticipatory and retrospective transitions can also be unarticulated. We have seen evidence of this in the examples of keyword or thematic transitions in Hebrews and Romans (§3.5). In those examples, new text units were introduced in relation to preceding text units by means of a transition in which the content of text-unit B was simply introduced at the point of transition, without an explicit indication that a text-unit transition is being made.[2] As will be shown, chain-link construction can also share this unarticulated feature with its anticipatory and retrospective cousins. In fact, most of the examples of chain-link construction in the New Testament are precisely of this unarticulated kind.

§4.3 Non-Defining Features of Chain-Link Interlock

It was seen in §3.5 and §3.6 that anticipatory and retrospective transitions can vary significantly in their length. Since neither Lucian nor Quintilian gives any indication that chain-link interlock is characterised by a given length, we might suspect that, like its anticipatory and retrospective cousins, a chain link is not constrained by considerations of length. In fact, in the examples offered in the following chapters, chain-link transitions vary in extent not only between different texts but also within single texts. Length appears, then, to have little part in defining chain-link interlock.

Similarly, just as anticipatory and reiterative transitions appear within the gamut of textual genres, so too we might suspect the same to be true of chain-link interlock. Neither Lucian nor Quintilian indicates that chain-link interlock is appropriate only to specific genres. Lucian mentions it in relation to the writing of history, but this does nothing to

---

[2] The same unarticulated character might mark out *transitio*-type transitions (A/a-b/B or A/a-b-B) in Hebrews. Guthrie (*Structure of Hebrews*, 146) argues that Hebrews 8:1-2 links the appointment of God's Son as high priest (as laid out in 5:1-7:28 = A) to his heavenly and superior offering (as laid out in 8:3-10:18 = B). With the "a-b" handoff at 8:1-2, Hebrews 5:1–10:18 comprises an A/a-b-B pattern, with the "a-b" of 8:1-2 acting as "the center point for the great central exposition on the high priestly ministry of Christ." If Guthrie is right, this transition would fall into the category of an unarticulated *transitio*. Guthrie finds the same construction in Hebrews 4:1-2, where the negative portrait of Israel's unbelief in the wilderness (laid out in 3:12-17) and the positive portrait of "rest" to those who believe (laid out in 4:3-11) meet in the intervening "a-b" transition. He identifies Hebrews 8:1-2 and 4:1-2 as examples of what he calls "direct intermediary transition" (106–7).

exclude it from use in other genres. Quintilian speaks of it in relation to recounting a case to others, and he uses it himself in the context of discourse. The survey of material in the following chapters confirms that matters of genre have little significance in determining the existence of chain-link interlock within a given text.

Finally, it is not the case that chain-link interlock always provides a smooth transition from one text unit to the next. Lucian thought that chain-link interlock ensured that "humps and hollows" could be avoided, and by this he seems to envisage the avoidance of abrupt starts-and-stops between self-contained and independent text units. But while chain-link interlock does avoid a boxy structure and ensures that two text units do not simply sit as "neighbours" next door to each other (Lucian again), nonetheless the very overlapping of material can at times result in some rather startling transitions. The interlocked transitions studied in this project could in theory be placed along a spectrum indicating the extent of transitional "smoothness" and "abruptness" for the respective examples. This will not be attempted, however, since it would be a rather subjective exercise. Nonetheless, at least two of the examples studied here have the effect of standing out prominently and starkly within the text, thereby blatantly grabbing the attention of the audience in order to demand conscious reflection on the rhetor's intended structure and the advancement of his case. Examples of this will be considered from both the Hebrew Bible (Isa 48, §5.6) and the New Testament (Rom 7, §6.2). For the most part, however, the instances of chain-link interlock considered in this project fall to the other side of the spectrum of transitional style, as examples of smooth transitions from one text unit to another.

§4.4   The Structural Levels of Chain-Link Interlock

It will be seen that chain-link construction can function at a variety of textual levels. By analogy, some interpreters who study the use of chiasm in ancient texts regularly make a distinction between "micro-chiasm" and "macro-chiasm," denoting differences in the extent of chiastic reflexivity in short sections of text (e.g., twelve verses) on the one hand and, on the other hand, as an organising structure of longer passages.[3] In practice, the distinction may not be valid with regard to chiasm, in that the existence of macro-level chiasm is itself a somewhat dubious phenomenon. But in theory, the distinction has merit, just as was shown above in relation to micro- and macro-level alternation (§3.3).

---

[3] See, for instance, M. J. Dahood, "Chiasmus," in *International Dictionary of the Bible Supplement* (ed. K. Crim; Nashville: Abingdon, 1976), 145; W. Brouwer, *The Literary Development of John 13–17: A Chiastic Reading* (Atlanta: Society of Biblical Literature, 2000), 49–85.

Precisely the same distinction between macro-levels and lesser structural levels is evident in the manner that the ancients made use of chain-link transition. In many instances it appears at the macro-level of texts as a transition from one major text-unit to the next. In some cases, however, it also appears at a lesser medial-level, serving as a transition from one textual subunit to the next.

§4.5   Structural Polyvalence and Concurrence

On occasion the transitional material at the centre of a chain-link interlock is not quite as cleanly demarcated as the theoretical pattern "b-a" might indicate. This is especially the case in those narratives (e.g., the Johannine Gospel) where themes and motifs are tightly interwoven throughout the whole of the narrative. For instance, a particular theme might appear in a transitional recapitulation section, although that same theme might also have relevance to the narrative that follows.[4] When faced with structural polyvalence of this kind, purists might throw up their hands and decry the arbitrariness and evidential selectively by which a thesis is proved. In practice, however, a purist's proper concern is less poignantly felt. In the following chapters, in the few cases in which "a" and "b" sections of the transition are not completely watertight, it is nonetheless clear in which direction the transitional sections have their respective "centres of gravity."[5]

Furthermore, on occasion a transition that incorporates chain-link interlock is also marked out by structural "concurrence"—that is, by the use of more than one structural technique acting simultaneously within a section of text.[6] This phenomenon of concurrence is evident, for example in the Johannine Prologue, which has been discussed above in relation to both chiasm (§3.1) and climax (§3.4). In the same way, interlocked transitional material will occasionally evidence the existence of other structural features as well. Even then, however, the features of text-unit interlock can be distilled without much effort.

In sum, the reader should not emerge from this theoretical discussion of chain-link interlock with the expectation that a pure pattern will be

---

[4] Cf. G. Mlakuzhyil (*The Christocentric Literary Structure of the Fourth Gospel* [Rome: Editrice Pontificio Instituto Biblico, 1987], 103), who notes a variety of cases in the Johannine Gospel in which "a summary serves simultaneously as a transition and as an introduction," and other cases in which "a summary functions both as a transition and a conclusion."

[5] That is, the distinctiveness of the overlapping sections of material is maintained, unlike the intertwining material of a bridge paragraph (studied in §3.8 above).

[6] The term "concurrence" in this sense derives from W. Holladay, "The Recovery of Poetic Passages of Jeremiah," *JBL* 85 (1966): 401–35, esp. 411.

evident in every case, like the cookie-cutter that repeatedly carves the same shape out of a batch of dough. Variation and diversity characterise the examples with regard to aspects of their structural pattern, their literary function, and the genre in which they appear. What unites all the examples is a perceptible conformity to the depiction of chain-link construction as mentioned by Lucian and Quintilian, with interlocking material appearing at text-unit boundaries and serving a transitional purpose.

§4.6   The Utility of Chain-Link Interlock in Oral/Aural Cultures

Occasionally a New Testament text reinforces the fact that its world was predominantly oral/aural. So Jesus exhorts his audience with the words, "Whoever has ears to hear, let him hear" (ὃς ἔχει ὦτα ἀκούειν ἀκουέτω, Mark 4:9, 23 [trans. mine]) and says to his disciples, "He who hears you hears me" (ὁ ἀκούων ὑμῶν ἐμοῦ ἀκούει, Luke 10:16). Similarly, Paul claims that "faith comes through hearing" (ἡ πίστις ἐξ ἀκοῆς, Rom 10:17 [trans. mine]; cf. 10:14; Gal 3:2, 5; 1 Thess 1:5; 2:13). He urges the Thessalonians that his letter be "read to all" of them (1 Thess 5:27) and urges the Colossians to "have it [his letter] read also in the church of the Laodiceans," adding that they should "read also the letter from Laodicea" (Col 4:16). The likely assumption here is that the reading will be a corporate reading, as in Revelation 1:3, which speaks of "one who reads aloud" (ὁ ἀναγινώσκων) for the benefit of "those who hear" (οἱ ἀκούοντες).[7]

Much work has been done in relation to oral/aural techniques within New Testament texts,[8] indicating their utility as tools for communication

---

[7] The exhortation "Let the reader understand" (ὁ ἀναγινώσκων νοείτω) of Mark 13:14 does not indicate that the Markan Gospel was to be read by individual readers on their own. See W. Shiner, *Proclaiming the Gospel: First-Century Performance of Mark* (Harrisburg: Trinity Press International, 2003), 177.

[8] See, for instance, P. J. Achtemeier, "*Omne Verbum Sonat*: The New Testament and the Oral Environment of Late Western Antiquity," *JBL* 109 (1990): 3–27; J. D. Harvey, *Listening to the Text: Oral Patterning in Paul's Letters* (Grand Rapids: Baker Books, 1998); J. Dewey, "Oral Methods of Structuring Narrative in Mark," *Interpretation* 53 (1989): 32–44; idem., "Textuality in an Oral Culture: A Survey of the Pauline Traditions," *Semeia* 65 (1995): 37–65; R. L. Rohrbaugh, "The Social Location of the Marcan Audience," *BTB* 23 (1993): 114–27; W. H. Kelber, *The Oral and Written Gospel: The Hermeneutics of Speaking and Writing in the Synoptic Tradition, Mark, Paul and Q* (Philadelphia: Fortress Press, 1983); T. E. Boomershine, "Jesus of Nazareth and the Watershed of Ancient Orality and Literacy," *Semeia* 65 (1995): 7–36. Background studies of particular importance are W. Harris, *Ancient Literacy* (Cambridge, MA: Harvard University Press, 1989); M. Bar-Ilan, "Illiteracy in the Land of Israel in the First

in the ancient world, in which only a very small percentage of people (usually elite men and/or their retainers) were literate.[9] In this regard we are frequently reminded that "[c]onventions of orality undergirded all composition, performance and reception of texts."[10] In a predominantly oral/aural culture, oral techniques "play much of the part which punctuation, highlighting, headings, and paragraphs play in a graphic text."[11] Scholars most sensitive to the oral/aural context in which ancient texts were written and conveyed frequently express frustration at "the linear nature of our thinking" in relation to these ancient texts.[12] As Walter Ong writes:

> In a primary oral culture, to solve effectively the problem of retaining and retrieving carefully articulated thought, you have to do your thinking in mnemonic patterns, shaped for ready oral recurrence. Your thought must come into being in heavily rhythmic, balanced patterns, in repetitions or antitheses, in alliterations and assonances, in epithetic and other formulary expressions, . . . in proverbs which are constantly heard by everyone so that they come to mind readily and which themselves are patterned for retention and ready recall, or in other mnemonic form.[13]

In the search for structural integrity within complete texts, post-Enlightenment interpreters often give voice to the discrepancy between

---

Centuries C.E.," in *Essays in the Social Scientific Study of Judaism and Jewish Society*, vol. 2 (ed. S. Fishbane and S. Schonfeld; Hoboken: KTAV, 1992); M. Beard. ed., *Literacy in the Roman World* (Ann Arbor: Journal of Roman Archaeology, 1991); and esp. C. Hezser, *Jewish Literacy in Roman Palestine* (Tübingen: Mohr Siebeck, 2001). Along different (and relatively uncritical) lines is A. Millard, *Reading and Writing in the Time of Jesus* (Sheffield: Sheffield Academic Press, 2000), who (like S. Safrai, J. Naveh, and A. Demsky before him) seeks to show that writing was widespread in first-century Roman Judaea.

[9] Estimates of two to four percent are frequent; see Rohrbaugh, "Social Location," 115; Dewey, "Oral Methods," 39–47; Bar-Ilan, "Illiteracy," 56. Hezser's *Jewish Literacy* helpfully offers a taxonomy of literacy according to social locations and social functions, rather than suggesting a simple percentage figure.

[10] J. Dewey, "The Gospel of John in Its Oral-Written Media World," in *Jesus in Johannine Tradition* (ed. R. T. Fortna and T. Thatcher; Louisville: Westminster John Knox Press, 2001), 243. So Plutarch maintained that instruction is achieved only through hearing (*Rect. rat. aud.* 2; 38a).

[11] C. Bryan, *A Preface to Mark: Notes on the Gospel in Its Literary and Cultural Settings* (Oxford: Oxford University Press, 1997), 78. Cf. his comments on p. 80: "Oral techniques perform . . . the tasks of punctuation, clarifying and emphasizing."

[12] J. L. White, *The Apostle of God: Paul and the Promise of Abraham* (Peabody: Hendrickson, 1999), 64.

[13] W. J. Ong, *Orality and Literacy: The Technologizing of the Word* (London: Routledge, 1988), 34.

the modern desire for neat and tidy textual outlines on the one hand, and on the other, the non-linear structures of the ancient world that assisted in the transmission of ideas in an oral/aural context. So with regard to Hebrews, Guthrie writes:

> Perhaps part of the difficulty with depicting Hebrews in outline form lies in the fact that Hebrews was originally delivered for its effect on hearers. The discourse was not crafted to fit our neat, thematically progressing outlines. It was meant to have an impact on hearers.[14]

Similarly, John Harvey indicates the following: "The predominantly oral nature of a rhetorical culture requires speakers to arrange their material in ways that can be followed easily by a listener. Clues to the organization of thought are, of necessity, based on sound rather than on sight."[15] That is, in the words of Joanna Dewey, "[a]ll ancient writers wrote for the ear."[16] So we read of Seneca's criticism of a colleague's writing style on the basis that "he was writing those words for the mind rather than for the ear" (*Ep.* 100.2). That "writing for the ear" includes chain-link construction is given added impetus from an observation by E. A. Havelock, who stresses that "it was the ear, not the eye, that had to be seduced," and to do this an author

> has to hint or to warn or to predict what the next thing he says is going to be like, or the next after that, even in the moment when he is saying the thing in front of it. So that the memory as it absorbs statement A is half-prepared to move on to statement B.[17]

This quotation roughly describes the function of the forward gesture involved in chain-link interlock, and it aptly illustrates the usefulness of cross-boundary gestures in facilitating the assimilation of texts in ancient oral/aural contexts.

The point is directly applicable to chain-link interlock. Although some forms of ancient chain-link interlock cause modern interpreters to balk (especially the unarticulated form), the technique seems to have been far more accessible and understandable within predominantly oral/aural cultures. According to Parunak, the delivery of ideas in an oral/aural context permitted features like material overlap to have a certain currency precisely as signals of transition. Although he does not discuss the chain-link technique in this regard, Parunak nonetheless

---

[14] Guthrie, *Structure of Hebrews*, 146.

[15] Harvey, Listening to the Text, xv.

[16] Dewey, "The Gospel of John," 249.

[17] E. A. Havelock, "The Alphabetization of Homer," in *Communication Arts in the Ancient World* (ed. E. A. Havelock and J. P. Herschbell; New York: Hastings House, 1978), 14.

offers an indication of how overlapping techniques in general assisted in
the dissemination of information in an oral/aural context:

> [Overlapping techniques were] especially effective in helping the
> reader [sic.; better "hearer"] of a text follow the writer's [or speaker's]
> shift in thought. . . . A speaker can help an audience follow a transition
> by hesitating at the point where the topic changes and hinting at the
> change before actually making it. . . . The effect is to slow down [sic.;
> better "prolong"] the transition and give listeners more opportunity to
> note that a change is taking place.[18]

So Richard Horsley also notes how the overlapping of material both contributes to the development of a narrative and aids in the process of
remembering that narrative. He writes:

> In a narrative style that assists memory, the earlier episodes suggest or
> forecast later episodes which in turn recall the earlier ones while carry-
> ing the story further and adding to the drama and conflict. The narra-
> tive thus establishes numerous interconnections that resonate with
> each other as they resonate with the hearers.[19]

Since transitional links enhance the audience's chance of assimilating
an author's meaning in an oral/aural culture, the ancient rhetoricians
considered them to fall well within the orbit of rhetorical interest.
Moreover, as was noted in §1.2, transitions have relation to four of the
five parts of rhetoric noted by the *Rhetorica ad Herennium*: arrangement,
style, memory, and delivery. Although it falls most naturally within the
category of style, its foothold within the other categories is not difficult
to discern. So, for instance, *Rhetorica ad Herennium* defines memory as
"the firm retention in the mind of the matter, word and arrangement"
(4.26.35). Although memory is assisted by the proper use of images in
one's rhetoric, proper structural clues within one's argumentation or
presentation would also have assisted the process of retaining the matter
within one's mind. This, at least, was Quintilian's view (*Inst.* 11.2.36), and
a common-sense one at that:

---

[18] Parunak, "Transitional Techniques," 546. Cf. W. Ong (*Interfaces of the
Word: Studies in the Evolution of Consciousness and Culture* [Ithaca: Cornell
University Press, 1977], 114) when discussing the importance of repetition in
general: "Oral cultures need repetition, redundancy, verboseness for several reasons. First . . . spoken words fly away. A reader can pause over a point he wants to
reflect on, or go back a few pages to return to it. The inscribed word is still there.
The spoken word [however] is gone. So the orator repeats himself, to help his
hearers think it over."

[19] R. A. Horsley, *Hearing the Whole Story: The Politics of Plot in Mark's Gospel*
(Louisville: Westminster John Knox, 2001), 70.

But it is Division and Composition which are important factors in memorizing what we have written, and almost uniquely important factors . . . in helping to retain what we compose mentally. The man who has got his Division right will never be able to make mistakes in the order of his ideas.

Verum et in iis quae scripsimus complectendis multum valent et in iis quae cogitamus continendis prope solae . . . divisio et compositio. Nam qui ercte diviserit, numquam poterit in rerum ordine errare.

To this end Richard Burridge rightly suggests that "the overall arrangement and structures noted in the Gospels, *as well as the links and relationships between individual units*, would help in both memory [cf. Horsley's comment above] and delivery" in an ancient context.[20] And it is precisely this observation that returns us to Quintilian's predilection (*Inst.* 9.4.129) that linking units together in an overlapped fashion ensures that one's audience is charmed by one's style, in order that the audience would surrender to the orator's case by means of sheer artistic and stylistic delight.[21]

That chain-link interlock served a significant purpose in cultures entrenched in oral/aural patterning is a view that is supported throughout the following chapters. There it will be repeatedly shown that the frequent inability of modern interpreters to appreciate the structure of interlocked transitions arises from a general inability to interpret ancient texts apart from modern expectations about the linear nature of a text's

---

[20] R. A. Burridge, "The Gospels and Acts," in *Handbook of Classical Rhetoric in the Hellenistic Period (330 B.C.–A.D. 400)* (ed. S. E. Porter; Leiden: Brill, 1997), 528, emphasis added. On p. 530, he writes: "Further consideration of the Gospels . . . designed to be read orally from the perspective of rhetorical delivery and memory might yield future benefit." Early exercises in this field include D. Rhoads, "Performing the Gospel of Mark," in *Body and Bible: Interpreting and Experiencing Biblical Narratives* (ed. B. Krondorfer; Philadelphia: Trinity Press International, 1992); Shiner, *Proclaiming the Gospel.* Like Burridge, Shiner (109) notes: "Ease of memorization is greatly facilitated by clear division and artistic structure." (See his important application of this insight to the issue of chiastic structures aiding the memory of the orator more than that of the audience, 114–16.) Shiner similarly discusses the importance of structure in relation to delivery ("structure would facilitate delivery since the performer could develop a particular narrative effect for each section" of an oration, 114)—thereby indicating the utility of structure for the purposes of both memory and delivery. Cf. also Horsley (*Hearing the Whole Story*, 7): certain literary patterns "aid the memory of the performer and the hearing of the audience."

[21] That delivery and style are closely related is clear from Isocrates's discussion of delivery in *Or.* 5.25-27, which flows naturally into discussion of "rhythmic flow and manifold graces of style . . . by which they [orators] might make their oratory more pleasing."

flow. As James Dunn suggests, "If we are to enter empathetically into such a [non-literary] culture it is essential that we become conscious of our literary paradigm and make deliberate efforts to step outside it and to free ourselves from its inherited predispositions."[22] As will be shown in the following chapters, freeing ourselves from the literary paradigm's modern presuppositions concerning the linear presentation of ideas enables fresh light to be shed on ancient texts. In particular, it will be shown that the non-linear patterns evident at a variety of transition points in New Testament texts have not resulted from an author's literary deficiency or from the inefficiency of some later weak-minded redactor who messed up the structure of the original text. Instead, those non-linear transitions are displays of rhetorical proficiency and effectiveness to benefit an audience residing within a predominantly non-literary culture.

As a final observation, however, it should be stressed that chain-link interlock need not be thought of as something belonging exclusively to cultures (past and present) dominated by orality. This is less obviously the case for unarticulated chain links, but it is obviously true for the articulated form of chain-link construction, both in oral[23] and printed contexts. (The appendix to this chapter offers an illustration of the continued utility of chain-link construction in modern print-culture.) If chain-link construction began life as a method for assisting transitional clarity in oral/aural cultures, it should not be surprising to find that it has not yet outlived its usefulness even in print-dominated cultures. Ong claims this to be the case for many techniques from oral contexts, of which chain-link interlock is only one example: "Of course, long after the invention of script and even of print, distinctively oral forms of thought and expression linger, competing with the forms introduced with script and print."[24]

---

[22] J. D. G. Dunn, "Altering the Default Setting: Re-envisaging the Early Transmission of the Jesus Tradition," *NTS* 49 (2003): 142.

[23] For instance, the news network CNN frequently ends a news programme with an advertisement for the programme that follows, then it starts that programme with a recap of the news highlights (i.e., A-b/a-B). Similarly, when chairing the discussion of a seminar paper after which coffee is scheduled to follow, I regularly say something like the following at the close of discussion: "In a moment we will break for coffee, but first it falls to me to thank our speaker for her interesting paper." If the paper/discussion = A and the coffee time = B, the closing words represent a clear chain-link transition (i.e., A-b-a/B) in this oral context.

[24] W. J. Ong, *The Presence of the Word* (New Haven: Yale University Press, 1967), 22; see his larger discussion on pp. 54–63. Cf. also Kelber, *Oral and Written Gospel*, 17, and especially the quotation from A. B. Lord already cited (see chapter 2) but worth repeating in this context as well ("Words Heard and Words Seen," 13): "There is a tendency for us in the European tradition to forget how extensive and how basic our literary heritage from the world of orality has been,

Chain-link interlock, involving the overlap of material at the point of text-unit transitions, appears to be one technique that has "overlapped" the oral, print and electronic eras of cultural development.

In the chapters that follow, however, we will concentrate on the appearance of chain-link interlock in a variety of ancient texts, thereby supplementing the evidence of Lucian and Quintilian in a process of evidential triangulation. So in chapter 5 a selection of examples of chain-link construction from the ancient world will be offered, laying the foundation for the more studied analysis of text-unit interlock in the New Testament in the four chapters that follow chapter 5. And so we move in the next chapter to the second triangulation point in this project.

---

and there is a corresponding tendency to believe that the world of literacy invented some of the characteristics of literature, which in reality originated in oral literature. Among them is a sense of form and structure . . . and many devices, later termed 'rhetorical' and attributed to schools, which actually were created in the crucible of the oral world." The point is made with specific regard to chiasm in Brouwer, *The Literary Development*, 23; I. H. Thomson, *Chiasmus in the Pauline Letters* (Sheffield: Sheffield Academic Press, 1995), 22–24; A. Stock, "Chiastic Awareness and Education in Antiquity," *Biblical Theology Bulletin* 14 (1984): 23–27; H. I. Marrou, *A History of Education in Antiquity* (New York: Sheed & Ward, 1956).

Appendix

§4.7   A Modern Example of Articulated Chain Links

In his 1980 extensive study of Galilee, Seán Freyne includes a number of chain links throughout his comprehensive survey, always at transition points from one topic to another. So, for instance, in a chapter entitled "The Galileans and the Temple," a first section (pp. 261–75) is entitled "Pagan Worship in Galilee." There the case is made that various religious centres in and around Galilee to which Galileans might have attached themselves held little attraction for most Galileans. Following on from that, a second section (pp. 275–93) is entitled "The Galileans and the Jerusalem Temple." There the case is made that Galileans in the first century CE demonstrated a surprising loyalty to the Jerusalem temple as the main centre of their affections. At the crossover point between these two sections Freyne makes a transition that would have pleased both Lucian and Quintilian. At the end of the first section, Freyne looks forward to the second, so that the final sentence of the first section reads as follows:

> As we shall presently see, later evidence in fact suggests the opposite and supports the evidence of *1 Macc* 5 that even from an early period Galilean attachment to the Jerusalem temple was unwavering.[25]

At the beginning of the second section, Freyne looks back to the first, so that the first sentence of the second section reads as follows:

> [O]ur investigation so far has not indicated any great desire for radical change on the part of the Galilean Jews in regard to their central religious symbol system. Contrary expectations notwithstanding, we have not been able to find any positive traces of serious inroads of hellenistic religious syncretism there.[26]

This is a perfect example of what Lucian considered to be a chain-link interlock, in which there is a certain strength of rhetorical force since, through the interweaving of their subject matter at their "boundaries," the separate sections are lending their respective forces to each other. The first section ends looking towards the next, and the following sentence ends by summarising the first. It is a perfect A-b/a-B construction.

Freyne uses the same chain-link technique at six other points in his book (pp. 170, 229, 323, 334 with 344, 372). But this is not the only tran-

---

[25] S. Freyne, *Galilee from Alexander the Great to Hadrian, 323 BCE to 135 CE: A Study of Second Temple Judaism* (Notre Dame: University of Notre Dame Press, 1980), 275.

[26] Freyne, *Galilee from Alexander the Great to Hadrian*, 275.

sition that he uses. Frequently his transitions are constructed according to a simple A-b/B construction of the anticipatory transition (pp. 26, 216, 356) or a simple A/a-B construction of the reiterative transition (pp. 121, 129, 138, 194, 293, 305, 329). The relationship between these simple anticipatory and reiterative transitions and chain-link interlock has been suggested in §4.1, with the interlock being formed by the coupling of anticipatory and reiterative features. Freyne's use of interlock is always articulated, although it was noted in §4.2 that unarticulated chain-link interlock is also possible, a form that Freyne does not utilise.

CHAPTER 5

Ancient Examples of Chain-Link Interlock

In this chapter, selected examples of chain-link interlock from sources outside the New Testament are briefly considered. These examples provide a second triangulation point for this project, demonstrating that chain-link construction is evident in textual predecessors to, and contemporaries of, the New Testament.

Although all of the examples of this chapter arise from antiquity, the texts that they are from span several centuries and a variety of genres. They also show no uniformity of provenance and demonstrate a variety of purposes. What unites all of the examples is that they conform to the principle of text-unit interlock that the Graeco-Roman rhetoricians Quintilian and Lucian praised as rhetorically attractive.

Each of the following examples illustrates the utility of chain-link interlock in a particular fashion. Examples of chain links operating at the macro-level of text units and in both articulated and unarticulated form will first be offered from six diverse texts (§5.1 to §5.6). One example of an unarticulated medial-level chain link will then be demonstrated (§5.7), with another example appearing in a later section (§5.9). Finally, two examples of chain link being constructed in the process of a text's compositional history will be considered (§5.8 and §5.9).

By briefly setting out a spattering of text-unit interlocks in texts beyond the New Testament and by illustrating the utility of this construction in a variety of ancient texts, this chapter prepares the way for the more in-depth analysis of New Testament texts in the chapters that follow. On occasion, discussion of those texts will refer explicitly back to the discussion of this chapter. A summary of findings appears at the end of this chapter, highlighting the significance of these examples in relation to the New Testament texts analysed in the following chapters.

Part 1: Macro-Level Chain-Link Interlocks

The following six sections illustrate the manner in which chain-link interlock frequently appears at a macro-level junction, serving to link two large text units.

§5.1   The Genesis-Exodus Textual Seam

The oldest example of chain-link construction in this survey comes from the Pentateuch of the Hebrew Bible. As the patriarchal narratives of Genesis give way to the narratives of the Hebrew people in Exodus, a chain-link construction is found at the point of transition. The patriarchal narratives proceed at a pace up through Genesis 50:21, but the final five verses of Genesis function as both a conclusion to the patriarchal narratives of Genesis and a transition to the Exodus narratives of the Hebrew people. As a conclusion to the patriarchal narratives, Genesis

50:22-26 tells the audience that Joseph remained in Egypt where he grew old and saw the coming of many descendants and eventually died. As a transition to the Exodus narrative, the same verses include Joseph's final words to his brothers (50:24) concerning the certain fact that God will lead his people out of the land of Egypt and bring them to the land that he has promised them—which of course is precisely the point of interest of the "exodus" narrative in the next major text unit. Moreover, it is recounted in Genesis 50:25 that Joseph committed the Israelites to carrying his bones from Egypt to the land that they would come to. This feature finds its fulfilment in Exodus 13:19: "And Moses took with him the bones of Joseph, who had required a solemn oath of the Israelites, saying, 'God will surely take notice of you, and then you must carry my bones with you from here.'" While this alone is not a strong transitional feature, in concert with the exodus motif of 50:24 it contributes to the transitional effect of the final verses of Genesis 50.

When the book of Exodus commences, its first feature is a list of the names of the sons of Jacob who came with him and relocated in Egypt. The list corresponds precisely to the list given in Genesis 35:23-26, and the relocation of Jacob and his eleven sons from Canaan to Egypt is recounted in Genesis 45–47. The audience is also reminded at the start of Exodus that Joseph was already in Egypt when his father and brothers relocated, as is evident from Genesis 39 onwards. Just as the book of Genesis concludes with Joseph's death (יוסף וימת, Gen 50:26), so too the start of the book of Exodus includes reference to Joseph's death (יוסף וימת, Exod 1:6). These features in the first five and a half verses of Exodus strongly link it to Genesis. But the Exodus narrative must begin, and does so, as the audience is told that although the whole generation of Joseph died off, "the Israelites were fruitful and prolific; they multiplied and grew exceedingly strong, so that the land was filled with them" (Exod 1:6-7). And so the Exodus story begins.

Here we see in practice the precise transition technique of interlock applauded by Quintilian and Lucian. At the point of intersection, the content of the two text units overlaps, interlocking the two units together in an A-b-a/a-B pattern. The link is "unarticulated," in that there is no explicit mention of the transition taking place within the text; the narrative itself carries the "back-and-forth" transition along without much difficulty or awkwardness.

This transition technique is not evident in any of the Pentateuch's further major text-unit divisions. At the seam between Exodus and Leviticus, for instance, there is absolutely no transition whatsoever; the narrative in Leviticus simply continues that of Exodus. The same is true for the following two books of the Pentateuch. Each have their own means of commencement and closure, but there is no transition from one text unit to the next at the point where the text units meet. So while the chain-link transition was thought to be helpful at the transition from Genesis to Exodus, transitions of this kind were seemingly not thought to be necessary at any of the subsequent text-unit boundaries.

It is interesting to note that the same technique of overlapping that marks out the transition in the final chapter of Genesis also marks out the structure of the first chapter of the same book. So, as Gordon Wenham has noted, the self-contained narrative of the first six days of creation is constructed so as to overlap its elements at the midpoint. He writes:

> The narrative has two poles, heaven and earth (1:1; 2:1), and its focus moves from heaven to earth, finishing with a close-up on man (vv 26-30). This shift of focus is again reflected in the arrangement of the creative acts.[1]

By this, Wenham refers to the focus on the heavens in the creative acts of days one, two, and four, and the focus on the earth in the creative acts of days three, five, and six (with the account of the seventh day standing "apart from the standard framework of each of the other six days"). According to Wenham, "Such crossover patterns are quite common in the OT." One such occurrence, as was shown above, is at the other end of the Genesis narrative where, unlike the overlap in Genesis 1, a transition to the next text unit (i.e., Exodus) is being made.

§5.2   Philo of Alexandria

Philo, the prolific Hellenistic Jewish author and theologian who lived in Alexandria from about 20 BCE to 50 CE, also made use of chain-link interlock as a transitional technique. His *Life of Moses* (*De Vita Mosis*) is a two-volume monograph that traces the early life and career of Moses (Book 1) and explores his character from various angles (Book 2, largely). Whereas early editors divided the double work into three treatises,[2] Philo himself speaks elsewhere of this work as comprising two books (*Vita* 52). This is confirmed within the work itself, when in 2.1 Philo speaks both of the "former treatise" (ἡ προτέρα σύνταξις) and of the "present treatise" (νυνὶ συντάττομεν, lit: "we now treatise"). It is precisely at this point that Philo makes use of the transitional technique that Lucian of Samosata identifies as involving linkage like that of a chain: the first book ends

---

[1] G. J. Wenham, *Genesis 1–15* (Waco: Word Books, 1987), 7, from where all of the Wenham quotations are taken.

[2] Noted by F. H. Colson, *Philo of Alexandria* (Loeb Classical Library; London: Heinemann; Cambridge, MA: Harvard University Press, 1934), 6:274.

introducing the subject matter of the second, and the second book begins recaping the subject matter of the first. So the first book ends in this fashion (1.334):

> We have now told the story of Moses' actions in his capacity of king. We must next deal with all that he achieved by his powers as high priest and legislator, powers which he possessed as the most fitting accompaniments of kingship.

τὰ μὲν δὲ κατὰ τὴν βασιλείαν πεπραγμένα αὐτῷ μεμήνυται· λεκτέον δ' ἑξῆς καὶ ὅσα διὰ τῆς ἀρχιερωσύνης καὶ νομοθετικῆς κατώρθωσε· καὶ γὰρ ταύτας περιεποιήσατο τάς δυνάμεις ὡς ἁρμοττούσας μάλιστα βασιλεια.

Having signalled the reader to move ahead into the next book, that book itself begins by reminding the reader of the contents of the first book (2.1):

> The former treatise dealt with the birth and nurture of Moses; also with his education and career as a ruler, in which capacity his conduct was not merely blameless but highly praiseworthy; also with the works which he performed in Egypt and during the journeys both at the Red Sea and in the wilderness—works which no words can adequately describe; further, with the troubles which he successfully surmounted, and with his partial distribution of territories to the combatants. The present treatise is concerned with matters allied and consequent to these.

ἡ μὲν προτέρα σύνταξίς ἐστι περὶ γενέσεως τῆς Μωυσέως καὶ τροφῆς, ἔτι δὲ παιδείας καὶ ἀρχῆς, ἣν οὐ μόνον ἀνεπιλήπτως ἀλλ' καὶ σφόδρα ἐπαινετῶς ἦρξε, καὶ τῶν ἕν τε Αἰγύπτῳ καὶ ταῖς ὁδοιπορίαις ἐπί τε τῆς ἐρυθρᾶς θαλάσσης καὶ κατὰ τὴν ἐρήμην πεπραγμένων, ἃ δύναμιν πᾶσαν λόγων ὑπερβάλλει, καὶ προσέτι πόνων οὓς κατώρθωσε καὶ κληρουχιῶν ἃς ἐκ μέρους ἀπένειμε τοῖς στρατευσαμένοις. ἣν δὲ νυνὶ συντάττομεν, περὶ τῶν ἑπομένων καὶ ἀκολούθων.

With these transitional features in place, Philo commences his essay with a conjunctive "for": "For it has been said . . ." (φασὶ γάρ τινες . . ., 2.2). The two-part hinge between the two books is comprised of (1) a preview of what follows at the end of the first book, and (2) a review of what has preceded at the beginning of the second book, followed by the beginning of the new topic already announced at the end of the first book. This conforms precisely to the text-unit interlock applauded by Quintillian and Lucian, with the transition in this case being explicitly articulated.

§5.3   Plutarch

We have already seen in §3.5 one example from *Adulator* in which
Plutarch (ca. 46–120 CE) makes use of an anticipatory transition at a text-
unit boundary. Elsewhere in the same work he couples the anticipatory
transition with a retrospective transition, thereby forming (as noted in
§4.1) a chain-linked interlock, much like the interlock evidenced in
Philo's *Life of Moses* (§5.2). This is evident in the transition from chapter
25 to 26 of *Adulator* (66E). The final paragraph of chapter 25 summarises
the points he has been making but then turns to a new subject towards
the end—that is, the need for balance between flattery and frank speech:

> [W]e ought to keep ourselves from both the one and the other
> extreme, and in frankness, as in anything else, achieve the right from
> the mean. The subject itself requiring, as it does, consequent elabora-
> tion, seems to determine that this be the final complement of our
> work.

> δεῖ δὲ μηδέτερον παθεῖν ἀλλ᾽ ὥσπερ ἄλλῳ τινὶ καὶ τῇ παρρησίᾳ τὸ
> καλὸν ἐκ τοῦ μετρίου λαβεῖν, αὐτὸς ἔοικεν ὁ λόγος ὁ τὸ ἐφεξῆς
> ἀπαιτῶν ἐπιτιθέναι τὴν κρωνίδα τῷ συγγράμματι.

Thus, in turning to his new subject of interest at the end of chapter 25
(66E),[3] Plutarch also explicitly directs the audience's attention to the following chapter. At the start of chapter 26, he first directs the audience's
attention back to his previous argument before starting his new topic
(i.e., the need to divest frankness of speech of self-regard). So he writes:
"Seeing, therefore, that there are certain fatal faults attending upon
frankness, let us in the first place divest it of all self-regard . . ." (ὥσπερ
οὖν κῆρας τινας ἐπούσας τῇ παρρησίᾳ πλείονας ὁρῶντες πρῶτον
ἀφαιρῶμεν αὐτῆς τὴν φιλαυτίαν . . .). The need to divest frank speech
of self-regard (φιλαυτία), with which the final text unit deals, arises from
the discourse of the previous text unit, in which it was shown that certain
faults easily attach themselves to frankness of speech. In this way
Plutarch states the point of the previous unit as the starting point of the
next main text unit. The technique of chain-link interlock is simple, and
here it is executed with simplicity of style.

---

[3] The transition may be said to begin even earlier than this. Mention in chapter 25 (66D) of the shame of avoiding flattery and destroying another by severe
criticism both recapitulates chapter 17–20 and introduces a theme that is highlighted in what follows, not least as early as chapter 26 (66E/F), where we find
repetition of the φιλικόν and κηδεμονικόν already mentioned in chapter 25
(66D).

§5.4 Josephus

Josephus's last surviving literary piece, *Against Apion* (*Contra Apionem*), was written to supplement his earlier and extensive *Jewish Antiquities* (cf. *Against Apion* 1.1–3). The latter had been written in 93/94 CE as an apology for Judaism, showing it to be an ancient and respectable religion. After the writing of that work, however, Josephus found it necessary to defend further the antiquity of his ancestral religion in the light of malicious counter-claims of others, one of whom was a famed Egyptian rhetorician, Apion. The work that resulted is an impassioned piece of powerful argument.

It is also a two-volume work, the two books being of approximate length and being inseparable. The hand-off from the first to the second book appears in 1.320 and 2.1–2. The first book comes to an abrupt end, simply pointing ahead to the second book (1.320):

> This book, however, having already run to a suitable length, I propose at this point to begin a second, in which I shall endeavour to supply the remaining portion of my subject.

> ἀλλ' ἐπειδὴ σύμμετρον ἤδη τὸ βιβλίον εἴληθε μέγεθος, ἑτέραν ποιησάμενος ἀρχὴν τὰ λοιπὰ τῶν εἰς τὸ προκείμενον πειράσομαι προσαποδοῦναι.

Having come to the end of one book, Josephus points his reader to the next. The second book does not just pick up where the first left off, but begins by retracing in miniature the argument of the first (2.1–2):

> In the first volume of this work, my most esteemed Epaphroditus, I demonstrated the antiquity of our race, corroborating my statements by the writings of Phoenicians, Chaldaeans, and Egyptians, besides citing as witnesses numerous Greek historians; I also challenged the statements of Manetho, Chaeromon, and some others. I shall now proceed to refute the rest of the authors who have attacked us.

> διὰ μὲν οὖν τοῦ προτέρου βιβλίου, τιμιώτατέ μοι Ἐπαφρόδιτε, περί τε τῆς ἀρχαιότητος ἡμῶν ἐπέδειξα, τοῖς Φοινίκων καὶ Χαλδαίων καὶ Αἰγυπτίων γράμμασι πιστωσάμενος τὴν ἀλήθειαν καὶ πολλοὺς τῶν Ἑλλήνων συγγραφεῖς παρασχόμενος μάρτυρας, τήν τε ἀντίρρησιν ἐποιησάμην πρὸς Μανεθῶνα καὶ Χαιρήμονα καί τινας ἑτέρους. ἄρξομαι δὲ νῦν τοὺς ὑπολειπομένους τῶν γεγραφότων τι καθ' ἡμῶν ἐλέγχειν.

This retracing of the argument of the prior book suggests that the closing words of the first book were not meant simply as a parenthetical signal to open the next book in order to continue the discussion. That is, the end of the first book is not the equivalent of modern signals such as "continued on next page." This impression is given in some secondary literature on Josephus. For instance, Steve Mason writes:

> Josephus ends the first volume rather suddenly, with the note that he has run out of space (*Ag. Ap.* 1.320). Evidently he became carried away and only now realized that he was at the end of his scroll. So the attack on Apion . . . simply continues the author-by-author analysis.[4]

In Mason's estimate, then, the manner in which volume 1 of *Against Apion* gives way abruptly to volume 2 illustrates Josephus's lack of presentational control at precisely the point of transition.

But this impression requires considerable qualification in view of Josephus's careful construction of the text overall. Josephus exhibits an obvious concern for structure throughout the two books of *Against Apion*. In my view, the forward-looking gesture at the end of volume 1 is not likely to indicate that Josephus had been caught off-guard by a sudden realisation that his scroll was coming to an end, as Mason suggests. Instead, it is an intricate part of a double gesture at the point of transition between the two books, serving as half of an interlocking hinge that binds the two volumes together. Josephus's comments at the end of volume one are not to be taken so much as a clue to Josephus's state of mind during the composing of his text. Instead, they are to be recognised as part of a rhetorical device illustrating Josephus's concern to mark a transition from volume 1 to volume 2 for the benefit of his audience and, importantly, permitting him to offer overview of his argument in the process.

It might be significant, then, that the second edition of Mason's book (in 2003) contains no hint of the above quotation (from the 1992 edition). Instead, in that supplementary edition Mason seeks to show in ways unprecedented in his first edition that Josephus has carefully crafted his work along rhetorically effective lines.[5] If Mason is right about this, then Josephus's use of chain-link interlock is simply another case to reinforce the viewpoint of the "mature" Mason.

Even if Mason's initial estimate is considered to have merit, however, it would nonetheless be significant that Josephus resorted to a chain-link transition precisely when realising that a transition had been forced upon him by his lack of compositional foresight. Either way, the utility of chain-link interlock is evident from the transition at the midpoint of Josephus's *Against Apion*.

---

[4] S. Mason, *Josephus and the New Testament* (Peabody: Hendrickson, 1992), 79.
[5] S. Mason, *Josephus and the New Testament* (2d ed.; Peabody: Hendrickson, 2003), 132–33.

§5.5   4 Ezra

Perhaps the "youngest" examples of chain-link construction in this survey come from the Jewish apocalyptic text 4 Ezra [chs. 3–14 of 2 Esdras], written at the end of the first century CE. Seven episodes comprise 4 Ezra's twelve chapters, the first three episodes (I–III) being a series of long and arduous dialogues between Ezra (the questioner) and the angel Uriel (the respondent), the final four episodes being comprised of a transitional episode (IV),[6] disclosure material (V–VI), and an epilogue (VII).

While 4 Ezra is a torturous book in many ways,[7] it usually makes for smooth reading at the point of transition between the episodes, precisely because it employs the chain-link construction that, as Lucian and Quintilian suggested, lends artistry to a narrative. This is true for at least three of its six main transitions.

The transition from episode II (5:21–6:34) to episode III (6:35–9:25) occurs on both sides of the text-unit boundary and is marked out by an interlocking overlap. Towards the end of episode II, Uriel, having finished his interaction with Ezra for the time being, says to him: "I have come to show you these things this night. If therefore you will pray again and fast again for seven days, I will again declare to you greater things than these" (*Haec veni tibi ostendere et venturae nocti. Si ergo iterum togaveris et iterum ieiunaveris septem diebus, iterum tibi renuntiabo horum maiora per diem*, 6:30-31). These verses point directly into the following episode, where in its first verse Ezra is said to weep and fast for seven days (6:35). Moreover, the promise of "greater things" (*horum maiora*) is fulfilled in the extensive and critical third episode that follows. But after Uriel's anticipatory promise in 6:30-31, he brings the episode to a fitting close with a retrospective analysis of the discussion they have just completed. Uriel tells Ezra that his uprightness and cry to the Lord has been the occasion for their discussion, and then Uriel concludes: "Therefore he [God] sent me to show you all these things, and to say to you, 'Believe and do not be afraid! Do not be quick to think vain thoughts concerning the former things, lest you be hasty concerning the last times'" (*Et propter hoc misit me demonstrare tibi haec omnia et dicere tibi: Confide et noli timere, et noli festinare in prioribus temporibus cogitare vana, ut non properes a novissimis temporibus*, 6:33-34). This has been the point of Uriel's case throughout

---

[6] M. E. Stone ("A Reconsideration of Apocalyptic Visions," *HTR* 96 [2003]: 167–80) makes a strong case for estimating that a profound religious experience lies behind episode IV, with the other episodes orbiting around this episode and its underlying mystical experience.

[7] See B. W. Longenecker, *Eschatology and the Covenant: A Comparison of 4 Ezra and Romans 1–11* (Sheffield: Sheffield Academic Press, 1991); and idem, *2 Esdras* (Sheffield: Sheffield Academic Press, 1995).

episode II, and as such recaps the basics of the discussion. With 6:30-31 pointing forward into episode III, 6:32-34 points backward to episode II before episode III begins in 6:35.

Here, then, is a typical chain-link interlock according to an unbalanced "A-b-a/B" pattern, with an overlap of material stretching over the text-unit boundary. The overlap is evident also at the start of episode III with the retrospective phrases "after this" (*post haec*), "again" (*iterum* in 6:35; *iterato* in 6:36), "as before" (*similiter*) and "as I had been told" (*quae dictae sunt mihi*)[8] in 6:35-36. With these backward glances, the chain-link pattern is enlarged to an "A-b-a/a-B" format, although this cannot be pressed since 6:35-36 have retrospective and prospective force simultaneously. But the principle of chain-link interlock is nonetheless evident in practice at this episodic transition point.

A similar chain-link transition appears in the movement from episode VI (4 Ezra 13) to episode VII (4 Ezra 14). After Ezra's vision and Uriel's interpretation in episode VI, Uriel says towards the end of the same episode: "And after three more days I will tell you other things, and explain weighty and wondrous matters to you" (*Erit enim post alios tres dies, ad te alia loquar et exponam tibi gracia et mirabilia*, 13:56). This points forward to episode VII. But before the episode concludes, two more verses serve to round off the sixth episode (13:57-58), with Ezra praising God for what he has just seen:

> Then I [Ezra] rose and walked in the field, giving great glory and praise to the Most High because of this wonders, which he did from time to time [i.e., "throughout the times"], and because he governs the times and whatever things come to pass in their seasons. And I stayed there three days.

> Et profectus sum et transii in campum multum glorificans et laudans Altissimum de mirabilibus, quae per tempus faciebat, et quoniam gubernat tempora et quae sunt in temporibus inlata. Et sedi ibi tribus diebus.

Here is a fitting point of closure to the sixth episode, in which Ezra finds consolation about the mysterious ways of God. At this point the seventh episode begins, so that the pattern that emerges at the point of transition is a standard unbalanced chain-link transition: A-b-a/B. The structure might be slightly more complicated if the phrase "on the third day" (*tertio die*) at the start of 14:1 is to be included in the chain-link, taking its cues as it does from material at the end of episode VI (13:56, 58). Again, then, the full chain-link appears to consist of an "A-b-a/a-B" pattern,

---

[8] Although this phrase is retrospective, its antecedent is nowhere in the extant text of 4 Ezra. The angel has said nothing about a three-week cycle.

conforming to the prescription for an easy interlocking transition as recommended by Lucian and Quintilian.

A third example from 4 Ezra comes at the transition between episode I (3:1–5:20) and episode II (5:21–6:34). It is complicated by the interruption of the main narrative and the introduction of subordinate material in 5:14-19, in which Ezra is joined by "Phaltiel, a chief of the people," who comes to plead with Ezra to intercede for the sake of the people of Israel. The text enclosing this separate incident is where the chain link lies. So, as Uriel's conversation with Ezra comes to a close at the end of episode 1, the angel concludes with these words: "And if you pray again, and weep as you do now, and fast for seven days, you shall hear yet greater things than these" (*Et si oraveris iterum et ploraveris sicut et nunc et ieiunaveris septem diebus, audies iterato horum maiora*, 5:13). The instructions to pray, weep and fast are anticipatory of the end of the episode (or the beginning of the next episode, depending on whether 5:20 should be included in the preceding unit or the following unit), where Ezra does precisely that, "as Uriel the angel had commanded me" (*sicut mihi mandavit Uriel angelus*, 5:20). The promise that "you shall hear yet greater things" (*horum maiora*) is anticipatory of episode II, with the A-b/B overlap emerging as a consequence. The matching part of the overlap appears at the start of episode II, which includes such phrases as "seven days after this" (*post dies septem*), and "again" (*iterum*, 5:21), and "once more" (*iterum*, 5:22). These are references back to episode I, and as such provide the transition with a complimentary overlap to the anticipatory overlap already noted. A balanced chain-link transition (A-b/a-B) emerges at the text-unit boundary between episodes I and II.

We have seen, then, that three of the six main text-unit boundaries in 4 Ezra are marked out by relatively straightforward chain-links with slight varieties in their patterns (i.e., balanced and unbalanced).

§5.6   Isaiah 48:16b-22

Isaiah 48:16b has posed difficulties for interpreters, since it seems to be so awkwardly out of place in its present position. The speaker throughout Isaiah 48 speaks on behalf of God, with the voice of God being heard in first-person format in 48:1-16a and in 48:17-22. Between these two blocks of text, however, falls the curious voice of one other than God and who also speaks in the first person: "And now the Lord God has sent me and his spirit" (ועתה **אדני** יהוה שלחני ורוחו).[9]

---

[9] This translation (NRSV) rightly takes "spirit" as a second object of the main verb "sent," not a new subject without an accompanying verb in a fragment that has been lost. So C. R. North, *The Second Isaiah* (Oxford: Clarendon Press, 1964), 182: "In the OT the spirit never sends but is always sent."

The majority of scholars have seen 48:16b to be a fragment that has inappropriately strayed into the text in one way or another. G. W. Wade identified it as "a parenthetic insertion" by a post-exilic redactor.[10] Charles Torrey found it to be "a later addition" due to "careless" scribe—an insertion that "must be omitted" when considering the original form of the text (a view accepted in the NEB, where 48:16b is omitted).[11] Christopher North articulated the problem in this way: "[W]hy should the Prophet interject a reference to himself [or the servant] into a context in which Yahweh is the speaker?" After considering several options, none of which proved convincing to him, North opted for taking this sentence as "a later interjection," although he notes that "there is no textual evidence" for this view.[12] Claus Westermann considered it to be the "unanimous" view of Isian scholars that this sentence "cannot possibly be explained in their present context."[13]

An exception to this unanimous view appears in the work of Franz Delitzsch, who in the mid-1800s argued that the words of 48:16b "form a prelude to the words of the One unequalled servant of Jehovah concerning Himself which occur in ch. xlix."[14] According to Delitzsch, this gesture to Isaiah 49 from within Isaiah 48 is one of the "often harsh transitions" evident in prophetic literature.[15]

Whereas Delitzsch's view had been ignored for at least a century, a handful of scholars have adopted positions consonant with it in recent years. Westermann noted that 48:16b fits well with the depiction of the servant of God in 49:1-6. But Westermann considered the words to have been "added in the margin at 49.1b . . . and were then inserted into the text at the wrong place. At the same time, to begin with, they may conceivably have formed part of 49.1-6."[16] Edward Young restated Delitzsch's position: "The Speaker is the Servant *par excellence*, [who is] about to be brought more prominently into the picture in chapters forty-nine, fifty, and fifty-three."[17] With Delitzsch, Young envisages 48:16b to have been original to the text, assisting in the transition to Isaiah 49, where the servant of the Lord emerges as an important figure.

---

[10] G. W. Wade, *The Book of the Prophet Isaiah* (London: Methuen, 1911), 310.

[11] C. C. Torrey, *The Second Isaiah* (Edinburgh: T&T Clark, 1928), 378.

[12] North, *Second Isaiah*, 182.

[13] C. Westermann, *Isaiah 40–66: A Commentary* (trans. David M. G. Stalker; London: SCM, 1969 [German original 1966]), 203.

[14] F. Delitzsch, *The Prophecies of Isaiah* (trans. J. Martin; Edinburgh: T&T Clark, 1867), 253.

[15] Delitzsch, *Prophecies of Isaiah*, 252.

[16] Westermann, *Isaiah 40–66: A Commentary*, 203.

[17] E. J. Young, *The Book of Isaiah* (Grand Rapids: Eerdmans, 1972), 3:259.

The same is true for Alec Motyer, who finds the transition to "take us by surprise."[18]

Perhaps the most outspoken advocates of the view that 48:16b introduces Isaiah 49 are Brevard Childs and Christopher Seitz. Childs writes concerning the speaker of 48:16b:

> [T]he reader is forced to wait until chapter 49 in order to understand the identity of the one sent (v. 16b). Then suddenly one is made aware that his identity is that of the servant, who now speaks autobiographically with the same first person pronoun of 48:16b to set forth in detail his calling and mission both to the house of Jacob and to the nations of the world. . . . The one sent by God [in 48:16b] . . . remains fully anonymous apart from his identity as the servant of chapter 49.[19]

Similarly, Seitz speaks of 48:16b as "the signature of the voice at work in [the following] chapters," with the "first-person poem" of 49:1-6 corresponding "to the signature of 48:16."[20] For Seitz, Westermann's "misplacement" theory misunderstands that 48:16b serves as "an intentional introduction to the servant's first-person speech, strongly prophetic in character, now found at 49:1-6." So 48:16b is a "very significant transition in the discourse."[21]

Far more needs be said about the identity of the person speaking in 48:16b within the narrative theology of Isaiah. For our purposes, however, it is enough to note that, whether original or a later insertion,[22]

---

[18] J. A. Motyer, *The Prophecy of Isaiah* (Leicester: InterVarsity, 1993), 381.

[19] B. S. Childs, *Isaiah* (Louisville: Westminster John Knox Press, 2001), 377–78.

[20] C. R. Seitz, "How is the Prophet Isaiah Present in the Latter Half of the Book? The Logic of Chapters 40–66 within the Book of Isaiah," *JBL* 115 (1996): 235. Seitz defends this view from the criticism that Isaiah 49 begins with its focus on Israel by interpreting 49:3 to mean "You are my servant; you are Israel, in whom I will be glorified." This bestows on the servant figure the functions expected of Israel. Here Seitz follows P. Wilcox and D. Paton-Williams, "The Servant Songs in Second Isaiah," *JSOT* 42 (1988): 79–102.

[21] C. R. Seitz, "The Book of Isaiah 40–66: Introduction, Commentary and Reflections," in *The New Interpreter's Bible* (ed. L. E. Keck et al.; Nashville: Abingdon Press, 2001), 319. The connection between 48:16 and Isaiah 49–55 is demonstrable also in the usage of the words אֲדֹנָי יְהוִה. They appear twenty-four times in Isaiah (by my count). Six of those occurrences (i.e., one quarter of the Isaian total) appear in Isaiah 49–55 (49:22; 50:4, 5, 7, 9; 52:4), as in 48:16b. The closest occurrence of these words prior to 48:16 is in 40:10. The other occurrences are: 3:15; 7:7; 10:23, 24; 22:12, 14, 15; 25:8; 28:16, 22; 30:15; 56:8; 61:1, 11; 65:13, 15.

[22] If 48:16b is a later insertion into Isaiah, this does nothing to undermine the fact that a chain-link interlock is evident in the anticipatory gesture of 48:16b and the closure of the preceding text-unit is evident in 48:17-22. It would only

48:16b serves the function as identified by Delitzsch and others: that is, it serves as an anticipatory gesture towards the new text-unit beginning at Isaiah 49, and towards 49:1-6 in particular. The sending described in 48:16b is enunciated further in 49:1-6, where the servant's calling and commissioning is described in detail at the start of the text-unit comprised of Isaiah 49–55, following on from Isaiah 40–48. So, at the virtual midpoint of deutero-Isaiah we find a construction conforming precisely to the chain-link interlock described by Lucian. Towards the end of text-unit A (Isa 40–48), a gesture is made to text-unit B (48:16b), before text-unit A comes to a close (48:17-22) and text-unit B begins properly (49:1-6, extending through to Isa 55). Whether it originated from the hand of the "author" or the hand of a later scribe, 48:16b seems to have been deliberately placed in its position in order to serve a transitional purpose, by means of chain-link overlap.

Isaiah 48:16b is, then, a "very significant transition" in the unfolding of the narrative of Isaiah. Modern scholars have often considered this to be a "careless" or "harsh" or "surprising" transition, and certainly it is one of the most abrupt and "eccentric" of the transitions in this project. But the ancient rhetoricians would likely have considered it to be a helpful means of signalling that a transition is in progress, a technique to endear one's case to one's audience by the overlapping of subject matter at the point of text-unit boundaries.[23]

Part 2: A Medial-Level Chain-Link Interlock

The six sections of Part 1 have outlined a variety of examples of chain-link interlock at the macro-level of a text's structure. In the following section, and in §5.9 of Part 3, two examples are offered that illustrate the manner in which chain-link interlock can also function at the medial-level of a text's structure.

§5.7   Isaiah 53:2b-6

Having noticed the presence of a chain-link interlock at the text-unit seam between Isaiah 40–48 and Isaiah 49–55 in §5.6, here we move to

---

suggest that a later scribe perceived that the transition from Isaiah 40–48 to Isaiah 49–55 would be aided by the insertion of the sentence in 48:16b, prior to the self-contained closure of Isaiah 40–48 in 48:17-22. In this case, Isaiah 48:16b-22 is an example of chain-link interlock being constructed in the process of a text's compositional history, as in Part 3 below.

[23] S. Terrien (*The Elusive Presence: Toward a New Biblical Theology* [New York: Harper & Row, 1978], 227–28) notes that "the prophets of Israel were true poets" who "cultivated all forms of rhetorical beauty and possessed a respect for the word that provokes thinking."

another Isaian passage in which the same overlapping construction appears: Isaiah 53:2b-6.

Nothing would be lost if these five verses from Isaiah were written in two distinct parts moving from the shame of the Servant of the Lord in the eyes of his community (part 1) to the honour of the Servant of the Lord in his saving role (part 2). So the text units would flow in an A-B movement, each unit consisting of seven lines, as follows:

> He had no form or majesty that we should look at him,
> nothing in his appearance that we should desire him.
> He was despised and rejected by others;
> a man of suffering and acquainted with infirmity;
> and as one from whom others hide their faces
> he was despised, and we held him of no account.
> We accounted him stricken, struck down by God, and afflicted.
>
> Surely he has borne our infirmities and carried our diseases;
> he was wounded for our transgressions, crushed for our iniquities;
> Upon him was the punishment that made us whole,
> and by his bruises we are healed.
> All we like sheep have gone astray;
> we have all turned to our own way,
> and the Lord has laid on him the iniquity of us all.

In this structure, each unit is self-contained. From start to finish the first stanza involves an assessment of the Servant of the Lord from an "uninformed" perspective, in which he is considered by his community to be the shameful object of derision who is weighed down by the enormous weight of his own dishonour and sin. And from start to finish the second stanza involves an assessment of the Servant of the Lord from an "informed" perspective, in which he is considered to be the honourable agent of salvation who is weighed down by the enormous weight of the dishonour and sin of his community, thereby acting for their salvation by his suffering.

Of course this proposed structure does not match the structure of the text itself. In Isaiah 53:4, the two stanzas meet, not in a straightforward manner but in overlapped form, so that the last line of the first text unit and the first line of the second text unit swap places, as follows:

> Surely he has borne our infirmities and carried our diseases;
> We accounted him stricken, struck down by God, and afflicted.

Consequently, while Isaiah 53:2b-3 depicts the servant of the Lord as the object of social scorn and rejection, and while 53:5-6 reveals that this same one has borne the iniquities of the people, between these two units lies 53:4, wherein the two perspectives on this suffering servant are combined in an overlapping fashion. Isaiah 53:4a introduces the theme of 53:5-6, and Isaiah 53:4b recalls the theme of 53:2b-3. The structure is consistent in both the MT and the LXX.

The A-b-a-B pattern conforms precisely to the chain-link overlap. There is no reason to see a new text unit beginning somewhere in Isaiah 53:4, and since there is no transition from one unit to the next, this transition falls at a "medial" level of the text's structure, although a significant theological transition is built upon it. The overlap is especially powerful in bringing the two perspectives on the Servant of the Lord together and intertwining them in ironic fashion, so that the contrast in the perspectives is shockingly felt when moving through Isaiah 53:4.

Another example of a medial-level interlock appears below in §5.9, which is also the second of two examples of a chain-link interlock being created in the process of a text's compositional history. This is the issue analysed now in Part 3.

Part 3: Chain-Link Interlock Constructed in the Process of Textual Development

In §5.6 above, it was noted that the chain-link interlock evident in Isaiah 48:16b-22 may have resulted from the compositional history of the Isaian text. In the two examples that follow, the same may well have been the case. For those who might argue against a composition-history approach to the texts studied below, the chain-link interlock can be accounted for in ways of their own choosing.

§5.8   *The Midpoint Seam in Daniel*

The book of Daniel is generally recognised as consisting of two main parts. The first is Daniel 1-6. This section recounts (in third-person format) a series of six legendary stories (or an introduction followed by five stories) about Daniel and/or his colleagues who are deported to Babylon but remain faithful to God even there. The second part of the book is Daniel 7-12, in which four of Daniel's visions[24] are recounted (in first-person format, except for 7:1 and 10:1) relating the outline of history from the time of Babylonian exile to the culmination of world history and the dawning of the final age.

With good reason, the handful of folk stories in Daniel 1-6 and of apocalyptic visions in Daniel 7-12 are generally thought to have circulated separately from each other originally, with each self-contained unit

---

[24] Visions appear in the first part of Daniel as well (Dan 2 and Dan 4), but they are not Daniel's and they are far simpler in form, content, and significance.

being brought into relationship with the other in a developing process of collection and redaction.[25] But as Philip Davies writes, "the challenge to critical scholarship is not only to distinguish carefully between the two contrasting parts of the book, but also to explore the positive aspect of this contrast: in other words, to do justice to the book of Daniel as a literary unit."[26] It will be suggested here that the bringing together of originally distinct units to form a single literary entity has resulted (intentionally or otherwise) in the construction of a chain-link transition at the seam where the folk stories of Daniel 1–6 meet the apocalyptic visions of Daniel 7–12. Through the overlapping of material at this textual seam, the final form of the book of Daniel has a stronger feel of unity than would otherwise have been the case.

Our first glance at this text-unit seam takes us to the last verse of Daniel 6 (identified here as 6:28, with the NRSV), in which we read: "So this Daniel prospered during the reign of Darius and the reign of Cyrus the Persian." According to Lars Hartman, this verse is a redactional insertion that permits Daniel 1–6 to link to Daniel 7–12, since the reference to Daniel within the reign of Darius pertains to the folktale of Daniel 6, while reference to Daniel within the reign of Cyrus pertains to the apocalyptic vision of Daniel 10 (i.e., "in the third year of King Cyrus of Persia . . .," 10:1). In this view, the final words of Daniel 6 are the springboard into Daniel 7–12 by means of the link with 10:1.[27] The transition in 6:28b, then, would look most like an anticipatory transition. But if it is a transition of this type, it is an awkward and feeble one, since Cyrus is not an important person in the second text unit and the link must cross over three full chapters. More satisfying, then, is John Collins's view that the mention of the reign of Cyrus in 6:28 "is a reprise of 1:21, which said that Daniel lived until the first year of Cyrus." For Collins, these two verses give balance to the first six chapters of the book, which comprise an introduction (Dan 1) and five folktales (Dan 2–6). Consequently, the mention of Cyrus and his reign in 6:28 is part of an *inclusio* around the folktales. He writes: "The balance between 6:29 [i.e., 6:28 in this study] and 1:21 supports the view that this point once marked the end of the Book of Daniel."[28] In other words, Daniel 6:28 serves

---

[25] The last prominent defender of Daniel's compositional unity was H. H. Rowley, "The Unity of the Book of Daniel," in *The Servant of the Lord and Other Essays on the Old Testament* (2d ed.; Oxford: Blackwell, 1965), 249–60. Conversely, see J. J. Collins, *Daniel* (Minneapolis: Augsburg Fortress, 1993), 24–38.

[26] P. R. Davies, *Daniel* (Sheffield: JSOT Press, 1985), 12.

[27] See L. F. Hartman and A. A. di Lella, *The Book of Daniel* (Garden City: Doubleday, 1978), 201. Hartman wrote the commentary on Daniel 1–9, di Lella on Daniel 10–12.

[28] Collins, *Daniel*, 272, from which all nearby quotations have also been taken.

primarily to unify the preceding text unit, rather than feebly introducing the following text unit.

If the last verse of Daniel 6 takes its cues from earlier material, so too does the second half of the preceding verse, in which the God of Daniel is praised for his mighty actions: "for he has saved Daniel from the power of the lions." This recounts the folktale of Daniel 6, of course, and as such is a good example of God working signs "on earth," as the preceding phrase mentions. It is arguable that the earlier parts of Darius's praise of God are also fitting conclusions of Daniel 6. Mention of God's ability to "deliver and rescue" in 6:27a summarises what the text has just related in relation to Daniel and the den of lions. And Darius' description of God as the "living God" in 6:26a follows on from his description of Daniel as the "servant of the living God" in 6:20. Even his acclamation of God as "enduring forever" in 6:26a[29] might be an inversion of the acclamation given to him by his courtiers in 6:6, where he is exhorted to "live forever." So there is enough that resonates with material earlier in the chapter to make Darius' final words a fitting conclusion to Daniel 6, and to Daniel 1–6 as a whole.

But it also needs to be recognised that, with Daniel 7–12 having been added to Daniel 1–6 (either as a complete unit or through a series of additions), certain elements in Darius' final words come to take on new significance within their new literary context, and they might in fact serve better as anticipatory pointers than as reiterative summaries. For instance, Darius praises God as one who "works signs and wonders in heaven and on earth." It has already been mentioned that the deliverance of Daniel from the lions is a natural follow-on from Darius' talk of signs and wonders "on earth" (בארעא), but that episode is not a fitting example of what Darius calls signs and wonders "in heaven" (בשמיא). What does qualify as a fitting example of those heavenly signs and wonders is what appears in the second text-unit, not least in Daniel 7 (e.g., 7:9-10, 13-14). Of course mention of "signs and wonders" has been made already by Nebuchadnezzar in 4:2 (see also 3:32-33), but he does not refer to these as "in heaven" as Darius does. In other words, while Darius' talk of "signs and wonders" has precedent within the first half of Daniel, the unprecedented phrase "in heaven" connects his words more with what comes in the second half of Daniel than with the first half.

When Dairus affirms that God's "kingdom shall never be destroyed" and that God's "dominion has no end" (6:26b), he is repeating themes learned already in the first half. Specifically, the same affirmations are uttered by Nebuchadnezzar in Daniel 4: "His kingdom is an everlasting kingdom, and his sovereignty is from generation to generation" (4:3). Or

---

[29] Cf. Nebuchadnezzar's "one who lives forever" in Daniel 4:34.

again: "For his sovereignty is an everlasting sovereignty, and his kingdom endures from generation to generation" (4:34). But the difference between the affirmations of these two kings is that Darius' affirmations have no relation to the story in which Darius himself figures (Dan 6), whereas Nebuchadnezzar's affirmations are precisely the point of the Nebuchadnezzar story, being driven home repeatedly (4:17, 25, 32, 35, 37; cf. 2:44). Daniel himself explicitly makes this the point that Nebuchadnezzar was to learn from the events that befell him (4:26; cf. 2:44).[30] Accordingly, while we might think that Darius' words are recalling themes from Daniel 4 since they have no direct relationship with any feature of the Daniel 6 story, it might be more appropriate to think of them as prefiguring what we find in Daniel 7–12, in which God's kingdom is shown to have no competent rival and thus will continue forever. So the affirmations of foreign kings Nebuchadnezzar and Darius in Daniel 4 and Daniel 6 respectively become graphically depicted in narrative format on the apocalyptic screen of Daniel 7–12. That Darius' words play a role in making this transition can be seen from the fact that the words of his affirmation, moreso than Nebuchadnezzar's, are replicated by Daniel in recounting his vision in Daniel 7. So Darius' pronouncement that "his kingdom shall never be destroyed (דִּי־לָא תִתְחַבַּל וּמַלְכוּתֵהּ) and his dominion has no end" in 6:26b is replicated in amplified form by Daniel in 7:14 ("his dominion is an everlasting dominion that shall not pass away, and his kingship is one that shall never be destroyed" [וּמַלְכוּתֵהּ דִּי־לָא תִתְחַבַּל]; cf. also 7:27).

In the light of these anticipatory features of Darius' words, other features of his speech might also take on transitional import. For instance, his depiction of God as one who is able to "deliver and rescue" [וּמְצִל מְשֵׁיזִב] might be easily expanded, in its larger literary context, to embrace not simply the micro-events of history (such as the episode with Daniel and the lions which Darius has as his primary referent) but also the macro-events of world history as described in Daniel 7–12. Those later chapters repeatedly give assurances that God will save his people at the culmination of all history (esp. "your people shall be delivered," עַמָּךְ יִמָּלֵט, 12:1). Similarly, whereas Darius depicts God's reign as a reign of deliverance (6:27), in Daniel 7–12 the reign of others who would usurp God's reign is, by contrast, shown to be a reign of destruction (8:24-25; 11:44).

If features at the end of Daniel 6 can be seen to point forwards to Daniel 7–12, so too, features at the start of Daniel 7 can be seen to be related to Daniel 1–6. So the third-person form that tends to unify

---

[30] In Daniel 4:26, clearly the phrase "Heaven is sovereign" equates to "The God of heaven is sovereign."

Daniel 1–6 but disappears almost completely in Daniel 7–12 appears in the very first verse of Daniel 7. This stylistic feature might be seen as a kind of residue from the first text-unit that has crept into the start of the second text-unit in order to help the audience make the transition from one unit to the next. Once the transition is made, the first-person format is replaced almost univocally by the third-person format.[31]

We have seen, then, a variety of anticipatory and reiterative features at the seam between Daniel 6 and Daniel 7. These stylistic and thematic features are precisely the sort of things that can help to mark out chain-link interlock. Specifically, the text-unit seam where Daniel 6 meets Daniel 7 contains an unbalanced and unarticulated chain-link construction (i.e., A-b-a/B).[32] It might be that the chain-link construction arose almost incidentally in the process of the text's composition history. Be that as it may, in the bringing together of the folktale cycle of Daniel 1–6 with the apocalyptic cycle of Daniel 7–12 (or at least in the first instance, Dan 7), a chain-link construction emerged as a transitional feature. If this occurred without the help of "authorial" or "redactional" intention, then it is simply a case of "the whole being greater than its parts."

If it is true that meaning is built on structure, then we can see how the creation of a chain-link construction in the Daniel material might have helped to reinforce the significance of Daniel for its early audiences. At the transition from folktale to apocalyptic vision, the confident words of Darius (especially those of 6:26b–27a) continue to ring in the ear of the audience even while the messy currents of world history are being read out in Daniel 7–12. In the centuries immediately prior to the turn of the Christian era, the Jewish people came under the influence of foreign rulers who failed to recognise the supremacy of the Jewish God and who worked against God's purposes, sometimes to the detriment of the Jewish people themselves. These kings were given literary embodiment within Daniel's own narrative in the description of the king who "shall exalt himself and consider himself greater than any god, and shall speak horrendous things against the God of gods" (Dan 11:36). In such alarming

---

[31] The same switch from third-person introductory material to first-person account appears again in 10:1, indicating that the format need not be explained as arising out of the placement of Daniel 7 next to Daniel 6. The point is simply that once that placement has been made, some of the features of the originally unrelated material begin to take on new significance. The switch in voice at 7:1-2 is a case in point, although the same cannot be said for the same feature in 10:1.

[32] This pattern does not take into account, however, that even at the point of introducing text-unit B an important characteristic from text-unit A has carried over for one verse—that is, the third-person voice. The problem with diagramming that feature is that the feature has been completely incorporated into B material and cannot be diagrammed itself.

contexts, the text of Daniel would have offered encouragement in a variety of ways, not least through the chain-link interlock at the midpoint text seam. There the text's audience would hear the voice of one foreign king whose acknowledgement of God's sovereignty rings out above the apocalyptic scenarios of Daniel 7–12 in which the foolish leaders of this world appear as ineffective usurpers of the sovereign God.

§5.9   Apocalypse of Abraham 7–8

Chain-link construction can almost inadvertently arise by combining texts that previously were independent of each other. This seems to have been the case in the compositional history of Daniel, as we have just seen. It also appears to be the case in the compositional history of the Apocalypse of Abraham (probably compiled for the most part by the first century CE). Like the book of Daniel, the Apocalypse of Abraham consists of two main parts, a cycle of folktales and extended apocalyptic revelations. The folktales of chapters 1–8 involve Abraham and his father Terah, with Abraham becoming increasingly dissatisfied with the idolatry of his father and seeking to discover the true creator God. In the second part of the text (chs. 9–32), we find the apocalyptic material in which the true creator God reveals himself to Abraham.

These two parts unevenly divide the thirty-two chapters of the book at the boundary between chapters 8 and 9. Within the first eight chapters, a smooth narrative flow between sections is ensured by means of backward glances at the start of new text-units. So chapter 3 begins, "As I was still walking on the road," as had been the case in chapter 2. Chapter 4 begins "And thinking thus" in relation to chapter 3. Chapter 5 begins "But having pondered my father's anger," referring to the last verse of chapter 4. Chapter 6 begins "When I, Abraham, heard words like this from my father," referring to the words in chapter 5. In each of these cases a retrospective transition is evident along the lines of an A/a-B pattern (cf. the discussion in §3.6).

The same technique is evident at the start of chapter 8, which begins, "And it came to pass as I was thinking things like these with regard to my father Terah in the court of my house," which refers back to chapters 6 and 7. But there is reason to think that chapter 7 is a later interpolation into the Apocalypse of Abraham.[33] If this is the case, then the words of 8:1 likely referred initially to the material in chapter 6, where Abraham is

---

[33] So R. Rubinkiewicz, "Apocalypse of Abraham," in *Old Testament Pseudepigrapha* (ed. J. H. Charlesworth; Garden City: Doubleday, 1983), 1:684. The point is defended in Rubinkiewicz, "La vision de l'homme dans l'Apocalypse d'Abraham," in *ANRW* 2.19.1 (ed. W. Hasse; Berlin: de Gruyter, 1979), 139–44.

shown as pondering much with regard to his father Terah, as described in
8:1. In the "final form" of the Apocalypse of Abraham, however, the connection between chapter 6 and chapter 8 has been altered by the introduction of chapter 7, so that the backward glance of 8:1 now refers to chapters
6 and 7 together, which seem to stand together as a single text unit.

Without chapter 7, the transition pattern would conform to that of
every other transition at the previous four text-unit boundaries (as mentioned above): A/a-B, with chapter 6 coming to an end, and chapter 8
beginning with a backward glance to chapter 6. With the addition of
chapter 7 to the apocalypse, however, a new transition pattern has been
introduced. In chapter 7, Abraham expresses his dissatisfaction with idolatry and desires to know "the God who created all the gods supposed by
us (to exist)" (7:10). Concerning this God Abraham exclaims in his closing words of this speech: "If only God would reveal himself by himself to
us!" (7:12). Of course, this is precisely what happens in chapter 8, where
almost immediately "the voice of the Mighty One came down from the
heavens in a stream of fire" (8:1) and speaks to Abraham. Consequently,
the final verse of chapter 7 performs a perfect gesture into chapter 8, with
Abraham's plea at the end of chapter 7 providing the occasion for God's
revelation of himself in chapter 8 (and in the remaining chapters of the
book). In this way, what originally had been an A/a-B transition has
become an A-b/a-B transition through the inclusion of additional material in chapter 7.

It needs to be noted that this change in structure causes the intensifi-
cation of, or perhaps even a change to, a theological strand within the
narrative. The last verse of chapter 7 is the first time in the text that
Abraham has expressed a desire for God to reveal himself; nothing of the
sort happens in any of the earlier (original) chapters. And the first time
that God reveals himself is in chapter 8. In other words, there is an implication in the final form of the narrative that God revealed himself to
Abraham as a consequence of Abraham's quest for God; only when
Abraham articulates his plea as a consequence of his own pursuit does
God become a character in the narrative. This theology is articulated
expressly in Apocalypse of Abraham 7:10, as Abraham says: "Listen,
Terah my father, I shall seek before you the God who created all the gods
supposed by us (to exist)." In the final form, human seeking is met by
divine revelation.

With chapter 7 removed, however, the first chapters of the Apocalypse of Abraham have no quest motif (at least explicitly so). Abraham
simply becomes progressively dissatisfied with the idolatry of his father
and culture, but nowhere does he express the view that a higher god must
exist whom he seeks. Until the Mighty One reveals himself to Abraham

and informs him, "You are searching for the God of gods, the Creator" in 8:3, the narrative might have gone in any direction. (For instance, Abraham might have simply voiced the view of Qohelet, affirming that "all is meaningless.") In the original storyline of the folktales, it is not so much his own quest that sets Abraham along his path as the father of God's people; instead, it is primarily the unsolicited, invading revelation of God to Abraham that results in that eventuality. Without chapter 7, the God of the folktales in the Apocalypse of Abraham is not so much a God who stands waiting to be discovered by those who would start down that long road toward enlightenment and fulfilment. Instead, he is more a God who invades people's lives in order to reveal the road to be followed for those who may simply be conscious of the fact that other roads lead nowhere, and one who meets them before they can even call out for him.[34] Whether one of these strands is theologically preferable is of no consequence here. The point is that the introduction of a new transitional structure has significantly affected the theology that that structure animates.

As with the chain link of Isaiah 53 (noted in §5.7), so too this chain-link interlock operates at a medial level, structurally speaking. The macro-level text-unit boundary is evident between chapter 8 and chapter 9 of the Apocalypse of Abraham, with the folktales of chapters 1–8 giving way to the apocalyptic revelations of chapters 9–32. The transitions between the chapters in the section of folktales are, then, medial-level transitions, with the chain-link interlock at the boundary between chapter 7 and chapter 8 falling into that category as well.

Part 4: Summary of Findings

§5.10   Overview and Relevance

Eleven examples of chain-link construction have been cited above. From those examples, four aspects of chain-link interlock are evident. These are listed below, along with a brief comment about their relevance to New Testament examples appearing in further chapters.

First, most of the examples offered above illustrate the usefulness of chain-link construction at macro-level transition points. This feature characterises all the examples cited in Part 1 above (§5.1–§5.6) and of the first example of Part 3 (§5.8). It also characterises the ten examples from the New Testament cited in chapters 7–10 below.

[34] A saying of Merritt Malloy goes as follows: "We look for God as though he were not already here."

Second, although chain links tend to appear at macro-level transition points, it is also the case that they appear at lesser transitions, such as the medial-level transition noted in Isaiah 53:2b-6 and at the boundary between Apocalypse of Abraham 7–8 (cf. §5.7 and §5.9). This form of construction will be considered in relation to five examples from Paul's letters in chapter 6 below.

Third, chain-link interlock can appear in both articulated and unarticulated form (cf. the discussion in §4.2). In articulated form, the author explicitly speaks about moving from one text-unit (i.e., book) to the next, whereas in the unarticulated form the transition is simply made without attention being explicitly drawn to that fact. Unarticulated interlocking transitions are evident, for instance, in the examples from Genesis–Exodus (§5.1), 4 Ezra (§5.5), Isaiah 48:16-22 (§5.6), Isaiah 53:2b-6 (§5.7), Daniel 6–7 (§5.8) and Apocalypse of Abraham 7–8 (§5.9). Articulated interlocking transitions are evident, for instance, in the examples from Josephus (§5.4) and Philo (§5.2) above. Clearly genre has relevance in determining whether the chain-link interlock is explicitly made. In tractates where the author incorporates himself within the discourse, the transition is easily articulated, as in the examples from Josephus (e.g., "In the first volume of this work, my most esteemed Epaphroditus, I demonstrated. . . . I shall now proceed to refute") and Philo (e.g., "We must next deal with. . . . The former treatise dealt with. . . . The present treatise is concerned with. . . ."). In these cases, the author explicitly alerts his audience to the fact that a transition is being made. In narratives describing events and characters without an obvious authorial presence, the transition is most naturally unarticulated. Most of the examples from the New Testament considered below conform to the latter case, and are consequently unarticulated. In only one case does a New Testament author (Luke) make it clear to his audience that a transition is in progress, where the chain-link interlock is explicitly made in articulated fashion (see §9.1).

Fourth, in Part 3 above, it was demonstrated that text-unit interlock could be influenced in the processes of a text's compositional history. In the cases studied here, the compositional history of two texts was shown to be the process by which chain-link interlock was created (§5.8 and §5.9; possibly also in Isa 48:16b-22 [§5.6]). When analysing the Johannine Gospel in chapter 8 below, it will be seen that the compositional history of that text has also influenced two of its chain links, enhancing one while unravelling the other (§8.8 and §8.9). Moreover, just as a theological shift was noted in the Apocalypse of Abraham in relation to the chain-link produced in the course of its compositional history, so too, it will be considered whether a theological shift is evident also in the compositional stages of the Johannine Gospel at precisely the point where the chain-link interlocks are evident.

A final word needs to be added here regarding the extent of the examples provided above. It has not been my intention in this project to trawl through the whole corpus of background (or contextual) literature, both Jewish and Graeco-Roman, looking for examples of chain-link interlock. This admission (if it is that) has two potential implications. First, it might be that there are no other examples of chain-link interlock in that extensive literature. This, however, is unlikely. As was noted in §2.1, the way that Quintilian and Lucian both discuss the interlocked transition suggests that it had currency in the ancient world to the extent that they found no reason to explain the mechanisms of the technique to their respective audiences. Consequently, the examples offered above are unlikely to exhaust the occurrences of chain-link interlock in the ancient world.

Second, it is likely that the database of chain-link interlock beyond the New Testament can be significantly extended. I have not deemed it my role to work through a variety of texts in which I have little expertise in order to increase the example database. That is the work of others to do, should they be so inclined. The impression that exhaustive work on texts outside of the New Testament must first be comprehensively conducted before work on the New Testament can commence is one that needs to be resisted in certain cases. The impression drawn from Quintilian's and Lucian's descriptions of chain-link interlock concerning its currency within the ancient world permits us to by-pass the comprehensive treatment of background literature. New Testament texts are themselves a rich source of information regarding the Graeco-Roman world, and as such they can be a starting point (but not an end point) for analysis of chain-link interlock in the ancient world. It is to a selection of those New Testament texts, themselves a segment of the extant literature from the Graeco-Roman world, that we now turn—our third point of triangulation in this project.

CHAPTER 6

Chain-Link Interlock
and the Logic of Romans

The third triangulation point in this study of "chain-link interlock" is the evidence from the New Testament, as laid out in the next five chapters (chs. 6–10). Demonstrating the existence of medial-level chain links in Paul's letters will prove to be a less complicated procedure than demonstrating the existence of the macro-level chain links in Revelation, in the Johannine Gospel, or in Luke-Acts. Consequently, of the five chapters dedicated to the study of chain-link interlock in New Testament texts, the first will involve an analysis of some passages in Paul's letters, especially Romans.

In chapter 3, a variety of structural techniques were surveyed in comparison to chain-link interlock. In that survey, several boundary-marking techniques, discourse arrangements, and text-unit transitions from Paul's letter to the Romans were noted: *inclusio*, climax, anticipatory transitions, retrospective transitions, and the bridge paragraph. In this chapter it will be shown that Paul also made use of chain-link transitions in his epistolary discourse. He does so not at macro-level text-unit boundaries but at medial-level text-unit boundaries (the kind demonstrated in §5.7 and §5.9 above).

In this chapter, cases of chain-link interlock in Paul will be noted and assessed for their structural and theological significance. Four examples of chain-link interlock will be offered from Romans. Prior to those examples, however, an example from 1 Corinthians will begin this overview.

Three of the passages studied in this chapter (§6.2–§6.4) are frequently thought to involve weak or anomalous structures that either (1) should not be credited to Paul (since they are beneath his expertise) or (2) reveal that he has a relatively poor grasp on the logic of his argument (since, in this view, the poorly structured logic is *not*, in fact, beneath his expertise). It will be shown, however, that the structure of these passages is not problematical and need not be credited to an unskilled rhetor. An ancient rhetor would have done all in his power to avoid the impression of amateurism, and a deficiency in controlling the structure of one's rhetorical logic would inevitably have advertised a consequent deficiency in persuasive ability. In fact, certain passages in which Paul is thought to lose control of his argumentative focus are precisely the passages in which he makes use of chain-link construction to assist his audience in assimilating his case. Scholars have failed to recognise that each of these passages share the same formal construction. Had that been recognised, they might have then asked whether this common structure underlying the passages in fact indicates the existence of a viable structural feature within Paul's day. That structure, as I have already suggested (esp. §4.6), was highly effective in oral/aural cultures in order to indicate that a transition is being made. Werner Kelber sought to sensitize modern students of Paul's letters to this phenomenon:

> His [Paul's] letters may in fact accommodate the requirements of oral speech more successfully than is commonly acknowledged. . . . [T]he letters, dictated by a speaker and intended for hearers, . . . will at least in part have been shaped by oral . . . speech patterns.[1]

If chain-link construction is one such speech pattern of the ancient world (as claimed in §4.6), and if Paul made use of it in his letters (as will be shown below), then Paul's efforts to assist his audience by means of this

---

[1] W. H. Kelber, *The Oral and Written Gospel: The Hermeneutics of Speaking and Writing in the Synoptic Tradition, Mark, Paul and Q* (Philadelphia: Fortress Press, 1983), 168. Cf. J. D. Harvey, *Listening to the Text: Oral Patterning in Paul's Letters* (Grand Rapids: Baker, 1998).

construction need to be recognised for what they are: first-rate examples of transitional construction.

§6.1   Chain-Link Interlock in 1 Corinthians 8:7-8

Dyke Parunak has argued that a chain-link construction (or as he calls it, an "inverted hinge" transition) underlies Paul's argument in 1 Corinthians 8:4-13.[2] The argument is as follows. First Corinthians 8 is the first of three chapters in which Paul considers issues pertaining to eating meat, participation in pagan banquets, and situations in which offending a Christian brother or sister might arise. In the first of these three chapters, Paul sets out two principles, the first pertaining to Christian "knowledge" and the second to Christian "love." These two principles are introduced in the first verse of Paul's exposition on these matters. So the word "knowledge" appears in 1 Corinthians 8:1a but is qualified with the notion of "love" in 8:1b. After coupling these two themes in a self-contained configuration in 8:2-3 (a kind of rhetorical aside), Paul begins a discourse in 8:4-13 that examines the issue of eating food offered to idols in two sections under the rubrics of knowledge (8:4-6; cf. "we know" in 8:4) and love (8:9-13, articulated in terms of modifying one's behaviour for the benefit of others). His statement in 8:7, however, relates more to 8:9-13 than to 8:4-6, including three features that suggest its relationship with the second half of the chapter:

(1) it introduces the pastoral note of concern for one's Christian brother or sister, which comes to full expression in 8:9-13;

(2) it introduces the notion of the "weak conscience" which appears later in 8:10 and 8:12; and

(3) it shifts out of the first person plural forms evident in the earlier section (as in 8:4, 6).

Similarly, just as 8:7 makes gestures towards 8:9-13, his statement in 8:8 relates more to 8:4-6 than to 8:9-13, including two features which suggest that it has close relationship with the earlier section:

(1) it reverts again to the first person plural forms, and

(2) it states for the first time the conclusion based on knowledge to which 8:4-6 has been leading.

---

[2] H. van Dyke Parunak, "Transitional Techniques in the Bible," *JBL* 102 (1983): 525–48, esp. 539–40.

TEXT-UNIT "A"	INTERLOCKED "b" (anticipatory)	INTERLOCKED "a" (retrospective)	TEXT-UNIT "B"
1 Cor 8:4-6/8	1 Cor 8:7	1 Cor 8:8	1 Cor 8:7/9-13

In this analysis, 1 Corinthians 8:7-8 looks to involve an overlap of material that is characteristic of chain-link construction, and the material overlap falls at what might be considered a medial-level transition between text units dealing with knowledge and love in the verses that surround 8:7-8. Accordingly, a chain-link interlock might well be evident here. With only slight adjustment to the beginning of 8:9, 1 Corinthians 8:7 and 8:8 could be inverted without loss, resulting in a more linear form of argument in which the topics are grouped together in self-contained fashion. As the text currently stands, however, we are left with the impression of a chain-link interlock at a medial-level of Paul's discourse. The same impression is given at three or four points in Paul's letter to the Christians at Rome, as demonstrated below.

§6.2   Chain-Link Interlock in Romans 7:25

Romans 7:25 stands at the point where the discourse of despair of the agonised "I" touches the sustained inventory of the blessings and promises given to those in Christ (7:7-25 and 8:1-39, respectively). So the last two verses of Romans 7 read as follows:

> Wretched man am I! Who will deliver me from this body of death? Thanks be to God through Jesus Christ our Lord. So then, with my mind I am a slave to the law of God, but with my flesh I am a slave to the law of sin (vv. 24–25).

Attracting scholarly attention, of course, is the whole of 7:25. The content and tone of 7:25a, for instance, seems ill-suited within the context of 7:7-25 while being wholly consonant with 8:1-39. So John Ziesler, assuming that Paul is not describing Christian experience in 7:14-25,[3] articulates the problem in simple terms: this exclamation "comes too early" in the arrangement of material.[4]

A variety of interpretative solutions have been proposed to rectify the apparently improper sequence of the text. C. H. Dodd surveys some of the options splendidly:

---

[3] For my own defence of this view, see my *Eschatology and the Covenant: A Comparison of 4 Ezra and Romans 1–11* (Sheffield: Sheffield Academic Press, 1991), 225–37, although some of my nuancing of the issue would now be different.

[4] J. Ziesler, *Paul's Letter to the Romans* (London: SCM Press, 1989), 199.

[I]t is scarcely conceivable that, after giving thanks to God for deliverance [i.e., 7:25a], Paul should describe himself as being in exactly the same position as before [i.e., 7:25b]. It is easy to conjecture various ways in which the displacement may have come about. For example, it is possible that an early reader of the epistle jotted down in the margin a more succinct and epigrammatic paraphrase of the somewhat cumbrous statement in verses 22-23, and that the next copyist incorporated the note in the text at the wrong place [i.e., at 7:25b]. Or again, the mistake may have arisen in the first writing of the epistle. Paul, we know, dictated his letters to *an amanuensis* (cf. xvi.22). At what a headlong speed must he have dictated this chapter, as he approached the emotional climax! It is conceivable that he himself repeated the statement of verses 22-23 in the more succinct form of verse 25, and that the amanuensis got confused, and made his fair copy in the wrong order.[5]

Dodd himself opted for seeing the "logical position" of 7:25b as being "before the climax of verse 24," with the text having been misconstrued in the process of its transmission. For him, this simple reordering of verses solves the problem of the text's illogical order. In his suggested re-ordered sequence (i.e., 7:23, 7:25b, 7:24, 7:25a), Romans 7:25a is placed directly next to Romans 8, the material that it is seen to introduce. According to Dodd, although there is no manuscript evidence in support of such a transposition in the order of the text, "we cannot avoid trusting our own judgment against [the manuscript] evidence," since the reputation of Paul's rhetorical skill is at stake.[6]

The other common view was the first solution mentioned by Dodd, in which scribal confusion has resulted in a later gloss being added to Paul's text. So Rudolf Bultmann, Ernst Käsemann, Ulrich Wilckens, John Ziesler, and John Ashton (to name a few) consider 7:25b to be, in Käsemann's words, "die Gloss eines später Lesers, . . . welche die erste *interpretatio christiana* von 7-24 bringt."[7] Alternatively, Brendan Byrne

[5] C. H. Dodd, *The Epistle of Paul to the Romans* (1932; repr., London: Hodder & Stoughton, 1947), 114–15.

[6] Dodd, *The Epistle of Paul*, 115.

[7] E. Käsemann, *An die Römer* (trans. G. W. Bromiley; 4th ed.; Tübingen: J.C.B. Mohr [Paul Siebeck], 1980), 203–4 ("the gloss of a later reader . . . which presents the first Christian interpretation of vv. 7–24," *Commentary on Romans* [trans. Geoffrey W. Bromiley; Grand Rapids: Eerdmans, 1980], 212). Cf. also R. Bultmann, "Glossen im Römerbrief," in *Exegetica: Aufsätze zur Erforschung des Neuen Testaments* (ed. E. Dinkler; Tübingen: J.C.B. Mohr [Paul Siebeck], 1967), 278–84, esp. 278–80; U. Wilckens, *Der Brief an die Römer (Röm 6–11)* (Zürich: Benziger Verlag, 1980; Neukirchen-Vluyn: Neukirchener Verlag, 1978–1982), 6:96 [giving an extensive list in n. 399 of others holding this view]; Ziesler, *Paul's Letter to the Romans*, 199; J. Ashton, *The Religion of Paul the Apostle* (New Haven: Yale University Press, 2000), 224. J. C. O'Neill (*Paul's Letter to the Romans* [Harmondsworth: Penguin Books, 1975], 133) advises us to "put these words

imagines 7:25a (rather than 7:25b) to be the later scribal addition.[8]

In ways of this sort, the peculiarities of the back and forth tussle within 7:25 are removed from Paul's orb of responsibility and apportioned to the disruptive influence of scribal copyists and meddlers. The fact that an evidential base for such proposals is, of course, beyond scholarly reconstruction is not seen as an impediment to such attempts, not least since Paul's reputation as one capable of effective persuasion is at stake, and the apparently convoluted text is not worthy of one such as him.

Peter Stuhlmacher takes a different route of explanation, in a manner that envisages no real structural deficiency in Paul's text. He notes the way that lament psalms sometimes erupt into strains of thanksgiving to God; something similar, he suggests is evident in Romans 7:25a, where thanksgiving breaks into the context of despair.[9] But the parallels are not precise, since the lament psalms noted by Stuhlmacher (Psa 22:22-23; 69:30-31) ultimately have their climax in praise without reverting once again to lament, as happens in 7:25b.

Instead of postulating fanciful textual reconstructions or the influence of scriptural precedents, most interpreters speak of 7:25a as an "anticipatory interjection," or something of the sort. The peculiar structure of the text is explained in relation to Paul's psychological demeanour and theological exuberance. The impression given in this view is that Paul has got slightly ahead of himself; he cannot maintain the sustained tones of despair without inserting a devotional note of praise before getting back to the point and concluding the unit in 7:25b.

For Paul's contemporaries, however, the implication of such a view would likely have been that Paul's rhetorical control is flawed here. Despite the antirhetorical rhetoric of 1 Corinthians 1–2, such an implication would not have helped to endear Paul's audience to his message. Neither is it enough to suggest that the phrase "thanks be to God, through Jesus Christ our Lord" is an example of rhetorical pathos, in which one wins over an audience through emotional involvement. (Compare, for example, Rom 9:2-3 or 10:1 where Paul's personal sentiments come to the fore.) Since the same effect could have been achieved by placing the phrase at the beginning of 8:1, an explanation of the struc-

---

[i.e., 7:25a] aside" when reconstructing what for him amounted to little more than Paul's original postcard to Roman Christians.

[8] B. Byrne, *S.J.*, *Romans* (Collegeville: Liturgical Press, 1996), 233.

[9] P. Stuhlmacher, *Paul's Letter to the Romans: A Commentary* (Louisville: Westminster John Knox; Edinburgh: T&T Clark, 1994), 113. Admittedly, Stuhlmacher tries to explain this problem by identifying 7:25b and 8:1 as two summarising conclusions (pp. 112–14). But this seems to run contrary to transitional marker ἄρα νῦν in 8:1, which does not serve to introduce a concluding note but a new section, not least in relation with the "then-now" contrast of 7:5-6.

ture of the last verse of Romans 7 fails to have a foothold in rhetoric pathos.

But there is a ready-made *structural* explanation for the passage that has so far been neglected in scholarly consideration. That is, in 7:25 we have an example of chain-link construction as a transition marker, with 7:25b stating an appropriate conclusion to 7:7-24 and 7:25a introducing the work of God through Jesus Christ that once again comes to the fore in 8:1ff.[10] In Romans the phrase "in/through Jesus Christ our Lord" occurs with locative or instrumental meaning only in Romans 5–8,[11] and always at key structural points (5:1, 11, 21; 6:23; 7:25; 8:39);[12] its inclusion at 7:25a signals that Paul is soon to make a transition back to discussing the eschatological work of God in Christ against the backdrop of the despair depicted so graphically in 7:7-24 and summed up in 7:25b.

The recognition that each part of 7:25 plays a role in an overlapped transition is not necessarily new. So, for instance, Ernest Best depicts the progression from Romans 7 to Romans 8 through the terrain of 7:25 in this manner:

> We have a long statement of the problem (7:7-24); a short statement of the answer (first half of verse 25); a short restatement of the problem (second half of verse 25); a long statement of the answer (chapter 8).[13]

When making this case, however, Best was unaware that this structural pattern describes precisely a transitional construction that had currency in antiquity, with 7:25 being the pivot point that leads from one text-unit to the next by means of chain-link interlock.

TEXT-UNIT "A"	INTERLOCKED "b" (anticipatory)	INTERLOCKED "a" (retrospective)	TEXT-UNIT "B"
Rom 7:7-25	Rom 7:25a	Rom 7:25b	Rom 8:1-39

---

[10] Here I differ from those who see 7:25b as an unsatisfactory summary of the earlier section (e.g., Franz J. Leenhardt, *The Epistles to the Romans* [trans. Harold Knight; London: Lutterworth Press, 1961], 195). 7:25b simply reiterates the kind of thought represented in 7:16 and 7:20.

[11] A prepositional phrase of this sort in connection with the tag "our Lord" appear elsewhere only at 15:30, where it has a different semantic force.

[12] In each case, a preposition (διά or ἐν) appears with "Jesus Christ" (or "Christ Jesus"), which itself is modified by "our Lord."

[13] E. Best, *The Letter of Paul to the Romans* (Cambridge: Cambridge University Press, 1967), 84. Cf. N. A. Dahl, "Missionary Theology in the Epistle to the Romans," (in his *Studies in Paul: Theology for the Early Christian Mission* [Minneapolis: Augsburg Press, 1977]) who calls 7:25b a "delayed conclusion" (85).

In other ways as well, Paul has taken great care to signal the transition from Romans 7 to Romans 8: first, by contrasting the "fleshly then" and the "spiritual now" in 7:5-6, two verses that provide the structural foundation for the movement from 7:7ff. and 8:1ff.; and second, by introducing the "spiritual now" in 8:1 with the emphatic "therefore now" (ἄρα νῦν). Such structural indicators are strengthened further by the intentional inclusion of a thematic overlap in 7:25.

It seems, then, that it was of crucial importance to Paul that his first hearers notice the significant shift in his presentation, including as he did three structural indicators to signal the transition. The chain-link construction at Romans 7:25 acts as a prod to ensure that his hearers move out of the context of Romans 7 to hear more of the things that God has done "through Jesus Christ our Lord" in Romans 8. Since in Paul's day chain-link construction was not an uncommon transitional device in assisting an audience (see §2.1), the placement of 7:25 within its surrounding context would not have been unusual or confusing. It would not have been seen as a structural anomaly requiring either textual reconstruction (à la Dodd, Bultmann, and others)[14] or psychological explanation. Instead, it would have been recognised as a transition marker used for the benefit of Paul's audience.

If I am right to see 7:25 in this light, more needs to be said about how Romans 7 is best interpreted. That is, the exclamation of 7:25a need not be understood as an articulation of the "I" of Romans 7. The chain-link construction in this case helps to juxtapose the two sections, 7:7-24 and 8:1ff. Consequently, the articulations of 7:25a and 7:25b are not to be understood as uttered by the same person. This is contrary to the argument of James Dunn, for instance, when he writes:

> It is precisely the one who knows that Jesus Christ provides the answer who goes on to observe calmly that the "I" continues to be divided between mind and flesh. As the conclusion to 7.7-25, v. 25b can hardly be read otherwise more naturally than as indicating a continuing state—a state of continuing dividedness of the "I" who says, "Thanks be to God through Jesus Christ our Lord."[15]

---

[14] Nor would the extant textual order have been the *lectio difficilior*, as it is for J. A. Fitzmyer (*Romans: A New Translation with Introduction and Commentary* [New York: Doubleday, 1993], 477). Fitzmyer calls the hypothetical textual reconstructions of Bultmann and others "more logical" than the extant text, but he adds that such reconstructions are "suspect for that very reason." In a society where chain-link construction is a recognised structural indicator, Fitzmyer's discussion would be perplexing.

[15] J. D. G. Dunn, *The Theology of Paul the Apostle* (Grand Rapids: Eerdmans, 1998), 474.

This reading, however, runs contrary to the dynamics of chain-link transition. The exclamation of 7:25a is simply a transitional feature spoken from the perspective of Romans 8 which looks back on the "I" of Romans 7 as "you" (σε, 8:2).[16] The one who speaks in 7:25a is not, then, the speaker of 7:7-24 and 25b.[17] Consequently, the view that Romans 7 is uttered by the "delivered" Christian who continues to be caught between the ages,[18] or by the immature Christian who continues to try to work for his own redemption in a legalistic or nomistic fashion, seems ill-founded.

§6.3   Chain-Link Interlock in Romans 10:16-17

Romans 10:16-17 has proved difficult to place within structural analyses of Paul's argument in Romans. For some, 10:16 marks the start of a minor text unit,[19] while for others that start is found in 10:18.[20] The problem of delimiting the text units surrounding 10:16-17 arises from the subject matter of those verses within their contexts. In 10:14-15 Paul sets in motion a series of cause and effect relationships in reverse order, from the desired result of calling on the name of the Lord (ἐπικαλέω; cf. 10:12-13), to the preceding act of believing (πιστεύω), to a preceding hearing of the message (ἀκούω), to a preceding act of gospel proclamation (κηρύσσω), to a preceding act of sending out the messengers (ἀποστέλλω). The train of thought concludes at 10:17 (cf. the concluding ἄρα), where Paul states: "So faith (πίστις) comes from what is heard (ἀκοή), and what is heard comes through the word (ῥῆμα) of Christ."

Prior to the conclusion of 10:17, Paul demonstrates that the outline of causality does not inevitably result in faith, and this is what 10:16 serves to indicate: "But not all have obeyed (ὑπακούω) the good news; for Isaiah says, 'Lord, who has believed (ἐπίστευσεν) our message?'" This qualifies the process of causality that surrounds it in 10:14-15 and 10:17.

---

[16] The presence of the first person plural form in 7:25a (ὑμῶν) lends confirmatory weight, since Paul's presentation throughout Romans 5-8 is (except in 7:7-25, of course) characterised by first person plural forms.

[17] According to C. Bryan (*A Preface to Romans: Notes on the Epistle in its Literary and Cultural Setting* [Oxford: Oxford University Press, 2000], 145), in 7:25a "Paul takes up the theme again in his own voice—a change that could easily be indicated by the reader's change of tone," citing Quintilian, *Inst.* 1.8.3.

[18] E.g., J. D. G. Dunn, *Romans* (Dallas: Word, 1988), 1:377. Cf. C. E. B. Cranfield, *The Epistle to the Romans* (Edinburgh: T&T Clark, 1975), 1:367-68.

[19] D. H. Lietzmann, *Einführung in die Textgeschichte des Paulusbriefe an die Römer* (5th ed.; Tübingen: J.C.B. Mohr, 1971), 101; O'Neill, *Paul's Letter to the Romans*, 176-80.

[20] M.-J. Lagrange, *Saint Paul Épitre aux Romains* (Paris: Gabalda, 1950), 262; O. Michel, *Der Brief an die Römer* (5th ed.; Göttingen: Vandenhoeck & Ruprecht, 1978), 333; Käsemann, *An die Römer*, 285-86; Dunn, *Romans*, 619-20.

And this qualification becomes the focus of Paul's attention in 10:18-21, where he discusses the lack of inevitability in the process of causality, explicitly with reference to Israel's lack of faith in 10:19-21. The fact that 10:16 relates most closely to 10:18-21 and 10:17 to 10:14-15 has been met by interpreters in a variety of ways. A number have resorted to the "scribal gloss" theory, speculating that 10:17 was added in the process of scribal transmission.[21] The removal of 10:17 from Paul's script removes the problem of material overlap within 10:16-17, as does the view that a scribe has awkwardly rearranged the verses, with 10:16 originally coming after 10:17.[22] Many interpreters, however, would agree with C. K. Barrett, who finds "not a sufficient reason for rearranging the text."[23]

But Barrett himself finds these verses to be awkward nonetheless. In his view, in 10:16 "Paul leaps to his conclusion, though it might more appropriately have been placed later." Moreover, 10:17 "would come more appropriately after v. 15a." According to Barrett:

> It is undoubtedly true that a rearrangement would improve the logic of the paragraph, for v. 17 summarizes the chain of connexions given in vv. 14f., and so would prepare the way for v. 16, with its disclosure that the chain was broken in the link of faith.

Consequently, in 10:16 "Paul leaps ahead to his main point, and then returns to fill up a gap in the argument" in 10:17.[24]

Others share similar estimates about the awkwardness of the text, the view being that, in the words of Tom Schreiner, Romans 10:16 "interrupts the sequence articulated in verses 14-15" and should be labelled an "interjection."[25] It is also worth quoting Hans Lietzmann's similar view,

---

[21] Bultmann, "Glossen im Römerbrief," 280; O. Michel, *Der Brief an die Römer* (5th ed.; Göttingen: Vandenhoeck & Ruprecht, 1978), 334; U. Luz, *Das Geschichtsverständnis des Paulus* (Munich: Kaiser Verlag, 1968), 32 n. 76; W. Schmithals, *Der Römerbrief* (Gütersloh: Gütersloher Verlag, 1988), 382–83.

[22] F. Müller, "Zwei Marginalien im Brief des Paulus an die Römer," *ZNW* 40 (1941): 249–54, esp. 252–54; cf. also O. Kuss, *Der Römerbrief* (Regensburg: Verlag Friedrich Pustet, 1963), 774.

[23] C. K. Barrett, *A Commentary on the Epistle to the Romans* (2d ed.; London: Adam & Charles Black, 1971), 205.

[24] All quotations in this paragraph are from Barrett, *Romans*, 204–5.

[25] T. R. Schreiner, *Romans* (Grand Rapids: Baker Books, 1998), 569. Dunn (*Romans*, 620) recognises a certain "awkwardness" in the structure of 10:16-17, but nonetheless seeks to illustrate a coherence to Paul's pattern of thought in these verses. First, he points out the link between ὑπακούω in 16, ἀκοή in 16-17 and ἀκούω in 18. (One might also refer to the connection between ῥῆμα in 10:17 and 10:18 and πιστεύω in 10:14 and 10:16 to illustrate an interconnectedness running throughout 10:14-18.) Second, he explains the awkwardness of the passage in the

not least in his comparison of the structure of this passage with that of
Romans 7:25:

> Mit v.16 tritt — zu früh — der Gedanke ein, dass nicht einmal alle,
> welche die Botschaft hören, zum Glauben kommen. Aber mit v. 17
> greift der Apostel, an das ἀκοή und ἐπίστευσεν des Zitats formell
> anknüpfend, wieder auf v. 14-15 zurück (ganz wie 7:25).[26]

When the passage is analysed with cognisance of chain-link construction
in mind, however, none of these attempts to "improve the logic of the
paragraph" by spurious theories are necessary, nor would it be necessary
to speak about interruption, interjection, and inappropriate ("too early")
arrangement—charges that would have been heard by Paul's contemporaries as slurs on his rhetorical ability. Paul's thought throughout 10:14-
21 incorporates a chain-link transition at 10:16-17, at which point the
causal linkage from sending messengers to calling on the name of the
Lord (10:14-15, 17) shifts to the problem of the lack of faith, especially
within Israel (10:16, 18-21). The presence of a chain link causes difficulties for linear outlines of Paul's thought, just as it has perturbed modern
interpreters. But presumably in view of the oral/aural nature of communication in the first century, the chain link of 10:16-17 aided the process-
ing of Paul's discourse by those who were his text's first recipients.

TEXT-UNIT "A"	INTERLOCKED "b" (anticipatory)	INTERLOCKED "a" (retrospective)	TEXT-UNIT "B"
Rom 10:14-17	Rom 10:16	Rom 10:17	Rom 10:18-21(ff.)

§6.4   Chain-Link Interlock in Romans 12:14-16

From a structural point of view, one of the passages in Romans that has
proved to be perennially problematical for interpreters is 12:9-21.
Douglas Moo highlights the problem clearly. Noting that it is typical for
interpreters to divide the passage into two main sections (12:9-13, 12:14-
21), he states:

---

following manner (p. 622): "V 16 therefore is best understood as a first response to
the sequence of vv 14-15, not intended to pick up on any particular link in the
chain, but simply asserting the fact that it has not worked in the case of 'all.' The
question why, or how has the breakdown occurred is not actually addressed until v
18." Dunn may well be right in all this, but the structural issue nonetheless still
remains. Why should Paul's "first response" of 10:16 precede the conclusion of
10:17 rather than follow it, as do his subsequent responses of 10:18-21?

[26] Lietzmann, *Einführung in die Textgeschichte*, 101.

But some uncertainty about this division was always present because the content of these sections did not seem to match this division. Particularly troublesome is the way in which Paul seems to move from inner-Christian relationships (vv. 9-13) to relationships with non-Christians (v. 14), back to inner-Christians relationships (vv. 15-16), and back again to relationships with non-Christians (vv. 17-21).[27]

Consequently, some interpreters prefer a different division of the textual structure, with the first section comprising 12:9-16 ("structured quite loosely")[28] and the second comprising 12:17-21.[29] The issue, then, is whether to group 12:14-16 with what precedes it or with what follows it, since the subject matter of those verses defies convenient categorisation.

There is little dispute, for instance, that 12:14 "cuts somewhat intrusively into the sequence" concerning the practice of love among Christians. Consequently, as Byrne states, "the perspective here [i.e., 12:14] . . . turn[s] for a time to the outside world (cf. vv.17-21)."[30] Clearly the term "persecutors" (διώκοντας) signals those outside the boundaries of Christian fellowship.

Nor is there much dispute that in 12:16 Paul has relations among Christians primarily in mind. This is suggested by the phrase εἰς ἀλλήλους, which has an internal corporate focus, recalling Paul's advice in 12:10 concerning Christian relationships: "In brotherly love show sincerity of love to one another" (εἰς ἀλλήλους). Similarly the heavy concentration of the verb φρονεῖν in 12:16 (three times, variously translated) recalls a similar concentration of the same verb in 12:3 (four times), where Paul begins his brief essay on diversity within the unity of the body of Christ (12:3-8). For such reasons, Pauline interpreters generally see 12:16 to be a carry-over of the corporate focus of 12:10-13.[31]

The same is generally conceded for 12:15 as well, although here the number of dissenters increases by one or two. Most think, however, that the notion of rejoicing with those who rejoice and weeping with those

---

[27] D. Moo, *The Epistle to the Romans* (Grand Rapids: Eerdmans, 1996), 773–74. Cf. his comments in the commentary proper: "A break in the passage occurs here [12:14], marked by a change in . . . topic—from relations among Christians in vv. 10-13 to relations of Christian with non-Christians in v. 14. . . . [At 12:15] Paul changes both style and topic yet again. . . . [T]he prohibition of retaliation in v. 17a expands on Paul's warning that we are not to curse our persecutors in v. 14b" (780, 781 and 784).

[28] Schreiner, *Romans*, 663.

[29] E.g., Schreiner, *Romans*, 662 and 671.

[30] Byrne, *Romans*, 377. Cf. Schreiner (*Romans*, 667): Romans 12:14 "shifts to the attitude that believers have for those who persecute and oppress them."

[31] For some, 12:9 is not linked with 12:10-13, since it is serving as a thematic statement of a general sort standing over much of the material that follows in Romans 12–13, and perhaps even Romans 14–15.

who weep, while having some application to outsiders of course, is intended primarily to instruct Christians in their mutual relationships. Other passages are sometimes referred to in this regard, not least 1 Corinthians 12:26: "If one member suffers, all the members suffer together, if one member is honoured, all the members rejoice together." Moreover, Paul's charge to "rejoice with those who rejoice, weep with those who weep" is common parlance in the *topos* of Graeco-Roman friendship (cf. 12:9-10), again suggesting that in 12:15 Christian internal relationships are in view.

For our purposes, however, a firm decision regarding the structural centre of gravity for 12:15 is not of ultimate concern, since almost all are agreed that 12:14 works with 12:17-21, while 12:16 works with 12:10-13, indicating that an overlap technique is in operation in these verses, regardless of which direction 12:15 is thought to point. The overlap conforms precisely to a chain-link interlock.[32]

TEXT-UNIT "A"	INTERLOCKED "b" (anticipatory)	INTERLOCKED "a" (retrospective)	TEXT-UNIT "B"
Rom 12:9-13/16	Rom 12:14(15?)	Rom 12:(15?)16	Rom 12:14/17-21

If it is right to find a chain-link interlock within 12:14-16, this explanation of the text renders other kinds of explanations unnecessary, particularly explanations involving Paul's thought processes in the course of composition. Thinking that Paul's structure is fragmented at this point, interpreters often feel compelled to explain the fragmentation in one of two ways. For some, Paul originally intended for 12:15-16 to follow directly on from 12:10-13, but the mention of διώκειν in 12:13 ("pursue") caused him to deviate from his intended course by including in 12:14 a version of the διώκειν saying ("persecute") from the Jesus tradition. For others, Paul originally intended to change topic at 12:14, but then remembered the important material of 12:15-16 and so included it, albeit outside the parameters of its natural context.[33]

[32] The A-b-a-B pattern of chain-link construction is likely to operate in the following manner: A = 12:10-13; b = 12:14; a = 12:15-16; and B = 12:17-21. Just as Bauckham's structural outline of Revelation places 22:6-9 within both 21:9–22:9 and 22:6-21 (noted in §7.3 below), so perhaps Romans 12:10-21 can only be outlined as 12:10-16 and 12:14-21.

[33] Both scenarios are entertained by K.-W. Peng, "[The] Structure of Romans 12.1-15.13" (Ph.D. diss., University of Sheffield, 1997), 101–2. The former solution is advocated by Fitzmyer, *Romans*, 655. Some try to minimise the problem by suggesting that the way Christians relate to each other pertains to the issue of how Christians relate to outsiders, since it affects the way outsiders perceive

Speculation of this sort is the natural result of the premise that the structure of Paul's case in 12:14-16 is problematical. But such speculation is unnecessary, precisely because the premise on which it rests is incorrect. Paul's structure is not problematical at this point, but it is constructed on the basis of the technique of chain-link overlap signalling a transition in the flow of thought. The very point at which *modern readers* think Paul has lost some argumentative control is precisely the point at which *ancient hearers* would have found Paul to be structuring the argument in order to assist them in assimilating his presentation most easily.

The difficulty that modern scholars have in appreciating the manner in which Paul ordered the text is illustrated well by Leon Morris in his discussion of 12:14 with regard to its larger context:

> It is possible that we move now to Paul's instructions about Christian behaviour toward outsiders; this is surely the meaning of the first injunction in this verse. But the following words seem to apply better to what Christians should do among themselves. In any case Paul is not dividing up his instructions to conform to a neat pattern.[34]

Morris's claim that Paul "is not dividing his instructions to conform to a neat pattern" assumes that a neat pattern can only be linear. But as is clear, non-linear structures were part of the range of "neat" structural patterns in the ancient world. So Moo's description of Paul's text moving between topics in a staggered manner (see above) would have been recognised by Quintilian and Lucian as meeting the qualifications of a chain-link transition. Although the back-and-forth structure that Paul employs in these verses may seem "particularly troublesome" to Moo and the majority of modern interpreters, it would not have been so to the first hearers of the letter, for whom it would have served the purpose of signalling a transition from one topic to another.

I have claimed that, for Paul's original audience, the shift in focus in 12:14-16 would have signalled that a transition is in process. Unlike the chain link of 7:25, however, the chain link of 12:14-16 does not serve a contrastive role (i.e., distinguishing 7:7-24 from 8:1ff.) but a correlative role, coupling two depictions of genuine love (12:9), the first with regard to the Christian community (12:10-13, 15-16) and the second with regard to those beyond the boundaries of that community (12:14, 17-21).

Christians. See Cranfield, *Romans*, 2:643; Bryan, *Preface to Romans*, 202. Better, perhaps, is Dunn's view (*Romans*, 739) that the discussion of internal relationships falls into this context because "some of the tensions within the Roman congregations . . . were a result of the persecution already suffered by the Roman Jews."

[34] L. L. Morris, *The Epistle to the Romans* (Grand Rapids: Eerdmans, 1988), 449.

In this case, the chain link seems not only to act as transition marker but, in its interweaving of the two aspects, also weds them closely together in the imagination of the Roman Christians, for whom relations both internally and externally may have been somewhat strained.[35]

Chain-link construction does not explain every structural feature throughout 12:9-21. That passage exhibits various structural techniques, such as: catchword links (e.g., διώκειν in 12:13-14),[36] formal connections (e.g., imperatival participles ending in –οι and –οντες [both homoeoptoton and homoeoteleuton] in 12:10-13; cf. 12:16), formal contrasts (e.g., imperatival verbs [as opposed to imperatival participles] are introduced at 12:14), an *inclusio* (κακόν in 12:17 and 12:21), a possible chiasm (in 12:17-21), and other structural features.[37] To these, one other structural feature simply needs to be added at the centre of the paragraph: chain-link interlock.

§6.5   Chain-Link Interlock in Romans 13:13-14

Towards the end of Romans 13, having pointed out that the end times are near and just before advising the "weak" and the "strong" regarding their responsibilities in corporate living, Paul exhorts his audience in the following fashion (13:12-14):

> Let us then lay aside the works of darkness and put on the armour of light; let us live honourably as in the day, not in revelling and drunkenness, not in debauchery and licentiousness, not in quarrelling and jealousy [μὴ ἔριδι καὶ ζήλῳ]. Instead, put on the Lord Jesus Christ, and make no provision for the flesh, to gratify its desires.

---

[35] Perhaps Paul's point can be summarised as follows: Offer care for other Christians in order to honour them and to walk in honour yourselves (12:10-13, 16); offer care for non-Christians in order to dishonour them (by your kindness) and to walk in honour yourselves (12:14, 17-21).

[36] M. Dibelius (*James* [Philadelphia: Fortress Press, 1976], 6–11) gives evidence of catchword linkage in paraenetic material, and on p. 10 lists Romans 12:13-14, 12:14a-14b, 12:16a-16b-16c and 12:17-18 as examples. Note O'Neill's handling of the catchword link in 12:13-14 as indicating the craftsmanship of a second-rate editor (*Paul's Letter to the Romans*, 204): "Here is clear proof that a collector of aphorisms is at work, not an author writing a continuous moral discourse. The verb "to persecute" also means "to pursue, devote oneself to," and has been used in that second sense at the end of v. 13. The compiler has mechanically put together a saying that ends by recommending devotion with another saying that begins by recommending persecutors to be blessed!"

[37] For fuller discussion of these techniques, see D. A. Black, "The Pauline Love Command: Structure, Style, and Ethics in Romans 12:9-21," *Filologia Neotestamentaria* 1 (1989): 3–21.

According to John O'Neill, the short vice list of 13:13 in the middle of this quotation "is not related to what follows or what precedes."[38] Others, however, have thought differently. According to Moo, Paul's mention of "quarrelling and jealousy" (ἔρις, ζῆλος) in 13:13 serves to introduce Paul's discussion of Romans 14–15: "Paul may have chosen them [i.e., the words "quarrelling" and "jealousy"] with a view ahead to his rebuke of the Roman Christians for their divisiveness and mutual criticism."[39] Similarly Jeremy Moiser argues that 13:11-14 consists of general paraenesis that has little to do with the situation of Christianity in Rome, except for the "last two vices included: quarrels and jealousy," which were particularly appropriate to Roman Christians, as is evident from Romans 14–15.[40]

There is some merit to this suggestion. Where Paul speaks in 13:13 of the strife and jealousy that shatters corporate living, he also highlights in 14:10 and 14:13 the tendency to "pass judgement on" and "despise" other Christians, a tendency that he obviously hopes the Roman Christians will shun. For Paul, the kingdom of God that is to animate Christian corporate behaviour promotes "peace and joy in the Holy Spirit" (14:17), as opposed to strife and jealousy. So Paul exhorts his audience to "pursue what makes for peace and for mutual edification" (14:19), and hopes that God will "grant you to live in such harmony with one another" (15:15). All this is in contradistinction to the "quarrelling and jealousy" that Paul encourages them to shun in the penultimate verse of Romans 13.

If the phrase "quarrelling and jealousy" of 13:13 can serve as a lead into the issues addressed in 14:1–15:13, the final verse of Romans 13 serves to round off the advice of the final paragraph of Romans 13. So just as Paul encouraged his audience in 13:12 to "put on the armour of light" (ἐνδυσώμεθα [δὲ] τὰ ὅπλα τοῦ φωτός), in 13:14 he also exhorts them to "put on the Lord Jesus Christ" (ἐνδύσασθε τὸν κύριον Ἰησοῦν Χριστόν). If 13:13 takes its cues from the impending discourse in Romans 14–15 and if 13:14 takes its cues from the earlier discourse of 13:11-14, we have here the makings of a chain-link transition.

TEXT-UNIT "A"	INTERLOCKED "b" (anticipatory)	INTERLOCKED "a" (retrospective)	TEXT-UNIT "B"
Rom 13:11-14	Rom 13:13	Rom 13:14	Rom 14:1–15:6

[38] O'Neill, *Paul's Letter to the Romans*, 218.

[39] Moo, *Romans*, 825. According to Moo, the two entries "do not so naturally fit here" and so have a forward-looking function. Unfortunately, Moo does not explain why ἔρις and ζῆλος are ill-matched to the context.

[40] J. Moiser, "Rethinking Romans 12–15," *NTS* 36 (1990): 571–82, esp. 578.

Mark Reasoner has suggested that the earlier vices listed in 13:13 also serve a role in relation to Paul's advice in Romans 14–15. He believes that there are indications in 14–15 that the "strong" are "gluttonous eaters" who are guilty of "consumptive excess" (cf. 14:2, 17, 21; 16:18).[41] Reasoner finds the "strong" characterised in 13:13 where Paul exhorts his audience to avoid "revelling and drunkenness," "debauchery and licentiousness," just as in 16:18 Paul warns against those who create dissensions in order to serve "their own appetites."[42] According to Reasoner, "Some members of the Roman churches were living as if the kingdom of God were food and drink [cf. 14:17], and justifying their excessive consumption by this dictum."[43] Consequently, Reasoner argues that the whole of 13:13 "should be taken into consideration when one is reading Rom. 14:1–15.13."[44]

Reasoner's suggestion is not wholly compelling, since there is no real indication in 14:2, 17 or 21 that the strong are gluttons, and since the polemic at 16:18 might be exaggerated polemic that cannot be used to mirror read the situation. But if "quarrelling and jealousy" can be said to gesture towards Romans 14–15 on the basis of a chain-link transition, then it is conceivable that the earlier clauses might also include similar forward gestures on the same basis (although for rhetorical effect rather than as a depiction of a particular group in Rome). Consequently, the forward gesture of 13:13 might apply to more than the single phrase "quarrelling and jealousy."

§6.6   Conclusions

Had he known of Paul's letter to the Romans, the second-century rhetorician Lucian of Samosata might have found the letter to have occasionally incorporated a transitional feature whereby material should be linked like a chain and "call out across the boundaries" (*History*, §55). It has been suggested here that this technique is visible in the following instances: Romans 7:25; 10:16-17; 12:14-16; and 13:13-14 (as well, perhaps, in 1 Cor 8:7-8). In the first three cases, scholarly dispute concerning the structure has arisen in one form or another due to what appears to be Paul's rather torturous structural arrangement. So A. D. Nock had this to say about Paul's manner of argument: "His words sometimes

---

[41] M. Reasoner, *The Strong and the Weak: Romans 14.1–15.13 in Context* (Cambridge: Cambridge University Press, 1999), 202 and 206 respectively.

[42] Reasoner, *The Strong and the Weak*, 202.

[43] Reasoner, *The Strong and the Weak*, 69.

[44] Reasoner, *The Strong and the Weak*, 67; the quotation applies to the whole of 13:8-14, but the force of Reasoner's claim pertains almost exclusively to 13:13.

tumble over one another: there are the brief, vivid violences which most men would, on later reflection, have removed."[45] But the impression shared by many interpreters that these passages involve structural mess-ups and "vivid violences" is often due simply to their own lack of aware-ness of chain-link interlock as a rhetorically efficient transitional structure. This structuring device had currency in ancient cultures where texts were encountered by hearers rather than readers and served to sig-nal a transition from one context of thought or perception to another.

Instead of losing control of his argument in these cases, Paul in effect is simultaneously demonstrating both mastery of his subject matter and concern for his audience. In both regards, he is proving himself to be an effective rhetor. Modern scholars have failed to recognise the point only because they have failed to include chain-link interlock within their own analytical toolbox. The Roman Christians to whom Paul was writing, however, would likely have readily recognised the rhetorical technique and been assisted by it in their aural reception of the letter.

This survey of chain-link interlock in New Testament texts turns now from medial-level examples to macro-level examples, as evidenced in Revelation (ch. 7), the Johannine Gospel (ch. 8), and Luke-Acts (ch. 9–10).

---

[45] A. D. Nock, *St. Paul* (London: Oxford University Press, 1938), 14.

CHAPTER 7

Chain-Link Interlock and the Structure of the Apocalypse

Having analysed medial-level examples of text-unit interlock in Paul's letters, our analysis of macro-level examples begins with the last book of the New Testament. This is because the book of Revelation provides one of the clearest examples of chain-link construction in the ancient world. The text-unit interlock of Revelation 22:6-9 is heavily studied—that is, it has been intentionally and extensively calculated and executed. And it provides further confirmation of the validity of the interpretation offered in chapter 2 concerning the construction described by Lucian as "linked

103

like a chain" and by Quintilian as "handholding." This is demonstrated in §7.1–§7.4. In §7.5–§7.7, three further chain links are examined, confirming that the author of the book of Revelation had a penchant for this construction, making use of it at key points in his literary enterprise.

Part 1: Chain-Link Interlock in Revelation 22:6-9

The book of Revelation is as much a work of art as it is religious literature. Part of its artistic impressiveness is the striking structural infrastructure that undergirds its narrative development. Structurally speaking, Revelation 22:6-9 must qualify as one of the richest and most complex passages in the apocalypse, let alone in the New Testament. In its current form, it shows evidence of having been carefully crafted in a way that connects it to the following material (22:10-21), the preceding material (17:1–19:10), and the opening of the book (1:1-3). As such, major features of Revelation dovetail within these four densely packed verses. The primary structural feature that animates them is an interlocking chain link, as demonstrated in §7.1 through §7.3 below.

§7.1   Thematic Closure in Revelation 22:6-9

The literary infrastructure of Revelation includes as one of its features the repetition of lexical signifiers at key points. This device frequently demarcates distinct text units within the overall narrative. Nowhere is this clearer than at the start of two related text units, 17:1–19:10 and 21:9–22:9. The following extracts reveal the extent of the lexical repetition:

> Then one of the seven angels who had the seven bowls came and said to me, "Come, I will show you. . . . " So he carried me away . . . in the spirit. (17:1-3)

> καὶ ἦλθεν εἷς ἐκ τῶν ἑπτὰ ἀγγέλων τῶν ἐχόντων τὰς ἑπτὰ φιάλας, καὶ ἐλάλησεν μετ' ἐμοῦ λέγων, Δεῦρο, δείξω σοι . . . καὶ ἀπήνεγκέν με . . . ἐν πνεύματι.

> Then one of the seven angels who had the seven bowls . . . came and said to me, "Come, I will show you. . . . " And he carried me away in the spirit. (21:9-10)

> καὶ ἦλθεν εἷς ἐκ τῶν ἑπτὰ ἀγγέλων τῶν ἐχόντων τὰς ἑπτὰ φιάλας . . ., καὶ ἐλάλησεν μετ' ἐμοῦ λέγων, Δεῦρο, δείξω σοι . . . καὶ ἀπήνεγκέν με ἐν πνεύματι.

In these passages, two of the text's visions (and text units) are introduced by means of lexical repetition to an extent that cannot be simply coincidental. No scholar has attributed this repetition to the influence of scribal meddlers. Even R. H. Charles, who delineated some forty-three redactional fragments within the text, did not find reason to include these passages within that number. Unless Charles's scepticism about the text's unity is to be exceeded, or unless new textual evidence arises to the contrary,[1] there is no reason to dispute that the lexical repetition is part of the architectural foundations of the structure of Revelation, rather than being attributable to a later redactor.

These same text units (17:1–19:10 and 21:9–22:9) are also marked out by lexical repetition at their closure. The following extracts reveal this:

> And he said to me, "These are true words. . . . " Then I fell down at his feet to worship him, but he said to me, "You must not do that! I am a fellow servant with you and your comrades. . . . Worship God!" (19:9-10)

> καὶ λέγει μοι, Οὗτοι οἱ λόγοι ἀληθινοί . . . ἔπεσα ἔμπροσθεν τῶν ποδῶν αὐτοῦ προσκυνῆσαι αὐτῷ. καὶ λέγει μοι, Ὅρα μή· σύνδουλός σού εἰμι καὶ τῶν ἀδελφῶν σου . . . τῷ θεῷ προσκύνησον.

> And he said to me, "These words are trustworthy and true. . . . " I fell down to worship at the feet of the angel . . . but he said to me, "You must not do that! I am a fellow servant with you and your comrades. . . . Worship God!" (22:6-9)

> καὶ εἶπέν μοι, Οὗτοι οἱ λόγοι πιστοὶ καὶ ἀληθινοι . . . ἔπεσα προσκυνῆσαι ἔμπροσθεν τῶν ποδῶν τοῦ ἀγγέλου . . . καὶ λέγει μοι, Ὅρα μή· σύνδουλός σού εἰμι καὶ τῶν ἀδελφῶν σου . . . τῷ θεῷ προσκύνησον.

Clearly, the substantive core of 22:8-9 embodies an almost word-for-word replication of 19:10, just as the first words of 22:6 repeat the first words of 19:9. So, just as the vision in 21:9–22:9 is introduced by means of linguistic repetition of the opening words of the vision in 17:1–19:10, so too the second of these two visions concludes by means of linguistic repetition of the closing words of the previous vision.[2]

Repetition of this sort cannot be simply coincidental. While the repetition at the start of the two visions has not been credited to the work of a redactor, the same is not the case for the repetition at the end of the two

---

[1] The discovery of ancient manuscripts continues to influence scholarly understanding of the book of Revelation. See, for instance, D. C. Parker, "A New Oxyrhynchus Papyrus of Revelation: P115 (P. Oxy. 4499)," *NTS* 46 (2000): 159–74.

[2] R. Bauckham (*The Climax of Prophecy: Studies on the Book of Revelation* [Edinburgh: T&T Clark, 1993], 18–21) shows that the intervening passage (19:11–21:8) serves a transitional function between 17:1–19:10 and 21:9–22:9, while at the same time weaving a web of intratextual cross-referencing that is critical to the book of Revelation, both theologically and structurally.

visions. Some interpreters have suggested that 19:10 (occasionally along with 19:9) is a redactional insertion duplicating 22:8-9,[3] while others invert the order of influence.[4] In a day where final-form studies are fashionable, interpolation theories of this kind are currently few and far between. Consequently, little effort has been made to refute views of this kind on their own terms.[5] As I have shown elsewhere, however, the view that 19:10 is a redactional insertion is problematical and cannot be sustained.[6] Nonetheless, a determination of the structural function of 22:8-9 remains a pressing issue, especially in view of the way in which 22:6-7 seems to relate primarily to 22:10-21, as illustrated below.

§7.2   Thematic Anticipation in Revelation 22:6-9

We have seen that 22:8-9 in particular serves as the structural closing of the New Jerusalem vision in 21:9–22:9. It is also evident, however, that 22:6-7 is primarily related to what follows in the epistolary epilogue of 22:10-21. Four simple features demonstrate this well:

(1) the declaration "Behold I am coming soon" (ἰδοὺ ἔρχομαι ταχύ) in 22:7 is repeated precisely in 22:12. Of Jesus' seven promises about his coming (2:5, 16; 3:11; 16:15; 22:7, 12, 20), only these two occurrences include both the command

---

[3] I. T. Beckwith (*The Apocalypse of John* [New York: Macmillan, 1919], 742): Revelation 19:10 "has crept into the text" from 22:8-9; R. H. Charles (*A Critical and Exegetical Commentary on the Revelation of St. John* [2 vols.; Edinburgh: T&T Clark, 1920], 2: 129): Revelation 19:9-10 was "inserted by the disciple who edited the whole work"; J. M. Ford (*The Revelation of John* [Garden City: Doubleday, 1975], 311): "a redactor's interpolation."

[4] On this, see H. Kraft, *Die Offenbarung des Johannes* (Tübingen: Mohr Siebeck, 1974), 227; D. E. Aune, *Revelation 17–22* (Nashville: Thomas Nelson Publishers, 1998), 1037, 1186. Aune thinks that 22:6-9 "was formulated, along with 1:1-3, at the last stage in the revision of the text of Revelation" (1146). M. Barker (*The Revelation of Jesus Christ* [Edinburgh: T&T Clark, 2000], 368–72) believes that the whole of 22:6-20, along with 21:5b-8, did not form part of the original apocalypse but was added from left-over fragments.

[5] In contemporary literature on 19:10, the views of "old-fashioned" source critics such as Charles and others are too often overlooked as inconsequential, usually without substantial supporting argument other than the expression of interest in the text's final form.

[6] B. W. Longenecker, "Revelation 19,10: One Verse in Search of an Author," *ZNW* 91 (2000): 230–37. I concluded: "Charles's confident case concerning the influence of a redactor in this verse is supportable only by impressionistic conjecture, by a reliance on insubstantial textual evidence, by misrepresentation of stylistic evidence, and by incorporating interpretative distinctions that have no contextual merit" (237).

"Behold" (cf. 16:15) and the adverb "soon" (cf. 2:16; 3:11). The same declaration of 22:7 is closely paralleled in 22:20 (ναί ἔρχομαι ταχύ), and becomes a prayer in 22:17 (twice) and 22:20 (ἔρχου);

(2) the warning/promise that all this "must soon take place" (δεῖ γενέσθαι ἐν τάχει) in 22:6 is articulated again in the words "the time is near" (ὁ καιρὸς γὰρ ἐγγύς ἐστιν) in 22:10;

(3) the sending of the angel of the Lord (or the angel of Jesus) is a theme of both 22:6 and 22:16;[7]

(4) the expression "the words of the prophecy of this book" (τοὺς λόγους τῆς προφητείας τοῦ βιβλίου τούτου) in 22:7 is repeated in 22:10 and 22:18 (cf. 22:19).

These four observations indicate a strong relationship between 22:6-7 and 22:10-21.

The fourth feature cited above plays a larger structural role than is suggested by the mere repetition of a phrase in 22:7 and 22:10-18. To demonstrate this, it is important to note also that this relationship between 22:6-7 and 22:10-21 is also established through the influence of the apocalypse's introductory verses. As Richard Bauckham notes, "[T]hose parts of 22:6-9 which are not verbally parallel to 19:9b-10 are verbally parallel to 1:1-3."[8] This is apparent from 22:6b-7, which repeats material from 1:1 and 1:3 in an almost word-for-word fashion (underlined words are repetitions of 1:1-3):

> the Lord, the God of the spirits of the prophets, has <u>sent his angel to show his servants what must soon take place</u>. See, I am coming soon! <u>Blessed is the one who</u> keeps <u>the words of the prophecy</u> of this book.
>
> ὁ κύριος, ὁ θεὸς τῶν πνευμάτων τῶν προφητῶν, <u>ἀπέστειλεν τὸν ἄγγελον αὐτοῦ δεῖξαι τοῖς δούλοις αὐτοῦ ἃ δεῖ γενέσθαι ἐν τάχει</u>. καὶ ἰδοὺ ἔρχομαι ταχύ. <u>μακάριος ὁ τηρῶν τοὺς λόγους τῆς προφητείας</u> τοῦ βιβλίου τούτου.

Whereas epistolary characteristics are obvious in the initial three chapters of Revelation (1:4-5, 11; 2:1–3:22), the final episode of the apocalypse closes with a similar epistolary tone (22:21), as if to provide a kind of "genre *inclusio*" within the text's overall structure. The repetition in 22:6-7 of complete phrases drawn directly from 1:1-3 reinforces a similar impression of structural *inclusio* precisely because the latter passage introduces the final section of the book. In particular, the blessing in 22:7 not only recasts the original blessing in 1:3 on those who read "the words

---

[7] Aune (*Revelation 17–22*, 1183–1184) elaborates this doublet further.

[8] Bauckham, *The Climax of Prophecy*, 5. The claim is only slightly overstated.

of the prophecy" and keep the things written therein, but also introduces the phrase "the words of the prophecy of this book." This phrase is then repeated in precise form twice in the final epilogue (22:10, 18), and it is the basis for the phrase "the words of the book of this prophecy" (τῶν λόγων τοῦ βιβλίου τῆς προφητείας ταύτης) in 22:19. In fact, the epilogue refers to the apocalypse of which it is a part on five occasions by means of the term βιβλίος (22:10, 18 [twice], 19 [twice]), a term which has the same referent nowhere else in the text except in the introductory material of chapter 1 (1.11)—again highlighting the concerns for *inclusio* within the first and last sections of the text. The grounding for this inclusio has already been laid in 22:6b-7, which introduces the passages that lie beyond 22:9.

§7.3   Chain-Link Interlock in Revelation 22:6-9

With these points in view, 22:6-9 seems to have been constructed in a back-and-forth manner, with 22:6-7 largely introducing later material and 22:8-9 largely concluding earlier material. Since the material overlap is so precise, with word-for-word correspondence with other text units of Revelation, there is not a "coincidence factor" to be taken account of in this case. The fact that these verses appear to be both highly studied and precise (i.e., the high degree of word repetition) and structurally "awkward" (i.e., the material overlap) has been explained by some as the result of a later textual corruption in 22:6-9. Here again the view of R. H. Charles requires mention. Charles attributes the ordering of the last chapter of Revelation (along with all the material after 20:3) to the work of an "unintelligent" and "shallow-brained" disciple who, characterised by "a hopeless mental confusion," introduced "a tissue of irreconcilable contradictions" to the text.[9] In Charles's view, the second-rate redactor threw together fragments of material towards the end of the book that the primary author would have wanted constructed in an altogether different manner. Accordingly, Charles suggests that 22:6-21 should be reconstructed in the following order: 22:6-7, 18a, 16, 13, 12, 10, then 22:8-9, 20, 21.[10] In this reordering, the structural overlap currently evi-

---

[9] Charles, *A Critical and Exegetical Commentary*, 1:1. Charles offers a fuller description, worthy of quotation: "He was apparently a Jew of the dispersion, a better Grecian than his master, but otherwise a person profoundly stupid and ignorant; a narrow fanatic and celibate, not quite loyal to his trust as editor; an arch-heretic, though, owing to his stupidity, probably an unconscious one" (1:xviii; this estimate is supported in vol. 1 on pp. l–lv and in vol. 2 on pp. 144–54).

[10] Charles, *A Critical and Exegetical Commentary*, 2:212–13, 219, 445–46. The remaining verses are seen as interpolations (e.g., 2:221–24).

dent in 22:6-9 is uncoupled, leaving a linear progression that is satisfying to the modern interpreter.

On this matter, Charles's view is not fashionable today. In Charles's own day, I. T. Beckwith shared similar views about the rather disjointed nature of the end of Revelation, speaking about it as "loosely connected" and full of "repetitions and interruptions." In Beckwith's view, however, and contrary to Charles, "irregularities" of this sort "are characteristic of the author [and] do not furnish unquestionable ground . . . for a rearrangement of the text."[11]

But 22:6-9 is not a problematical text in structural terms. It is not to be explained either with reference to the misguided sloppiness of a later redactor (Charles) or to the slightly "irregular" mind of the author (Beckwith). Neither "stupid" redactors nor "irregular" minds need to be entertained to explain the structure of these verses.

Revelation 22:6-9 plays a notable structural role in the overall layout of Revelation, doing double duty in relation to what comes before and after. For many modern commentators, however, this makes for difficulty when placing these verses in a structural outline that follows a linear sequence. Some consider 22:6-9 to belong with 22:10-21 as a complete unit, forming the epilogue of Revelation (22:6-21).[12] Others place 22:6-9 with what precedes it, so that the epilogue proper begins at 22:10.[13] Elizabeth Schüssler Fiorenza has changed her mind on the matter, early on seeing 22:6 as the beginning of the epilogue of 22:6-21,[14] then later identifying 21:9–22:9 as a self-contained unit.[15]

The "either-or" of this debate has been side-stepped by a minority of scholars. Both Richard Bauckham and David Aune, for instance, suggest

---

[11] Beckwith, *The Apocalypse of John*, 771.

[12] E.g., G. K. Beale, *The Book of Revelation* (Grand Rapids: Eerdmans, 1999), 150, 1123 (although he finds 22:6-21 to have "no explicit flow of thought," being composed of five unrelated sections); U. Vanni, *La Struttura Letteraria dell'Apocalisse* (Rome: Herder, 1971), 107–15; J. Lambrecht, "A Structuration of Rev 4.1–22.5," in *L'Apocalypse johannique et l'Apocalyptique dans le Nouveau Testament* (ed. J. Lambrecht; Leuven: Leuven University, 1980), 77–104, esp. 78–79. D. Mathewson (*A New Heaven and a New Earth: The Meaning and Function of the Old Testament in Revelation 21.1–22.5* [London: Sheffield Academic Press, 2003]) simply assumes this structural division throughout, without defence.

[13] E.g., C. H. Giblin, "Structural and Thematic Correlations in the Theology of Revelation 16–22," *Biblica* 55 (1974): 487–504, esp. 491. Giblin struggles to explain the structure of 22:6-9, referring to the vision of the New Jerusalem as "inclusive and open-ended rather than delimited" in its final stages (491). He regularly defines the vision somewhat ambiguously as falling within "21.9–22.6ff."

[14] E. Schüssler Fiorenza, "The Eschatology and Composition of the Apocalypse," *CBQ* 30 (1968): 537–69, esp. 561–63.

[15] E. Schüssler Fiorenza, "Composition and Structure of the Revelation of John," *CBQ* 39 (1977): 344–66, esp. 361.

that 22:6-9 functions "both as the conclusion to the major section of 21:9–22:9 and as the beginning of the [epistolary] epilogue" of the apocalypse in 22:6-21.[16] According to Bauckham, structural overlap of this sort is not to be seen as problematical. In fact, as he states,

> [To assign] these verses only to one or other of these sections, as most previous scholars have done, is to misunderstand John's literary methods, among which are the overlapping and interweaving of the sections of his work. John has skilfully formed this section as both the conclusion to the vision of the New Jerusalem [21:9–22:9] and the beginning of the epilogue [22:6-21].[17]

Views of this sort do not underplay the amount of structural overlap within 22:6-9 but take full account of it. In explaining this feature, Bauckham does not view these verses as an occasion of redactional meddling or authorial loss of control over the material. For him, they simply indicate how the author's mind works, as revealed in similar ways throughout his text. This represents a healthy advance in the study of this passage. That the author had a penchant for overlapping techniques is evident from any analysis of Revelation that moves past a rudimentary level. So Aune speaks of Revelation as "a sequence of episodes marked by various literary markers . . . [and] literary devices," one of which is cited as "the technique of interlocking (the use of transitional texts that conclude one section and introduce another)."[18]

---

[16] Bauckham, *The Climax of Prophecy*, 5. Cf. Aune, *Revelation 17–22*, 1144, 1148, 1182, 1188, although Aune identifies 21:9–22:9 as a singe textual unit with 22:6-9 as its transitional conclusion (although elsewhere he takes 22:6-21 to be a unit; e.g., p. 1148 [incorrectly written as "26:6-21"], p. 1186). Cf. also P. Prigent, (*Commentary on the Apocalypse of St. John* [trans. W. Pradels; Tübingen: Mohr Siebeck, 2001], 95), although he too is apparently not wholly consistent in speaking of 22:6-9 as doing double structural duty. On p. 92 he argues that "22:6-9 is not the conclusion to the vision of the new Jerusalem . . . but [the beginning of] the conclusion to the book of Revelation," and on p. 96 he states that "21:1–22:5 is composed as a unit!" In his outline of the book of Revelation (p. 102), he groups 22:6-21 together as the epilogue. In none of these cases is 22:6-9 shown to have any relation to the preceding text unit.

[17] Bauckham, *The Climax of Prophecy*, 5. Cf. J. A. Filho ("The Apocalypse of John as an Account of a Visionary Experience: Notes on the Book's Structure," *JSNT* 25 [2002]: 213–34, esp. 231): "Revelation 22.6-9 is both the end of the section on the New Jerusalem and the beginning of the epilogue, which is given over to the juxtaposition and interweaving of these sections."

[18] D. E. Aune, *The New Testament in Its Literary Environment* (Philadelphia: Westminster, 1987), 241. Elsewhere (*Revelation 1–5* [Dallas: Word, 1998], cviii) Aune speaks of Revelation as exemplifying "a plethora of literary devices linking the various parts of the text together, though not always in a completely successful manner. Revelation is a "unity" because the author has worked diligently, even

Evidently, then, the transitional overlap evident in 22:6-9 appears untidy to many modern eyes since it threatens to disrupt the linear progression in the presentation of ideas. Nonetheless it conforms precisely to Lucian's advice about chain-link interlock in which one achieves "clarity . . . by the interweaving of subjects," precisely the feature of Revelation highlighted by Bauckham and Aune. Despite its structural complexity, 22:6-9 provides one of the clearest examples of chain-link interlock from the ancient world. There, the author's concern for stylistic artistry is matched by his concern for structural clarity (*contra* Charles and Beckwith). This is an author whose craftsmanship seems studied and considered rather than haphazard and confused.[19]

TEXT-UNIT "A"	INTERLOCKED "b" (anticipatory)	INTERLOCKED "a" (retrospective)	TEXT-UNIT "B"
Rev 21:9–22:5/9	Rev 22:6-7a	Rev 22:7b-9	Rev 22:6/10-21

§7.4   Structural Features beyond the Chain-Link Interlock

Although I have argued that Revelation 22:6-9 involves a chain-link construction, the structure of these four verses is more complicated and cannot be contained wholly within that single construction. That other structural features also appear (e.g., the passage involves "concurrence," as described in §4.5 above) is apparent from the close of 22:9, where the phrase "those who keep the words of this book" (τῶν τηρούντων τοὺς λόγους τοῦ βιβλίου τούτου) is picked up from 22:7 in order to lead directly into 22:10-21. This phrase, then, falls outside of the chain-link construction. It functions as an anticipatory phrase that introduces the next section. Moreover, the first phrase of 22:6 (οὗτοι οἱ λόγοι πιστοὶ καὶ ἀληθινοί), while repeating in precise form the words of 21:5, is also reminiscent of 19:9b (οὗτοι οἱ λόγοι ἀληθινοὶ τοῦ θεοῦ εἰσιν), thereby acting as a structural marker signalling the close of a section.

Neither of these phrases, then, is included in the chain-link construction that lies at the heart of 22:6-9; Revelation 22:6a relates to the

---

ingeniously, at the task of linking units of texts that were not originally designed to fit together." For further discussion, see also A. Yarbro Collins, *The Combat Myth in the Book of Revelation* (Missoula: Scholars, 1976), 16–18.

[19] The relevance of chain-link construction in an oral/aural culture was noted in chapter 4 (§4.6). On Revelation as a text intended to be read orally to small groups, see discussions by David Barr, *Tales of the End: A Narrative Commentary on the Book of Revelation* (Santa Rosa: Polebridge Press, 1998), 171–80; Alan Garrow, *Revelation* (London: Routledge, 1997).

preceding material and signals the closure of the structural unit, while 22:9b anticipates the section which follows. Nonetheless, while other structural features are present within 22:6-9, the chain-link construction (evident in 22:6b-9a specifically) is dominant within these transitional verses. A translation of 22:6-9 appears below, indicating (1) those features that act as structural markers of text-unit closure (marked with single underlining), and (2) those features that act as structural springboards to the text-unit that follows (marked with double underlining):

> And he said to me, "These words are trustworthy and true, for the Lord, the God of the spirits of the prophets, has sent his angel to show his servants what must soon take place." "See, I am coming soon! Blessed is the one who keeps the words of the prophecy of this book." I John am he who heard and saw these things. And when I heard and saw them, I fell down to worship at the feet of the angel . . . , but he said to me, "You must not do that! I am a fellow-servant with you and your comrades the prophets, and with those who keep the words of this book. Worship God."

Part 2: Other Examples of Chain-Link Interlock in Revelation

This chapter began with a description of the chain-link construction in Revalation 22:6-9 as "studied" or intentionally and extensively calculated. But what would Lucian or Quintilian think of the author's use of the technique? Would they applaud him for his most masterful execution, or would they scorn him for his somewhat puerile and slavish adherence to the "rules" of chain-link interlock, resulting in a ponderous and lacklustre formulation?

However his execution would have been assessed, his apocalypse evidences three other cases of the same construction, each in a far less studied form than that of 22:6-9. These three further cases illustrate that the structure of 22:6-9 is not itself exceptional within the book of Revelation. This may consequently suggest that 22:6-9 is not to be attributed to the hand of a later redactor who failed to exercise a strong structural grip on his material. The fact that four chain links appear at significant junctures of the apocalypse may well suggest that the technique is attributable to the apocalypse's main author.[20] It is to these three other cases that we turn now.

[20] If this is the case, theories about the compositional history of the text need to be bracketed by the compositional influence of a single person. So, for instance, Aune (Revelation) proposes that Revelation 4:1–22:5 was composed by 70 CE (itself the product of extensive historical development), later being redacted during the time of Trajan with the inclusion of the letters to the seven

§7.5   Revelation 3:21-22

If the author of Revelation made use of chain-link construction at 22:6-9, the same transition technique is also evident elsewhere in this text. Chain-link construction appears, for instance, at the juncture between the messages to the seven churches (Rev 2–3) and the vision of the heavenly throne room (Rev 4–5). At the close of each message to the seven churches, the exalted Jesus gives a brief instruction germane to the particular church addressed. In each case, the instruction is directed to those who "conquer" and is associated with the phrase "Let anyone who has an ear listen to what the Spirit is saying to the churches" (2:7, 11, 17, 26-29; 3:5-6, 12-13, 21). In the seventh case of this occurrence, however, the "conquer" clause is crafted with reference to Revelation 4–5, in which the author depicts the heavenly throne room and recounts Christ's victorious death and subsequent enthronement. So 3:21 makes a gesture to the following chapters: "To the one who conquers I will give a place with me on my throne, just as I myself conquered and sat down with my Father on his throne." This is distinctly different from the previous six "conquer" clauses, each of which takes its cues from the context immediately preceding; the seventh, by contrast, is informed by the material following it.[21] With 3:22, however, we find a structural terminus for the final message (3:14-22), repeating again the saying about hearing the Spirit's message to the churches, the saying that has repeatedly acted as an indicator of closure throughout Revelation 2–3 (2:7, 11, 17; esp. 2:29; 3:6, 13). Once again, then, the overlap technique spoken of by Lucian and Quintilian emerges here. Specifically, in 3:21 the author introduces the content of Revelation 4–5 (3:21) and in 3:22 closes the previous section (i.e., Rev 2–3 on a macro-level, 3:14-22 on a medial-level), before starting a new section (i.e., Rev 4–5).[22]

---

churches, the long introduction, and the conclusion of 22:6-21. Conversely Prigent (*Commentary on the Apocalypse*, 633), while advocating a similar formation process, suspects that the one responsible for the additions at the beginning and the end was "probably the author himself." Our findings concerning the use of chain-link interlock throughout the compositional process would suggest that Prigent's view has more to commend itself.

[21] Cf. Bauckham, *The Climax of Prophecy*, 6; E. Schüssler Fiorenza, *The Book of Revelation: Justice and Judgement* (Philadelphia: Fortress Press, 1985), 173; Filho, "The Apocalypse of John," 230.

[22] Revelation 4–5 itself begins with a gesture to the previous section ("After this . . . ," 4:1a), so that the whole transition falls into an A-b-a/a-B pattern.

TEXT-UNIT "A"	INTERLOCKED "b" (anticipatory)	INTERLOCKED "a" (retrospective)	TEXT-UNIT "B"
Rev 2:1–3:22	Rev 3:21	Rev 3:22	Rev 4:1ff.

§7.6   Revelation 8:2-5

The beginning verses of Revelation 8 comprise another passage in which chain-link construction is evident. Charles felt that the half-hour silence in heaven upon opening the seventh seal, depicted in 8:1, corresponds with the offering of incense and the prayers of the saints in the heavenly throne room, depicted in 8:3-5. He found 8:2, which introduces the seven angels with seven trumpets, to be out of position, since it disrupts the flow from 8:1 to 8:3-5 and pertains to the narrative of the trumpets that begins in 8:6. Considering the extant structure of the text to be unsuitable to logical presentation, Charles blamed his postulated redactor for the allegedly second-rate construction in these verses. In his opinion 8:2 "is an intrusion in its present context and not original in its present form."[23]

The link between 8:1 and 8:3-5 is accepted by many interpreters, whose handling of the consequent overlap of material in 8:2 is occasionally at variance. Some interpreters simply note the structure without further comment. So José Filho writes:

> Revelation 8.1 states that, when the seventh seal was opened, "there was silence in heaven for about half an hour." At 8.3-5 we find the prayer of the saints, the response to which is judgment (8.5). In between the silence in heaven and the offering made by the saints, the seven angels with their trumpets are introduced (8.2), as a preparation for the beginning of the series in 8.6.[24]

Others note the significance of the structure in relation to the author's style. So Bauckham directly rejects Charles's suggestion that 8:2 is an awkwardly placed redactional insertion: "Charles . . . failed to appreciate that v. 2 is an example of the characteristic "interlocking" by which John links the sections of his vision together."[25] Although Bauckham does not

---

[23] Revelation, 2:218. He defends this later (2:221–22), thinking 8:2 originally to have stood alongside 8:5.

[24] Filho, "The Apocalypse of John," 219.

[25] Bauckham, *The Climax of Prophecy*, 70. Cf. also Beale, *The Book of Revelation*, 454, 460–64. Bauckham's quotations continues in this way: "the seven angels with their trumpets are introduced in the midst of the account of the opening of the

share Lucian's language of chain-link construction or Quintilian's imagery of handholding, he interprets the passage in ways wholly consistent with both.[26]

TEXT-UNIT "A"	INTERLOCKED "b" (anticipatory)	INTERLOCKED "a" (retrospective)	TEXT-UNIT "B"
Rev 6:1–8:5	Rev 8:2	Rev 8:3-5	Rev 8:6ff.

As is the case for 22:6-9, so too, for 8:1-5 the passage is structurally complex and cannot be easily contained within a straightforward linear outline. This is evident in the variety of text-unit demarcations offered by structural analysts of Revelation. Some maintain that a new text unit begins at 8:1.[27] Others see 8:1 as the final verse of one text unit with 8:2 introducing another.[28] Still others place the text-unit break between these two sections at the end of 8:5.[29] These three structural options are all attempts to deal with an ancient structural technique that does not lend itself easily to modern linear outlining strategies. For our purposes it is enough to note that the narrative of the seven seals concludes with 8:1 along with 8:3-5, while the narrative of the seven trumpets is introduced in 8:2 and is picked up again in 8:6ff. This arrangement conforms to the textual interlock described by Quintilian and Lucian.

---

seventh seal in order to indicate that the account, which follows (8:6–11:19), of the seven trumpet blasts is in some sense included in the events that follow the opening of the seventh seal."

[26] Schüssler Fiorenza (*Book of Revelation*, 172), while noting the link between 8:2 and 8:6, leaves the link between 8:1 and 8:3-5 undeveloped. Consequently, she incorrectly identifies the author's construction at this point as an "intercalation," following an A-B-A¹ structure (8:2, 8:3-5, 8:6ff) rather than an A-b-a-B structure natural to chain-link construction.

[27] J. Sweet, *Revelation* (London: SCM Press, 1979), vii; Ford (*Revelation*, 47) identifies 8:1-5 as preparatory to 8:6–11:14.

[28] J. W. Bowman, "The Revelation to John: Its Dramatic Structure and Message," *Interpretation* 9 (1955): 436–53; F. Rosseau, *L'Apocalypse et le milieu prophétique du Nouveau Testament: Structure et préhistoire du texte* (Montreal: Bellarmin, 1971); Aune, *The New Testament in its Literary Environment*, 242. Similarly, R. H. Mounce (*The Book of Revelation* [Grand Rapids: Eerdmans, 1977], 48, 178–79) identifies 8:1 as "a dramatic pause" prior to 8:2–11:19.

[29] N. W. Lund, *Chiasmus in the New Testament: A Study in the Form and Function of Chiastic Structures* (Chapel Hill: University of North Carolina, 1942), 327–28.

§7.7   *Revelation 15:1-4*

Just as a chain-link construction appears at the text-unit boundary between the seven seals and seven trumpet narratives (i.e., 8:1-5), so it also appears at the beginning of the cycle of the seven bowls (15:1-4). After the narratives of conflict between the people of God and the enemies of God in Revelation 12–14, the seer sees "another portent in heaven [of] seven angels with seven plagues, which are the last, for with them the wrath of God is ended" (15:1). This introduces the material in 15:5–16:21, in which seven angels pour out the contents of their bowls on the earth.[30] Sandwiched between 15:1 and 15:5, the three verses of 15:2-4 form the conclusion to the narrative in chapters 12–14. The conflict of those chapters reaches its apex in the song of triumphant praise in 15:3b-4, following from the victory described in Revelation 14 and sung by "those who had conquered the beast [13:1-10] and its image [13:15] and the number of its name [13:16-18]" (15:2).[31] In this way, the verses at the beginning of Revelation 15 form the basis of the A-b-a-B structure that characterises chain-link construction (A = 12:1–14:20; b = 15:1; a = 15:2-4; B = 15:5-21). Consequently, "in spite of the intervention of chs. 12–14, the sequence of bowls clearly follows on from the final trumpet."[32]

TEXT-UNIT "A"	INTERLOCKED "b" (anticipatory)	INTERLOCKED "a" (retrospective)	TEXT-UNIT "B"
to Rev 15:4	Rev 15:1	Rev 15:2-4	Rev 15:5ff.

The recognition of the presence of chain-link interlock in this passage suggests the need for a slight qualification to one of Pierre Prigent's conclusions concerning the author's composition of this passage. Prigent finds that since 15:5 "relates to the vision introduced in v.1 . . . , we can conclude that verses 2 to 4 have been inserted by our author into a tradition that was originally devoted to the seven angels alone."[33] Instead of being a bald (and seemingly arbitrary) insertion of material, however, 15:2-4 needs to be put into a larger structural perspective. As such, it is seen to form one part of an interlocking structure at the text-unit seam between Revelation 14 and Revelation 15.

[30] The articular forms in 15:6 (οἱ ἑπτὰ ἄγγελοι, τὰς ἑπτὰ πληγάς) are anaphoric with reference back to the anarthrous forms of the same in 15:1.

[31] See especially Beale, *The Book of Revelation*, 112–13, 462, 621–22, 784; Yarbro Collins, *Combat Myth*, 18–19; Bauckham, *Climax of Prophecy*, 16.

[32] Filho, "The Apocalypse of John," 220; cf. Bauckham, *The Climax of Prophecy*, 8–9.

[33] Prigent, *Commentary on the Apocalypse*, ad loc.

§7.8   Structural and Theological Implications

From this survey it is evident that, as one commentator notes, "most of the major literary 'joints' of Revelation have an interlocking function."[34] We have seen this to be the case with regard to four transition points in Revelation (3:21-22; 8:1-5; 15:1-4; 22:6-9). Each case coincides wholly with the chain-link or handholding analogies of Graeco-Roman rhetoricians. The last of these cases is the most studied by its composer.

No attempt will be made here to offer a structural outline of the whole of Revelation, since this investigation has not qualified me for that task, not least since this apocalypse may indeed be "more structurally complex than any other Jewish or Christian apocalypse."[35] Nonetheless, three things need to be noted about the placement and function of these chain-link transitions. First, the author of Revelation has impressed chain-link interlock upon virtually all of the main components of the text, including the epistolary frame, the "letters" section, and the visions of God's unfolding sovereignty coming to bear on a world embroiled in chaotic depravity.

Second, the two interlocks at 8:1-5 and 15:1-4 appear at the transition points that both demarcate and unite the three series of seven-fold plagues against the earth. So, the narrative of the seven seals hands off to that of the seven trumpets (8:1-5) and the narrative of the seven trumpets hands off to that of the seven bowls (15:1-4). The author has constructed a kind of literary triptych, the three scenes of which are joined together by means of chain-link hinges at their meeting points. In this way, the impressiveness of their content is matched by the impressiveness of their artistic linkage.

Third, the first and last occurrences of chain-link interlock fall at significant seams in the text's construction and have significant import in relation to the text's genre. The first chain link appears at the transition from the seven ecclesial letters to the vision of the heavenly throne room (3:21-22), and the last appears at the transition from the apocalyptic scenario of God's triumph over evil to the epistolary closure of the book (22:6-9). The importance of these two interlocks can hardly be overemphasised, since it is through them that the author creates a new generic hybrid, fusing together both the epistolary and the apocalyptic genres (not to mention prophecy) in tight linkage and wholly unprecedented fashion.[36] Chain-link interlock operates as the pivot point from the

---

[34] Beale, *The Book of Revelation*, 114.

[35] Aune, *The New Testament in its Literary Environment*, 241.

[36] In §5.8, it was noted that the book of Daniel is itself a generic hybrid with chain-link construction falling at the point where the genres meet (i.e., Dan 6–7). In this way, the book of Revelation compares favourably with its apocalyptic

epistolary genre to the apocalyptic genre (3:21-22) and back again (22:6-9). Just as Dorothy in the Wizard of Oz is swept up into another world and then returns again to Kansas, so too, the original recipients were to have been swept up from their localised settings into the apocalyptic narrative that follows and then set down again into their ordinary lives. And just as Dorothy is changed by her travels to the land of Oz, so too, the audience of the apocalypse is to be changed after being immersed in John's apocalyptic adventures, with the narrative of Revelation 4:1–22:5(9) having a dramatic impact on their lives in ways that correspond to the pronouncements of Revelation 2–3.[37] This theological interest appears in structural format in the two outer chain-link interlocks of the apocalypse.

Here the book of Revelation goes in a direction contrary to that of some apocalypticists of the ancient world. Frequently the apocalyptic mysteries of God were deemed to be worthy topics of reflection for only a select group of initiates who alone were worthy of handling those mysteries with responsible care and insight. So, for instance, the Jewish apocalypse 4 Ezra (i.e., 2 Esdras 3–14, a contemporary apocalypse to that of John, ca. 100 CE) includes within its lengthy episodes the instruction that apocalyptic mysteries are to be hidden from the people (12:37) but taught "to the wise among your people, whose hearts . . . are able to comprehend and keep these secrets" (12:38; cf. 14:6, 26). The whole of the apocalypse ends with this same note, in which Ezra is exhorted to reveal the apocalyptic mysteries concerning the ways of God only to "the wise among your people," rather than to the people as a whole, both "the worthy and the unworthy" (14:45-46).[38]

---

predecessor in the Christian Bible. The differences between the two books, however, have to do with (1) intentionality (i.e., the generic hybrid of Revelation seemingly having been constructed intentionally by means of chain-link interlock, whereas the generic hybrid of Daniel probably resulted consequently in the construction of a chain-link interlock), (2) type of genre (with Revelation linking epistolary and apocalyptic genres and Daniel linking folktale and apocalyptic genres), and (3) type of interlock (with Revelation incorporating a double interlock at its epistolary seams and Daniel incorporating a single interlock at its virtual midpoint).

[37] On the theological challenge of Revelation 2–3, see B. W. Longenecker, "Rome, Provincial Cities and the Seven Churches of Revelation 2–3," in *The New Testament in Its First Century Setting* (ed. P. Williams et al.; Grand Rapids: Eerdmans, 2004), 281–91.

[38] For an in-depth discussion of this feature in 4 Ezra and other Jewish apocalypses, see B. W. Longenecker, *Eschatology and the Covenant: A Comparison of 4 Ezra and Romans 1–11* (Sheffield: Sheffield Academic Press, 1991), 138–47.

But the book of Revelation advocates a view that runs directly counter to this differentiation between those worthy and those unworthy to receive divine wisdom. In Revelation, the worthy and the unworthy (e.g., Rev 2–3) are the target recipients for learning the apocalyptic secrets of God's ways, and the outer interlocks of the text are the structural corollaries of the seer's "democratising" interests. By means of chain-link interlock, the author not only links apocalyptic and epistolary genres together, but does so precisely in order that the visionary scenarios of supra-human phenomena might be seen as relevant to the ordinary lives of those who would seek to follow the Lamb.

We have seen that the author of Revelation favours chain-link construction as a transitional pivot point that bears significant structural weight. In this, that author can be likened to the author of the Johannine Gospel. Although the point is disputed, many scholars suspect that the two authors were likely to have moved in similar circles. So, for instance, in his comparison of the two texts Moody Smith has written:

> One would not want to claim too much common ground in view of their wide-ranging differences, but the similarities that are distinctive and not widely shared by other New Testament books suggest that the communities (or individuals) that produced the Gospel and Revelation had some overlap or area of contact.[39]

Similarly, in the Qumran scrolls, the Community Rule (1QS) 9.17-18 reads as follows: the master of the community is one to "hide the counsel of the law in the midst of the men of sin" and to "reproach (with truthful knowledge and (with) just judgment those who choose the path/Way." So too 1QS 11.5-7 reads: "My eyes have observed what always is, wisdom that has been hidden from mankind, knowledge and understanding (hidden) from the assembly of flesh." Translations are from F. García Martínez, *The Dead Sea Scrolls Translated: The Qumran Texts in English* (2d ed.; Grand Rapids: Eerdmans, 1996), 14, 18.

[39] D. M. Smith, *The Theology of the Gospel of John* (Cambridge: Cambridge University Press, 1995), 61. Cf. R. Brown, *The Community of the Beloved Disciple: The Life, Loves, and Hates of an Individual Church in New Testament Times* (New York: Paulist Press, 1979), xxx; M. Hengel, *The Johannine Question* (London: SCM Press, 1989), 124–35; D. L. Stamps, "The Johannine Writings," in *Handbook of Classical Rhetoric in the Hellenistic Period (330 B.C–A.D. 400)* (ed. S. E. Porter; Leiden: Brill, 1997), 609–32, esp. 613. Prigent (*Commentary on the Apocalypse*, 36–50, esp. 49) offers the following conclusion: "we find in the background of the fourth Gospel and the book of Revelation the same theological presuppositions. On these bases were constructed two original literary edifices (though it was surely not the same hand at work), each possessing its specificity." For an opposing voice, see A. Heinze, *Johannesapokalypse und johanneische Schriften* (Stuttgart: Kohlhammer, 1998).

The features of "overlap" between the book of Revelation and the Johannine Gospel are not to be found simply in common theological themes and motifs, but also in their common use of transitional markers, since their texts both favour chain-link interlock at key transition points. Demonstrating the significant placement and function of chain-link construction within the Fourth Gospel will be the task of the next chapter.

CHAPTER 8

Chain-Link Interlock and the Theology of the Fourth Gospel

In his important article "The Man from Heaven in Johannine Sectarianism," Wayne Meeks wrote concerning the Johannine Gospel that the "major literary problem of John is its combination of remarkable stylistic unity and thematic coherence with glaringly bad transitions between episodes at many points."[1] In this chapter we will study two of the main transitions of the Johannine Gospel, at least one of which has frequently been characterised as "glaringly bad." As will be shown, a chain-link construction has formed the basis for both of these transitions. If the discussion of these Johannine transitions takes us a little way into the complex and extensive debate concerning the Gospel's composition history, readers of this chapter might take encouragement from John Ashton's suspicion that "the study of the awkward transitions in the Gospel could prove a useful tool for determining how it was composed."[2] Although that target evades our grasp due to its complexity, an analysis of the two chain links of the Johannine Gospel nonetheless moves us a little way in its direction.

One aspect of Johannine chain-link construction will be demonstrated in this chapter. That is, Johannine text-unit interlock establishes an interpretative lens through which aspects of the larger narrative are to be viewed and understood. Johannine chain links highlight particular themes and crystallise the main ingredients of the narrative in a densely compacted form. This function of chain-link transitions in the Johannine Gospel, which plays no part in Lucian's or Quintilian's description of the function of text-unit interlock, will not be set out as a hypothesis to be tested. To proceed in this fashion would be to lengthen the discussion unnecessarily and redundantly. Instead, the claim is simply made at the outset, and the supporting evidence appears in the process of assessing the relevant material.

In Part 1, the case for seeing a chain link in John 12:20-50 will be set out, while in Part 2 the same will be established for the original transition prior to John 18. Along the way the chain links are analysed in relation to the Gospel's composition history, and consideration is given to the relevance of chain-link interlock for certain kinds of narrative and theological readings of the Johannine Gospel.

Part 1: Chain-Link Interlock in John 12:20-50

A chain-link interlock can be seen in John 12:20-50, at the point where the public ministry of Jesus comes to a close, giving way to the second half of the narrative, which involves his final instructions to his disciples (John 13–17) and the crucifixion-resurrection narratives (John 18–21).

---

[1] W. A. Meeks, "The Man from Heaven in Johannine Sectarianism," in *The Interpretation of John* (2d ed.; ed. J. Ashton; Edinburgh: T&T Clark, 1997), 172. He continues: "The countless displacement, source, and redaction theories that litter the graveyards of Johannine research are voluble testimony to this difficulty."

[2] J. Ashton, *Understanding the Fourth Gospel* (London: Clarendon Press, 1991), 81.

Few would dispute that the Johannine Gospel consists of two prominent text units that meet at the boundary between John 12 and John 13. According to John Ashton, there are "four simple but strong reasons for retaining the break at the end of chapter 12," these being:

> (1) that chapter's particularly solemn conclusion, which rounds off what Jesus has to say to the world; (2) the exceptionally weighty and measured introduction to chapter 13; (3) the change of audience from "the Jews" to Jesus' disciples, to which corresponds to a shift in mood from confrontation to consolation and encouragement; (4) the sense of finality signalled by the word τέλος ([13:1] not found elsewhere, but echoed in Jesus' dying τετέλεσται—"it is accomplished" [19:30]).[3]

To the best of my knowledge, C. H. Talbert first proposed that chain-link construction underlies 12:20-50 as a transition from the first main text unit to the second.[4] The case for a chain-link interlock at this point is quite simple: (1) the final paragraphs of John 12 offer a retrospective summary of what the audience has heard throughout the first twelve chapters (this is the case for 12:37-50, and in particular 12:44-50); and (2) much of 12:20-36 serves to point the audience's attention to the events that follow in John 13–21. This combination of thematic anticipation followed by thematic recapitulation is what we have come to expect of chain-link interlock. The evidence for this structure needs now to be considered.

TEXT-UNIT "A"	INTERLOCKED (anticipatory) "b"	INTERLOCKED (retrospective) "a"	TEXT-UNIT "B"
John 1:1–12:50	John 12:20-36	John 12:37-50	John 13:1 to end

---

[3] J. Ashton, "Narrative Criticism," in *Studying John: Approaches to the Fourth Gospel* (Oxford: Clarendon Press, 1994), 149; cf. D. A. Carson, *The Gospel according to John* (Grand Rapids: Eerdmans, 1991), 103–4. Only a few have argued differently. Cf. M. Rissi, "Der Aufbau des vierten Evangliums," *NTS* 29 (1983): 48–53; J. L. Staley, *The Print's First Kiss: A Rhetorical Investigation of the Implied Reader in the Fourth Gospel* (Atlanta: Scholars Press, 1988), 67; C. H. Giblin, "The Tripartite Narrative Structure of John's Gospel," *Biblica* 71 (1990): 449–67; F. F. Segovia, "The Journey(s) of the Word of God: A Reading of the Plot of the Fourth Gospel," *Semeia* 53 (1991): 23–54.

[4] Cf. C. H. Talbert, *Reading John: A Literary and Theological Commentary on the Fourth Gospel and the Johannine Epistles* (London: SPCK, 1992), 179–80. In fact, the origins of the present project lie in my first reading of these pages not long after their publication.

§8.1   Thematic Reiteration in John 12:37-50

John 12:37-50, with its initial recollection of the "many signs" Jesus had done among his contemporaries (12:37), stands primarily in relation to what has preceded it. This is especially the case for Jesus' words in 12:44-50, in which several theological themes and motifs that Jesus has expressed during his public ministry are recalled and summarised in brief. The verb "cry out" (κράζω) that stands at the top of this section (12:44) serves to heighten the significance of the words that follow, in which at least six points of thematic recapitulation may be noted.

(1) Jesus' first words of his speech correlate belief in and seeing Jesus with belief in and seeing "the one who sent me" (12:44-45). With this we might compare specifically 5:24 ("anyone who hears my word and believes him who sent me"). But in general the designation of God as "the one who sent me" (τὸν πέμψαντά με) is one of the two favoured designations throughout the first half of the Johannine Gospel (the other being "Father"). Its three appearances in the last verses of John 12 (12:44, 45, 49) all are part of Jesus' public speech, corresponding to its sixteen occurrences throughout the first half of the Gospel, all of which are included in public speech (4:34; 5:23, 30, 37; 6:38, 39, 44; 7:16, 18, 28, 33; 8:16, 18, 26, 29; 9:4; cf. 3:17, 34; 9:33).[5] Its five occurrences in the second half of the Gospel (13:20; 14:24; 15:21; 16:5; 20:21) are all included in private speeches to his disciples behind closed doors. Here, then, when Jesus offers his parting words to the world, he reiterates three times one of the favourite designations for God in Jesus' public speeches of the Johannine Gospel: "the one who sent me." It is a designation that underlines Jesus' subordination and obedience to the Father, themes that permeate Jesus' public proclamation in the first half of the Gospel.[6]

(2) Jesus likens himself to light that has come into the world for the benefit of those in darkness (12:46). This powerful

---

[5] In John 9:4 the appellation appears in Jesus' speech in answer to his disciples but in a public context.

[6] Ashton (*Understanding the Fourth Gospel*, 544) suggests that John 12:44-45 "looks like a compressed reminder" of the healing of the blind man episode of John 9, "with which it shares the themes of faith, mission, sight, light, darkness, and judgement."

image of light has already been incorporated into the first half of the Gospel numerous times (1:4, 5, 7, 8, 9; 3:19; 8:12; 9:5; cf. 3:20, 21; 11:9, 10), where it serves as a key theological image. Within the second half of the Johannine Gospel, however, it has little place (although the imagery of darkness and artificial light in 13:30 and 18:3 probably play into these theological metaphors). As such, the image relates to material in the preceding chapters particularly well, but has little relation to the chapters that follow.

(3) The theme of judgement (κρίσις, κρίνω) has a strong foothold in the first half of the Johannine Gospel (3:17, 18, 19; 5:22, 24, 27, 29, 30; 8:15, 16, 26, 50; cf. 7:24; 12:31), with only two occurrences of the theme in the second half (16:8, 11). Its appearance in the retrospective paragraph (12:47-48) places it among the key themes of the first half of the Johannine Gospel.

(4) Although the verb "to save" (σώζω) is not common within the Johannine Gospel, its occurrences fall only within the first half of the narrative (3:17; 5:34; 10:9; cf. 4:22) where it is reinforced by a number of supporting concepts (e.g., belief, life, judgement, light, darkness, truth, testimony, Jesus as "the door" and "the good shepherd"). Consequently, its appearance in a paragraph summarising the first half of the Gospel (12:47) should not be surprising.

(5) John 12:48 makes reference to "the last day": "On the last day (τῇ ἐσχάτῃ ἡμέρᾳ), the word that I have spoken will serve as judge" (12:48). This motif itself makes no appearance in John 13–21, although Jesus' return is referred to there (e.g., 14:3, 28; 16:16, 22). The motif of "the last day" makes occasional appearances within John 1–12, especially in John 6 (6:39, 40, 44, 54) and elsewhere (11:24; cf. 5:25-29). Since the theological emphasis of the Johannine Gospel falls primarily on the coming of Jesus into the world and his departure from it, and since a future eschatology involving "the last day" is not strongly paraded, these eschatological passages have been variously explained. Some attribute them to an early stage of Johannine theology that later became overshadowed by an incarnational eschatology, while others attribute them to a later redactor who sought to bring Johannine theology more into line with mainstream Christian beliefs. But regardless of this matter, it is significant that a future eschatology was

deemed significant enough to include within the summary paragraph of 12:44-50.[7]

(6) Towards the close of Jesus' final words to the public, he makes mention of "eternal life" (ζωὴ αἰώνιος). This term appears in John 13–21 only at 17:2-3, but it appears fourteen times in John 1–12 prior to Jesus' closing words of John 12 (3:15, 16, 36; 4:14, 36; 5:24, 39; 6:27, 40, 47, 54, 68; 10:28; 12:25). Although "life" is said to be the goal of Jesus' ministry in 14:6 and the result of faith in 20:31, the occurrences of this term converge almost exclusively in John 1–12 (noun form: 30 out of 36 times; verbal form: 18 out of 20 times). So in the climax of Jesus' final public address (12:50), it is fitting that his words are linked to eternal life (cf. 3:17) in summary of Jesus' public ministry of John 1–12.

In view of these data, it is not surprising that virtually every interpreter recognises 12:44-50 to be "an epilogue in the proper sense, rounding off and summing up the preceding revelation,"[8] "a restatement of the leading concepts" of the previous twelve chapters,[9] an "(e)valuation and summary of the revelation of Jesus" which has been narrated throughout John 1-12,[10] or "a final public speech summarizing the significance of his words and deeds."[11] Here the public ministry of Jesus finds its close and its constitutional recapitulation.[12] As Graham Stanton writes, "[A]t the

[7] Cf. C. K. Barrett (*Essays on John* [London: SPCK, 1982], 5): "The theme of futurist eschatology runs deeper into Johannine thought than is often supposed." Cf. M. Hengel, *The Johannine Question* (London: SCM Press, 1989), 104. Ashton (*Understanding the Fourth Gospel*, 544), who accepts that a future eschatology is not central to Johannine theology, nonetheless rejects R. Bultmann's view (*Das Evangelium des Johannes* [Göttingen: Vandenhoeck & Ruprecht, 1957], 262–63) that John 12:48 should be attributed to a later redactor, suggesting that "one may surmise that the author of the Epilogue [i.e., the epilogue of John 12] (who may well be the Johannine prophet himself) is more interested in completeness than consistency."

[8] Ashton, *Understanding the Fourth Gospel*, 541. Cf. C. H. Dodd, *Historical Tradition in the Fourth Gospel* (Cambridge: Cambridge University Press, 1965), 26; G. R. Beasley-Murray, *John* (Waco: Word Books, 1987), 207.

[9] M. Stibbe, *John* (Sheffield: Sheffield Academic Press, 1993), 139.

[10] J. W. Pryor, *John: Evangelist of the Covenant People* (London: Darton, Longman & Todd, 1992), 53. Cf. D. M. Smith, *The Theology of the Gospel of John* (Cambridge: Cambridge University Press, 1995), 38: "[T]his passage offers as neat a summary of the theology of the Fourth Gospel as one could ask."

[11] D. Rensberger, "The Messiah Who Has Come into the World: The Message of the Gospel of John," in *Jesus in Johannine Tradition* (ed. R. T. Fortna and T. Thatcher; Louisville: Westminster John Knox, 2001), 15–23, 18.

[12] Cf. E. Haenchen (*Die Johannesevangelium: Ein Kommentar* [Tübingen:

end of the first main section of the gospel the evangelist sums up nearly all the themes which have been developed in the preceding chapters."[13]

But Stanton also notes that Jesus' words in 12:44-50 "not only summarize neatly the whole of the first half of the gospel" but "also turn out, on closer inspection, to be related to the immediately preceding verses"—that is, to 12:37-43. This connection with the preceding verses is through the theme of belief and unbelief. The social implications of belief in Jesus Christ are evident in 12:37-43, where the audience is told about some authorities whose belief is stifled by a fear of the Pharisees and expulsion from synagogue (12:42; cf. 9:22; 16:2). In this regard, it needs to be noted that the Pharisees are mentioned in 12:42 as if they were the main opponents to belief, something that is especially true of John 1-12, where they are mentioned eighteen times prior to 12:42 (1:24; 3:1; 4:1; 7:32 [twice], 45, 47, 48; 8:3, 13; 9:13, 15, 16, 40; 11:46, 47, 57; 12:19). By contrast, in John 13–21 they are mentioned only once (18:3).

The theme of belief and its opposite that unites both sections of 12:37-50 is treated both historically and theologically in 12:37-43. The simple historical observation that appears in 12:37 and 12:42-43 is that some believed while most did not. The theological treatment of the motif appears in 12:38-41, in which lack of faith itself is shown to be a fulfilment of scriptural prophecy. In this way, the dynamics of belief and unbelief that animate the preceding twelve chapters are all depicted in 12:37-43 as an essential part of God's unfolding plan. Since belief and unbelief have emerged largely in relation to Jesus' public performance of signs (2:11, 18, 23; 3:2; 4:48, 54; 6:2, 14, 26, 30; 7:31; 9:16; 10:41; 11:47; 12:18; cf. 20:30), John 12:37 recollects the preceding chapters of the Gospel by mentioning Jesus' performance of "many signs in their presence." So 12:38-41 serves to interpret the narrative of the preceding chapters by placing the conflict that animates much of John 1–12 within a larger scriptural and explanatory context. Significantly, the whole of the story that those chapters contains is framed on either side by quotations from Isaiah. The first prepares the reader for the narrative to follow,

---

Mohr, 1980], 96): "Eine letzte kurze Rede Jesu (V. 44-50), welche die wichtigsten Themen noch einmal anklingen läßt, beschließt die öffentliche Tätigkeit Jesu."

[13] G. N. Stanton, *Jesus and the Gospels* (Oxford: Oxford University Press, 1989), 116. For Stanton, a variety of themes that appear in concentrated form throughout 12:44-50 "are already found in the Prologue." He lists the following themes: light and darkness (cf. 1:4-5, 9 and 12:46); life (cf. 1:4-5 and 12:50); the coming of Jesus leads to his rejection (by some) (cf. 1:10f. and 12:47-48); to believe in Jesus is to believe in God (cf. 1:12 and 12:44); and seeing the Father (cf. 1:18 and 12:45). As Stanton admits, "[S]ome of these parallels are closer than others." Nonetheless, he makes the point that the evangelist sets out a small range of themes already "in his Prologue and sums them up in these verses which close the first main part of his gospel."

identifying its protagonist as "the Lord" (1:23, quoting Isa 40:3) while the second explains how the failure of many to believe in Jesus "the Lord" is itself a fulfilment of scripture (12:38 and 12:40, citing Isa 53:1 and 6:10).[14] This scriptural *inclusio*, then, contributes to the sense of closure in 12:37-50.

Consequently, there is good reason to identify 12:37-50 as "an epilogue in two parts."[15] As Andrew Lincoln aptly notes, the two-part conclusion to John 1–12 is comprised of the following components:

> In vv. 37-43 the narrator summarizes the response to Jesus' signs, and in vv. 44-50 the protagonist himself summarizes what has been at stake in the response to his words. The two sections sum up the trial of the public ministry. In the first, the narrator acts as counsel for the defense as he provides an apology for the response to Jesus' deeds; in the second, the person who is on trial is allowed to give a final statement about his teaching and its significance.[16]

It needs to be noted, however, that this epilogue is itself a part of a larger interlocking construction, the corresponding half of which appears in 12:20-36, where thematic anticipation of later chapters appears in condensed fashion, a matter to which we now turn.

§8.2 Thematic Anticipation in John 12:20-36

John 12:20-22 sets up a narrative situation in which Jesus expounds the meaning and implications of his impending death and resurrection throughout 12:23-36. The arrival of some Greeks in order to see Jesus signals to Jesus that the time for his "hour," with its universal significance, has come. By its very nature, then, this section points forward to Jesus' death and resurrection in the second half of the Johannine Gospel. A variety of themes appear in 12:20-36 to highlight that connection, expanding on the theological significance of Jesus' impending crucifixion and resurrection. As Gail O'Day notes, "John 12:20-36 is the most

---

[14] On the christological significance of this, see n. 91 below.

[15] Ashton, *Understanding the Fourth Gospel*, 494. Cf. G. Mlakuzhyil (*The Christocentric Literary Structure of the Fourth Gospel* [Rome: Editrice Pontificio Instituto Biblico, 1987], 89–90), who provides an extensive list of summarising themes in 12:37-50. As Ashton suggests, the verb "see" in 12:45 serves to link 12:44-45 "with the blindness motif that precedes and the light motif that follows," indicating the intended connection between 12:37-43 and 12:44-50.

[16] A. T. Lincoln, *Truth on Trial: The Lawsuit Motif in the Fourth Gospel* (Peabody: Hendrickson Publishers, 2000), 105. Cf. Ashton (*Understanding the Fourth Gospel*, 543): "The first (12:37-43) comments ruefully on the blindness of Israel in a verse from Isaiah (6:10) drawn from the common stock of the gospel tradition. The second summarizes the content of what has been revealed so far."

concentrated collection of sayings on the death of Jesus in John."[17] In the data that will be surveyed below, my contention will be that 12:20-36 acts as the interpretative lens through which the events of the crucifixion and resurrection are to be viewed.

(1) Jesus' words of this section begin as follows: "The hour has come [ἐλήλυθεν ἡ ὥρα] for the Son of Man to be glorified [δοξασθῇ]" (12:23; cf. 12:27, where reference to "the hour" appears twice). The coming of the hour is a signal to the narrative of crucifixion and resurrection in the second half of the Johannine Gospel,[18] which itself begins "Now before the festival of the Passover, Jesus knew that his hour had come [ἦλθεν αὐτοῦ ἡ ὥρα] to depart from this world and go to the Father" (13:1). The theme is repeated again in 17:1, when Jesus prays "Father, the hour has come [ἐλήλυθεν ἡ ὥρα]; glorify your Son [δόξασόν του τὸν υἱόν], so that the Son might glorify you." The coming of the hour in these passages is especially significant in light of the fact that on three previous occasions the audience was told that Jesus' hour has not yet come: οὔπω ἥκει ἡ ὥρα μου (2:4), οὔπω ἐληλύθει ἡ ὥρα αὐτοῦ (7:30; 8:20). To say at John 12:23 and 12:27 that his hour has come is to open the narrative floodgates to John 13–21.

(2) In association with the coming of the hour in which the Son of Man is glorified, this section also speaks of the "lifting up" and departure of the Son of Man (12:32, 34). The imagery of lifting up is specifically stated to refer "to the kind of death that he was about to die" (τοῦτο δὲ ἔλεγεν σημαίνων ποίῳ θανάτῳ ἤμελλεν ἀποθνῄσκειν, 12:33)—an explicitly forward-looking reference that reappears almost exactly in 18:32 (ἵνα ὁ λόγος τοῦ Ἰησοῦ πληρωθῇ ὃν εἶπεν σημαίνων ποίῳ θανάτῳ ἤμελλεν ἀποθνῄσκειν).[19] The imagery of lifting up has already appeared in the narrative

---

[17] G. O'Day, "Johannine Theology as Sectarian Theology," in *Readers and Readings of the Fourth Gospel* (vol. 1 of *"What is John?"*; ed. F. F. Segovia; Atlanta: Scholars Press, 1996), 199–203, esp. 200.

[18] It is a commonplace to identify Jesus' hour with his death, resurrection and ascension; cf. G. R. O'Day, "The Gospel of John: Reading the Incarnate Words," in Fortna and Thatcher, (eds.), *Jesus in Johannine Tradition*, 25–32, esp. 30.

[19] John 18:32 is sometimes thought to be a redactional insertion; cf. Bultmann, *Das Evangelium des Johannes*, 505; R. Schnackenburg, *Das Johannesevangelium* (Freiburg: Herder, 1976), 3:281.

on two occasions (3:14; 8:28), each of these occasions being tantalisingly undeveloped in their referent and meaning; it is only in John 12 that the theological significance of that image is fully cultivated. So Richard Bauckham notes that, in the earlier occurrences of the imagery, the Johannine evangelist

> explains the literal meaning, leaving the paradox of its concurrence with the figurative meaning to be inferred, but it is only on the last occasion when Jesus uses the figure that he provides this explanation. . . . [To those] who have not managed to penetrate the meaning through the first two occurrences of the figure "lifted up," he gives substantial help on its third occurrence but avoids depotentiating the riddle by giving too much help too soon.[20]

Consequently, the final and fullest development of the "lifted up" image appears in the section that functions as the interpretative lens of the narrative of Jesus' death and resurrection in the chapters that follow.

(3) The lifting up of Jesus is interpreted in this section as a moment in the process of Jesus' glorification (i.e., "the hour has come for the Son of Man to be glorified," 12:23; cf. 7:39; 17:4).[21] If a causal relationship is evident between 12:27b and 12:28, then Jesus' hour is ultimately to result in the glorification of God's name (12:28),[22] just as in 17:1 the coming of the hour pertains to the glorification of the Son and, in turn, of the Father (cf. 17:4). The Johannine Gospel polemicises against the need for mystical ascents into heaven in order to catch a vision of the "glory of the Lord" (cf. 1:18), since to see Jesus is to see his heavenly Father

---

[20] R. Bauckham, "The Audience of the Fourth Gospel," in Fortna and Thatcher (eds.), *Jesus in Johannine Tradition*, 101–11, esp. 109. Cf. Ashton, *Understanding the Fourth Gospel*, 493, and (here) 540: in 8:28 "the full significance of ὑψοῦν is still obscure (and will not be fully clarified until 12:23-5)."

[21] Although the crucifixion is to be seen as an important moment of Jesus' glorification, that glorification encompasses a broader association of events, including the betrayal that sets the crucifixion in motion (13:31), Jesus' resurrection and/or return to his Father (cf. 12:16; 17:5; 11:4, in which the resurrection of Lazarus foreshadows Jesus' own resurrection), and the divine guidance of Jesus' followers after his return to his Father (16:14).

[22] The divine response to Jesus in 12:28 ("I have glorified it [the divine name], and I will glorify it again") pertains to Jesus' obedient life in the first instance and his crucifixion and resurrection in the second.

(14:8-9), and the glory of the Father is reflected in the glory of the Son, which is evident in his crucifixion and resurrection. It is not surprising, then, that the theme of glorification appears in a section that points to and interprets Jesus' death and resurrection, narrated in later chapters of the Johannine Gospel.

(4) The coming of Jesus' hour is also said to be the occasion for the casting out of the ruler of this world (12:31). Reference to "the ruler of this world" (ὁ ἄρχων τοῦ κόσμου τούτου) also appears in 14:30, where the betrayal/arrest/crucifixion of Jesus is prefaced by the phrase "the ruler of the world is coming" (ἔρχεται γὰρ ὁ τοῦ κόσμου ἄρχων), and where it is pointed out that this ruler has no power over Jesus. If the ruler of this world is the spiritual power that drives the actions of the human players in the arrest and crucifixion of Jesus (cf. 13:2-3, 27), ironically he is also the one whose plans are thwarted precisely in the act of Jesus' crucifixion. For that is the primary moment of Jesus' own glorification, to the glory of the Father. The power of the ruler of this world is thereby shown to be ineffectual against the power of Jesus' Father, the inevitable result being that "the ruler of this world will be cast out" (12:31; cf. 16:11).[23] If 12:20-36 is acting as an interpretative lens through which to view the events that follow in the second half of the Johannine Gospel, it is significant that this theme of cosmic conflict and divine victory should make an appearance within the passage.

---

[23] G. H. Twelftree ("Exorcisms in the Fourth Gospel and the Synoptics," in Fortna and Thatcher (eds.), *Jesus in Johannine Tradition*, 135–43, esp. 141–42) makes the following point of interest: "[O]n the one hand, in the synoptic traditions the battle with Satan is centered during the public ministry of Jesus in his exorcisms. But then it is severely attenuated in the passion narrative. The reverse is the case for FG [the Fourth Gospel]. The battle with Satan permeates the proleptic ministry of Jesus, reaching its climax and realization in the cross event—the grand cosmic exorcism. In this way FE [the fourth evangelist] is able to affirm that the lie of Satan's control of this world is far more pervasive than the possession of some sick individuals and that the defeat of Satan requires more than isolated exorcisms. . . . In turn, the Jesus of FG liberates people not from demons but from unbelief. . . . FE radically reinterprets Jesus' mission as one of liberating people from the demonic darkness of unbelief rather than freeing them from demonic sickness." On the absence of exorcisms in the Johannine Gospel, see R. A. Piper, "Satan, Demons and the Absence of Exorcisms in the Fourth Gospel," in *Christology, Controversy and Community: New Testament Essays in Honour of David R. Catchpole* (ed. D. G. Horrell and C. M. Tuckett; Leiden: Brill, 2000), 253–78.

(5) The motif of divine victory is expanded further by means of other motifs appearing in 12:20-36. So the lifting up of Jesus is said to be the means whereby Jesus will "draw all people" to himself (12:32). Similarly his death is likened to a grain of wheat that "bears much fruit" (πολὺν καρπὸν φέρει, 12:24), in which a universal harvest is intimated.[24] This imagery is picked up in the metaphor of the vine and the branches in John 15. There Jesus equates being his disciple with bearing much fruit (ἵνα καρπὸν πολὺν φέρητε καὶ γένησθε ἐμοί μαθηταί, 15:8; cf. 15:16), which itself glorifies the Father (15:8). The bearing of fruit within the lives of Jesus' followers occurs as they "remain in me" (ὁ μένων ἐν ἐμοὶ κἀγὼ ἐν αὐτῷ οὗτος φέρει καρπὸν πολύν, 15:5; cf. 15:2, 4). It needs to be noted that the imagery of bearing fruit in both John 12 and John 15 is not wholly congruous in the two chapters. In the earlier chapter it is Jesus' death that is said to bear much fruit (12:24), while in the later chapter it is the disciples who bear much fruit as they live out their lives "in me." The imagery differs, but can also be correlated as associated harvests.

Expanding the theme of divine victory over the ruler of this world, these images of drawing all people to Jesus and bearing much fruit contribute to the interpretative lens of 12:20-36, verses that help to ensure that the audience interprets the events that follow in a manner consonant with the author's own interpretation.

(6) If the Johannine story of divine victory through the lifting up of Jesus is played out in the lives of Jesus' own followers who bear fruit, 12:20-36 also defines the nature of that story as it is replicated in the lives of Jesus' followers. So, following in the wake of the story of Jesus' own life, Jesus' followers are dramatically expected to "hate their own life in this world" in order to "keep it for eternal life" (12:25). The (potentially disturbing) metaphor of hating one's own life outlines the cruciform pattern that is expected to mark out the lives of Jesus' followers. In this way, the metaphor

---

[24] The universal resonance in these verses (12:24, 32) relate easily to the appearance of "some Greeks" who wished "to see Jesus" in 12:20-21. In the evangelist's thought, that "seeing" is associated with the "hour" of the Son's "glorification," as in 12:23. Cf. Haenchen (*Das Johannesevangelium*, 96): "Griechische Proselyten begehren, Jesus zu sehen: das ist für den Evangelisten das Zeichen, daß nun die Stunde der Verherrlichung gekommen ist." See also F. J. Moloney, *Signs and Shadows: Reading John 5–12* (Minneapolis: Fortress, 1996), 188.

correlates with Jesus' graphic action in 13:3-20 of washing his disciples' feet, another image of service that both interprets Jesus' own "service" on the cross (cf. 13:7) and imprints itself as the pattern of life for his followers (cf. 13:14-15).[25] The point is brought home in 12:20-36 by means of Jesus' words "Whoever serves me must follow me," in parallel with Jesus' words later in 13:14-15. Since, then, the Johannine theology of divine victory does not bypass but includes a cruciform lifestyle for Jesus' followers, it is appropriate that this feature should make an appearance at 12:20-36, in which the events of Jesus' death and resurrection are interpreted *in nuce*.

(7) Finally, John 12:20-36 appropriately includes the promise of a reward awaiting Jesus' followers: "Whoever serves me, the Father will honour" (12:26). This honour involves "being with Jesus," expressed in the phrase "where I am, there will my servant be also" (ὅπου εἰμὶ ἐγὼ ἐκεῖ καὶ ὁ διάκονος ὁ ἐμὸς ἔσται, 12:26). The phrase "where I am" is repeated with similar effect on two occasions in the narrative that follows. So in 14:3 Jesus promises his disciples that his departure will be to their benefit: "so that where I am, there you will be also" (ἵνα ὅπου εἰμὶ ἐγὼ καὶ ὑμεῖς ἦτε). And in 17:24 Jesus expresses his wish to his Father concerning his followers: "that where I am, there they may be" (ἵνα ὅπου εἰμὶ ἐγὼ κἀκεῖνοι ὦσιν μετ' ἐμοῦ, transl. mine). So the aspect of honour through being with Jesus is a theme that makes an appearance in the second half of the Johannine Gospel and, appropriately, appears within 12:20-36 to instil a sense of hope within Jesus' followers. If the function of 12:20-36 is to act as the interpretative lens through which to view the narrative of Jesus' crucifixion and resurrection, it is little wonder that that passage ends with the promise for Jesus' followers of being honourably numbered among the "children of light" (υἱοὶ φωτός, 12:36).

With these seven features of anticipation clustered together in 12:20-36, the evangelist expects his audience to be predisposed to read the follow-

---

[25] So Ashton, *Understanding the Fourth Gospel*, 491: Jesus' washing of the disciples' feet is "widely, and I think rightly, interpreted as a sacrificial gesture." Cf. S. J. Beutler, "Die Heilsbedeutung des Todes Jesu im Johannesevangelium nach Joh 13,1-20," in *Der Tod Jesu: Deutungen im Neuen Testament* (ed. K. Kertelge; Freiburg im Breisgau: Herder, 1976), 188–204.

ing chapters in a particular light. So concerning 12:20-36 Barnabas Lindars perceptively writes:

> The reader is now in a position to understand the chapters which follow. He will know that they are more than the history of a brave man who was condemned to death and was crucified and rose again from the dead. He will know that it is a history in which his own destiny before God is involved.[26]

§8.3   Summary and Supporting Evidence

It would be improper to suggest that 12:20-36 serves only as a forward gesture to the narrative that follows it, or that 12:37-50 serves only as a backward gesture to the narrative that preceded it.[27] The various themes of the Johannine narrative interpenetrate in such a way that pathways forward can be found in 12:37-50 and pathways backward can be found in 12:20-36.[28] Nonetheless, despite this interpenetration of themes in the Johannine Gospel, the gravitational pull of the two sections is predominately overlapping. Strong evidence suggests that 12:37-50 serves primarily to provide a précis or a concentrated recapitulation of major themes of the preceding twelve chapters. Similarly 12:20-36 serves primarily as a densely packaged synopsis of the leading themes pertaining to the events that unfold in the following nine chapters. In this way, the thematic overlap of 12:20-36 and 12:37-50 provides a significant example of chain-link interlock, serving not only as a transitional marker but, as has been suggested throughout, as a concentration point that brings together many of the primary themes of the Fourth Gospel. The presence of a chain-link transition in these two neighbouring passages serves to crystallise the main motifs of the narrative and to establish in clear and concise terms the primary dynamics that animate the two main text units that surround

---

[26] B. Lindars, *The Gospel of John* (London: Oliphants, 1972), 426.

[27] Cf. Ashton (*Understanding the Fourth Gospel*, 545) on 12:44-50 as a summary of John 1-12: "[T]he piece was designed as a coping-stone to crown all that has gone before—and perhaps with just a glimpse of what lies ahead." So the notion of "eternal life" appears in both the forward-glancing 12:25 and in the backward-glancing 12:50. Moreover, while 12:45 compares well with 1:18, it also parallels 14:9; and 12:50 parallels 14:31. These are testimonies to the way in which Johannine themes cross text-unit boundaries with ease, since they are so tightly interwoven. Since the material in John 14 probably derives from the first edition and 12:44-50 from a later edition (see §8.5 below), the earlier features (diachronically speaking) of John 14 seem to have influenced the backward-looking epilogue (synchronically speaking) of 12:44-50.

[28] Ashton (*Understanding the Fourth Gospel*, 52 [cf. 67]): "[T]he central themes are . . . tightly interlocked and intertwined."

the interlock.[29] The interlock serves as a prime structural location in which to assemble leading themes of the Johannine Gospel. In essence, the chain-link interlock at John 12:20-50 functions virtually as a mini-version of the Johannine Gospel, outstripping even John 1:1-18 in this regard.

One further feature of the final paragraph of John 12 needs also to be noted. Within 12:44-50 lies the hint of a chain link within a chain link. Ashton notes that the paragraph constitutes two sections, comprising

> 44b-48a and 49-50, with an intervening line, 48b, which points back-wards to the first section (κρινεῖ) and forwards to the second (ὁ λόγος ὃν ἐλάλησα). . . . Both the key words, κρίνειν and λαλεῖν, occur in the intervening line, 48b."[30]

Just as 12:44-50 plays a role as the second of two parts of a chain-link overlap, so it itself consists of two parts that are fused in the middle by way of a thematic overlap. So, the four occurrences of λαλέω in 12:49-50 correspond with the substantive that begins the sentence of 12:48b (ὁ λόγος ὃν ἐλάλησα ἐκεῖνος), while the three occurrences of κρίνω in 12:47-48a correspond with the main verb that follows the substantive of 12:48b.

12:47-48a:	κρίνω (3x)
12:48b:	ὁ λόγος ὃν ἐλάλησα ἐκεῖνος
12:48b:	κρίνω
12:49-50:	λαλέω (4x)

If 12:48b plays a transitional role within the final paragraph of John 12, it needs to be noted, then, that the author chose to construct that part of the paragraph in such a way that an overlapping forward and backward gestures make a further appearance at a lesser structural level. This may be mere coincidence, since the positioning of a verb after a substantive is not at all surprising. But Greek permits other constructions as well, and the transitional effect could have been served without loss of effect if κρίνω had preceded λαλέω in 12:48b. In that envisaged structure, a miniature "bridge paragraph" effect would have been produced (i.e., A/a+b/B, as discussed in §3.8). That the author chose instead to overlap

---

[29] Since 12:20-36 and 12:27-50 form two parts of a single transition, it is not adequate to note, as Ashton does (*Understanding the Fourth Gospel*, 546; cf. 547), "some surprising omissions" from 12:37-50 (such as "the cross and the passion—and even the resurrection") and then to build theological meaning on those omissions. These features appear within the summarising chain link, just in the earlier part, 12:20-36. By reducing the relevant summary passage to 12:37-50, Ashton skews the evidence.

[30] Ashton, *Understanding the Fourth Gospel*, 452 n. 40.

the key words adds weight to the suggestion that he is in "chain-link mode" in the final paragraphs of John 12.

§8.4   The Significance for Narrative and Theological Analysis

I have suggested that the chain link of 12:20-50 functions not merely as a transition from the first half of the Johannine Gospel to the second half, but also that 12:20-36 operates as the interpretative lens through which the second half of the Gospel is to be read. This has certain implications for the way in which the narrative of the second half is to be interpreted.

For instance, in his discussion of the terms "to lift up" and "to glorify," John Ashton senses that the evangelist has a theological preference for the term "glorify" over the term "lift up," since "glorify" seems to overshadow "lift up" in the second half of the Johannine Gospel. So the term "to lift up" makes no appearance after 12:20-36, with the term "to glorify" becoming the preferred term (as in 13:31-32, where it appears five times without "to life up"). Ashton draws the following conclusions from this:

> [S]uch allusions to Jesus' death as it [i.e., the verb ὑψοῦν, "to lift up"] ever carried have been transferred to δοξάζειν ["to glorify"]. It is as if the evangelist is gradually eliminating all the more painful and shameful associations of the death of Jesus. . . . What pain and shame there is in the chapters that follow is reserved for the disciples. Jesus' farewell and departure are tranquil and assured. . . . Used as it was earlier (12:23, 28) in close connection with ὑψοῦν, the verb δοξάζειν may continue to suggest, however obliquely, the death that Jesus is to die. But by now [i.e., John 13–17] the suggestion is at best very tenuous and all the emphasis is laid upon the bright, epiphanic conclusion to Jesus' mission.[31]

But in view of the interpretative function of 12:20-36 for the narrative that follows, arguments of this kind are problematical. Ashton's reading operates with an implicit prejudice favouring linear development within narrative, resting upon the assumption that later features of the narrative can serve to reinterpret earlier features. On this basis he is able to suggest a prioritisation of the term "to glorify" over "to lift up," along with a consequent prioritisation of certain theological convictions—not least in making Jesus' death little more than a prerequisite for his return to glory, the latter receiving the greater emphasis.[32] But this runs contrary to the

---

[31] Ashton, *Understanding the Fourth Gospel*, 496–97. See also G. Nicholson, *Death as Departure: The Johannine Descent-Ascent Schema* (Chico: Scholars Press, 1983), esp. 128, 163.

[32] For a critique of this kind of exegetical move, see G. R. Beasley-Murray, *Gospel of Life: Theology in the Fourth Gospel* (Peabody: Hendrickson Publishers, 1991), 46–47. For a more extensive treatment along similar lines, see W.

function of the non-linear chain link at 12:20-50. There, the chain link serves to bind these two concepts together so that wherever the verb "to glorify" appears in the later chapters, it is to be interpreted in relation to (although not simply synonymously with) the verb "to lift up" in relation to Jesus" death (as 12:32-33 makes plain).[33] In this way, the recognition of the interpretative function of the chain link at 12:20-50 places certain restrictions on the kind of narrative readings that can be entertained in the later chapters of the Johannine Gospel.[34]

One further point emerges from Ashton's comment, cited above, in which the following view is expressed: "It is as if the evangelist is gradually eliminating all the more painful and shameful associations of the death of Jesus."[35] Ashton is right, of course, with regard to the "shameful" aspect of Jesus' death. The Johannine Gospel gives little hint of the shame associated with crucifixion, although presumably such was obvious

---

Thüsing, *Die Erhöhung und Verherrlichung Jesu im Johannesevangelium* (Münster: Aschendorff, 1970). Cf. F. J. Moloney ("Raymond Brown's New Introduction to the Gospel of John: A Presentation—And Some Questions," *CBQ* 65 [2003]: 1–21, esp. 9): "In the Fourth Gospel, the expression 'glory' is associated with the cross. There Jesus is both lifted up on a stake and exalted . . . ; there he reveals the glory of God. But the event of the cross initiates the 'glorification' of the Son of Man." So too, R. Bauckham, *God Crucified: Monotheism and Christology in the New Testament* (Carlisle: Paternoster, 1998), 65.

[33] So, for instance, B. Lindars ("The Passion in the Fourth Gospel," in *Essays on John* [Leuven: Leuven University Press, 1992], 67–85, esp. 68): "the themes of the lifting up of the Son of Man and of Jesus' going to the Father certainly include reference to the passion in some sense." Smith (*Theology of the Gospel of John*, 117; cf. also 119) reduces the arena of Jesus' glorification too much when stating that "the death of Jesus is important for John as the moment of his glorification," but he rightly holds Jesus' glorification and death together in a way that Ashton downplays.

[34] Ashton, of course, is not an advocate of narrative readings, as his essay "Narrative Criticism" (in *Studying John*, 141–65) makes plain. What he opposes there tends to be a fully fledged narrative approach, as opposed to simply reading the narrative sensitively.

[35] That Ashton is committed to this position is clear from the fact that he had taken the same position a few pages earlier (*Understanding the Fourth Gospel*, 489). Cf. D. F. Strauss (*Das Leben Jesu*, cited and translated by Ashton, 37): According to the Fourth Gospel, "although he [Jesus] foreknew them [his sufferings], and also in one instance had a foretaste of them (John 12:27ff.), he had yet long beforehand completely triumphed over them, and when they stood immediately before him, he looked them in the face with unperturbed serenity." Similarly R. Bultmann's famous assertion (*Theology of the New Testament* [New York: Charles Scribner & Sons, 1955], 2:52–53): "While for Paul the incarnation is secondary to [Jesus'] death in importance, one might say that the reverse is true in John. . . . In John, Jesus' death has no pre-eminent importance for salvation."

to any first-century audience. But regarding the "painful" aspect of Jesus' death, Ashton's case needs to be severely qualified in light of the interpretative function of the chain link of 12:20-50. The forward gesture of 12:20-36 includes within it the announcement from Jesus' own lips "Now my soul is troubled" (νῦν ἡ ψυχή μου τετάρακται, 12:27), which is reminiscent of the tradition shared by Mark and Matthew of Jesus being "distressed and agitated" (Mark 14:33) and saying to his disciples "I am deeply grieved, even to death" (Mark 14:34; cf. Matt. 26:37-38). Although the tradition of Jesus' troubled soul is somewhat suppressed by Luke (unless Luke 22:43-44 is deemed original),[36] it is nonetheless maintained in the Johannine Gospel. This is true not only in 12:27 but also in Jesus' likening of his ordeal to a "cup" in 18:11 (cf. Mark 14:26, where Jesus' impending agonising death is said to be his "cup"). Granted, the Gethsemane story of the synoptic tradition per se is not recounted in John, and features of that story may be polemicised against in the Johannine account. So Ashton writes: "Jesus' acceptance of 'the cup which the Father has given me' (18: 11) reminds us of his refusal to plead to be saved 'from this hour' (12: 27); in the same breath these saying both recall and reject the Gethsemane tradition."[37] But the Gethsemane tradition is not rejected *in toto*. Ashton himself notes that the mention of Jesus' troubled soul in 12:27 is the Johannine "tipping of the hat" to that tradition.[38] But he also suggests that one of "the most striking omissions" in the Johannine Gospel in relation to the synoptic tradition is Jesus' "agony in the garden," repeating the oft-cited view that "[i]n the case of the Fourth Gospel 'passion' is a misnomer."[39] Granted, the Gethsemane garden makes no appearance in the Johannine Gospel, but the real point

---

[36] See, for instance, R. W. Moberly, "Proclaiming Christ Crucified: Some Reflections on the Use and Abuse of the Gospels," in *From Eden to Golgotha: Essays in Biblical Theology* (Atlanta: Scholars Press, 1992), 83–104.

[37] Ashton, *Understanding the Fourth Gospel*, 487.

[38] Ashton, *Understanding the Fourth Gospel*, 36: The Gethsemane tradition "is not found as such in the Fourth Gospel, but 12:27ff. clearly depends upon the same tradition."

[39] Ashton, *Understanding the Fourth Gospel*, 489, this being a common claim in secondary literature. I have no intention here of denying the phrase that follows this quotation from Ashton: "Jesus controls and orchestrates the whole performance." From Jesus' words in 12:27, however, it is not clear that Jesus' calm orchestration of events in John 18-19 rules out a "passion" element. E. Käsemann (*Jesu Letzter Wille nach Johannes 17* [Tübingen: J. C. B. Mohr (Paul Siebeck)], 1966) famously argues that the primary theological tendencies of the Johannine Gospel denude Jesus' humanity and consequently by-pass Jesus' passion. But this only highlights the fact that the Gospel does not abandon a passion aspect altogether, including the note of passion in prime location, structurally speaking. See also n. 41 below.

of debate here, of course, involves Jesus' agony. The fact that this aspect of the traditional Gethsemane story has been moved ahead in the Johannine narrative to a position before Jesus' last meal with his disciples does not undermine its narrative effectiveness or theological significance in relation to the crucifixion. Nor is the passion aspect of Jesus' crucifixion minimised or defective as a consequence of this re-placement. In fact, by its repositioning to a point on structural high ground, this feature serves as both a forward gesture to, and an interpretative lens for, Jesus' crucifixion. This affords it a far more important role within the narrative than its single and brief occurrence might otherwise suggest.[40]

Because of its placement within the chain link, the little phrase "Now my soul is troubled" plays a part in establishing one of the keys with which the audience is expected to interpret the crucifixion narrative. However much the Johannine Gospel errs on the side of highlighting the divine over against the human component of Jesus' identity, the chain-link transition of 12:20-50 keeps one foot solidly rooted in the Gethsemane tradition,[41] thereby ensuring that that tradition acts as a contributing influence for interpreting the narrative of Jesus' death even within the Johannine Gospel.[42]

[40] Cf. Beasley-Murray (*John*, 212): "The brevity of this description of the agony of Jesus as he faces his 'glorification' in no way diminishes its gravity in the eyes of the Evangelist." The highly significant use of chain-link construction of 12:20-50 to interpret the Johannine Gospel gives claims such as this the structural foundation that they otherwise lack. The use of that construction also qualifies a suggestion made by Lindars ("The Passion in the Fourth Gospel," 68) that "the importance of the passion has penetrated the gospel far more deeply than in the arrangement of the contents." In fact it has also penetrated the arrangement of the contents as well, giving it primacy of structural place.

[41] In contrast to claims that the Johannine Gospel is "naively docetic," Hengel (*The Johannine Question*, 104) emphasises that the author's high christology was maintained without "playing down the true humanity of Jesus." See esp. M. Meye Thompson, *The Humanity of Jesus in the Fourth Gospel* (Philadelphia: Fortress Press, 1988), 87–115. Since Ashton himself argues strongly along the same lines (*Understanding the Fourth Gospel*, 74), my quarrel with him is simply in relation to his handling of the Gethsemane and "passion" aspect of the Johannine Gospel. M. W. G. Stibbe (*John as Storyteller: Narrative Criticism and the Fourth Gospel* [Cambridge: Cambridge University Press, 1992], 129–47) relates Jesus' passion to the tragic "killing of the king" genre, as found also in the Bacchae. Having little force is M. C. de Boer's case (*Johannine Perspectives on the Death of Jesus* [Kampen: Pharos Publishing House, 1996], 195) in which, applying a "two-level drama" reading of John to 12:27, he argues that "[t]he point of relating [Jesus'] anguish is not to acknowledge Jesus' humanity, which is scarcely emphasised at all, but the humanity of the readers" (emphasis in original).

[42] For a further theological implication of this study of text-unit interlock at John 12, see n. 91 below.

Part 2: Chain-Link Interlock at the Original Seam
Prior to John 18

At this point, our attention shifts to material several chapters after John 12, where again chain-link interlock seems to present itself. Before this can be demonstrated, it is necessary to outline aspects of the compositional history of John 15–17, as in §8.5 below.

§8.5   John 14:30-31 in Its Contexts

The Johannine Gospel as a whole has been the subject of intense scrutiny with regard to its composition history. In that enterprise, a variety of stages have been proposed through which the Gospel as we know it has emerged. Even scholars on the conservative end of the spectrum participate in this enterprise. So Gary Burge writes that "every scholar senses that FG [the Fourth Gospel] offers hints of its history, tantalizing bits of data that point to stages of literary development."[43] Scholarly proposals frequently depict the Gospel as incorporating material that, following an initial oral period, straddles three or four distinct but related stages of literary development. With a final redactional edition completing the processes for the written compilation, two or three earlier literary predecessors are frequently envisaged.[44] For many interpreters, since this process of composition history has significantly shaped the final literary product, an appreciation of the compositional process is integral to an appreciation of the ensuing literary product.

The Johannine Gospel leaves itself open to the study of its composition history in some parts of the narrative more than others. The composition history of John 15–17 has been a matter of importance in Johannine studies. Theories regarding the composition history of the Johannine Gospel have a notable interest in these chapters, especially in view of two curious features contained within them:

(1)   When noting that "I will no longer talk much with you, for the ruler of this world is coming" (14:30), Jesus then says to his followers, "Rise, let us be on our way out from here"

---

[43] G. M. Burge, "Situating John's Gospel in History," in Fortna and Thatcher (eds.), *Jesus in Johannine Tradition*, 35–46, esp. 44. Cf. L. W. Hurtado, *Lord Jesus Christ: Devotion to Jesus in Earliest Christianity* (Grand Rapids: Eerdmans, 2003), 354.

[44] Three editions and a redactional update are argued for by J. Painter, *The Quest for the Messiah: The History, Literature and Theology of the Johannine Community* (Edinburgh: T&T Clark, 1991); M.-E. Boismard (and A. Lamouille), *L'Evangile de Jean* (Paris: Éditions du Cerf, 1977); Thatcher, "Introduction," in Fortna and Thatcher (eds.), *Jesus in Johannine Tradition*, 1–9, esp. 8.

(14:31, transl. mine). It is not until 18:1, however, that we hear about a departure: "After Jesus had spoken these things Jesus went out [i.e., out of the house] with his disciples. . . ." The departure that Jesus orchestrates seems to have been delayed by three lengthy chapters of speech on his part. Consequently, many hold the view that "the conclusion of chapter 14 . . . offers an impossible transition to the beginning of chapter 15,"[45] and that it is at 14:31 that "the farewell discourse really ends"[46]—that is, in the Gospel's original form.

(2) In 16:5 Jesus says to his disciples, "But now I am going to him who sent me; yet none of you asks me, "Where are you going?" (νῦν δὲ ὑπάγω πρὸς τὸν πέμψαντά με, καὶ οὐδεὶς ἐξ ὑμῶν ἐρωτᾷ με, Ποῦ ὑπάγεις;). Jesus' statement is awkward, however, since Peter already asked precisely this question in 13:36: "Simon Peter said to him, 'Lord, where are you going?'" (λέγει αὐτῷ Σίμων Πέτρος, Κύριε, ποῦ ὑπάγεις;). Moreover, in 14:5 Thomas has asked a question that builds on precisely this query: "Thomas said to him, 'Lord, we do not know where you are going. How can we know the way?'" (λέγει αὐτῷ Θωμᾶς, Κύριε, οὐκ οἴδαμεν ποῦ ὑπάγεις· πῶς δυνάμεθα τὴν ὁδὸν εἰδέναι;).

These narrative discrepancies have suggested to many that the text's assemblage was not wholly straightforward. Theories of compositional development explain these apparent aporias by depicting John 15–17 (sometimes only John 15–16) as having been inserted into their present position at a later developmental stage.[47] This insertion broke apart the natural link between 14:31 and 18:1ff., and similarly created the narrative awkwardness between Jesus' statement in 16:5 and those of his disciples in 13:36 and 14:5. John 15–17 is frequently thought to be comprised of traditions that take account of changing historical situations known to the Johannine evangelist. As C. K. Barrett explains:

[45] Ashton, *Understanding the Fourth Gospel*, 29. Cf. similar estimates on 46 ("the intolerably awkward transition at the end of chapter 14") and 87 ("the notorious puzzle of the conclusion of chapter 14").

[46] Hengel, *The Johannine Question*, 100.

[47] D. E. Aune (*The Westminster Dictionary of the New Testament and Early Christian Literature and Rhetoric* [Louisville: Westminster John Knox Press], 54) defines aporia as a term "used of literary inconsistencies, contradictions, interruptions, sudden turns, non sequiturs, and doublets . . . in texts that suggest the original order of the text has somehow been interrupted in the editorial process."

The most probable explanation is that in ch. 14 (or 13.31–14.31) and chs. 15–17 (16) we have alternative versions of the last discourse. This hypothesis is easily credible if we may suppose that the gospel material was collected over a period of time, and particularly so if some of it was first delivered orally.[48]

So, according to Johannes Beutler, "John 13–17 was written over a period of a decade or more . . . as the Johannine Community faced new experiences of persecution and internal doctrinal strife."[49] In the estimate of Joanna Dewey, a situation of this sort is the result of the Gospel's composition in an "oral-written media world." So she explains:

> Updated or corrected material would naturally be added as the Gospel was continually readapted to new situations, without the old necessarily dropping out. In a totally oral world, the old would probably be lost altogether. In a manuscript world, the text maintains some stability, so the old is more likely to remain.[50]

---

[48] C. K. Barrett, *The Gospel according to St John* (2d ed.; London: SPCK, 1978), 454. Cf. Painter (*The Quest for the Messiah*, 350–51): "[E]ach stratum of the discourses [of John 13–17] reflects a situation of crisis in the history of Johannine Christianity, and . . . this is the focus of the evangelist's reformulation of the teaching material." So, too, Meeks ("The Man from Heaven in Johannine Sectarianism," 173): the discourse material in John 14 and John 15–16 "seem to be alternate interpretations of the same group of themes belonging to different stages in the history of redaction of the Gospel."

[49] J. Beutler, S.J., "Synoptic Jesus Tradition in the Johannine Farewell Discourse," in Fortna and Thatcher (eds.), *Jesus in Johannine Tradition*, 165–73, esp. 166. Even with this multiple source solution, John 17 is sometimes thought to have been part of the early form of the Gospel. Most think this unlikely. Cf. Ashton (*Understanding the Fourth Gospel*, 498): John 17 "probably did not figure in the first edition"; Painter (*The Quest for the Messiah*, 367): "The situation reflected in this section [John 17] appears to be slightly later than the third version and slightly earlier than 1 Jn." Hengel (*The Johannine Question*, 95), who is not keen on elaborate compositional development theories in relation to the Johannine Gospel, articulates a series of five "basic assumptions" with regard to the Johannine Gospel and heads the list with the following: along with the Prologue, "John 17 was also added at a later stage" by the author (not by a redactor). With regard to John 13–17 in general, Hengel entertains "the possibility that the author had sometimes written several outlines side by side which his pupils then incorporated in to the work after his death. In this way, for example, we could explain the much-discussed break between 14.31, where the farewell discourse really ends, having a smooth continuation in 18.1f. and the abrupt new beginning in 15.1ff."

[50] J. Dewey, "The Gospel of John in Its Oral-Written Media World," in Fortna and Thatcher (eds.), *Jesus in Johannine Tradition*, 251. Cf. Painter, *The Quest for the Messiah*, 368–69.

Whether the insertion of John 15–17 was made by the Johannine evangelist or a later redactor who inherited them relatively intact and simply incorporated them into the narrative after the evangelist's death is a matter of continued debate among compositional theorists.

But compositional development theories do not hold universal assent. The weakness that plagues them involves the motivation of the author. As Wayne Brouwer writes,

> Why should a single author pen significantly different accounts of the same incident, and then splice them together so poorly? Beside [sic], what reason would there be for having the three discourses appear in chronological order, when, over the course of time, a thematic arrangement would probably provide a better exhortation?[51]

R. E. Brown thought that the explanation to this lies in the very character of the Fourth Gospel, in which "new insights are placed next to old insights," the result being that "the new insights reinterpreted the old."[52] Similarly, attributing the insertion to the redactor in the last stage of composition takes the sting out of the tail for some scholars. But others have not been satisfied with solutions of that kind, and have provided

---

[51] W. Brouwer, *The Literary Development of John 13–17: A Chiastic Reading* (Atlanta: Society of Biblical Literature, 2000), 18. Despite this observation, however, Brouwer does not abandon a compositional development view but supplements it with a further literary theory regarding the text's chiastic structure. In this way, he advances his own solution to the problem of "the dangling command of 14:31b" without abandoning a developmental undergirding. See, for instance, 152–53.

[52] R. E. Brown, *The Community of the Beloved Disciple: The Life, Loves, and Hates of an Individual Church in New Testament Times* (New York: Paulist Press, 1979), 51–52. In his earlier commentary (*The Gospel according to John* [2 vols. New York/London: Doubleday, 1966, 1970], 656–67) Brown wrote: "[T]he final editor simply made the best of a difficult situation and did not seek to force a new meaning" on 14:31 when adding the new material.

In an interesting article ("Raymond Brown's New Introduction to the Gospel of John," 14), Moloney has demonstrated that Brown's own work was marked out by certain tensions that Moloney, as the editor of Brown's final posthumous work, handled in different ways: footnoting them, altering them, or leaving them to stand unaltered. Moloney then notes (15): "If Brown's own work—obviously the work of a single author working on the same material across a span of thirty years—can reflect these . . . tensions and internal contradictions, is it necessary to develop a hypothesis involving a series of different 'authors' (Beloved Disciple, evangelist, redactor) to account for the compositional history of the Gospel of John?" In fact, Moloney's own redactional practice of allowing some tensions to remain within Brown's work might serve as one of several examples in support of a compositional history approach.

alternative solutions to the relationship of John 15–17 to the dangling command of 14:31. Three of these solutions are outlined below.[53]

A handful of interpreters argue that Jesus spoke John 15–17 while he and his disciples were getting up to leave.[54] So L. L. Morris writes:

> Anyone who has tried to get a group of a dozen or so to leave a particular place at a particular time will appreciate that it usually takes more than one brief exhortation to accomplish this. There is nothing at all unlikely in an interval between the uttering of the words and the

[53] A fourth solution sees the whole of John 13–17 as operating according to a chiastic structure. So J. Frey, *Die johanneische Eschatologie* (Tübingen: Mohr Siebeck, 2000), 3:110; Mlakuzhyil, *The Christocentric Literary Structure of the Fourth Gospel*; Brouwer, *The Literary Development of John 13–17*; F. J. Moloney, "The Function of John 13–17 within the Johannine Narrative," in *Literary and Social Readings of the Fourth Gospel* (vol. 2 of *"What is John?"*; ed. F. F. Segovia; Atlanta: Scholars Press, 1998), 43–66, esp. 66. But as is evident in the work of Brouwer and Moloney, this solution can easily piggy-back a theory of compositional development. See n. 51 above.

The same kind of piggy-backing is evident in the solution that sees the narrative of 14:30–18:1 replicating the experience of Johannine Christians in the "between time," expecting to move on (14:30) but having to wait before they can do so (18:1), with ethical and ecclesiastical guidance provided in the meantime (John 15–17). Those who postulate this view do not dispute that originally 18:1 followed 14:31. So, F. J. Moloney, *Glory Not Dishonour: Reading John 13–21* (Minneapolis: Fortress Press, 1998), 52–53; idem, "The Function of John 13-17," 51. Cf. also U. Schnelle, "Die Abschiedsreden im Johannesevangelium," *ZNW* 80 (1989): 64–79, 70–73, although he rejects the composition history solution (71).

Other kinds of solutions have also been suggested but are not widely accepted. T. Thatcher (*The Riddles of Jesus in John: A Study in Tradition and Folklore* [Atlanta: Society of Biblical Literature, 2000], 204) argues that 14:31 is meant as a riddle "to further confuse the disciples" because it "contradicts everything Jesus has said" in the preceding verse. Cf. also the rather contrived suggestions of T. L. Brodie (*The Gospel according to John: A Literary and Theological Commentary* [Oxford: Oxford University Press, 1993], 470–71), who postulates that a new spiritual plateau is envisaged in 14:31; and F. F. Segovia (*The Farewell of the Word* [Minneapolis: Fortress Press, 1991], 116–17), who postulates a psychological development within Jesus. Others attribute the problem to John's elderly age, imagining him to have disrupted his own composition as a consequence of an ageing and weakened mind; cf. G. Hoffmann, *Das Johannesevangelium ein Alterswerk: Eine psychologische Studie* (Gütersloh: Kaiser, 1933); E. Renan, *Les Origines du Christianisme, v. Les Évangiles; vi. L'Église chrétienne* (Paris: Calmann Lévy, 1877/79), 429–30.

[54] E.g., W. Hendriksen, *The New Testament Commentary: Exposition of the Gospel according to John* (Grand Rapids: Baker Books, 1953), 290; L. L. Morris, *The Gospel according to John* (Grand Rapids: Eerdmans, 1971), 661.

departure of the group. And if an interval, then there is no reason why Jesus should not have continued to speak during it.[55]

This view has not convinced many since, for instance, Jesus' prayer of John 17 "is not the kind of extended petition one tosses off while straightening up the room."[56]

Consequently, others have considered Jesus and his disciples to be already on the move in John 15–17, either walking through the Kidron valley,[57] or passing by the Temple,[58] with the vineyards and temple architecture serving as object lessons along the way. But these views, too, have failed to convince many, for similar reasons. With regard to John 17, for instance, many find it unlikely "that the prayer of chapter 17 would be uttered while the group is in motion in public places. Even with the shelter of night or the devotional surroundings of the Temple precincts, the prayer is too intimate."[59] In Brouwer's view, the "walking through Jerusalem" interpretation has "two significant problems that militate against it."

> First, if the evangelist takes such pains to identify temporal surroundings of significance to the rest of the discourse [i.e., 13:1-2, 30; 18:1], it is very strange that there is no narrative explanation of Jesus' comment in 14:31 as these developments occur, nor any suggestion of Jesus' gestures toward either the vines of nearby vineyards or the vine emblems carved into the capstones of the Temple buildings as he expresses the thoughts of 15:1-8. Second, all of the other prayers of Jesus recorded in the Fourth Gospel are introduced with a specific set of circumstances. It is out of character for this prayer, particularly with the intimacy conveyed in it, to have a setting other than the one assumed by the text as a continuation of the meeting room discourse.[60]

For reasons of this sort, solutions that envisage an unstated plot development in John 14–17 have not been widely accepted as solutions to the first apparent aporia noted above (i.e., Jesus' command to rise and leave). And with regard to the second aporia (i.e., Jesus' question about not being asked where he is going), Brouwer rightly queries: "Why, in such a

---

[55] Morris, *The Gospel according to John*, 661.

[56] Brouwer, *The Literary Development of John 13–17*, 105 n. 58.

[57] Carson, *The Gospel according to John*, 479; Haenchen (*Das Johannesevangelium*, 479): "Die Kapitel 15–17 müßten dementsprechend unterwegs, auf dem Gang zum Kidron, gesprochene Rede Jesu sein."

[58] B. F. Westcott, *The Gospel according to St. John* (Grand Rapids: Eerdmans, 1954), 187.

[59] Brouwer, *The Literary Development of John 13–17*, 18. Cf. also Ashton, *Understanding the Fourth Gospel*, 29 n. 62; J. Beutler, *Habt keine Angst: Die erste johanneische Aschiedsrede (Joh 14)* (Stuttgart: Katholisches Bibelwerk, 1984), 9 n. 4.

[60] Brouwer, *The Literary Development*, 108–9.

moment of profound intimacy with his closest friends, does Jesus ignore these forthright questions, apparently pretending they have not been asked?"[61]

Yet another solution, operating on the basis that 14:31 should in fact be followed by 18:1, is the displacement theory. In explanations of this kind, somewhere in the process of its transmission the Johannine Gospel became jumbled, resulting in a confusing and unnatural flow in the narrative of the Gospel as we now have it. B. H. Streeter explained the situation in the following manner:

> Everyone who has ever sent manuscript to be copied on a large scale knows that either through his own inadvertence or that of the copyist, sheets often get transposed, and paragraphs added by way of correction get inserted in the wrong place. The same kind of thing is frequently to be observed in ancient MSS of classical authors; and there is not the slightest improbability in its having happened in one of the earliest, or even in the earliest, copy of this Gospel. At any rate there are certain places where the connection is immensely improved if we suppose there has been an accidental transposition of paragraphs or sections. Thus it is difficult to believe that Jn. xiv.25-31, which reads like a concluding summary, leading up to the words "Arise, let us depart hence," was intended by the author to be followed by chap. xv-xvi. But move these seven verses to the end of ch. 16, and they make a magnificent close to the discourse, xiv.1-24, xv, xvi.[62]

But whereas Streeter found the solution to involve the re-placement of a mere seven verses, most suggested reconstructions are more radical in extent. So J. H. Bernard suggested the following reordering of the material within John 13–18:

13:1-31a: The last supper: feetwashing and betrayal
15:1–16:33, 13:31b-38, 14:1-31: The discourse proper
17:1-26: The prayer of Jesus[63]

Rudolf Bultmann suggested a similar reconstruction, but considered that the prayer of John 17 should precede the discourse rather than follow it, since it is most natural to assume that it was spoken as part of the final meal after the departure of Judas. So Bultmann reordered the sequence in the following manner:

---

[61] Brouwer, *The Literary Development*, 113.

[62] B. H. Streeter, *The Four Gospels: A Study in Origins* (5th ed.; London: Macmillan, 1936), 380–81. The view has been extensively critiqued in D. Moody Smith, *The Composition and Order of the Fourth Gospel* (New Haven: Yale University Press, 1965), 175–79.

[63] J. H. Bernard, *The Gospel according to St John* (Edinburgh: T&T Clark, 1928), xvi–xxx.

13:1-30: Jesus' last meal with his disciples
17:1-26: Jesus' farewell prayer
13:31-35; 15:1–16:33; 13:36–14:31: Jesus' farewell discourses and
conversations[64]

The weakness of displacement theories of this kind is that they provide little explanation as to the mechanics of how the displacement came to be in the first place. The shuffled leaves of text would in some cases have to involve some very small fragments of papyrus in order for the textual mix-up to have occurred. For instance on Bultmann's view, if the five verses of 13:31-35 ended up in a context so different from their original placement, the piece of papyrus on which they would have been written would have been a self-contained piece of an unusually small size. But other weaknesses attend to theories of this sort, as has been capably demonstrated by others, to the extent that Ernst Haenchen speaks for many in relegating such theories to the past ("Die Zeit der Umstellungshypothesen ist vorbei").[65]

Of the four main solutions on offer, those involving the text's compositional development (unlike the compositional disruption theories of Bultmann and others) seem to be operating along the most satisfactory lines. They set out in a single theory a plausible explanation of two of the Gospel's most curious features, not only the unfulfilled expectation of closure in 14:31 but also the awkward narrative discrepancies existing between 13:35 and 14:5 on the one hand and 16:5 on the other. Jesus' words in John 15–17 appear to have been included at what was originally a text-unit boundary between what we now know as John 14:31 and 18:1. The significance of this for the study of chain-link transitions in the New Testament will be illustrated next in §8.6 and §8.7.

§8.6   The Chain-Link Interlock at John 14:31/18:1-8

If John 15–17 was not part of the earliest form of the Johannine Gospel, a transition from 14:31 to 18:1 would have been evident. In 14:31, Jesus completes his words to his followers in an intimate private setting in which little action takes place. In 18:1, the intimate private setting gives way to a public setting in which Jesus' arrest, trial, and crucifixion (all public events) are set in motion.

Of particular interest is the manner in which forward and backward gestures lie across the boundary of these two text units, the characterising feature of chain-link interlock. Three forward gestures are evident.

---

[64] Bultmann, *Das Evangelium des Johannes*, 348–51.
[65] Haenchen, *Die Johannesevangelium*, 57, with his extensive analysis appearing on 48–57.

(1) Jesus' charge "Let us be on our way" (ἄγωμεν ἐντεῦθεν) in
14:31 corresponds to the action of 18:1 in which he "went
out [of the house] with his disciples" (ἐξῆλθεν σὺν τοῖς
μαθηταῖς) across the Kidron valley.

(2) Jesus' revelation that "the ruler of the world is coming
[ἔρχομαι]" (14:30) is matched in 18:3 by the coming
[ἔρχομαι] of Judas and the soldiers to arrest Jesus, with a
theology of suprahuman embodiment animating the link.

(3) Jesus' claim that "the ruler of this world . . . has no power
over me" (14:30) is graphically confirmed in the prostrate
position of Judas and the soldiers after Jesus' assertion
ἐγώ εἰμι (narratively: "I am he"; theologically: the divine
name).[66]

In light of these forward gestures, Jesus' words in 14:30-31 find their fitting continuation in the events of 18:1ff.

The backward gesture at this text-unit seam is not as strong as its forward gestures, but it is evident nonetheless. The NRSV translates the
first clause of 18:1 in the following way: "After Jesus had spoken these
words." This apt translation is a rendition of a simple two-word construction in Greek: ταῦτα εἰπών. The fact that this looks like a weak
transitional marker might induce reticence with regard to the existence
of a chain-link construction at the John 14/John 18 text-unit boundary. It
might be that the strong forward gestures alone should be thought of as
comprising the transition marker, with the transition conforming to the
pattern of a simple anticipatory transition. But when a larger collection
of Johannine transition markers are taken into consideration, this
impression is not compelling. It is not the Johannine norm to incorporate substantial transition markers when moving from one section to the

---

[66] Cf. Beutler, "Synoptic Jesus Tradition in the Johannine Farewell Discourse," 171: He adds: "Is this Satan, in a sense, asking permission to proceed?"
On ἐγώ εἰμι in 18:5-8 as connoting the divine name, see esp. C. H. Williams, *I
am He: The Interpretation of "Anî Hû" in Jewish and Early Christian Literature*
(Tübingen: Mohr Siebeck, 2000).

Beutler notes two other ways in which the material of John 14 crosses over
into John 18ff.: (1) "Judas' actions are more clearly the means by which Jesus is to
return to his father (14:28)." (2) "Also, could it be that Jesus' words that their
hearts should not be troubled or afraid [14:27] are in fact fulfilled in Peter's
action of withdrawing the sword and cutting off the ear of Malchus. What is
required is the coming of the Spirit who will 'teach you all things,' including,
presumably, how a heart untroubled and unafraid is to act — not militaristically
(i.e., Peter), but sacrificially (i.e., Jesus' footwashings)." I am not convinced by
either of these suggestions. In my view, the overlapping material starts at 14:30,
not earlier.

next. When one section builds on the next in the Johannine Gospel, it is often the case that the transition is relatively brief and uninvolved.[67] The following Johannine transition markers appear at the beginning of text units that take their temporal bearings from the previous text units, and all of them are comprised of a minimal number of words:

τῇ ἐπαύριον ("the next day," 1:29, 35, 43; 6:22; 12:12);

τῇ ἡμέρα τῇ τρίτῃ ("on the third day," 2:1);

μετὰ ταῦτα ("after these things," 3:22; 5:1; 6:1; 7:1; 19:28 [μετὰ τοῦτο], 38; 21:1);

μετὰ δὲ τὰς δύο ἡμέρας ("when the two days were over," 4:43);

ὡς δὲ ὀψία ἐγένετο ("when evening came," 6:16);

πάλιν ("again," 8:12, 21; 10:7);

καὶ παράγων ("as he walked along," 9:1);

ἐλθών ("when Jesus arrived," 11:17);

καὶ τοῦτο εἰποῦσα ("when she had said this," 11:28);

ὅτε οὖν ἐξῆλθεν ("when he had gone out," 13:31);

ὅτε ἐσταύρωσαν τὸν Ἰησοῦν ("when the soldiers had crucified Jesus," 19:23);

ὅτε οὖν ἠρίστησαν ("when they had finished breakfast," 21:15).

Short transitional markers with temporal bearings in the preceding text unit are, then, not at all uncommon in the Johannine Gospel. Accordingly, the brief phrase ταῦτα εἰπών of 18:1 is in good Johannine company in performing the function of a backward transition marker. In fact, this phrase has already been used in the Johannine Gospel as a backward transition marker, although unaccompanied by any corresponding forward gestures (thereby forming a retrospective transition, as described in §3.6). So John 13:21 reads: ταῦτα εἰπών [ὁ] Ἰησοῦς ἐταράχθη τῷ πνεύματι καὶ ("After saying this Jesus was troubled in spirit"). Although the backward gesture of 18:1 is not as strong as the forward gestures of 14:30-31, it both conforms to the predilection for brief backward gestures noted throughout the Johannine Gospel and has precedent already in that function within the narrative. The combination of both forward and backward gestures, then, corresponds to the pattern of text-unit interlock that Lucian and Quintilian admired.

---

[67] Short backward gestures functioning as transition markers have already been noted in §3.6 above, where fourteen Matthean examples appeared.

TEXT-UNIT "A"	INTERLOCKED "b" (anticipatory)	INTERLOCKED "a" (retrospective)	TEXT-UNIT "B" "B"
John 13:1–14:31	John 14:30-31	John 18:1, 6	John 18:1ff.

§8.7   The Theological Lens of the John 14/John 18 Chain-Link Interlock

The theological significance of this interlock is as simple as it is profound. In the earliest version of the Johannine Gospel, prior to the insertion of John 15–17, steps were taken to ensure that the narrative of Jesus' death and resurrection was placed within the broadest frame of reference possible—the cosmic battle between suprahuman forces. This was accomplished through the reference to "the ruler of this world" in 14:30 in connection to the coming of Judas and his entourage in the opening verses of John 18 (cf. 13:2, 27). The narrative of Jesus' arrest, trial, crucifixion, and resurrection is not played out simply in relation to human power. It is a two-level drama in which suprahuman forces are shown to be at work. The audience is encouraged to use a kind of "stereoscopic vision" in order to perceive the rich dimensions of the narrative.[68] In this way, the forward gestures of the text-unit interlock help to establish the cosmic parameters around which the ensuing narrative is to be interpreted, with Jesus' death and resurrection straddling two spheres of influence, the human and the suprahuman.

Moreover, the forward gestures of the interlock make it clear that this is not a battle in which the opposing forces are equal to each other. Jesus' claim in 14:30 that "the ruler of this world . . . has no power over me" is dramatically depicted in the submissive posture of Judas before Jesus in 18:6. That the ruler of this world is merely a pawn in the sover-

---

[68] So Beutler ("Synoptic Jesus Tradition in the Johannine Farewell Discourse," 171): the Johannine Gospel "gives Judas's arrival in the garden an eschatological dimension." Cf. Lindars ("The Passion in the Fourth Gospel," 83–84): one theological feature that the Johannine evangelist shares with Paul is "the apocalyptic struggle with the forces of evil" that is won by Christ in his death and resurrection, with John's contribution to the myth being that Jesus' "cross is the arena for this struggle precisely because it is a moral battle, rather than the phantasmagoric bloodbath of apocalyptic fancy." Cf. Bultmann (*Das Evangelium des Johannes*, 330): "Seit diesem Jetzt ist der "Fürst der Welt" gerichtet (16:11) und das Schicksal des Menschen ein definitives geworden, je nachdem, ob sie den Sinn dieses Jetzt erfallen, ob sie glauben oder nicht (3:36, 5:25). Keine Zukunft des Weltgeschehens wird Neues bringen, und alle apokalyptischen Zukunftsbilder sind nichtige Träume."

eign activity of God is evident from the interlock at 14:30-31, where the events that are about to unfold are said to belong to God's own strategy. Just as the interlock of John 12:20-50 interprets both human and suprahuman opposition as contained within the sovereignty of God (12:31 and 12:37-43), so too does the original interlock of John 14/18. It is little wonder, then, that God's own glory and honour are bound up with the events that are soon to take place in the account of Jesus' death, and that they will be vindicated in those events over and above competing forces, as both interlocks demonstrate. As Judith Kovacs writes, "the cross is not merely the metaphorical jumping off point for Jesus' renascent to his heavenly Father. It is the locus of a cosmic battle, in which Jesus achieves a decisive victory over Satan."[69]

In the course of the composition history of the Johannine Gospel, the tight narrative intrareferentiality between suprahuman and human characters in 14:30-31 and 18:1-8 was somewhat broken apart in order for the audience to hear further words of exhortation and encouragement from their departed Lord. The narrative correspondence between "the ruler of this world" and Judas became lessened when the chain-link was decoupled through the inclusion of John 15–17. The severing of the interlock did not, however, decouple this correspondence between suprahuman and human figures altogether, since that correspondence can still be recognised, now just postponed by a few chapters. But the inclusion of later material does seem to have resulted in a shift in emphasis, so that a story of divine sovereignty (i.e., the cosmic battle) is supplanted somewhat by (or perhaps, "focussed more specifically in") a story of the on-going life of Jesus' followers.

§8.8   The Effects of Compositional History on the Theology of the Interlocks

In the appendix to this chapter (§8.9), it is suggested that the chain link of 12:20-50 probably existed in abbreviated form even in the first edition of the Johannine Gospel. Moreover, it was suggested above that the first edition of the Johannine Gospel also included a chain link at the seam between 14:31 and 18:1. If these points have merit, then the original version of the Johannine Gospel bracketed the intimate moments of the last gathering of Jesus and his disciples in John 13–14 by means of text-unit interlocks on either side. But it is also suggested in the appendix below that editorial adjustments to the Johannine Gospel saw the chain link of 12:20-50 elaborated with additional material expanding the original elements of the interlock somewhat. From this, a curious feature emerges.

[69] J. L. Kovacs, "'Now Shall the Ruler of this World be Driven Out': Jesus' Death as Cosmic Battle in John 12:20-36," *JBL* 114 (1995): 227–47.

Whereas the later edition(s) saw material inserted between John 14 and John 18, thereby breaking apart the chain link that had originally existed there, those same later editions also saw material added to John 12 in a manner that enhanced the chain link that had originally existed there (e.g., 12:44-50).

It was noted in relation to the Apocalypse of Abraham (§5.9) that a theological modification resulted in the course of the compositional history of that text, with a chain-link interlock bearing the weight of that modification. Whether a similar shift in narrative and theological import resulted in the Johannine Gospel as a consequence of its own compositional history is a matter that I am unsuited to address fully at this stage, not least since a variety of possible narrative adjustments between the versions would need to be considered which cannot be entertained here.[70] Nonetheless, I offer some tentative observations in relation to the adjustments affecting the two chain-link interlocks considered in this chapter.

In the later version(s) of the Johannine Gospel, the heightening of the chain-link interlock of 12:20-50 and the eradication of the interlock at John 14/18 might well have two interrelated effects. First, in its original (and shorter) edition, the Johannine Gospel could be thought of as a literary triptych, in which three main blocks of material were hinged by chain-link interlock (roughly speaking, John 1–12; 13–14; 18–20). In its later edition(s), however, that Gospel appears to operate more like a two-panel diptych (John 1–12; 13–21), with the first twelve chapters being structurally set off from the nine that follow them, virtually as a single literary unit (John 13–21).

The second effect flows from this. In the later edition(s) of the Gospel, the account of the death and resurrection of Jesus in John 18–20 falls within the second literary panel, which itself is bounded by internal corporate concerns (i.e., John 13–17, 21). Whereas in the original triptych structure the glorification of Jesus played its part in relation to Jesus' ministry to the world in general (John 1–12) and to his followers in

---

[70] For instance, the apparent transfer of the temple episode from its position just prior to the chain link of John 12 to its current position in 2:13-22 would need also to be taken into account in any in-depth analysis of changes in narrative impact between early and later editions. Cf. Lindars ("The Passion in the Fourth Gospel," 71): "It is significant that the only place where the theme of destruction and renewal is taken up again is in the traditional saying of Jesus in 12.24, immediately after the point which this pericope [the temple incident] is likely to have occupied in his [the evangelist's] original scheme." The view that 12:24-26 was inserted at a later stage problematises Lindars's point (unless the later insertion is simply 12:25-26, as I think likely, if an insertion theory has merit here), but that insertion might itself have some relation to the transfer of the temple incident to John 2.

particular (John 13–14), in the later diptych structure Jesus' glorification is structurally situated almost exclusively in relation to his followers.[71] This shift of emphasis might be reflected in the Johannine Prologue, itself a feature of a later edition of the Gospel. There we read of the contrast between those in the world who fail to know him, on the one hand and, on the other, those who receive him and behold his glory:

> He was in the world . . . , yet the world did not know him. He came to what was his own, and his own people did not accept him [John 1–12].

> But to all who received him, who believed in his name, he gave power to become children of God. . . . And we have seen his glory [John 13–21].

If a Christian community's experience of the world is progressively one of alienation, as seems to have been the case as much for the Johannine community as for some other Christian communities, the glorification of the Son of Man might, over the course of time, come to be perceived as having more to do with the corporate life of his followers than with the world itself (except in relation to judgement).[72] The eradication of the chain-link interlock of John 14/18 and the building up of the chain-link interlock at John 12/13 might itself be a structural equivalent to the subtle shift in such a community's theological perspective and sentiment.

Appendix

§8.9   The Compositional History of the John 12 Chain Link

Having analysed the chain-link structure in 12:20–50 (§8.1–§8.3) and considered its implications for narrative and theological analysis of the Johannine Gospel (§8.4), the text-unit interlock prior to John 13 needs to be considered in relation to the Gospel's composition history.[73] Since this

---

[71] Cf. Aune (*The Westminster Dictionary of New Testament*, 245): "The two main sections of John clearly intended by the author are John 1:19–12:50, which narrates the public ministry of Jesus, and 13:1–20:29, which narrates Jesus' private ministry to his own disciples in preparation for his death."

[72] Compare a similar estimate of Johannine ethics, which J. T. Sanders (*Ethics in the New Testament* [Philadelphia: Fortress, 1975], 91–100) famously and poignantly depicts as morally deficient.

[73] Compositional history is often eschewed by those seeking to interpret the final form of the text. In my view, enquiries into both the text's compositional history and its final-form are valid. Cf. Moloney ("Raymond Brown's New Introduction to the Gospel of John," 3): "However committed a newer generation may be to the impact a text makes upon a reader (the world in front of the text), the serious consideration of what may have generated that text (the world behind the text) must still be part of the biblical scholar's activity."

is an extremely complicated matter, its consideration has been delayed until this appendix so as not to clutter the discussion of other important matters in the sections above. Here our interest will be guided by the following issue: to what stage of the text's compositional development is the chain link of 12:20-50 to be attributed?

For the discussion that follows, I have chosen to assess the chain link of 12:20-50 in relation to one of the more complex models of the text's composition history. It needs to be emphasised that, despite making use of this model, I am not necessarily of the view that it is the most accurate on offer. The model is used here simply for pragmatic purposes. That is, the task before us involves assessing the origin of the chain link of 12:20-50 in relation to a model of compositional development. If a less complex model were to be adopted to meet that task, the results arrived at might have little potency for those who advocate a more complex model. The task is best served, then, by adopting one of the more complex models currently on offer and assessing the material in the light of that model. If, by adopting a complex model, the chain link is shown to have existed at (one of) the earliest stage(s) of compositional development, the same would presumably be the case in a less complex model. If a less complex model were adopted, however, the same results would presumably not be compelling for those who favour a more complex model. So it is pragmatically expedient to adopt the more complex model for this exercise.

For heuristic, analytical purposes, then, I have chosen to adopt the model of composition history advocated by John Painter. He envisages the Johannine Gospel to have undergone "three consecutive editions and a final redaction."[74] The redactional edition involved the inclusion of John 21 to a narrative that originally ended at John 20, a view shared by most.[75] Where Painter advocates a more complex model than some is in seeing three rather than two versions of the Gospel lying between the final redacted version and the early period of oral tradition. Painter characterises these three editions as follows:

> The first edition contains the traditions shaped in the period of open dialogue with the synagogue concerning the *messiahship of Jesus*. . . . The second edition is bounded by the experience of *expulsion from the synagogue* and also contains the tradition of dispute and conflict leading up to that expulsion. . . . The third edition manifests the issues bound up with a growing *schism within the Johannine community*.[76]

[74] Painter, *The Quest for the Messiah*, 45.

[75] The exceptions include H. Thyen, "Aus der Literatur zum Johannesevangelium," *Theologische Rundshau* 42 (1977): 211-70; and P. Minear, "The Original Function of John 21," *JBL* 102 (1983): 85-98.

[76] Painter, *The Quest for the Messiah*, 45 (emphasis mine). There Painter also argues that to speak of editions can give a rather static impression of what was

To generalise, what differentiates the more complex three-edition model from the less complex two-edition model is the estimate that the first of the three editions preceded the "experience of expulsion from the synagogue." Interpreters such as Lou Martyn, Raymond Brown, and John Ashton envisage the first edition to have been compiled after that experience rather than befor it. Accordingly they advocate a simpler model of compositional development than Painter does.[77]

A telling example of the application of the three-edition model is Painter's relegation of the material in John 15–17 to differing strata in the development of Johannine Christianity and different editions of the evangelist.[78] As we have seen (§8.5), for many interpreters Jesus' farewell discourse in 13:1–14:31 belongs to the first edition, and provided something of a template for the revised discourse material that was later included in further editions. For Painter, 15:1–16:4a derives from the second-edition period in which conflict with the synagogue was of primary concern, while 16:4b–17:26 likely derives from the third-edition period in which alienation from the world was profoundly felt within Johannine Christianity and the potential for intercommunal schism was mounting.

Presently I will attempt to assess the chain-link construction of 12:20–50 in light of a three-part taxonomy of this kind in order to trace that construction roughly through the various stages of composition history. In this exercise, I will take account of interpreters' views regarding the

---

likely a far more dynamic process. So he writes: "Very likely the editions represent a process of ongoing revision, but one in which certain watersheds can be perceived in [t]he way the tradition has been shaped. The "editions" represent these perceived watersheds."

[77] J. L. Martyn, *History and Theology in the Fourth Gospel* (Nashville: Abingdon, 1968); Brown, *The Community of the Beloved Disciple*; Ashton, *Understanding the Fourth Gospel*, 162–66 (although he accepts that a signs source predates the first edition). On this, I incline more to the two-edition model. As Hengel has demonstrated (*The Johannine Question*, 115), the expulsion from the synagogue need not be dated as late as the 80s and 90s, since the Hellenists and other figures within the earliest decades of the Christian movement were likely to have been expelled from local synagogues as well. Consequently, this experience may have been earlier for Johannine Christians than is often suggested, and it may be reflected already in the first edition of the Johannine Gospel. In this case, the motif of Christians being cast out of the synagogue need not postdate the motif in 12:31 of the "ruler of this world" being "cast out"—a motif likely to have stood within the first edition. So Lincoln (*Truth on Trial*, 106) writes: "The one behind the world's casting out of Jesus and the synagogue's casting out of Jesus' followers (cf. 9:34) is himself cast out."

[78] Cf. also J. Becker, "Die Abschiedsreden Jesu im Johannesevangelium," *ZNW* 61 (1970): 215–46.

existence of late additions to 12:20-50 and strip away those suspected late additions in order to see what the chain link might have looked like in an early developmental stage.[79]

Before engaging in that exercise, however, consideration needs to be given as to whether the chain link itself makes gestures to material that is best attributed to later stages of the text's compositional development. If this is the case, then the issue of the chain link's origin is almost certainly to be resolved in favour of a later stage of composition. But in fact, most of the themes involved in the chain link of 12:20-50 are not dependent on a particular section of text that might be considered a late addition. The chain-link themes appear in relation to a spattering of themes to one side or the other. In general, a variety of passages support the chain-link themes at any given point.

The possible exception might be themes pertaining exclusively to material in John 15-17, material that appears not to belong to the Gospel's early compositional strata. Consequently, it needs to be considered whether the envisaged omission of John 15-17 would affect the chain-link interlock at the seam of John 12 and 13. To what extent are the anticipatory themes of that chain link dependent on corresponding themes in John 15-17? If the chain link of 12:20-50 is heavily dependent on material in those chapters, and if that material does not belong to the earliest strata of the Gospel, then the likelihood is that forward gestures of the chain-link interlock came into existence only at a later stage in the composition history of the Gospel.

In fact, however, very little of the forward gestures at the interlock in 12:20-50 actually relates to the material in John 15-17. In 12:23 (cf. 12:27) there is mention of Jesus' "hour" having come, and this corresponds with the same in 17:1. But the omission of John 17 from an envisaged first version does not reduce the narrative and theological effect of the chain link since mention of Jesus' hour having come also appears in 13:1 and since the reference to Jesus' hour is a general reference to the crucifixion-resurrection narrative of John 18-20.

Some features of the chain link are supplemented by material in John 15-17, most significantly the correlation between "bearing much fruit" in 12:24 and 15:2-16. But as noted above, the metaphor of those two chapters, while associated, is used somewhat differently in each case. In the first instance, the metaphor is used in relation to Jesus and his death;

---

[79] I am not persuaded by attempts to delineate Johannine Christianity as having high walls over and against other strands of early Christianity. Nonetheless, there does seem to have been a "Johannine" social grouping that (a) was distinctive within the panoply of early Christian groups of the first century, and (b) was marked out by influences that may not have been shared by all of the early Christian groups.

in the second instance, it is used in relation to the lives of Jesus' followers. The second use of the metaphor may itself be a development of the first. In the absence of John 15–17, then, this anticipatory theme might be slightly truncated in its effect, but not significantly. Even if the metaphor of "bearing fruit" in 12:24 was itself added at a late stage in the Gospel's composition history, as some suspect (see below), the removal of this theme altogether from the link would weaken only the fifth point of "thematic anticipation" noted in §8.2 above, and even then only slightly.

Other narrative features that appear both in the chain link and in John 15–17 also appear outside of those three chapters in question. So, for instance, while the motif of God's cosmological battle with Satan appears in both 12:31 and 16:11, it also appears in 13:2-3, 13:27 and 14:30. The absence of 16:11 from an envisaged early compositional stage slightly reduces the effect of the anticipatory aspect of Jesus' words in 12:31 ("now shall the ruler of this world be cast out"), but the anticipatory link is nonetheless maintained in relation to four verses from John 13–14. Similarly the promise in 12:26 of being where Jesus is corresponds well with 17:24, where the same promise appears, but it also appears earlier in 14:3, so that the chain link is relatively unaffected by the removal of John 15–17.

In sum, then, the chain-link transition of 12:20-50 is not heavily indebted to John 15–17, chapters that likely derive from one or more of the later editions of the Johannine Gospel. Consequently, we can now move to the related issue of determining whether the chain link of 12:20-50 itself shows signs of having been constructed in the later stages of the text's composition history.

One part of the chain-link interlock that has been credited to a late stage of development is 12:24-26:

> Very truly, I tell you, unless a grain of wheat falls into the earth and dies, it remains just a single grain; but if it dies, it bears much fruit. Those who love their life lose it, and those who hate their life in this world will keep it for eternal life. Whoever serves me must follow me, and where I am, there will my servant be also. Whoever serves me, the Father will honor.

For some, this block of material interrupts the sequence of thought in the verses that surround it, indicating its late inclusion.[80] Similar estimates have been offered for 12:34-36a:

[80] Cf. Brown, *John*, 1:471; Ashton, *Understanding the Fourth Gospel*, 491, 494. For my part, if an insertion is to be found here, it is likely to be found only in 12:25-26, not in 12:24-26. John 12:24 involves a metaphorical description of Jesus' words in 12:23, and links easily to 12:27. In this case, 12:25-26 are, if really a later insertion, a moralising application in which the story of Jesus' self-giving is applied to the lives of his followers, as in the footwashing account of John 13.

> The crowd answered him, "We have heard from the law that the
> Messiah remains forever. How can you say that the Son of Man must
> be lifted up? Who is this Son of Man?" Jesus said to them, "The light
> is with you for a little longer. Walk while you have the light, so that the
> darkness may not overtake you. If you walk in the darkness, you do not
> know where you are going. While you have the light, believe in the
> light, so that you may become children of light."

Finding that these verses rightly belong after 8:29, Rudolf Bultmann esti-
mated that they had been misplaced from their proper place by the hand
of the redactor (although few have accepted this rather subjective judgement).[81]

The most significant chunk of text that falls victim to a composition-
history approach includes the final seven verses of 12:20-50. Whereas
Bultmann thought that these verses originally belonged after 8:12 (and
before 8:21),[82] others have advanced the case for seeing this "carefully
constructed piece" (i.e., 12:44-50) as belonging to a late stage in the
Gospel's composition. Rudolf Schnackenburg and John Ashton assign it
to the hand of the redactor in "the last stage of composition," while
Barnabas Lindars considers it either to belong the evangelist's last edition
or to the redactional edition.[83] Estimates of this kind arise from the
observation that in 12:36b Jesus is said to have hidden himself from the
public; whereas, after a commentary on the unbelief of Jesus' contemporaries (12:37-43), the Jesus who has supposedly removed himself from
the scene suddenly makes an outburst of great theological magnitude in
12:44-50. There he either speaks to no one in his continued state of soli-
tude or has returned to public view momentarily—the audience is not
told which. If this is deemed to be an awkward narrative wrinkle (which is
not a view that I maintain myself),[84] it is easy to see why some scholars

---

[81] Bultmann, *Das Evangelium des Johannes*, 264–72. Other suggestions, such as
moving 3:14-21 after 12:31, will not be considered here. See further discussion in
F. J. Moloney, *The Johannine Son of Man* (2d ed.; Rome: Bibliotea di Scienze
Religiose, 1978), 161–64.

[82] Bultmann, *Das Evangelium des Johannes*, 260–64.

[83] Schnackenburg, *Das Johannesevangelium*, 2:513–14, 523; Ashton, *Understanding the Fourth Gospel*, 542; Lindars, *John*, 411, 436–37. Arguments against
this view appear in Moloney, *The Johannine Son of Man*, 163–64.

[84] It could be, for example, that we are simply to imagine the eternal Word of
God incarnated in Jesus as articulating the core of the Johannine message apart
from a specific spacio-temporal location (cf. 1:1-3), precisely because it is a message for all time and all places. Cf. Mlakuzhyil (*The Christocentric Literary
Structure of the Fourth Gospel*, 217 and 323 respectively), who speaks of this discourse being spoken "from behind the stage where he [Jesus] has disappeared"
and "from behind the curtain." He notes (217) that "[s]peaking invisibly from
behind the stage was common in ancient Greek tragedies," so that this "is a good

attribute the awkwardness to "editorial fatigue" at a later stage in the Gospel's composition than to imagine it having been part of a paragraph in an earlier edition without being smoothed out in further compositional stages.[85]

Other verses of 12:20-50 have also been cited as representing a late-edition inclusion. In 12:31-32 Jesus states, "Now is the judgement of this world; now the ruler of this world will be driven out. And I, when I am lifted up from the earth, will draw all people to myself." Painter considers these verses to derive from the (proposed) third edition of the Johannine Gospel, in which the lifting up of the Son of Man is understood as "the moment of judgement for the power of darkness, shattering that power and enabling men to come to the light, 12.31f."[86] But while Painter's

---

dramatic technique the author has used to create a mysterious atmosphere (as of an invisible voice) to make the reader reflect on the last public discourse of Jesus."

[85] In my view, however, 12:44-50 probably is not to be attributed to the editor but to the evangelist, albeit at a late stage of composition. These seven verses manage to condense so many themes into such a short and well-constructed unit, suggesting that they were composed by one whose genius is more prone to the crafting of the theologically acute Prologue (which itself was likely to have been a late inclusion by the primary author) than the comparatively simplistic narrative of John 21 that was included at the redactional stage. In fact, parallels between 12:44-50 and the theologically pronounced 3:16-19 are easy to spot. Here I differ from Lindars (*John*, 436), for instance, who considers 12:44-50 to be substandard. Brown (*John*, 1:490) credits these verses to the hand of a redactor, although he applauds the redactor for his fine judgement in including the verses where they now appear: "Actually, the redactor's judgement was a good one, for this little discourse, which now comes at the end of the Book of Signs, nicely summarizes Jesus' message." But if the content approximates other solidly Johannine content, and if the placement is creatively considered, what merit is there is attributing them to a redactor? For my part (unlike some interpreters), the redactor/s probably did not play a very significant role in the production of the final form of the Gospel, except for the inclusion of John 21 and a few other bits and pieces. Nor was boldness and creativity a characteristic of his/their work. If the aporia of 14:31 had been left behind from the evangelist's final edition, he/they either did not notice it or did not have the confidence to rework the text in order to remove the problem. Or conversely, it may have been that his/their lack of boldness caused the aporia of 14:31 to appear in the first place. Cf. Brown (*John*, 2:656): "the final editor did not want to tamper with this ending and so, despite the fact that he was creating an awkward sequence, added additional forms of the Last Discourse after 31." Either way, the characterisation that emerges of the redactor/s is one of a "hands-off" approach in which only the most pressing of adjustments were deemed appropriate. The addition of 12:44-50 would not seem to fall under this category, making it likely that these verses are to be credited to the evangelist, in his last edition.

[86] Painter, *The Quest for the Messiah*, 364.

model has merit enough to have been chosen as the heuristic template for our assessment here, Painter overworks the model in this case and consequently attributes too much material exclusively to the proposed third edition, thereby excluding it from the second. In all models of the Gospel's composition history (including Painter's), John 14:30-31 is allocated to the first edition, and there we read about "the ruler of the world" who "has no power over me" (14:30). Consequently, there is no need to assign the motif of driving out "the ruler of this world" in 12:31 to the third edition. Its partner verse in 14:30 qualifies it for inclusion within the first edition.[87] Moreover, I find it unlikely that the "lifting up" theme is to be relegated to the third edition in all of its appearances in the Johannine Gospel (3:14; 8:28), and consequently I see no basis for removing it from 12:32 in a rough attempt to reconstruct the second edition. Within Painter's model, there is reason to think that "the judgement of the world" theme originates only in the third version (cf. 16:8-11, 33) as a consequence of a sense of alienation from the world, so that this self-contained phrase might be attributed to that late stratum. But the same cannot be said for the remainder of 12:31-32.

We have seen, then, that several passages are suspected of being insertions into 12:20-50 in later editions of the Johannine Gospel (i.e., the third and the redactional editions in Painter's model). Excluding these suspected late additions from 12:20-50 permits us to estimate the force of the chain link at earlier stages of the Gospel's development. To this end, the text of 12:20-50 appears below in truncated fashion. The contents of this truncated version have been informed by the suggestions noted above:

(1) that the redactor(s) inserted 12:24-26 into its current position;

(2) that 12:34-36 has been uprooted from its original position following 8:29, where it originally belonged;

(3) that 12:44-50 was included at a late stage of the Gospel's composition; and

(4) that the "judgement of the world" theme of 12:31 belongs to the third edition in Painter's model.

It is not my intention to demonstrate that all of these suggestions have merit. (The second, especially, has very little force.) My intention is simply to evaluate whether a chain-link interlock would have been evident in the second edition of the Gospel (in Painter's model) after removing the material that is suspected to have arisen in the third and redactional editions. To that end, in what follows I have simply cut-and-pasted the

[87] See also n. 77 above.

NRSV's reading of 12:20-50 and removed the blocks of text that have been suspected of being later additions of one kind or another. The end result is an approximation of what the second edition of the Gospel (again, according to Painter's model) might have looked like at this point in the narrative. Both the forward gestures of the first paragraph and the backward gestures of the second paragraph are highlighted to indicate the extent of a second-edition chain-link interlock. Backward gestures are marked by single underlining and forward gestures by double underlining.

> 12:20Now among those who went up to worship at the festival were some Greeks. 21They came to Philip, who was from Bethsaida in Galilee, and said to him, "Sir, we wish to see Jesus." 22Philip went and told Andrew; then Andrew and Philip went and told Jesus. 23Jesus answered them, "The hour has come for the Son of Man to be glorified. 27Now my soul is troubled. And what should I say—'Father, save me from this hour'? No, it is for this reason that I have come to this hour. 28Father, glorify your name." Then a voice came from heaven, "I have glorified it, and I will glorify it again." 29The crowd standing there heard it and said that it was thunder. Others said, "An angel has spoken to him." 30Jesus answered, "This voice has come for your sake, not for mine. 31Now the ruler of this world will be driven out. 32And I, when I am lifted up from the earth, will draw all people to myself." 33He said this to indicate the kind of death he was to die. When Jesus had said this, he departed and hid himself from them.
> 12:37Although he had performed so many signs in their presence, they did not believe in him. 38This was to fulfil the word spoken by the prophet Isaiah: "Lord, who has believed our message, and to whom has the arm of the Lord been revealed?" 39And so they could not believe, because Isaiah also said, 40"He has blinded their eyes and hardened their heart, so that they might not look with their eyes, and understand with their heart and turn—and I would heal them." 41Isaiah said this because he saw his glory and spoke about him. 42Nevertheless many, even of the authorities, believed in him. But because of the Pharisees they did not confess it, for fear that they would be put out of the synagogue; 43for they loved human glory more than the glory that comes from God.

This reconstruction yields the following conclusions concerning the chain link in what is identified in Painter's model as the second edition of the Gospel.

(1) If 12:44-50 was incorporated at a late stage of the Gospel's composition history, a chain link in the earlier editions would have been significantly truncated, comparatively speaking, by the fewer gestures of thematic recapitulation in the second half of the chain link. Other thematic recapit-

ulations in 12:37-43, however, have been unaffected by this exercise, especially those of 12:37-41, where the scriptural legitimisation of the preceding narrative appears. John 12:37-43 carries enough structural weight to permit a chain link transition if also accompanied by elements of thematic anticipation in 12:20-36.

(2) If 12:24-26 is a late insertion, the effect of the chain link in the earlier editions would have been reduced with regard to the anticipatory features considered in points 5 through 7 of the "thematic anticipation" section above (§8.2). However, the removal of these verses would not obliterate the anticipatory features altogether, since a significant number of such features remain in the anticipatory section of the chain link.

(3) If 12:34-36 has been misplaced from its proper narrative position late in the development of the Gospel, the impact on the chain link of earlier editions is relatively minimal, with only a slight reduction of the effect outlined in point 7 of the "thematic anticipation" section above (§8.2).

(4) If the "judgement of the world" theme of 12:31 is a third-edition addition, its exclusion from earlier versions does little to truncate the chain link's effect.

In sum, then, while the chain link of 12:20-50 suffers somewhat from the removal of these suspect passages, the chain link nonetheless remains intact in this exercise of approximating the passage's content in the second edition of the Gospel, according to Painter's adopted model.[88] A sig-

---

[88] If John 12:41-43 is also a late insertion, then the backward gestures of the chain link would be truncated enough to suggest that the chain link arose only in the latest stages of the Gospel's composition. But the argument for such an insertion is a very weak one and, consequently, I have not permitted it to disturb the results of this exercise. It is argued by Ashton (*Understanding the Fourth Gospel*, 203), who makes his case on the basis that 12:41-43 refers to "the Pharisees" only, rather than to "the chief priests and Pharisees." His point seems to be that these verses were added when the Pharisees represented the evangelist's (or redactor's) main antagonists, the chief priests having long since fallen away in significance (i.e., post-70 CE). But the argument is not strong. The Pharisees are referred to alone on eleven occasions prior to 12:42 (1:24; 3:1; 4:1; 7:47; 8:13; 9:13, 15, 16, 40; 11:46; 12:19). The Pharisees and chief priests appear together on four occasions prior to 12:42 but always whenever Jesus' arrest is in view (7:32, 45; 11:47; 11:57; cf. 18:3). Since 12:41-43 is not an "arrest" passage, the case for its inclusion at a late stage carries little weight. Moreover, these verses include one of the three famous "synagogual expulsion" passages that was likely incorporated in the

nificant amount of interlocking material remains in the undisputed passages of that version. Evidently in later stages of the Gospel's development the chain link that already existed there was given a more pronounced structural profile, consonant with the structural transition that was imprinted on the material at an earlier stage.[89]

Two things need to be noted further. First, had a less complex two-edition model been adopted for our analysis instead of a three-edition model, the reconstructed chain link (above) would have been identified as belonging to the first edition. Only in the more complex three-edition model, in which the expulsion from the synagogue represents the interests of the second edition as opposed to the first, is this not the case.

Second, if we attempt to move from Painter's proposed second edition to the first edition, the material to be excluded from the reconstructed chain link above is 12:42-43, with its polemic against the Pharisees and the theme of exclusion from the synagogue. Without these verses, the chain link is still intact and effective, with 12:37-41 functioning as an epilogue to the narrative of John 1–12. Those verses sit well within an envisaged first edition, which Painter characterises as one of open dialogue with synagogual Judaism in which the evangelist sought "to understand Jesus in relation to the Old Testament and salvation history."[90] This is precisely the nature of 12:37-41, comprised overwhelmingly of citations from Isaiah.[91] If the final-form version of 12:37-50 is

first edition (or at least the second edition) of the Gospel. On this, see n. 77 above and n. 91 below.

[89] For a similar phenomenon, compare the way that the chiastic Logos-poem of John 1:1-18 was likely supplemented by material concerning John the Baptist in such a manner as to keep the pre-existing chiastic structure intact. That is, the addition of 1:6-8 to the existing poem required a complementary addition of John the Baptist material on the other side of the chiasm's centre-point, thus falling at 1:15. On the chiastic structure of the Logos-poem, see §3.1 above.

[90] Painter, *The Quest for the Messiah*, 358.

[91] Although the theological significance of John 12:41 cannot be considered in detail here, it needs to be noted that a very high Christology is evident there, intrinsically embedded within the summarising chain-link interlock. So, the indication in Isaiah 6:1 that Isaiah "saw the Lord sitting on a throne, high and lofty; and the hem of his robe filled the temple" is now given a christological interpretation in the Johannine Gospel. The heavenly "Lord" is identified as Jesus Christ, the one who "dwelt among us" and whom the authorities have failed to "see." (Hurtado [*Lord Jesus Christ*, 73–74] calls this a "striking case" of "charismatic exegesis" in which new christological insights resulted from the interpretation of scriptural texts. See also 374–75.) That claims of this sort are embedded within the all-important chain-link interlock in the Gospel's first edition calls into question any scheme of compositional history that credits a high Christology to a late edition and the product of later controversies with the synagogue. Significant christological assertions and devotional practices seem to

rightly characterised as "an epilogue in two parts,"[92] the assigning of 12:42-43 to the second edition and of 12:44-50 to a later edition means that the remaining verses (12:37-41) served simply as a one-part epilogue of the first edition. And this epilogue is marked out by backward glances enough to enable it to qualify as one half of a chain-link construction.

It would seem, then, that although the chain link has likely developed to one degree or another throughout the text's composition history, the chain link just prior to John 13 has nonetheless been a relatively stable feature of the Johannine Gospel throughout most, and probably all, of the stages of its composition history.

---

have characterised earliest Christians virtually from the start of the Christian movement; see in particular, Hurtado, *Lord Jesus Christ*, esp. ch. 2–3.

[92] Ashton, *Understanding the Fourth Gospel*, 494; cf. Aune, *The Westminster Dictionary of New Testament*, 247.

Chain-Link Interlock in the Narrative of Acts

Mikeal Parsons and Martin Culy have recently expressed surprise at "the lack of studies that attend to Acts from the perspective of ancient rhetorical criticism," imagining that "studies that read the narrative portions of Acts in light of ancient rhetoric . . . would hold great promise in further illuminating Luke's rhetorical strategies."[1] In the study of the Acts of the Apostles, Luke's historical, theological, and literary interests have dominated scholarly discussion, without significant concern to showcase his rhetorical interests.

---

[1] M. C. Parsons and M. M. Culy, *Acts: A Handbook on the Greek Text* (Waco: Baylor University Press, 2003), xxi.

C. K. Barrett has summarised Luke's literary and historical interests in the following manner:

> There is little more to say than that his literary and historical work was controlled by two practical motives: he wished to paint a picture of the life and preaching of the earliest church that would provide instruction and inspiration for his contemporaries, and he wished to show how the Gospel had been taken beyond the Judaism in which it was cradled into the Gentile world.[2]

With regard to the rhetorical aspect of Luke's project,[3] however, much could also be said. As will be shown in the paragraphs that follow, one of Luke's rhetorical concerns was to ensure that his original audiences would recognise main text-unit divisions within the narrative of Acts by means of discernible transitions comprised of text-unit interlock. Moreover, as will also be shown, the demarcation of these text units governed Luke's historical and literary interests, at least at certain key points where Luke's rhetorical interests are seen to take precedence over other interests.

In this chapter it will be demonstrated that chain-link constructions underlie a number of significant transition points in the Lukan writings. In particular, chain-link transitions are evident (1) at the seam shared by the Lukan Gospel and Acts (§9.1), (2) at the text-unit seam just prior to Acts 13 (§9.2), and (3) at Acts 19:21-41 (§9.4). Furthermore, it will be shown that a complex chain link appears in an important transition in the early verses of Acts 8 (§9.3). In the light of these four transition passages, Chapter 10 will then proceed to consider their implications in relation to (1) the unity of the Lukan Gospel and Acts (§10.1), (2) the structure of Acts (§10.2), (3) the theology of Acts (§10.3) and (4) Pauline chronology (§10.4).

§9.1   The Chain-Link Interlock at the Luke-Acts Seam

The transition from the first Lukan volume (the Lukan Gospel) to the second (the Acts of the Apostles) evidences a chain-link construction. It offers the only instance in which a New Testament chain-link interlock is "articulated," although it is only partially articulated, with the textual

---

[2] C. K. Barrett, *The Acts of the Apostles* (Edinburgh: T&T Clark, 1994), 56.

[3] In what follows, the name "Luke" will be used to identify the third canonical evangelist. Although this ascription is disputed, I concur with the estimate of L. Alexander ("Acts," in *The Oxford Bible Commentary* [ed. J. Barton and J. Muddiman; Oxford: Oxford University Press, 2001], 1028–61, esp. 1028): "it is difficult to find any alternative which makes more sense of all the data than the traditional ascription."

interlock being explicitly drawn to the audience's attention in Acts 1:1. Although the Lukan Gospel and the Acts of the Apostles have for long been separated from each other in the Christian canon, it is arguable, and will be argued in §10.1 below, that Luke envisaged them as a single literary unity. This view does not command universal assent among interpreters since it is possible that, despite their similarities, the two texts were written independently of each other and without a shared overarching programme. But as will be shown in chapter 10 below, the two texts are best considered to be interdependent volumes of a single monograph. In this section, then, the "final Lukan form" of these two texts will be analysed in relation to chain-link construction.

Close to the end of Luke's Gospel, at least four "forwards" gestures point to the narrative in the early chapters of Acts.

(1) Jesus' prediction towards the end of the Lukan Gospel that "repentance and/unto[4] the forgiveness of sins will be preached . . . to all nations beginning in Jerusalem" (Luke 24:47) correlates initially to the events narrated in the early chapters of Acts and subsequently to the events of later chapters.[5] So on three occasions while in Jerusalem, Peter exhorts others to repent in order to be forgiven (2:38; 3:19) or he speaks of Jesus' ministry as offering "repentance to Israel and forgiveness of sins" (5:31). Forgiveness of sins continues to be preached to gentiles spread beyond the confines of Jerusalem as the narrative progresses, by both Peter (10:43) and Paul (13:38; 26:18). With the charge to repent having initially been taken to the gentiles by others (11:18), Paul then carried on the task in his own ministry to the gentiles (20:21; 26:20).

(2) Jesus' instruction that the disciples are to "stay in the city until . . ." (Luke 24:49) finds its narrative fulfilment in the early chapters of Acts. This is evident from the first post-ascension event narrated in Acts (1:12-26) and continues through the first seven chapters of Acts in which Jerusalem is the geographical centre for the action of the main narrative, before the geographical focus begins to broaden out.

Jesus' instruction to remain in Jerusalem is initially fulfilled in the final sentence of the Lukan Gospel, where we

---

[4] The textual evidence is almost evenly divided between εἰς and καί in 24:47.

[5] For a study of Luke 24:47 in relation to the whole of Acts, see G. Betori, "Luke 24:47: Jerusalem and the Beginning of the Preaching to the Pagans in the Acts of the Apostles," in *Luke and Acts* (ed. G. O'Collins and G. Marconi; New York: Paulist Press, 1993), 103–20.

read: "And they returned [from Bethany] to Jerusalem with great joy, and were continually in the temple blessing God" (24:52-53). But the early chapters of Acts amplify that depiction, so that Luke 24:52-53 takes on something of a double function. On the one hand, these verses, together with 24:50-51, round off the Gospel's narrative, providing it with a sense of closure. Luke's Gospel is marked out by an *inclusio* centred on the temple, with the narrative proper beginning and ending in the Jerusalem temple (cf. 1:5-23 and 24:51).[6] On the other hand, since these verses overlap with the material content of the first chapters of Acts, which amplifies and expands the closing verses of Luke's Gospel, they also serve as a springboard to the story of the disciples' experiences in Jerusalem as recounted in Luke's second volume.[7]

(3) The commission to "stay in the city" includes the temporal qualification "until you are endowed with power from on high," a phrase that is most likely synonymous with Jesus' mention of the "promise of my Father" (Luke 24:29). The "power from on high" that is "promised" by Jesus' Father corresponds to the bestowal of the Spirit upon the followers of Jesus at Pentecost in Acts 2:1-42.

(4) The disciples' role as "witnesses of these things" (Luke 24:48) serves as a transitional foothold to their role as "witnesses in Jerusalem and in all Judea and Samaria and to the end of the earth" (Acts 1:8), as played out repeatedly throughout the Acts narrative (1:22; 2:32; 3:15; 4:33; 5:32; 10:39, 41; 13:31; cf. 22:15, 20; 26:16).

In at least four ways, then, the end of the Lukan Gospel introduces features that are given their full showing only in the Acts narrative. These features foreshadow events that come to pass after Jesus' own public ministry has been completed, as narrated in Acts. But since they appear at a text-unit boundary (assuming here the unity of Luke-Acts),

---

[6] According to D. Juel (*Luke-Acts* [London: SCM Press, 1983], 7), "there may even be grounds to suspect that someone tampered with the ending of the Gospel to make it more suitable as an independent volume."

[7] A. George ("Les récits d'apparitions aux Onze à partir de Luc 24,36-53," in *La résurrection du Christ et l'exégèse moderne* [ed. P. de Surgy et al.; Paris: Éditions du Cerf, 1969], 75–94) illustrates how this passage serves both a concluding and forward-looking role. On the theological significance of Luke 24:50-53, see A. G. Mekkattukunnel, *The Priestly Blessing of the Risen Christ: An Exigetico-Theological Analysis of Luke 24,50-53* (Bern: Peter Lang, 2001).

these features do more than simply foreshadow later events; they serve also as transitional features between the two text units.[8] According to the early work of Mikael Parsons, "By so connecting these two accounts, the narrator strengthens the retrospective patterning of the reader," with the end of Luke's Gospel being summarised as "to be continued."[9]

The text unit that follows (i.e., the Acts of the Apostles) includes within its first five verses especially (but also as far as Acts 1:11) a series of glances back to the Lukan Gospel.[10] It begins with an articulated reference to "the first book" (τὸν πρῶτον λόγον, 1:1), and then provides an out-of-sequence summary of late highlights in Jesus' public career.[11] These include:

(a) Jesus' ascension (i.e., "the day when he was taken up," 1:2; cf. 1:9-11),

(b) Jesus' resurrection appearances ("he presented himself alive to them," 1:3; cf. 1:4-8),

(c) Jesus' passion ("after his passion," 1:3),

(d) Jesus' command not to depart from Jerusalem (1:2, 4), and

(e) Jesus' promise of the Spirit, "the promise of the Father" (1:4-5).

Moreover, reference is made to John's baptism with water (1:5), with John first making an appearance in Luke 1 (1:57-66), and his baptismal ministry being outlined in Luke 3 (3:1-22). Consequently, virtually the whole of the Lukan Gospel falls between the events referred to in the backward gestures of the first five verses of Acts.

---

[8] That narrative "foreshadowing" can function separately from, as well as part of, chain link construction was discussed in §3.2.

[9] M. C. Parsons, *The Departure of Jesus: The Ascension Narratives in Context* (Sheffield: Sheffield Academic, 1987), 192–93.

[10] Although P.-H Menoud ("Remarques sur les textes de l'ascension dans Luk–Acts," in *Neutestamentliche Studien für Rudolf Bultmann* [ed. W. Eltester; Berlin: Töpelmann, 1957], 148–56) queried the authenticity of Acts 1:1-5, he later renounced his challenge ("During Forty Days," in his *Jesus Christ and the Faith: A Collection of Studies by Philippe Menoud* [Pittsburgh: Pickwick Press, 1978], 167–79).

[11] See further V. K. Robbins, "The Claims of the Prologues and Greco-Roman Rhetoric: The Prefaces to Luke and Acts in Light of Greco-Roman Rhetorical Strategies," in *Jesus and the Heritage of Israel: Luke's Narrative Claim upon Israel's Legacy* (ed. D. P. Moessner; Harrisburg: Trinity Press International, 1999), 63–83, esp. 76–83. His conclusion is as follows: The preface to Acts exhibits "how the words and deeds of Jesus" followers in Acts "grow out" of the words and deeds of Jesus in the Gospel."

This combination of forward gestures at the end of the Lukan Gospel and backward gestures at the start of Acts are the ingredients of a chain-link structure that help to enhance the unity of the two Lukan volumes.[12] They are what Lucian would describe a century later as a means of bringing entities together into essential connection, permitting no possibility of separation and ensuring a smooth transition within a narrative's progression. Or as C. K. Barrett writes, "In Luke's thought, the end of the story of Jesus is the Church; and the story of Jesus is the beginning of the Church."[13] This theological connection has been concretised in literary form in the interlocked transition between the two Lukan volumes.

TEXT-UNIT "A"	INTERLOCKED "b" (anticipatory)	INTERLOCKED "a" (retrospective)	TEXT-UNIT "B"
Luke 1:1–24:53	Luke 24:47-49 (52-53)	Luke 24:50–Acts 1:12	Acts 1:1–8:3 (28:31)

As noted above, that these overlaps in material between the Lukan volumes amount to a chain-link transition is a view dependent on the conviction that Luke and Acts are two volumes of a single literary unity. This conviction will be given significant consideration in §10.1, where evidence for it will be presented. In the meantime, three further cases of Lukan chain-link will be studied, demonstrating Luke's aversion to narrative "humps and hollows" (Lucian) in general.[14] The first of these is the text-unit boundary between the first and second halves of Acts.

---

[12] According to D. W. Palmer ("The Literary Background of Acts 1.1-14," *NTS* 33 [1987]: 427–38, esp. 435), the transition from the Lukan Gospel to Acts enables their author to combine "features of a commission-appearance [i.e., Luke 24] with those of a farewell scene [i.e., Acts 1]," noting that this linkage "has been made possible by the almost unparalleled literary situation, where Luke portrays the assumption of a figure who has already risen from the dead." We saw how the use of chain-link construction similarly afforded the author of Revelation the opportunity to link the epistolary and apocalyptic genres in a similarly unprecedented fashion. For further evidence of overlap between the end of Lukan Gospel and the beginning of Acts, see A. W. Zwiep, *The Ascension of the Messiah in Lukan Christology* (Leiden: Brill, 1997), 118.

[13] C. K. Barrett, *Luke the Historian in Recent Study* (Philadelphia: Fortress Press, 1970), 57.

[14] C. H. Talbert, who was the first to notice the chain-link construction in John 12 (*Reading John: A Literary and Theological Commentary on the Fourth Gospel and the Johannine Epistles* [New York: Crossroad Press, 1992], 179–80), did not mention it in his earlier study of the arrangement of Luke-Acts (*Literary Patterns, Theological Themes and The Genre of Luke-Acts* [Missoula: Scholars Press, 1974]), unless I have inadvertently failed to notice it.

§9.2   The Chain-Link Interlock at the Peter-Paul Seam

The Transition prior to 13:1

A good number of scholars consider that, to one extent or another, "a major shift in the narrative" of Acts begins somewhere in the vicinity of Acts 13:1.[15] Some perceive it as a shift into a new main-text unit while others perceive it as a shift within a main-text unit. Some identify the new text unit as commencing at 12:24;[16] others at 12:25;[17] and others at 13:1.[18] At least one interpreter has even suggested that the transition to the new text unit is to be found as far back as 11:27.[19] As will be shown, although Acts 11:27 appears a long way from Acts 13:1, in structural terms it is virtually "just next door," and serves the function of beginning the transition that builds towards 13:1—a verse which in my view is rightly characterised as "a major departure in Luke's story."[20]

There is some merit in perceiving the narrative of Acts as comprised of two main parts: Acts 1–12 and Acts 13–28 (although each of these large text units are to be further subdivided, not least by means of further text-unit interlocks, as will be shown in §9.3 and §9.4). This is evident from the shifts in focus of the two parts. Although the book of Acts is not a biographical study of personages per se, the history that it recounts is intricately connected to key figures in the early Christian movement. Without dispute, two of those figures are far and away the most prominent: Peter and Paul. Each figure holds prominence in relatively self-contained sections of the text. In Acts 1–12 the main figure is Peter, who

---

[15] So, S. Cunningham, "Through Many Tribulations," in *The Theology of Persecution in Luke-Acts* (Sheffield: Sheffield Academic Press, 1997), 242.

[16] E.g., C. Burchard, "Fußnoten zum neutestamentlichen Griechisch," *ZNT* 61 (1970): 157–71, esp. 165–66. M. Hengel and A. M. Schwemer (*Paul between Damascus and Antioch* [London: SCM Press, 1997], 244) suggest "there is a quite new beginning in 12.24," and the phrase "The word of God grew and increased" of 12:24 "may be taken as the title of chs. 13 and 14." But the content of 12:24 is a standard Lukan summary which is used to close text units; cf. Acts 6:7; 19:20.

[17] E.g., C. H. Turner, "Chronology of the Bible," in *A Dictionary of the Bible* (ed. J. Hastings; Edinburgh: T&T Clark, 1898), 1:403–25, esp. 421; M. Goulder, *Type and History in Acts* (London: SPCK, 1964), 65, 98; F. F. Bruce, *The Book of Acts* (Grand Rapids: Eerdmans, 1988), 243; R. N. Longenecker, "The Acts of the Apostles," in *The Expositor's Bible Commentary* (Grand Rapids: Zondervan, 1981), 9:205–573, esp. 234.

[18] E.g., D. Marguerat, *The First Christian Historian: Writing the "Acts of the Apostles"* (Cambridge: Cambridge University Press, 2002), 111.

[19] C. Perrot, "Les Actes des Apôtres," in *Introduction critique au Nouveau Testament* (ed. A. George and P. Grelot; Paris: Desclée, 1976), 2:239–99, esp. 253–55.

[20] Barrett, *The Acts of the Apostles*, 598.

evidently oversees both the Jerusalem-based community and the initial expansion into other geographical areas. Even the events that do not have a Petrine focus (e.g., Stephen in Acts 7; Philip in Acts 8; and Paul in Acts 9 and 11) nonetheless appear within a Petrine frame that extends to Acts 12, with Petrine material interspersed throughout the whole of Acts 1–12 (e.g., 1:15–5:42; 8:14-25; 9:32–10:48; 12:1-19).[21] In Acts 13–28, however, the narrative focuses primarily on Paul, depicted as a great missionary working for the spread of Christian communities throughout the Mediterranean basin.[22]

A quick statistical survey illustrates well the Lukan shift in character focus. By my count, the first twelve chapters of Acts include fifty-five references to Peter, while the sixteen final chapters of Acts (13–28) include only one (15:7). Similarly, whenever referring to the great apostle to the gentiles in Acts 1–12, Luke names him as "Saul" (Σαῦλος or Σαούλ); as of 13:9, however, the name used of this figure throughout Acts 13–28 is "Paul." The only exceptions to this are in Acts 22 (vv. 7, 13) and Acts 26 (v. 14). But since these occurrences appear in Paul's accounts of his conversion, they indicate that Luke prefers the name "Saul" when describing him within the time-frame of events in Acts 1–12 and the name "Paul" when describing him within the time-frame of events in Acts 13–28. The differentiation of the two sections is virtually water-tight with regard to the naming of Luke's main (human) protagonist, and it illustrates that the boundary between Acts 12 and Acts 13 is important for Luke.[23]

If it is correct to think of a major text-unit shift at the boundary of Acts 12 and Acts 13 (identified by Joseph Fitzmyer as the beginning of "the second part of Acts"),[24] and if we are to expect that Luke might have

[21] In fact, the name Peter appears 19 times in Acts 1–7, and 36 times in 8–12 (by my count), so even though Philip and Paul and others distract the Petrine focus at times in the latter chapters, a strictly numerical analysis suggests that Peter takes an even higher profile in the five chapters of Acts 8–12 than in the seven chapters of Acts 1–7.

[22] T. Bergholz (*Der Augbau des lukanischen Doppelwerkes* [Frankfurt am Main: Peter Lang, 1995], 26) only slightly overstates the point: ". . . weil ab Apg 13 ganz allein Paulus im Vordergrund steht."

[23] Moreover, Acts 13–28 marks itself off from Acts 1–12 with regard to the leadership of the Jerusalem community. Whereas Peter seems to function as the primary figure within the Jerusalem church in Acts 1–12 (a point generally accepted, but a contrary views have been suggested; see J. Painter, *Just James: The Brother of Jesus in History and Tradition* [Columbia: University of South Carolina Press, 1997], 44; P.-A. Bernheim, *James, Brother of Jesus* [London: SCM Press, 1997], 193), this function is taken up by James the brother of Jesus in Acts 13–28. So in Acts 15 James speaks last in order to summarise the discussion and point the way forward.

[24] J. A. Fitzmyer, *The Acts of the Apostles* (New York: Doubleday, 1998), 494.

concerned himself with providing a transition from one text unit to the next, we cannot find much transitional material in the opening verse of Acts 13, which simply begins: "Now in the church at Antioch there were prophets and teachers. . . ." There is little here to provide a smooth transition to the new text-unit that begins in 13:1. Instead, Luke seems to expect his readers to have been prepared for the the beginning of the new text-unit by what precedes 13:1. That preparation has already been laid by the narrative in Acts 11–12, and it is there that we find the transition from the predominantly Petrine material (Acts 1–12) to the predominantly Pauline material (Acts 13–28).

Acts 12:25 plays a role in that transition, laying some of the foundations for the new text unit. It depicts the conscription of John Mark within the partnership of Barnabas and Saul (cf. 13:5, 13; 15:37, 39).[25] Moreover, unless the variant "to Jerusalem" is to be preferred in 12:25, it describes the return of Barnabas and Saul to Antioch, from where the narrative of 13:1 begins.

These are not particularly strong transitional features, however, especially when compared to the effective interlock at the seam of Luke's Gospel and the Acts of the Apostles (cf. §9.1 above and §9.5 below). But the transition appears to be relatively weak only when 12:25 is artificially dissociated from its larger context. That is, preparation for the transition in Acts 13:1 occurs as far back as Acts 11, with 12:25 being the continuation of the story told in 11:27-30 (this being true no matter the view one takes on the variant readings in 12:25).[26] Having recounted the founding

---

Talbert (*Literary Patterns*, 23–26) differentiates Acts 1–12 and 13–28 on the basis of seven literary parallels occurring throughout both sections of the text. Cf. also his *Acts* (Atlanta: John Knox Press, 1984).

[25] John Mark has already made an appearance in Acts 12:12, but his place within the partnership of Barnabas and Paul is not established until 12:25.

[26] Textual discrepancy exists in 12:25 as to whether Barnabas and Saul returned "to" Jerusalem (NRSV, based on the εἰς of manuscript ℵ, B, etc.) or "from" Jerusalem (RSV, based on the ἐξ of manuscript A, P⁷⁴, etc.; or the ἀπό of manuscripts D, E). The point made in the main text above is simply that 12:25 continues the story in 11:27-30 no matter what view one takes of the textual variants. This is especially evident if the Antiochene emissaries returned "from" (ἐξ) Jerusalem, in which case 12:25 is the conclusion to 11:27-30. But that 12:25 continues on from 11:27-30 is also clearly the case if the Antiochene emissaries are said to have returned "to" (εἰς) Jerusalem. That reading gives 12:25 less relation to the events of 13:1ff., since the emissaries would then be in different geographical locations in the two passages; that is, it operates as a one sentence story, more related to 11:27-30 (where the partnership of Barnabas and Saul and their movement from Antioch to Jerusalem have already been established) than to 13:1ff. So in either case, 12:25 is a continuation of the story in 11:27-30.

of the Christian community at Antioch in 11:19-26,[27] Luke then highlights in 11:27-30 the initiative of that community in delivering a gift of aid through Barnabas and Saul to the community in Jerusalem. In this narrative lies a reservoir of transitional oil that lubricates the structural pivot from the predominantly Petrine to the Pauline material. In particular Luke introduces four features in 11:27-30 that lay the narrative foundations for the next text unit: (1) the partnership of Barnabas and Saul, or "Paul" as he will be referred to here (11:30; cf. Acts 13–15); (2) the status of Barnabas and Paul as "apostles" (i.e., commissioned ones) of the Antioch community (11:30; cf. specifically 14:4, 14, but generally throughout Acts 13–15);[28] (3) the role of Barnabas and Paul as cotravellers whose movements serve a declared purpose (11:30; cf. 13:2); and (4) the leadership group in Jerusalem known to Luke as "the elders" (11:30; cf. 15:2, 4, 6, 22-23; 16:4; 21:18). Here then we have four further anticipatory features that contribute to the narrative of Acts 13ff. If 12:25 plays a structural role in anticipating certain features of the chapters that follow, it does so especially in relation to the narrative of 11:27-30—a section that concludes in 12:25 and that carries anticipatory weight in the transition to the Pauline narratives of Acts 13ff.

If 11:27-30 and 12:25 act together to assist in the transition to Acts 13, the function of 12:1-24 needs to be explained, for it is curious that Luke should have interrupted the journey(s) of Barnabas and Paul by including a long intervening narrative. The continuation of the narrative already begun in 11:27-30 has been significantly delayed, appearing only in a single short verse prior to 13:1. Between 11:30 and 12:25 Luke recounts the events surrounding Agrippa's persecution of the early church and, in particular, of Peter.[29] This is a somewhat unusual manner

---

[27] L. T. Johnson (*The Acts of the Apostles* [Collegeville: The Liturgical Press, 1992], 206–7): "By devoting special attention to the foundation of the Church at Antioch (the only new community described so fully since the Jerusalem narrative), he prepares the way for the latter commissioning of Barnabas and Saul (13:1-4)."

[28] The partnership of Barnabas and Saul is not necessarily evident already in 11:26, where they both are said to have "met with" (συναχθῆναι) many in the Antiochene communities and "taught" (διδάξαι) a significant number of people. That they did this in partnership is not stated. The two may have had separate responsibility for two distinct Christian communities in Antioch, for instance, and may have taught independently of each other. This is, in fact, the implication of 13:1, where the list of five prophets and teachers keeps Barnabas and Saul separate, with Barnabas at the head of the list and Saul at its closure.

[29] Also in this material is a depiction of the death of Herod Agrippa. On this, see O. W. Allen, Jr, *The Death of Herod: The Narrative and Theological Function of Retribution in Luke-Acts* (Atlanta: Society of Biblical Literature, 1997).

of storytelling, with a transitional unit being split into two parts, separated by a significant block of text.

The "interrupted story" technique has already been used by Luke in Luke 9, of course, where he inherits it from his Markan source. So the sending out of the twelve in Luke 9:1-6 finds its conclusion in 9:10 (cf. Mark 6:6-13, 30), having been "interrupted" by the story of Herod's beheading of John the Baptist in 9:7-9 (cf. Mark 6:14-29). In the case of the stories of Acts 11 and 12, however, Luke's structure cannot be explained in terms of his indebtedness to the structure of a preexisting source. Luke has probably inherited two main traditions in these two chapters and has sought to meld them together: i.e., the Antiochene collection of 11:27-30/12:25[30] and the Herodian persecution of 12:1-24. So the "Petrine sandwich" that appears in Acts 11–12 was most likely constructed by Luke himself (unlike Luke 9:1-9), who inserted the Petrine story into the narrative about the Antiochene collection.

The simple recognition of a common literary technique in both Luke 9:1-9 and Acts 11:27–12:25 provides little explanation as to why Luke chose to replicate the pattern in the latter instance.[31] And in the secondary literature on Acts 11–12, such explanations are few and far between. Those explanations that do appear are, to my mind, four in number, and these four require consideration.

[30] For instance, Barrett (*The Acts of the Apostles*, 546, with further defence there and pp. 559–60): Luke "has traditional material at his disposal and it is probable that he collected it in Antioch, or at least through Antiochene contacts." Cf. also his later comments (p. 599): "Luke was able to draw at Antioch on a story that recounted the founding and establishing there of a mixed Jewish Gentile church which traced its spiritual ancestry back to the work of Stephen and his associates in Jerusalem, and continued with missionary work based on that church." Barrett does not envisage this "Antiochene story" to involve a sustained, documented, written "Antiochene Source" that many have postulated. So, for instance, R. Jewett (*Dating Paul's Life* [London: SCM Press, 1979], 10) thinks that an Antiochene Source of this sort underlies the following sections: 6:1–8:4; 9:1-30; 11:19-30; 12:25–14:23; 15:35ff. Moreover, he finds this source to include polemic that "is clearly aimed against Jerusalem" (12). The suggestion may be intriguing, but suffers from a noticeable over-reading on Jewett's part. With Jewett, however, I am not persuaded that 12:25 is simply redactional, despite the presence of redactional influence. Luke received it as the conclusion to the account of 11:27-30, and as such it formed part of a tradition that Luke inherited.

[31] So G. Lüdemann (*Das frühe Christentum nach den Traditionen der Apostelgeschichte* [Göttingen: Vandenhoeck & Ruprecht, 1987], 146) does not press the issue far enough when he writes: "Die Technik, zwischen Aussendung und Rückkehr der Boten eine andere Geschichte einzuschieben, wird auch Mk 6,7–13.30 (par. Lk 9,1-9) angewandt und mag Lukas zur Komposition dieser Szene inspiriert haben."

A First Explanation: Alleviating Historical Confusion

Some have suggested that the story of Herod Agrippa's persecution of
James and Peter has been moved to Acts 12 in order "to gloss over the
confusion caused by the mention in XI:30 of a visit by Paul to
Jerusalem,"[32] in apparent contradiction to Paul's account in Galatians 1–2
where such a visit seems to be ruled out (assuming that Gal 2:1-10
equates to Acts 15). But this explanation is hardly satisfying, since it is
unclear how the insertion of Petrine material into the story of the
Antiochene collection is meant to help gloss over the historical "confusion." In fact, the sandwich effect causes Paul's visit(s) to Jerusalem to be
doubly highlighted, at both 11:30 and 12:25, potentially drawing the
audience's attention to the apparent discrepancy between the Acts and
Galatians accounts rather than minimising it.

A Second Explanation: A Lukan Chiasm

A literary-historical explanation for the conspicuous placement of the
conclusion of the Antiochene collection story has been proposed by
Walter Schmithals.[33] He argues that the whole of 11:27–12:25 is animated by a chiastic structure. The outer components of the chiasm are
comprised of traditions about the Antiochene collection (11:27-30;
12:24-25). The intermediary components are comprised of traditions
about Herod (12:2-3/5; 12:18/20-23). The centre of the chiasm is comprised of the tradition about Peter's persecution and deliverance (12:6-
19). The function of this chiasm, according to Schmithals, is to link Paul
and Jerusalem closely, in that John Mark appears in Peter's orbit in the
chiastic centre (12:12) and in Paul's orbit in the chiastic conclusion
(12:25). In Schmithals's view, then, a historical interest drives Luke's literary structure.

    Despite its attraction, this explanation places structural weight on the
figure of John Mark in a manner that the text does not easily support.
The mention of John Mark at 12:12 is relatively insignificant within the
extensive narrative of 12:1-24.[34] Moreover, the same result (i.e., the link-

---

[32] A. Q. Morton and G. H. C. MacGregor, *The Structure of Luke and Acts*
(London: Hodder & Stoughton, 1964), 47.

[33] W. Schmithals, *Die Apostelgeschichte des Lukas* (Zürich: Theologischer
Verlag, 1982), 115.

[34] For a discussion of the "essentials of chiasm," see W. Brouwer, *The Literary
Development of John 13–17: A Chiastic Reading* (Atlanta: Society of Biblical
Literature, 2000), 29–45. A point made repeatedly there is that the "centre [of the
chiasm], rather than the beginning or ending, holds the interpretive key" (35; cf.
33 and 41). That John Mark falls within the long centre of Schmithals's chiastic

ing of Paul and Jerusalem through the figure of John Mark) could just as easily have been achieved by placing the Petrine material of 12:1-24 prior to the Antiochene material of 11:19-30. Moreover, while it is true that John Mark provides Luke with yet another line of connection between Paul and Jerusalem Christianity, it is not wholly clear that John Mark is a reliable enough figure in the Lukan narrative to enhance that connection by making him the structural glue for the whole of 11:27–12:25. If Schmithals is right to seek an explanation for Luke's intriguing structure in 11:27–12:25, his solution is not ultimately compelling.

A Third Explanation: Temporal Simultaneity

More compelling is a third solution, which has some currency among German interpreters especially. In this explanation, by splicing the story of the Antiochene collection so that its conclusion appears after the Petrine story of 12:1-24, Luke intended to suggest that Barnabas and Paul were in Jerusalem at the time of the Herodian persecution. The vague temporal indicator at the beginning of 12:1 ("about that time," κατ᾽ ἐκεῖνον δὲ τὸν καιρόν) permits this interpretation. According to Ernst Haenchen, a leading advocate of this view, in constructing the distinct stories in this way Luke demonstrates "wie eng die junge heidenchristliche Kirche Antiochias mit der Muttergemeinde verbunden ist."[35] This close association between the two communities is evidenced

---

proposal is clear; that John Mark holds the "interpretive key" for the whole of 11:27–12:25 is not.

[35] E. Haenchen, *Die Apostelgeschichte* (Göttingen: Vandenhoeck & Ruprecht, 1977), 361, from which the following quotations are also taken. Cf. also J. Roloff (*Die Apostelgeschichte* [Göttingen: Vandenhoeck & Ruprecht, 1988], 192; cf. 182): "Lukas will den Eindruck erwecken, als seien Barnabas und Paulus unmittelbar vor der Agrippa-Verfolgung nach Jerusalem gekommen und bis zu deren Ende dort geblieben . . . Er wollte zeigen, daß gerade in der Stunde der Not die Gemeinden von Jerusalem und Antiochia trotz aller ihrer Verschiedenheit eng zusammenstanden." Others accept that Luke portrays Barnabas and Saul as being in Jerusalem at the time of the Herodian persecution without any of the further implications that Haenchen draws out. For instance, Schmithals, *Die Apostelgeschichte des Lukas*, 119; J. Jervell, *Die Apostelgeschichte* (Göttingen: Vandenhoeck & Ruprecht, 1998), 337; H.-J. Klauck, *Magic and Paganism in Early Christianity: The World of the Acts of the Apostles* (trans. B. McNeil; Edinburgh: T&T Clark, 2000), 45. E. Trocmé (*Le "Livre des Actes" et l'histoire* [Paris: Presses Universitaires de France, 1957], 90–91) puts a somewhat different spin on things when he states that Luke placed 12:1-24 within the narrative of the Antiochene collection "peut-être pour rejecter la thèse selon laquelle Pierre avait quitté Jérusalem avant que Barnabas et Saul y fussent parvenus," although he does not state why the sequence of departures is necessarily important.

(1) in the Antiochene community's contribution towards alleviating the material impoverishment ("die materielle Not") of the Jerusalem community, and (2) in Antioch's participation in danger alongside the Jerusalem community ("die Gefahr mit der jerusalemischen Gemeinde"): "ihre Abgesandten, Barnabas und Paulus, weilen mitten in der Verfolgungszeit in Jerusalem!" Thus, by concluding the account of the Antiochene collection as late as 12:25, Luke binds together "das Ende wieder mit dem Anfang . . . und gibt damit der ganzen Komposition ihre erstaunliche Geschlossenheit."[36]

This is an intriguing interpretation, and one that falls within the orbit of Luke's concerns, since the connection between the two Christian communities is toward the top of his agenda. Nonetheless, this interpretation is not wholly compelling. While Luke's temporal indicators at 12:1 ("about that time") and 12:25 ("after completing their mission") are vague and therefore permit the kind of interpretation that Haenchen and others propose, it is precisely their vagueness that counts heavily against that interpretation. Luke is a master of transitional linkages of a variety of kinds, and when he wants to overlap two episodes temporally so that they are seen as having some simultaneity, he does so explicitly.

Consider, for example, what he does in the transition from the story of Paul and Silas in Beroea (17:10-15) to the story of Paul in Athens (17:16-34). The final verse of the first story places Paul in Athens: "Those who conducted Paul brought him as far as Athens, and after receiving instructions to have Silas and Timothy join him as soon as possible, they left him." The first verse of the second story begins by linking it to the first in a temporal overlap: "While Paul was waiting for them in Athens . . ." (ἐν δὲ ταῖς Ἀθήναις ἐκδεχομένου αὐτοὺς τοῦ Παύλου). Or consider Luke's transition in 19:1. Having recounted the Ephesian ministry of Apollos and his subsequent travel to Achaia in 18:24-28, Luke introduces Paul to the Ephesian scene beginning in 19:1 with the transitional phrase "While Apollos was in Corinth [i.e., in Achaia] . . ." (ἐν τῷ τὸν Ἀπολλῶ εἶναι ἐν Κορίνθῳ).

In view of these examples it would seem that, had Luke intended for his audience to envisage Barnabas and Paul in Jerusalem when the events of 12:1-24 occurred, we would expect him to have made this important point explicitly. Perhaps Luke would have said something along the lines of "While Barnabas and Saul were in Jerusalem (ἐν τῷ τὸν Βαρναβᾶν καὶ τὸν Σαῦλον εἶναι ἐν Ἰερουσαλήμ), Herod laid violent hands upon some who belonged to the church." Instead, by means of the ambiguous phrase "about that time" in 12:1, Luke leaves his audience with the impression that the two events have some temporal proximity, perhaps,

---

[36] Haenchen, *Die Apostelgeschichte*, 377.

but he does not go so far as to suggest their temporal overlap, as he does in other cases.

Moreover, if Luke expected his audience to read between the lines by temporally overlapping these two accounts in their imagination, he left no controls on the kind of imaginative reading that they could be permitted to devise. If Paul and Barnabas are to be seen as present in Jerusalem at the time of the Herodian persecution, readers could easily draw out implications that run contrary to Luke's agenda. So, one might well arrive at the conclusion that Paul had become a relatively insignificant figure by the time that he arrived in Jerusalem. After all, according to the Lukan account, Paul had previously been empowered by "the high priest and the whole council of elders" to act as their representative and instrument in the persecution of Christians (22:5; cf. 9:1-2; 26:10, 12). In Luke's view, Paul had enjoyed a high profile among the Jewish leadership in Jerusalem prior to his encounter with the risen Lord. So in 26:10 Paul speaks of his previous influence in Jerusalem to the extent that he is depicted as having a vote among the Jewish leaders.[37] What better for the Jewish leadership than to ensure that, upon Paul's return to Jerusalem, the former persecutor of stature and now prominent renegade became the target of a humiliating Herodian persecution. And the Acts narrative has already recounted how, on his first return to Jerusalem after his conversion, Paul was regarded as a significant figure to be removed from the scene: "He spoke and argued with the Hellenists; but they were attempting to kill him" (οἱ δὲ ἐπεχείρουν ἀνελεῖν αὐτόν, 9:29). This attempt on Paul's life replicated the one recounted earlier in 9:23 in which the Jews (i.e., Jewish leaders) whom Paul "confounded" in the Damascus synagogue "plotted to kill him" (συνεβουλεύσαντο οἱ Ἰουδαῖοι ἀνελεῖν αὐτόν). By the time Paul arrives in Jerusalem in 11:30 the Jewish leadership of Jerusalem and Damascus have already been united in their attempts to kill him on two occasions.

But, if Paul is really to be thought of as present in Jerusalem during the Herodian persecution, the Lukan account can be read as suggesting that Paul's stature had significantly diminished in the time since his previous visit to Jerusalem.[38] The one who was the target of enmity and persecution on his first visit is no longer significant enough to merit the same effort on his subsequent visit. So, seeing how the murder of the prominent apostle James was pleasing to "the Jews" (i.e., the Jewish lead-

[37] Does Luke suggest here that Paul was a member of the Sanhedrin, or at least had occasional influence on its decision making?

[38] We might imagine Paul hiding away from public notice in Jerusalem. But it is unlikely that this strategy could have been sustained for long, since news of Paul's arrival in Jerusalem would likely have leaked out.

ership in particular),[39] Herod Agrippa decides to turn his aggression against Peter, not Paul. Since Herod would have acted in a fashion that endeared him to the Jewish leadership, his selection of a next victim would have been calculated with their sentiments in mind. Since Herod's victim was Peter and not the newly arrived renegade Paul (accepting the Haenchen reconstruction of events momentarily), the clear implication is that Peter outstrips Paul in significance and profile in the eyes of the Jewish authorities in Jerusalem.[40]

It does not take a degree in social-scientific or anthropological interpretation to recognise the simple point made by Martin Hengel and Anna Maria Schwemer: "Agrippa could not have made an example of an insignificant member of the messianic sect."[41] Similarly it could be said that those who did not hold a high profile in the Christian movement would have naturally escaped Herod Agrippa's persecution. But if we are to envisage Paul, a former member of the Jewish leadership (as Luke depicts him), returning to Jerusalem and remaining there untouched during Agrippa's persecution of prominent Jewish Christians, then Luke has left his narrative unguarded from the conclusion that the Jewish leaders in Jerusalem no longer considered Paul to be a significant figure, despite the fact that he had escaped two earlier efforts by Jewish leaders to kill him (9:23, 29). A narrative of this kind is simply implausible. And even if Luke had intended to take his narrative along implausible lines, it is unthinkable that Luke would have jeopardised Paul's stature in this way in the paragraph just prior to the sixteen chapters in which Paul takes

---

[39] J. J. Kilallen ("Persecution in the Acts of the Apostles," in *Luke and Acts* [ed. G. O'Collins and G. Marconi; New York: Paulist Press, 1993], 143–60, esp. 148) rightly notes that it is "inconceivable that every Jew in Israel was concerned with Peter and James," but he identifies "the Jews" of 12:3 and 12:11 simply as "certain groups or strata of Jews" who "were becoming impatient with the continuous and insistent preaching of Jesus as messiah." Although Kilallen fails to say so, this must have been the Jewish leadership based in Jerusalem.

[40] It might be argued that this argument is fallacious since, in the events of 6:8–8:2, Stephen the deacon is martyred rather than Peter the apostle, suggesting that it is not always the senior figure that is the target of attack. But this envisaged argument is itself fallacious, since it was Stephen, not Peter or the other apostles, who "spoke blasphemous words" against the temple and the Law (6:11; cf. 6:13-14, 48-49). The situation in 6:8–8:2 is wholly different from that of Acts 12. Moreover, where the persecution described in 8:1 and 8:3 targeted Christians in general (probably including the apostles; see n. 73 below), the Herodian persecution of 12:1-5 targeted precisely Christian leaders in order to curry favour with the Jewish leadership among whom Paul had previously been numbered (according to Luke). Again, the two persecutions operate along different lines and rationales, undermining the counterargument envisaged here.

[41] Hengel and Schwemer, *Paul between Damascus and Antioch*, 247.

centre stage. To leave his narrative open to this eventuality would have been to compromise his own literary and theological goals.

Consequently, for both stylist and literary-theological reasons, the solution of Haenchen and others is not compelling as an explication of the placement of 12:1-24 in relation to 11:27-30 and 12:25. The same is the impression of Richard Bauckham, who writes that "Luke certainly does not mean that the events of 12:1-24 happened while Barnabas and Saul were in Jerusalem."[42] The Haenchen interpretation is one that, I suspect, Luke did not foresee as a possibility. Its merit lies in attempting to explain an apparently awkward structural construction, but it falters as a compelling explanation of that construction.

A Fourth Explanation: Temporal Reversal

The fourth solution to the narrative's curious structure in 11:27–12:25 sees 12:1-24 as a "flashback" that offers the audience an explanation for a feature of the narrative in 11:30. There it is said that Barnabas and Paul delivered the Antiochene collection to "the elders," a group previously unmentioned in the narrative but one that plays an important role in the narrative of Acts 13–28, being referred to there on six occasions in important developments of the storyline (15:2, 4, 6, 22–23; 16:4; 21:18). That Acts 12 might be called an explanatory flashback depends on the view that the events of Acts 12 (Agrippa's persecution of the Jerusalem church) historically precede the events of Acts 11:27-30 (the Antiochene collection for Jerusalem). This historical arrangement has for long been the consensus view. Only the actual dates for the two episodes remain debated. For my part, we can do little better than to observe the strong convergence of dates in the exemplary historical work of Rainer Riesner on the one hand and of Hengel and Schwemer on the other. Riesner dates Agrippa's persecution to the year 41 (or at the latest 42) CE and the Antiochene collection to somewhere between 42 and 45 CE.[43] Hengel

---

[42] Cf. R. J. Bauckham, "James and the Jerusalem Church," in *The Book of Acts in Its Palestinian Setting* (ed. R.J. Bauckham; Grand Rapids: Eerdmans, 1995), 433.

[43] R. Riesner, *Paul's Early Period: Chronology, Mission Strategy, Theology* (Grand Rapids: Eerdmans, 1998), 118–22 and 134–36 respectively. The earlier dating presumes that Agabus's prophecy was not concerned so much with an empire-wide "famine" per se, which occurred in the late 40s, but with local food shortages resulting in massive price increases that consequently would have meant that the poor could not afford even basic foodstuffs. Such localised situations were apparent throughout the 40s CE, and not simply the late 40s (see esp. Riesner, *Paul's Early Period*, 127–34). Jewish communities in Jerusalem would have been affected by them, owing also to the refusal of many Jews of Judaea to sow their autumn seed in 40 CE in reaction to Caligula's threat to establish a statue of himself in the Jerusalem temple (Josephus, *Life*, 2.200; *Ant.* 18.272).

and Schwemer date Agrippa's persecution to the year 43, and the Antiochene collection to somewhere in the years 44/45 CE.[44]

If the temporal location of Acts 11 and Acts 12 is to be reversed, it is possible to explain why Barnabas and Paul are said to deliver the Antiochene collection "to the elders" (11:30) rather than laying it "at the apostles' feet," which is where donations were placed previously in the narrative (4:37; 5:2). That is, "a major change"[45] in the leadership structures of Jerusalem Christianity had resulted from Agrippa's persecution, with James the son of Zebedee being martyred and Peter leaving the city (12:17). Little wonder, then, that the Antiochene delegation that arrived after these persecutions was met by "the elders,"[46] a new leadership group whom the audience has not heard of previously in the narrative.[47]

Historical reconstructions of this kind are eminently sensible and may well shed light on historical developments in nascent Christianity.[48] Moreover, this reconstruction offers a potential solution to the apparently

---

Moreover, 41/42 CE was a Sabbatical Year during which the production of food in Judaea was severely restricted. On "Acts and Food Shortages," see the article of the same name by B. W. Winter in *The Book of Acts in Its Graeco-Roman Setting* (ed. D. W. J. Gill and C. Gempf; Grand Rapids: Eerdmans, 1994), 59–78.

[44] Hengel and Schwemer, *Paul between Damascus and Antioch*, 257 and 243 respectively. Bauckham ("James and the Jerusalem Church," 433 n. 59) nonetheless offers the following caution: "The decision to send famine relief to Jerusalem (11:29) was based on Agabus's prediction of the famine (11:28), and so the visit of Barnabas and Saul to Jerusalem could have preceded the famine, even by some years," although he admits that "it would be more natural to assume that the narrative means it arrived not long before it was needed."

[45] Hengel and Schwemer, *Paul between Damascus and Antioch*, 464 n. 1264.

[46] See, e.g., Hengel and Schwemer, *Paul between Damascus and Antioch*, 245.

[47] According to Hengel and Schwemer (*Paul between Damascus and Antioch*, 256), in Acts 11:27–12:24 we see all the key ingredients of a shift of power in Jerusalem Christianity: "[t]he execution of James the son of Zebedee, Peter's flight from the territory ruled over by Agrippa I, and the transfer of the leadership of the Jerusalem community from Peter and the apostles to James and the elders." Cf. W. Pratscher, *Der Herrenbruder Jakobus und die Jacobustradition* (Göttingen: Vandenhoeck & Ruprecht, 1987), 74–77; and especially Bauckham, "James and Jerusalem Church," 427–41. A different view has been offered by Painter, *Just James*, 44.

[48] Moreover, from reconstructions of this sort the historian might go on to draw causal lines between the events of Acts 12 and the later events of Acts 11 that are not explicit in Luke's narrative. For instance, Hengel and Schwemer (*Paul between Damascus and Antioch*, 243 and 251) consider the possibility that the persecution of Agrippa against the leadership of the Jerusalem church was a contributing factor in motivating the later Antiochene collection, since the Jerusalem community was depleted not only of material resources but also of corporate leadership.

awkward insertion of the Petrine material (12:1-24) within the story of the Antiochene collection that currently enfolds that material (11:27-30/12:25). For instance, Hengel and Schwemer speak of Luke needing to offer "an explanatory 'recapitulation'" so that his readers might "catch up" with the historical background necessary to understand the reference to the elders in 11:30. The insertion of the Petrine tradition just after 11:30 and before 12:25 allows for this explanatory flashback.

But even if the events of 12:1-24 historically precede those of 11:27-30 (which I do not intend to dispute), it is nonetheless questionable whether Luke intended 12:1-24 to function as a flashback to explain the reference to "the elders" in 11:30. That the elders rose to prominence in the wake of a power vacuum within the Jerusalem *apostleship* is one interpretative option, but it is not the only one and probably not the most natural one within the context of the Lukan narrative. The view that Acts 12 depicts "the disintegration of the Twelve" apostles[49] by means of their martyrdom and/or exodus from Jerusalem is not well rooted in the text itself. We hear only of a persecution of James and the arrest of Peter; nothing else. And Acts 15 speaks of Christian apostles being in Jerusalem (15:2, 4, 6, 22-23; cf. 16:4) without suggesting that they have returned from elsewhere (although that is the implication in Peter's case [cf. 12:17 and 15:7]).

A different, and perhaps more likely, interpretation of the identity of the elders arises from within the narrative. Luke's audience might well have imagined that the Antiochene donation was handed over to the elders simply because they, at that time, administered the corporate resources of the Jerusalem community. In the course of the Acts narrative, the Lukan audience has watched that responsibility being administered first by the apostles themselves in 4:36-37 and 5:1-11, and then being divested to the seven deacons specifically appointed for this task in 6:1-7. But the audience has also been told in 7:54–8:2 that Stephen, one of those seven deacons, was martyred. And in 8:1 the audience hears that an ensuing persecution caused all except the apostles to flee from Jerusalem. The implication within the Lukan narrative is clear: the administrative position that the deacons had previously filled was left vacant in the wake of Stephen's martyrdom and the departure of the other six. When the audience hears in 11:30 that the *elders* received the Antiochene donation, the most immediate interpretation is that they are undertaking the position left vacant by the departure of the financial administrators of the community, as described in 8:1. There is no reason to think of them assuming power in the wake of an *apostolic* power vacuum in Jerusalem (which is not what is described in 12:1-24 anyway). As inheritors of the administrative duties previously performed by the

---

[49] Allen, *The Death of Herod*, 135.

apostles and then the deacons, the elders are the ones rightly placed to accept the Antiochene donation.

This interpretation of the identity of the elders makes good sense of other features of the Lukan narrative. Are we to imagine, for instance, that the apostles, who had previously divested themselves of this responsibility, had taken the role back upon themselves at the same time that they are scurrying off to other places for significant blocks of time? Peter and John are sent to Samaria (8:14-25); Peter is said to have gone "here and there among all the believers" (9:30), including places "throughout Judea, Galilee and Samaria" (9:31), specifically Lydda (9:32-35), Joppa (9:36-43), and Caesarea (10:1-48). If the administration of the community's resources had proved an onerous task in the earliest period of the Christian movement, the apostles' later responsibilities in various places outside of Jerusalem must have made it absolutely imperative that oversight of the community's resources be given to others once the deaconate of seven had been depleted/disbanded (as implied in 8:1).[50] That is, the implication most immediately presenting itself from the narrative is that the elders of 11:30 are those who filled the administrative vacuum left behind by the seven deacons, and who therefore are the ones rightly placed to accept the Antiochene donation.

It is arguable, of course, that Luke intended to counter precisely this most natural interpretation, and so he included Acts 12 as a correctional explanatory flashback—a flashback that explains the origins of the elders not in relation to the dispersed deacons but in relation to an apostolic power vacuum left behind after the Herodian persecution. But it is not wholly clear that Luke expects his audience to envisage the formation of an apostolic power vacuum of this kind, since that is not what is depicted in 12:1-24. Moreover, Luke does not present Acts 12 as an explanatory flashback in explicit terms. If Luke intended his audience to invert the order of 11:27-30/12:25 and 12:1-24, this should either be evident from the narrative itself or be explained by means of strong temporal indicators. But Luke offers his audience neither. The only other occasion in Acts where an explanatory flashback appears is in 1:18-19. There the audience can easily recognise the flashback effect without requiring the assistance of temporal indicators. So Judas' final initiative is described in a literary context in which Judas has already died; the flashback effect is perceptible without the assistance of strong temporal indicators. But the

---

[50] The departure of "all" Christians in 8:1 is clearly hyperbolic, as 8:3 confirms. Paul's persecution of Christians in 8:3 seems to be a wiping-up operation to root out the Christian movement and does nothing to suggest that the remaining deacons continued to reside in Jerusalem. Presumably Luke would have envisaged the elders arising from the constituency described in 8:3, no matter how we are to envisage their rise to prominence.

narrative of Acts 11–12 is different. There Luke does offer temporal indicators, but they are vague and ambiguous and do little to suggest that the events that follow them are to be temporally inverted. Luke writes simply "in those days" (ἐν ταύταις ταῖς ἡμέραις) in 11:27 and "about that time" (κατ᾽ ἐκεῖνον τὸν καιρόν) in 12:1.[51] These are not the temporal indicators expected of an explanatory flashback.

We have seen, then, that mention of the elders in 11:30 does not require an explanatory flashback in order to be interpreted within the confines of the Lukan narrative and that the transitions at both 11:27 and 12:1 are poorly qualified to support an explanatory flashback interpretation. Consequently, even if historical research reveals that the events of 11:27-30 are likely to have followed those of 12:1-24, it is unlikely that Acts 12 functions as an explanatory flashback. That is, Luke probably did not expect his audience to invert the events of 11:27-30/12:25 and 12:1-24 in their imagination in order to understand the origins of the elders mentioned in 11:30 in relation to an apostolic power vacuum left behind in the wake of the Herodian persecution. The "apostolic power vacuum" interpretation of the origins of the elders seems to play no role in Luke's literary project.

I have suggested that Luke did not expect his audience (1) to by-pass a natural interpretation of the elders' origins, (2) to invert the order of events of his narrative, and consequently (3) to devise an explanation of the origins of the elders. But even if he did expect these things of his audience, we are still no closer to explaining why he chose to structure the text in the surprising way that he did. Precisely the same explanatory function could have been achieved by placing the account of Acts 12 prior to the events of 11:19-30. This envisaged placement would have no loss of narrative effect and could have potential narrative gains (see below). As Richard Bauckham notes, the traditions of Acts 12 "could have been inserted between 11:18 and 11:19, appropriately completing the account of Peter's leadership of the Jerusalem church before proceeding to the events at Antioch that lead directly to the first missionary journey of Paul and Barnabas."[52] In the unlikely event that Luke expected

---

[51] The phrase κατ᾽ ἐκεῖνον τὸν καιρόν of 12:1 is paralleled in 19:23 (κατὰ τὸν καιρὸν ἐκεῖνον) where it is again temporally ambiguous. Only Luke's transition statement in 20:1 ("after the uproar had ceased," μετὰ δὲ τὸ παύσασθαι τὸν θόρυβον) indicates that the events of 19:23-41 were subsequent to earlier Ephesian episodes.

[52] Bauckham, "James and the Jerusalem Church," 433–34 (and cf. also his n. 62). Bauckham suggests that Luke constructed things the way he did in order "to emphasise the links between Jerusalem and Antioch." But Luke's interest in links between these two cities could have been facilitated just as easily if 12:1-24 had been structured to follow immediately after 11:18.

Acts 12 to explain the identity of the elders of 11:30, we would still need to explain why he chose one of at least two structural possibilities. The explanatory flashback theory, then, provides no solution to the text's literary structure. It seems simply that Luke wanted his audience to imagine the events of 11:27-30 and 12:1-24 as falling within a certain broad time period, but he did not necessarily expect his audience to order these events in any particular fashion.

The Proposed Explanation: Chain-Link Interlock

The solution to the intriguing structure of 11:27–12:25 that is proposed here involves, of course, text-unit interlock as its basis. The surprising interruption of the story of Barnabas and Paul in 11:27-30/12:25 by a story about Peter in 12:1-24 is not the result of some historical interest on Luke's part (as in the four explanations considered above); it is simply the result of Luke's concern to establish a literary transition from the Petrine to the Pauline cycle of his narrative.

It has already been shown that the story narrated in 11:27-30/12:25 serves a strong anticipatory function in the transition to the new text-unit that begins in 13:1. Before that text-unit commences, however, a story about the central protagonist of the first twelve chapters is recounted in 12:1-24. Luke Johnson rightly characterises the account in 12:1-24 as a moment in which "Luke pauses to look for a last time at events concerning the Church in Jerusalem and especially concerning the figure who until now had so dominated the story that it could fairly have been called 'The Acts of Peter.'"[53] Since Herod's persecution results in Peter going to another place (12:17), the closure of the Petrine cycle is facilitated, with Peter dropping out of the narrative almost completely, except for a brief reappearance in 15:7-11.

Other features within 12:1-24 also act as indicators of text-unit closure. So, the story of Herod's persecution of the Jerusalem leadership is an appropriate one to round off the narratives of Acts 1–12. As Wesley Allen demonstrates, "the Lukan narrator presents persecution as increasing" within Acts 1–12, beginning with a simple rebuke of Peter and John as apostolic representatives in 4:1-22 and progressing to the eventual martyrdom of James and the persecution of Peter in Acts 12. In this way, Herod's persecution in Acts 12 "marks the climax of increasing persecution during this portion of the narrative [i.e., Acts 1–12]."[54] Moreover,

---

[53] Johnson, *The Acts of the Apostles*, 216–17. Cf. D. T. N. Parry ("Release of the Captives: Reflections on Acts 12," in *Luke's Literary Achievement: Collected Essays* [ed. C. M. Tuckett; Sheffield: Sheffield Academic, 1995], 156–64, esp. 158): Acts 12 "provides a fitting final Acts story about Peter."

[54] Allen, *The Death of Herod*, 135.

the aftermath of James' martyrdom itself indicates that the end of an era has been reached. As Gerd Lüdemann states, "Die Tatsache, daß für den Zebedaiden Jakobus keine Ersatzwahl stattfindet, zeigt, daß, heilsgeschichtlich gesehen, die Phase der Urgemeinde vorüber ist."[55] Whereas the apostolic vacancy that resulted from Judas' death had been filled in Acts 1, the vacancy that resulted from James' martyrdom was not filled, with this lacuna in the narration of Acts 12 indicating that the earliest apostolic period had come to a close.

Consequently, Acts 12:1-24 serves the function of text-unit closure (1) by explaining why the one who acted as the central protagonist in the narrative's first twelve chapters disappears (for the most part) thereafter, (2) by bringing the motif of opposition to the twelve to its zenith, and (3) by indicating that the period of earliest apostolic Christianity no longer continues.

It is clear, then, that at the text-unit boundary just prior to Acts 13, Luke's narrative shifts its focus from Barnabas and Paul (esp. 11:27-30), back to Peter (12:1-24) and then back again to Barnabas and Paul (12:25ff.). Since, regardless of their other purposes, the various parts serve the dual roles of text-unit closure (12:1-24) and transition (11:27-30/12:25), what we have here is chain-link construction at precisely the point where the Petrine material hands off to the Pauline material.

TEXT-UNIT "A"	INTERLOCKED "b" (anticipatory)	INTERLOCKED "a" (retrospective)	TEXT-UNIT "B"
to Acts 12:25	Acts 11:27-30/12:25	Acts 12:1-24	Acts 13:1ff.

In order to test the force of this suggestion, it is helpful to imagine how an "unlinked" structural arrangement would have affected the narrative. As Barrett notes, with the exception of Acts 12:25, Acts 12 "is more easily detachable from the main thread of narrative in Acts than any other" section in Acts.[56] In accordance with this observation, I have already raised an envisaged scenario in which 12:1-24 might have been placed just prior to the Antiochene narrative that begins in 11:19. Six potential advantages of such an arrangement present themselves.

First, the unlinked arrangement would have permitted the Antiochene traditions of 11:19-30 to have flowed naturally and directly into the Antiochene traditional material of Acts 13-15 without interruption by traditional Petrine material.[57]

---

[55] Lüdemann, *Das frühe Christentum nach den Traditionen der Apostelgeschichte*, 146.

[56] Barrett, *The Acts of the Apostles*, 568.

[57] If Luke inherited material in Acts 11 and 13-15 from the Antiochene

Second, in similar fashion, an unlinked arrangement would also have kept the Petrine material together in a tight block, with the Petrine narratives of 9:32–11:18 being followed immediately by the Petrine narrative that forms 12:1-24. Interpreters often note that Luke has a preference for grouping related material together in textual blocks. In the "linked" text as we currently have it, however, the opportunity to group Petrine material together has not been taken.[58]

Third, the unlinked arrangement would imply a causal relationship between the controversial "law-free" mission to gentiles sponsored by Peter in Acts 10–11 and Herod's persecution against Peter and James in Acts 12. The fact that even "circumcised believers" of 11:2 are said to have criticised Peter for eating with gentiles (11:3) and for breaking down the "distinction between them and us" (11:12) leads naturally to the persecution of Peter by Herod in Acts 12 in order to please "the Jews" (12:3). In the linked text as we have it, however, while this causal connection can still be made, it is less obvious than would have been the case in the envisaged unlinked version.

Fourth, this causal connection between Peter's acceptance of a law-free mission and his persecution by Agrippa in an attempt to curry favour with the Jews would have laid strong foundations for subsequent chapters of Acts. There the audience discovers that Jewish opposition to Paul arises not so much with regard to his Christology or any other theological tenet of belief, but in relation to his law-free mission and its attraction to gentiles.[59] In the overlapped text as we have it, the relationship between Peter and Paul on this score is harder to recognise than it otherwise might be in a hypothetical unlinked text.

Fifth, the unlinked arrangement would have avoided the otherwise awkward postponement of the continuation of the Antiochene collection story. In the envisaged unlinked version, 12:25 would have followed immediately on what is currently 11:30.

Christian community, he has introduced the non-Antiochene Petrine material of 12:1-24 into that inherited Antiochene tradition.

[58] Perhaps all this Petrine material was originally grouped in a single block and has subsequently been disrupted by Luke's insertion of Antiochene material in 11:19-30. This is the view of Ben Witherington (*The Acts of the Apostles: A Socio-Rhetorical Commentary* [Grand Rapids: Eerdmans, 1998], 77), who speaks of the Petrine block of material having originally consisted of 9:32–11:18 and 12:1-24, with Luke having "interrupted this block of material with an Antioch block found in 11:19-30."

[59] See, for instance, B. W. Longenecker, "Moral Character and Divine Generosity: Acts 13:13-52 and the Narrative Dynamics of Luke-Acts," in *New Testament Greek and Exegesis: A Festschrift for Gerald F. Hawthorne* (ed. A. M. Donaldson and T. B. Sailors; Grand Rapids: Eerdmans, 2003), 141–64, esp. 143–48.

Sixth, the unlinked arrangement might have contributed to ensuring a more satisfactory and promising conclusion to the Peter story. That is, in the current arrangement, when Peter is threatened with death he simply is said to go "to another place" (12:17). Had Acts 12:1-24 followed on from Acts 10:1–11:18, the Lukan audience would quite naturally imagine that this other place would be somewhere like Joppa, where he had just been, or in some other city carrying out a Christian mission, as in 10:1–11:18. But when the two Peter stories are separated, as in the received text, Peter's going to another place is not as naturally linked to a further mission in cities beyond Jerusalem.[60]

It seems evident, then, that a handful of narrative advantages might have yielded themselves had Luke chosen an unlinked arrangement at this point. That these advantages were foresworn by Luke suggests that he preferred the linked arrangement for other advantages. It is suggested here that rhetorical advantages pertaining to chain-link transitions in oral/aural contexts outweighed the six potential advantages of an unlinked arrangement outlined above. For this suggestion to have its intended force, however, it must also be considered whether the proposed unlinked arrangement of the narrative might have been accompanied by its own narrative complications. In my view, the proposed unlinked sequence of material would have caused no complications to the narrative.

For instance, it is frequently observed that, in the transitional section of Acts 11–12, Luke "intends to convince his audience that a legitimate succession took place"[61] from Peter to James in leadership of the Jerusalem church (cf. 12:17)[62] and to Paul in leadership of the gentile ministry.[63] But the same effect could have been just as easily achieved in

[60] I take the ambiguous subject of 12:19 to be Herod, not Peter (contra NRSV). This is the consensus view, so much so that the point is barely noted in the commentaries. Cf. Barrett, *The Acts of the Aposles*, 588; R. Pesch, *Die Apostelgeschichte* (Neukirchen-Vluyn:Neukirchener Verlag, 1986), 1:367; Jervell, *Die Apostelgeschichte*, 336.

[61] R. W. Wall, "Successors to "the Twelve" according to Acts 12:1-17," *CBQ* 53 (1991): 628–43. Cf. also Parry, "Release of the Captives," 158; Bauckham, "James and the Jerusalem Church," 435.

[62] See especially Allen, *The Death of Herod*, 130–36, where Acts 12:1-24 is shown to have significance for the chapters that follow it. Cf. also Barrett, *The Acts of the Apostles*, 572–73. While this is true, the structural centre of gravity for this passage leans primarily to the chapters that precede it, as has been indicated here. It would not be surprising if 12:1-24 incorporates some structural polyvalence, as discussed in §4.5.

[63] So also, Peter reappears in Acts 15 largely to confirm that the mission to the gentiles that originated under his oversight is now capably overseen by Paul and Barnabas.

an unlinked version as in the extant "linked" version, with the point simply being made earlier in the narrative.

Furthermore, the "linked" arrangement of the text offers a short profile of John Mark in 12:12 prior to his mention in 12:25. But obviously the same would be the case in the envisaged unlinked arrangement, which has no advantage over the "linked" version as it currently stands.

Two critical observations have therefore presented themselves: (1) an envisaged unlinked sequence in Acts 11–12 would not have posed any narrative complications, and (2) the unlinked sequence might well have had significant benefits for the narrative in several ways (six being suggested above). In light of these observations, it seems best to conclude that Luke preferred the "linked" sequence for an overwhelmingly strong reason. That reason, I suggest, is that he was committed to constructing a chain-link interlock at this point in the narrative in order to signal a transition from the Petrine to the Pauline material. Luke, it seems, considered the linked interlocked transition to carry substantial transitional weight. This should not be surprising in view of the fact that, as we have already seen (§9.1 above; cf. §10.1 below), Luke made use of chain-link construction in the most significant transition of his two-volume monograph—at the end of his Gospel and the beginning of Acts, precisely the point where the narrative shifts its focus from Jesus (the central character of the Gospel narrative) to Jesus' followers (central characters in the narrative of Acts). Luke's second volume also has a noticeable shift in focus at its approximate midpoint, and it is precisely at this transition point that a chain-link construction appears once again. In each case chain-link interlock seems to serve the purpose of narrative transition in a way that accords precisely with Lucian and Quintilian's view about how narrative transitions should be constructed in historical writing.

It might be argued that, since the extent of material considered here is relatively large, the case for seeing chain-link interlock just prior to Acts 13 is thereby undermined. But this objection needs to be put in its proper perspective. First, the tradition of 11:27-30/12:25 that serves an anticipatory role to Acts 13 is comprised of only five verses, and as such is not in and of itself inordinate in extent. Second, although the Petrine story of 12:1-23 (with a Lukan conclusion in 12:24) is longer than the retrospective component in other chain-link interlocks, this is simply because Luke is making use of traditional material that, evidently, he chose not to abbreviate. This fact alone explains the length of the retrospective component of the chain-link interlock. Third, other Lukan passages that are comprised of chain-link interlock evidence precisely the same character: a relatively brief anticipatory component is followed by a much more extensive retrospective component. So, as was shown above (§9.1), the three anticipatory verses of Luke 24:47-49 are followed by twelve to sixteen retrospective verses (Acts 1:1-12, with Luke 24:50-53). Similarly, as will be shown below (§9.4), the two anticipatory verses of Acts 19:21-22 are followed by a further retrospective component of nineteen verses (19:23-41). In each of these cases, the retrospective components are likely to be comprised of traditional material that Luke preserves while simultaneously using that material in an interlocked transition that, consequently, extends to greater lengths than would otherwise be the case. Fourth, the interlock of Acts 11:27–12:25 is comprised of 557 Greek words, virtually identical in extent to the strong interlock in the final form of John 12:20-50 (studied above in §8.1–§8.4), which is comprised of 560 Greek words. Lengthy chain-link interlocks therefore are not beyond the pale for authors of this study, not least those for who made use of traditional materials as the components of the interlock.

The view that a chain-link construction underlies Acts 11:27–12:25 offers a solution to the somewhat awkward narrative placement of 12:25—a solution that is free from the weaknesses of the solutions considered above. This solution has no historical component but operates wholly on the basis of rhetorical considerations concerning the artistic flow of the narrative and the importance of transitions. In this solution, Luke is seen simply to have reserved the conclusion of the Antiochene collection story for the very end of the text unit (i.e., 12:25)[64] in order to draw further attention to the fact that a text-unit transition is underway. That is, he has deemed it necessary, perhaps in the light of the extent of the transition, to reinforce the transition by allowing the anticipatory gestures of 12:25 to come into play just prior to 13:1. In this way, the anticipatory effects of 12:25 (re)activate the anticipatory effects of 11:27-30 to which 12:25 is organically related, thereby placing the whole of 11:27–12:25 in the role of transitional material, composed of both anticipatory and retrospective gestures.

Consequently Acts 12:25 assists the interlocked transition by adding transitional force just prior to 13:1. Luke might have considered the concentrated focus on events in Jerusalem in Acts 12 to have required a delay in the conclusion of the Antioch material of 11:27-30, so that the focus can shift back to Antioch at the end of Acts 12 (i.e., 12:25), from where the action of Acts 13ff. begins. In addition, he might have thought this combination of transitional features to have been necessary since an alternation between Paul and Peter has already appeared at an earlier

---

[64] The same technique is evident in Luke's reservation of the end of the Stephen story until Acts 8:2 instead of 8:1. The difference is that the postponement of the conclusion of the Stephen story until 8:2 allows the chain-link interlock to be created, whereas the postponement of the conclusion of the Antiochene collection story until 12:25 (re)activates the force of the chain-link overlap in 11:27–12:24.

point in Luke's narrative, with 9:1-31 focussing on Paul and 9:32–11:18 focussing on Peter.[65] By compounding transitional devises just prior to 13:1, Luke is signalling to his audience that this alternating pattern, which has twice made an appearance in the narrative (9:1-31, with 9:32–11:18; and 11:25-30 with 12:1-24) terminates at this point. The somewhat surprising continuation of the Antiochene collection story in 12:25 alerts the audience to the fact that something new is happening. These expectations are fulfilled in the narrative that follows, which, unlike the earlier chapters of Acts 9–12, has no alternation between Paul and Peter. The transition that precedes Acts 13 is, then, not like the transition between the earlier Petrine and Pauline episodes (i.e., 9:31-32). Instead, it is a transition terminating the alternation between Peter and Paul that has characterised the four chapters prior to Acts 13.

In light of this, it seems that Luke took a variety of precautions to ensure that the transition to Acts 13 was clearly evident to his audience. His decision to compose the narrative in a linked as opposed to an unlinked fashion testifies to this, as does his somewhat surprising placement of the material in 12:25 that supports the interlock.

§9.3   The Chain-Link Interlock in Acts 8:1b-3

If chain-link interlock is evident at the midpoint of Luke's two volumes (Luke 24 and Acts 1) and at the midpoint of Luke's second volume (Acts 11–13), it is also evident at the approximate midpoint of the first half of Acts. There the Jerusalem narrative of Acts 1–7 concludes with the account of Stephen, prior to handing off to a new narrative focus at Acts 8.

Luke's account of Stephen's ministry concludes in the consecutive verses Acts 7:60 and 8:1a with two references to Stephen's death (i.e., he "fell asleep" [ἐκοιμήθη]; "his killing" [τῇ ἀναιρέσει αὐτοῦ]). Acts 8:2 then brings the Stephen material to a close: "Devout men buried Stephen and made loud lamentation over him." But between the reference to Stephen's death and his burial a full sentence appears that refers to things outside the Stephen account: "That day a severe persecution began against the church in Jerusalem, and all except the apostles were scattered (διεσπάρησαν) throughout the countryside of Judaea and Samaria." This sentence of Acts 8:1b introduces 8:4: "Now those who were scattered [διασπαρέντες] went from place to place, proclaiming the word." Acts 8:4 itself serves as the introduction to the account of missionary activity in Samaria (8:5-25)[66] and beyond (8:26-40)—both sections focussing pri-

---

[65] See also §3.3, where alternation of this sort was noted as a common feature in the Graeco-Roman world.

[66] F. S. Spencer (*The Portrait of Philip in Acts: A Study of Roles and Relations* [Sheffield: Sheffield Academic Press, 1992], 26–27) notes that "Luke clearly cor-

marily on Philip, along with Peter and John (8:14-25), all of whom serve as apostolic models for the non-apostles who had been scattered but who preached "throughout the region of Judaea and Samaria" (8:1). Consequently, the material of Acts 7 and Acts 8 respectively overlaps in these transitional verses, with the account of Acts 7 having its closure in 8:2, and the account of Acts 8 having its broad starting point in a new situation introduced in 8:1b. The apparent awkwardness of the transition at a narrative level is evident especially in the placement of 8:2. As Barrett notes, it is "suprising that Luke should allow this verse to separate vv. 1b and 3."[67] (Or, alternatively, one might say that it is surprising that Luke should allow 8:1b to separate 8:1a and 8:2.)

If a chain-link interlock is evident in the early verses of Acts 8, assisting in the transition from the Stephen to the Philip narratives, those verses also indicate that Luke has introduced a multiple interlock at this point in his narrative. We have not had reason to consider this kind of construction previously, but the complexity of Luke's narrative indicates that a multiplication of chain-link construction occurs at precisely this point.

This additional dimension of the chain-link transition revolves in the first instance around the figure of Saul and links Acts 9 to this textual intersection. Luke introduces Saul for the first time in Acts 7:58, where he is said to have been "a young man" before whom those stoning Stephen laid their coats. Three verses later (8:1a) we are told that Saul consented to Stephen's death. Then in 8:3 we are told that Saul himself began persecuting the church, "ravaging" it "by entering house after house: dragging off both men and women, he committed them to prison." The next time we hear of Saul is in Acts 9, where the narrative begun in 8:3 is expanded upon: "Meanwhile, Saul, still breathing threats and murder against the disciples of the Lord . . ." (9:1).[68] It is possible, of

---

dons off Acts 8.4-25 as a single literary unit by a favourite *inclusio* technique involving vv. 4-5 and 25," referring especially to themes of proclamation, the word, and Samaria.

[67] Barrett, *The Acts of the Apostles*, 389. Cf. his comments on 391: "The verse interrupts the connection between vv. 1 and 3." He suggests that the verse "may be Luke's insertion of what seemed a suitable close for his account of Stephen" (392), but this only begs the question as to why Luke would place the conclusion at this point in the narrative.

[68] K. Löning (*Die Saulustradition in der Apostelgeschichte* [Münster: Aschendorff, 1973], 25) is probably right to speak of Luke himself having brought together the Saul and Stephen traditions. E. Richard (*Acts 6:1–8:4: The Author's Method of Composition* [Missoula: Scholars Press, 1978], 303) counters this view by pointing to Acts 22:19-20 where Paul himself makes the connection: but Richard's is a weak case since the Paul that speaks there is himself a Lukan construct.

course, to see the description of Saul's persecution of the church in 8:3 as simply an additional conclusion to the stoning of Stephen, with the first conclusion being the mention of Stephen's burial in 8:2. In this case, both 8:2 and 8:3 might be seen as conclusions to Acts 7, with Saul's persecution of the church belonging to an earlier text unit as a fitting climax to the stoning of Stephen. But since the temporal location of Saul's persecution as recorded in 8:3 corresponds to the temporal location of 8:1b (i.e., they both arise after Stephen's martyrdom), 8:3 has forward momentum within the text and links itself not to the material in Acts 8 but, in this case, to that in Acts 9. So in the estimate of Hengel and Schwemer, for instance, the Philip narrative "interrupts the sequence between 8:3 and 9.1."[69]

Instead of speaking of one pericope "interrupting" the other, however, it is arguable that Luke employs a complex chain-link construction in the transition material of Acts 8:1-3, with that chain link forming the transitional springboard to both 8:4-25 and 9:1-31. Luke uses the martyrdom of Stephen in Acts 7 as the pivot point to discuss two further features: (1) the expansion of the proclamation of the gospel, as recorded initially in Acts 8, and (2) the expansion of persecution against the church, as recorded in relation to Saul's own persecutions. Ironically, even the latter (i.e., persecution) results in the former (i.e., expansion): that is, in this case the persecutor *par excellence* becomes the proclaimer— i.e., the proclaimer *par excellence*, as the second half of Acts illustrates.

TEXT-UNIT "A"	INTERLOCKED "b" (anticipatory)	INTERLOCKED "a" (retrospective)	TEXT-UNIT "B"
Acts 1:1–8:3	Acts 8:1b, 3	Acts 8:2	Acts 8:4–12:25

But the complexity of Luke's transition has a further dimension to it, since 11:19 is also structurally related to the chain link at the transitional junction in 8:1-3. We have already seen how 8:1b and 8:4 reinforce each

---

[69] Hengel and Schwemer, *Paul between Damascus and Antioch*, 466 n. 1276. Johnson (*The Acts of the Apostles*, 166) makes the interesting observation that by inserting Acts 8:4-40 between the accounts of Paul in 8:1-3 and 9:1ff., Luke "accomplished two things: first, he prepared the reader to imagine Christians existing in other places, so that without ever telling us about a mission to Damascus, we can picture Saul going to find some there; second, he allowed some time to elapse so that it makes sense for Saul to seek new territories for persecution beyond Jerusalem. When we therefore read in 9:1 that Saul was 'still breathing threat and murder,' we find no difficulty in picking up the story just as Luke intended."

other. In Acts 8:1b the audience hears of "a severe persecution" (διωγμὸς μέγας) that arose and caused "all except the apostles" to be "scattered (διεσπάρησαν) throughout the countryside of Judaea and Samaria." This material relates to 8:4, the introductory verse of the Philip narrative: "Now those who were scattered (διασπαρέντες) went from place to place (διῆλθον), proclaiming the word (εὐαγγελιζόμενοι τὸν λόγον)." In a similar fashion to 8:4, Acts 11:19 also links the material that follows it to 8:1b. So 11:19 mentions "those who were scattered (οἱ διασπαρέντες)[70] because of the persecution (ἀπὸ τῆς θλίψεως) that arose over Stephen," the result being that they "went from place to place" (διῆλθον) and "spoke the word" (λαλοῦντες τὸν λόγον). Acts 8:1b has already introduced the motif of the spread of Christian leaders through "Judaea and Samaria" because of the post-Stephen persecution, and in 11:19 we are told that churches "as far as Phoenicia and Cyprus and Antioch" were founded as a consequence of the same persecution. In particular, it is the church at Antioch that takes pride of place throughout 11:20-30, introduced by 11:19. And, as was demonstrated above, with the story of the Antiochene collection in 11:27-30 we are brought to the point of yet another chain-link construction.

Throughout Acts 8–12, then, we see Luke setting out a variety of important scenarios in the wake of Stephen's death and linking those scenarios by means of chain-link construction to the post-martyrdom developments that are introduced in 8:1b. With the larger narrative sweep of Acts 8–12 in view, the Stephen material of 6:8–8:2 is linked by means of the thematic overlap in 8:1b with later sections throughout Acts 8–12. First, 8:1b is expanded in the Philip panel of 8:4-40, then in the Saul panel of 9:1-31 (itself an expansion of 8:3, which itself expands 8:1b), and finally in the Antioch panel of 11:19-30.[71] With the Philip, Saul and Antiochene panels being structurally hinged to the chain link evident in the early verses of Acts 8, virtually the whole of Acts 8–12 is lashed together as a single text unit.

The only material in Acts 8–12 that is not connected to the chain-link hinge are the Petrine narratives of Acts 9:32–11:18 and 12:1-24.

---

[70] This word appears in Acts only at 8:1, 4, and 11:19.

[71] F. Ó Fearghail (*The Introduction to Luke-Acts: A Study of the Role of Lk 1,1–4,44 in the Composition of Luke's Two-Volume Work* [Rome: Editrice Pontificio Instituto Biblico, 1991], 77 n. 197) writes: "Acts 8,1b-3 represents a good example of the overlapping, ἀνακεκρᾶσθαι κατὰ τὰ ἄκρα, recommended by Lucian (*Hist.* §55): 8,2 concludes the story of Stephen; 8,1bc anticipates that of Philip in 8,4-40; 8,3 anticipates 9,1-2 on Saul; the writer thus achieves a certain interweaving of matter, συμπεριπλοκὴ τῶν πραγμάτων, in keeping with Lucian's advice." This observation requires only the additional mention of the link to the material in 11:19-30.

Although not directly incorporated into the chain-link interlock of Acts 8, these Petrine traditions do not upset what otherwise emerges as the unifying thematic thread throughout Acts 8–12, as revealed primarily in the chain-link connectives. That thread is the motif of the "scattering" of Christian leaders throughout the Mediterranean basin because of the persecution against the Christian movement.[72] In fact, the Petrine section of 12:1-24 plays a role in the development of precisely that narrative strand. Although the "thematic header" of 8:1b indicates that the Jerusalem apostles alone remained in Jerusalem in the wake of the persecution that arose, the audience watches as Peter is, in effect, "scattered" to another place (cf. 12:17), in parallel with what the audience is told about non-apostolic Christian leaders in 8:4 and 11:19. Consequently it can be said that a plot line that begins in 8:1b with the clause "all were scattered . . . except the apostles" comes to a climax in the Peter material of 12:1-24; whereas the persecution of 8:1 did not result in the diminution of the Jerusalem apostolate,[73] the persecution of 12:1-24 did, at least with regard to James and Peter. Since the first "non-linked" Petrine narrative (i.e., 9:32–11:18) provides the most obvious background for the continuation and rise of resentment against Peter among the non-Christian Jewish leadership (as implied in 12:1-3),[74] so that narrative, too, plays a role in what appears to be the unifying theme throughout Acts 8–12.[75]

[72] The "flip-side" to this plot line is the motif of "conversion" that runs throughout this text unit. Cf. Marguerat (*The First Christian Historian*, 189): "Acts 9 comes at the climax of a series of conversions (Simon, then the Ethiopian eunuch, then Saul) which show how God has widened the circle of the elect; the decisive step will be made in the encounter of Peter and Cornelius (cf. 10.34-6). . . . The common theme is God's surprising initiative in the choice of converts: Simon the greedy magician, the mutilated Ethiopian excluded from the covenant, Saul the persecutor, Cornelius the impure one." Cf. B. R. Gaventa, *From Darkness to Light: Aspects of Conversion in the New Testament* (Philadelphia: Fortress Press, 1986), 52–129.

[73] When 8:1 hyperbolically states that all the Christians except the apostles fled Jerusalem, this does not mean that the apostles were not the target of persecution at that point. As Bauckham ("James and the Jerusalem Church," 429) rightly notes, "[a]ll that Luke maintains is that the persecution did not bring their [apostolic] leadership to an end." Cf. L. W. Hurtado, *Lord Jesus Christ: Devotion to Jesus in Earliest Christianity* (Grand Rapids: Eerdmans, 2003), 211.

[74] Earlier in Acts the Jewish leadership are shown to have a significant grudge against Peter (Acts 4:1-22), but their grudge is not nearly as pronounced as in the events of Acts 12, in which Herod's persecution of Peter is the calculated outworking of his attempt to please "the Jews"—in particular, we should imagine, the Jewish leadership.

[75] Of course, Acts 9:32–11:18 also serves a role with regard to the mission to the gentiles that is occurring even within Acts 8–12 and is ready to burst onto the

There is reason to think, then, that Acts 8–12 forms a single literary unit consisting of smaller subunits. A chain-link interlock stands at the start of the text unit (8:1b-3), linking Acts 8–12 to the previous text unit (ending in Acts 7). Moreover, the chain-link interlock at the start of Acts 8–12 links most of the individual subunits of Acts 8–12 together. Furthermore, a chain-link interlock stands at the end of Acts 8–12, introducing the subsequent text unit that begins in Acts 13. In these three ways, Luke's commitment to transitional interlock at major text-unit boundaries is clearly evident.

As a consequence of Luke's extensive use of chain-link construction throughout Acts 8–12, it should not be surprising to find temporal discrepancies within that text unit. We have already seen how the chain link of Acts 11–12 may result in a temporal disordering of events leading up to Acts 13, with the events of 12:1-24 preceding those of 11:27-30 (cf. §9.2). The same might well be involved in the three chain links that operate in Acts 8–11. For instance, when Hengel and Schwemer speak of potential "chronological overlaps" in Acts, the examples that they use to illustrate the point all come from the three chain-linked materials of Acts 8–11. They write:

> [T]he delay between 8.2, 4 and 11.19 is striking. This does not mean that everything reported in the meantime in 8.5–11.18 also took place in the interim period, so that Paul arrived in Tarsus [i.e., 9:30] essentially earlier than the Hellenists who had been driven out to Phoenicia, Cyprus and Antioch [i.e., 11:19]. The activity of Philip from Samaria through Ashdod to Caesarea (8.4-40) also need not have taken place before the conversion of Paul (ch. 9).[76]

Once again, then, it seems that concerns for rhetorical effectiveness characterise the arrangement of Luke's material over and above those for historical sequence.

It remains only to discuss the structure at the hub of the chain-link junction in 8:1-3. For some interpreters a new text unit in the Acts narrative begins at 8:4.[77] If this is correct, then 8:1b-3 should be seen to conclude the previous text unit, with overlapping forward gestures found in 8:1b and 8:3 and closing backward gestures in 8:2 and 8:3 (Acts 8:3

---

scene in Acts 13ff., thereby rooting that mission in the ministry of a truly "apostolic" figure, Peter.

[76] Hengel and Schwemer, *Paul between Damascus and Antioch*, 466 n. 1276.

[77] W. G. Kümmel, *Introduction to the New Testament* (trans. Howard Clark Lee; Nashville: Abingdon Press, 1975), 155; J. C. O'Neill, *The Theology of Acts in Its Historical Setting* (rev. ed.; London: SPCK, 1970), 66, 72; E. Haenchen, "The Book of Acts as Source Material for the History of Early Christianity," in *Studies in Luke-Acts* (ed. L. E. Keck and J. L. Martyn; Nashville: Abingdon Press, 1966), 258–78, esp. 259.

connects backwards with 7:58 and forwards with 9:1-2). This would suggest that the passage is to be structured according to an unbalanced A-b-
a/B pattern. But it is also possible to argue that the new text unit begins
not at 8:4 but at 8:1b.[78] In this case, overlapping backward gestures
should be seen in 8:2 and 8:3, with the forward-looking gestures appearing within the new text unit at 8:1b and 8:3. This would suggest that the
passage is to be structured according to an unbalanced A/b-a-B pattern.

One piece of evidence tips the balance in favour of 8:4 as the beginning of a new text unit. The Greek construction μὲν οὖν appears at the
start of that verse (translated simply "now" in the NRSV), a construction
that appears once in Luke and twenty-seven times in Acts. Seventeen of
those instances bear no structural weight in the narrative (Luke 3:18;
Acts 1:18; 2:41; 5:41; 12:5; 14:3; 15:3; 17:12, 17, 30; 19:32, 38; 23:18;
25:4, 11; 26:9; 28:5). In four cases it is given structural weight as a signi-
fier of text-unit closure (Acts 8:25; 9:31; 16:5; 23:22). In 11:19, however,
the construction μὲν οὖν introduces a text unit (11:19), and in five other
instances it appears at the start of a text unit of one kind or another (1:6;
13:4; 15:30; 23:31; 26:4). So in ten of twenty-eight instances in the Lukan
volumes this construction is given some structural weight, with more
than half of those instances involving the introduction of a text unit.
Since there is nothing to indicate the beginning of a text unit at 8:1b,[79]
the start of the new text unit is best identified in 8:4, where an introductory μὲν οὖν appears.

§9.4   The Chain-Link Interlock at Acts 19:21-41

In the three preceding sections it has been demonstrated that chain-link
interlock is evident (1) at the midpoint of Luke's two volumes, (2) at the
approximate midpoint of Luke's second volume, and (3) at the approximate midpoint of the first half of Acts. There is reason to think that the
same construction is evident in Acts 19–20, the approximate midpoint of
the second half of Acts. The evidence for this view appears as follows.

The Acts narrative has Paul in Ephesus as of 19:1, and it includes five
Ephesian episodes in an Ephesian block of material: in 18:24-28 Apollos
preaches to the Ephesians; in 19:1-7 Paul baptises Ephesians; in 19:8-10
Paul defends the gospel in the synagogue and in the Ephesian hall of
Tyrannus; in 19:11-20 the Ephesian magic of the sons of Sceva takes cen-
tre stage; and in 19:23-41 a riot at Ephesus is depicted as arising from

---

[78] Bergholz (*Der Aufbau des lukanischen Doppelwerkes*, 139) takes this view,
making 8:1b–12:25 a single unit, followed by Acts 13–28.

[79] The phrase "on that day" (ἐν ἐκείνῃ τῇ ἡμέρᾳ) appears nowhere else in
Acts, and only six times in Luke's Gospel (5:35; 6:23; 9:36; 12:46; 17:31; 21:23),
never with any structural significance.

Paul's ministry there. Between the fourth and fifth episodes lie two verses (19:21-22) that are difficult to place in this outline and are independent of the other episodes. On either side of these two verses are distinct signs of paragraph closure and opening. So, 19:11-20 closes with the statement "The word of the Lord grew mightily and prevailed," a Lukan summary with parallels elsewhere at text-unit closures.[80] And 19:23-41 begins with the same temporally ambiguous statement that began Acts 13, "about that time" (κατα τὸν καιρὸν ἐκεῖνον).[81] With these two structural markers appearing on either side of 19:21-22, those verses stand on their own, forming a passage that is structurally independent from the material immediately surrounding it.

But 19:21-22 also makes gestures beyond the Ephesus narrative in Acts 19 towards the narrative that occurs in Acts 20ff. In fact, the travel plan for Acts 20–28 is laid out in nuce in 19:21: "Paul resolved in the Spirit[82] to go through Macedonia and Achaia, and then to go to Jerusalem. He said, 'After I have gone there, I must also see Rome.'" So Luke Johnson notes: "The actual journey will not begin until 20:1-5, but Paul's announcement of his intention [in 19:21] begins the process and functions as a programmatic prophecy for the narrative to follow."[83] Paul sets his colleagues in motion in 19:22, although for some unexplained reason "he himself stayed for some time longer in Asia," which permits the narrative to keep its Ephesian focus for one further event (19:23-41). Consequently, the self-contained unit of 19:21-22 includes strong forward gestures[84] and is followed by another unit of material in 19:23-41 that continues the series of episodes dedicated to elaborating dimensions of Christian ministry in Ephesus.

In this way, the forward and backward movement of chain-link interlock that we have witnessed already at three points in the Lukan narrative seems to recur here as well. That construction involves both 19:23-41, in which the final Ephesian story is recounted and gives closure to the Ephesian cycle, and the forward-looking features of 19:21-22, which fill out the geographical movement of Acts 20–28 where Paul goes from Macedonia, through Achaia, to Jerusalem and ultimately to Rome.

---

[80] Cf. also mention of "the word of the Lord" in 19:10, acting loosely as literary frame to the minor paragraph 19:11-20.

[81] Acts 20:1 makes it clear that the events of 19:23-41 are subsequent to other events of Acts 19, since they are the last events of Paul's time in Ephesus.

[82] Like most, I take the expression ἐν τῷ πνεύματι to refer to the Holy Spirit. Contrast Parsons and Culy, *Acts*, 370.

[83] Johnson, *The Acts of the Apostles*, 351. This observation has no influence on Johnson's structural outline of Acts.

[84] G. Schneider (*Die Apostelgeschichte* [Freiburg: Herder, 1982], 2:273): Acts 19:21-22 "finden in 20,1-6 ihre sachliche Fortsetzung."

TEXT-UNIT "A"	INTERLOCKED "b" (anticipatory)	INTERLOCKED "a" (retrospective)	TEXT-UNIT "B"
Acts 13:1–19:41	Acts 19:21-22	Acts 19:23-41	Acts 20:1–28:31

Without an appreciation of this chain-link construction in 19:21-41, scholars frequently engage in speculation regarding the placement of those verses that simply cannot be substantiated. For instance, Robert Jewett articulates the relatively common view that the "account of Paul's plans to leave Ephesus (19:21-22) is pointedly included before the story of the riot, with the apparent intention of spiking any suspicion that Paul was driven out of town by the disturbance."[85] But this is not a convincing interpretation, since in four earlier episodes Luke depicts Paul departing from a city precisely because of opposition against him (13:50-51; 14:5-6; 17:5-10, 13-14). Consequently, the positioning of 19:21-22 is unlikely to be explained in these terms, since Luke does not indicate an aversion to similar depictions elsewhere in his narrative. Instead, the structural placement of 19:21-22 is to be explained simply with regard to its function within a larger chain-link construction.

In light of the fact that the previous three chain-link constructions evident in Luke's writings seem also to serve as macro-level transitions from one main text unit to another, we might suppose that the same function is evident in the chain-link interlock in operation in 19:21-41. It is also possible to argue that this chain-link construction carries no macro-level transitional weight in relation to main text units, but is a medial-level transition between two subunits within a larger text unit. Determining the extent to which the chain link of 19:21-41 carries transitional weight is bound up with larger issues about delimiting the main text units themselves, suggesting that this case might be plagued by the age-old "chicken or egg" dilemma. Does the presence of a chain-link construction inevitably signal a macro-level transition from one main text unit to another? Although it has been argued that this is, in fact, the case in the previous three Lukan examples (and in the majority of cases studied in earlier chapters of this project), the assumption itself is not self-evident, and in fact is not the case for all examples of chain-link con-

---

[85] Jewett, *Dating Paul's Life*, 19. Cf. Schneider, *Die Apostelgeschichte*, 2:273; Haenchen, *Die Apostelgeschichte*, 546. G. Ogg (*The Chronology of the Life of Paul* [London: Epworth Press, 1968], 135) writes: "The writer of Acts appears to minimize, perhaps he even attempts to conceal, the extent to which the riot was the occasion of Paul's departure from Ephesus." Along with others, Jewett suggests that, in fact, "an Ephesian imprisonment provided the conclusion of his ministry there" (*Dating Paul's Life*, 19).

struction suggested in this project (see §5.7, §5.9, and §6.1–§6.4). In practice, however, things are not arbitrary in this case, since, as will be shown, there is good evidence for seeing Luke as being in "main unit transitional mode" in and around 19:21. (See §10.2, where 19:21 is univocally recognised as the start of a main text unit for virtually all structural proposals of Acts involving more than four main text units.)

Not all scholars hold this view, of course. For some, Acts 19:21-22 appears not at the boundary of a main text unit but in the middle of a main text unit. In this case, the chain-link transition of 19:21-41 should be identified as a medial-level transition between textual subunits. So, for instance, Jacob Jervell, following Haenchen, delineates the main text unit of which 19:21-41 is a part of as beginning in 15:36 and ending in 21:26.[86] Jervell claims that his outline of Acts attempts to take full account of "die verschiedenen Etappen in dieser Geschichte."[87] In seeking to do justice to these different historical stages, Jervell identifies the final three main text units as beginning at 9:1, 15:36, and 21:27 respectively. But this seems to open up a curious tension within Jervell's own work, since his comment on 19:21-22 is as follows: "Die paulinische Mission ist jetzt beendet. Ab 19,21 kommt der Übergang zum letzten Abschnitt der Apostelgeschichte, der sich überwiegend mit dem Prozess des Paulus beschäftigt, 21,27–28,31."[88] But 19:21-22 outlines Paul's movements as of 20:1, not merely as of 21:27, weakening Jervell's case that 19:21-22 forms a transition ("Übergang") to a new main text unit that begins at 21:27. If Jervell's concern to outline the book of Acts according to the different stages of salvation history is applied rigorously, and if he is right to say that the Pauline mission comes to an end with 19:21, the final section of the book needs to be moved back from Acts 21 to the textual interlock of Acts 19–20, in relation to the transitional function that 19:21 serves, as Jervell rightly notes.

It is precisely at 19:21 that a good number of interpreters identify the beginning of a new main text unit comprised of 19:21–28:31, a self-contained unit that forms the "Höhepunkt" of the book of Acts. So

---

[86] Cf. Jervell, *Die Apostelgeschichte*, 5–7; Haenchen, "The Book of Acts as Source Material," 259. Johnson (*The Acts of the Apostles*, v–vii) identifies the text unit as 15:36–22:29. It was at one point common to identify 18:23–21:16 as a major text unit, since those verses encompass the start and completion of "Paul's third missionary journey." But textual delineation of this sort is determined by considerations (i.e., missionary journeys) other than literary features per se, and it has largely been abandoned (although see P. W. Walaskay, *Acts* [Louisville: Westminster John Knox Press, 1998], where the "missionary journey" outline is replicated).

[87] Jervell, *Die Apostelgeschichte*, 53.

[88] Jervell, *Die Apostelgeschichte*, 486.

argues Jürgen Roloff, for instance, for whom 19:21-22 marks out "einen entscheidenden Wendepunkt . . . Das missionarische Werk des Paulus is abgeschlossen; nun soll der neue, letzte Abschnitt seines Weges beginnen, der von zwei Stationen bestimmt sein wird: Jerusalem und Rom."[89] So, too, Hans-Joseph Klauck believes that Paul's "farewell journey . . . begins at Acts 19:21f. with a programmatic introduction that matches the beginning of the narrative of Jesus' journey to Jerusalem (Luke 9:51f.); the definitive departure (Acts 20:1) is delayed by the uprising of the silversmiths (19:23-40)."[90]

With Paul's missionary work lying behind and the travel to Jerusalem and Rome lying ahead, 19:21-22 indeed qualifies as a significant turning point ("Wendepunkt") in the Lukan narrative equal to that of the shift from the Petrine to the Pauline cycle in Acts 13. Consequently the chain-link construction of 19:21-41 seems to carry structural weight as a macro-level transition marker, as was the case with all three previous instances of chain-link construction in Luke's writings.

If a macro-level chain-link transition is evident in 19:21-41, can the text unit boundary be identified? A case can be made for identifying the beginning of that text unit at either 19:21 or 20:1. If a definite text-unit boundary presents itself, it will do so in one of two ways. If Acts 19:21 is the start of the text-unit, then the chain link follows an A/b-a-B pattern, with the overlap in 19:21-22 (i.e., "b") and 19:23-41 (i.e., "a") occurring after the commencement of that new text unit. If Acts 20:1 is the start of the text unit, then the chain link follows an A-b-a/B pattern, with the text unit boundary coming after the overlap in 19:21-22 (i.e., "a") and 19:23-41 (i.e., "b").[91]

In favour of the A/b-a-B structure is the fact that 19:20 includes a summarising statement that could qualify as the closure to a main text unit: "So the word of the Lord continued to grow and prevail" (my reworking of NRSV, οὕτως κατὰ κράτος τοῦ κυρίου ὁ λόγος ηὔξανεν καὶ ἴσχυεν). On a previous occasion Luke has used the verb "to grow" (αὐξάνω) in connection with the phrase "the word of God/the Lord" (ὁ λόγος τοῦ θεου/τοῦ κυρίου) in a summary statement within the context of a chain-link interlock and near to the end of a main text unit. So in

---

[89] Jervell, *Die Apostelgeschichte*, 288. Cf. his comment on p. 13: "Und in 19,21f. klingt . . . ein neuer Ton an." Cf. Kümmel, *Introduction to the New Testament*, 156; O'Neill, *The Theology of Acts*, 67–68 and 72 ("a new stage begins at 19.21"); Turner, "Chronology of the Bible," 421. See also the NRSV's eight text units, the last of which is 19:21–28:31.

[90] Klauck, *Magic and Paganism in Early Christianity*, 97.

[91] A balanced chain link (i.e. A-b/a-B) would not seem likely here, since that would place the start of the new text unit at 19:23, a view that (I venture to say) no interpreter has ever suggested, and for good reason.

12:24 Luke writes: "But the word of God continued to grow and gain adherents" (my reworking of NRSV, ὁ δὲ λόγος τοῦ θεοῦ ηὔξανεν καὶ ἐπληθύνετο). In 19:20, then, we find Luke employing terms that he has previously used to close one main text unit and to start another. Weakening this observation is the fact that Luke uses a similar summarising statement in 6:7 to make a medial-level transition: "The word of God continued to spread; the number of the disciples increased greatly in Jerusalem" (καὶ ὁ λόγος τοῦ θεοῦ ηὔξανεν καὶ ἐπληθύνετο ὁ ἀριθμὸς τῶν μαθητῶν ἐν Ἰερουσαλὴμ σφόδρα). There is no inevitability, then, in seeing summary statements of this kind as markers of main text-unit boundaries.[92]

In favour of the A-b-a/B structure, however, are four other considerations suggesting that 20:1 is best seen as the start of the new main text unit. First, this A-b-a/B pattern matches the pattern of Lukan chain links in each of the previous three occasions in which "b" material is brought before the text-unit boundary. At the Luke-Acts seam and at the Acts 7–8 and 11–13 transitions, Luke has consistently brought "b" material over the text-unit boundary prior to the commencement of the new text unit.[93] The consistency of this pattern favours 20:1 as the opening of the fourth main section, rather than 19:21.

Second, since the account in 19:23-41 is a rather long episode of "a" material, it is not well placed towards the start of a new text unit. Kicking off a new text unit with a lengthy narrative that is more closely associated with the previous text unit does not make for a strong start.

Third, since the story of opposition in 19:23-41, like its predecessors, occurs in Ephesus, and since Paul barely makes an appearance within it, it is rather ill-suited to be the first main episode of a text unit concerned with Paul's movement throughout Macedonia and Achaia, to Jerusalem and ultimately to Rome.

[92] The case for seeing summary statements of this kind as main text-unit closures was advanced by Turner ("Chronology of the Bible," 421), and argued for by H. J. Cadbury ("The Summaries in Acts," in *The Beginnings of Christianity* [ed. F. J. Foakes-Jackson and K. Lake; London: Macmillan, 1920–33], 5:392–402). The attempt to see main text units demarcated by these summary statements has since been severely criticised. See for instance O'Neill, *The Theology of Acts*, 64–65. Few today advocate it. J. P. Polhill (*The Acts of the Apostles* [Nashville: Broadman, 1992], 72–74) continues to overlook the weaknesses of this structural scheme.

[93] So, the "b" material of Luke 24:47-49 appears before the text-unit boundary at Acts 1:1; the motif of "scattering caused by persecution" in 8:4 and 11:19 appears already in 8:1, prior to the beginning of a text unit at 8:4 (cf. also 9:1 in relation to 8:3); and the Pauline mission of Acts 13ff. has a solid springboard in Acts 11:27-30/12:25, prior to the commencement of a new text unit at 13:1.

Fourth, the story of 19:23-41 is itself the fitting conclusion to the immediately preceding narrative. In his work on the structure of Acts, G. H. C. MacGregor argued that the summary statement of 19:20 should probably be "transferred to follow XIX:10," since it "looks strangely out of place at XIX:20"; according to him, "one would not expect it [the summary statement of 19:20] *in the middle of the account* of the dramatic events at Ephesus."[94] With no text-critical basis for this suggestion, MacGregor's argument is weakly founded. But MacGregor's observation about the relationship of the accounts in 19:11-20 and in 19:23-41 has a bearing on this discussion. For MacGregor, these two paragraphs comprise a single account of "dramatic events at Ephesus." This might be to overstate their relationship, making the two paragraphs more unified than they might in fact be. But their close relationship is nonetheless undeniable, with the whole premise of the later paragraph being laid out in the earlier paragraph. The great success of Christianity in Ephesus is spectacularly outlined in the three concluding verses of the earlier paragraph (19:18-20), and this forms the context out of which arises the "no little disturbance" of the later paragraph (19:23). So Demetrius the Ephesian silversmith gathers the opposition against Paul by highlighting how "this Paul has persuaded and drawn away a considerable number of people" (19:26). Paul's Ephesian success as outlined in 19:11-20 leads directly into the Ephesian opposition against Paul in 19:23-41. The two paragraphs are not a single account, but they are strongly related. To place a main text unit break between them would be awkward.

Evidently, then, the summary of 19:20 is not acting as main text-unit boundary marker; it is to be seen as operating at a less significant structural level. And consequently, Acts 20:1 is best qualified as the start of the main text unit that 19:21-22 has set up. In fact, Demetrius' description of Paul's success could well function as a Lukan summary of Paul's public ministry since Acts 13 (itself introduced by a chain link): "in almost the whole of Asia this Paul has persuaded and drawn away a considerable number of people" (19:26). In Lukan perspective, Demetrius' criticism of Paul is in fact a testimony to the great success of Paul's public ministry, begun officially in Acts 13 and ending in Acts 19. To put a text-unit break before this testimony creates an awkward rupture in the narrative that began in Acts 13.

For these reasons, if the start of a text unit is to be demarcated in this chain-link transition, it would seem best to place that starting point at Acts 20:1, with Paul's departure from Ephesus and his resolve "in the Spirit" to travel "through Macedonia and Achaia" to Jerusalem and ultimately to Rome—a travel itinerary laid out in 19:21 but only initiated at

---

[94] Morton and MacGregor, *The Structure of Luke and Acts*, p. 41, emphasis added.

20:1.[95] For Luke, the initiating of the action, rather than its earlier devising, is the start of the final main text unit of his narrative.

Four passages in Acts have been shown to include chain-link interlock as part of their underlying structure. The following chapter addresses a variety of implications that ensue from the exegetical observations noted above.

---

[95] Paul's travel plan as laid out in 19:21-22 plays a role in an interlocking transition in a way that the mention of Jesus' travel plan in Luke 9:51 does not.

Appendix 1

§9.5   The Significance of Variant Readings in Acts 12:25

It has been argued in §9.2 that (1) a chain-link interlock animates the two main sections of Acts 11:27–12:24 (i.e., 11:27-30; 12:1-24), and (2) Luke probably delayed the conclusion to the first section in order to permit 12:25 to function as an additional transitional feature to the material of Acts 13ff. But since ancient manuscripts of 12:25 vary so significantly in one respect, it is necessary to demonstrate how the proposed interpretation of Luke's technique is affected by those variants. Although the difficult text-critical problem of Acts 12:25 is often overlooked or underplayed in scholarly literature,[96] it must be attended to in any theory of the transitional elements prior to Acts 13. As will be shown, none of the variants can muster enough weight to dislodge the interpretation advanced in §9.2.

Two actions of Barnabas and Saul are described in 12:25 and are not disputed in the textual variants: i.e., Barnabas and Saul (1) fulfilled their service/mission and (2) returned. What is disputed in the textual variants of 12:25 is (1) whether Jerusalem was the "starting point" (i.e., "from [ἐξ or ἀπό] Jerusalem") or the "telic point" (i.e., "to [εἰς] Jerusalem") of their movements, and (2) whether the clause about Jerusalem modifies the verb "return" (ὑπέστρεψαν) or the participial clause "fulfilled their service" (πληρώσαντες τὴν διακονίαν). There are other variant readings that raise further possibilities, but these are generally recognised as the main interpretative data. Three translational options arise as a consequence:

1. Barnabas and Saul returned from (ἐξ or ἀπό) Jerusalem [i.e., to Antioch], having fulfilled their service, bringing with them John, whose other name was Mark.

2. Barnabas and Saul, having fulfilled their service to (εἰς) Jerusalem, returned [i.e., to Antioch], bringing with them John, whose other name was Mark.[97]

---

[96] Perhaps this is because of its cumbersome complexities. Cf. Parsons and Culy (*Acts*, 242): "The [text-critical] problem [of Acts 12:25] . . . can easily lead text critics to despair."

[97] Cf. Pesch (*Die Apostelgeschichte*, 1:370): "Barnabas aber und Saulus kehrten zurück, nachdem sie in Jerusalem den Dienst erfüllt hatten." This interpretation was probably first proposed by H. H. Wendt, *Die Apostelgeschichte* (Göttingen: Vandenhoech & Reprecht, 1899). See esp. J. Dupont, *Nouvelles Études sur les Actes des Apôtres* (Paris: Éditions du Cerf, 1984), 217–41. For an opposing view, see P. Parker, "Three Variant Readings in Luke-Acts," *JBL* 83 (1964): 165–70. This reading is sometimes thought to transgress the expected structure of the sen-

3. Barnabas and Saul returned to (εἰς) Jerusalem, having fulfilled their service, bringing with them John, whose other
name was Mark.

If either the first or the second reading represents the original, the interpretation of Luke's transition technique suggested in §9.2 is unaffected:
that is, the narrative pattern involves a movement from Jerusalem to
Antioch in a way that eases the transition from Acts 12 to Acts 13.

In the third reading, the narrative pattern is quite complicated. It
involves understanding Barnabas and Saul to have returned to Antioch
after 11:30 and, as of 12:25, to have undertaken yet another journey to
Jerusalem, without mention of a return to Antioch, where the narrative
picks up in 13:1. Even in this complicated narrative, however, the interpretation of Luke's technique postulated in §9.2 is unaffected. That is, if
the third reading represents the original, then Luke simply included a
mini-episode at 12:25 that, however convoluted it might be narratively,
served the transition from Acts 12 to Acts 13 by reintroducing the close
connection between Jerusalem Christianity and Antiochene Christianity
—centres of Christianity that fall on either side of the text-unit boundary. Consequently, no matter which of the three variants is to be preferred, the interpretation of Luke's rhetorical strategy postulated in §9.2
encounters no insurmountable difficulties.

When the issue is broadened out from Luke's strategy to the way in
which Luke's text was interpreted by Christian scribes, however, the issue
might be more complex. If the third reading is to be attributed to the
influence of scribal activity, it might be that Luke's interest in compounding transitional techniques was simply not understood by some later
scribes. They may have failed to see the purpose of mentioning a journey
from Jerusalem to Antioch at this point in the narrative, and so they
changed the text to speak of a journey from Antioch to Jerusalem. For
these scribes, the journey described in 12:25 did not represent the conclusion to the story of 11:27-30 that was delayed in order to assist in a
transition. For them it seems simply to have been a self-contained mini-
narrative that required the introduction of the preposition "to" (εἰς) in
order to make sense in its own terms (no matter the amount of complications it introduced to the wider narrative; see below).

It is possible, then, that the rhetorical strategy motivating Luke's
placement of 12:25 (as proposed in §9.2) was not apparent to some scribes
who handled his text in the centuries that followed. Perhaps Luke was too

---

tence. In defence of this reading, however, Barrett (*The Acts of the Apostles*, 596)
notes: "Luke did not always adopt the 'correct' order of words." The same point
was made to me in private conversation with Martin Hengel, who finds the word
order to fall within the bounds of Lukan style.

optimistic in thinking that his compounded transitional devices (i.e., chain-link interlock in 11:27–12:24 and anticipatory gestures inherent within the closure of 12:25) would be readily noticed. This conclusion commends itself to those who accept that the third reading represents a later scribal change that was motivated by some need to straighten out the narrative (although actually achieving the opposite effect).

In my view, the third reading is to be credited to a scribal hand. The case for this follows, briefly laid out. None of the prepositions is without some good support when judged on the basis of "external" manuscript evidence.[98] The third reading, in which εἰς is understood to modify the verb "return," is notably the harder reading when judged on the basis of "internal evidence." While text-critical decisions frequently favour the harder reading,[99] in this case the harder reading is *so* hard as to be virtually non-sensical. So, for instance, Barrett speaks for many when he says: "it [i.e., the reading "they returned to Jerusalem"] is too difficult to be accepted. It does not make sense."[100] Weighty reasoning lies behind this judgement:

1. If the third reading is to be preferred, the motivation for the return to Jerusalem in 12:25 is left unstated, unlike the motivation laid out clearly in 11:27-30.

2. If the third reading is to be preferred, the events that transpired in Jerusalem are left unstated.

3. If the third reading is to be preferred, the return of Barnabas, Saul, and John Mark to Antioch between 12:25 and 13:1 is left unstated.

4. If the third reading is to be preferred, the reference to the "mission/service" (διακονία) of Barnabas and Saul in 12:25

---

[98] See n. 26 for the major witnesses. Although manuscript P[74], which supports the reading ἐξ, is not an early manuscript, the Introduction to the Nestle-Aland *Greek-English New Testament* (Stuttgart: Deutsche Bibelgesellschaft, 1993, 13) notes that it is "a particularly significant" textual witness "despite its VII century date."

[99] This is evident, for instance, in the NRSV reading, as well as the NET Bible, both of which prioritise external over internal evidence, thereby favouring the preposition "to." But of course textual criticism is as much an art as a science, as in the NET Bible's preference for the internal over the external evidence in other places, such as Romans 5:1. There it is noted that "[I]f the problem were to be solved on an external basis only, the subjunctive would be preferred. Nevertheless, the indicative is probably correct. . . . [A]lthough the external evidence is stronger in support of the subjunctive, the internal evidence points to the indicative."

[100] Barrett, *The Acts of the Apostles*, 595.

has to be taken to include their unstated return to Antioch after going to Jerusalem in 11:27-30. But their service is better understood simply in the terms laid out in 11:29: i.e., "to send relief to the brothers [and sisters] who lived in Judaea."

For these reasons, I find it difficult to accept the originality of the third reading and consider it to be a scribal contribution.[101]

This conclusion might suggest that Luke's strategy for the placement of 12:25 was misunderstood by later scribes who intentionally changed the preposition. But it is not wholly evident that the change arose out of scribal intentionality as opposed to a simple scribal error. So Mikeal Parsons and Martin Culy have recently suggested that there was no scribal intentionality involved in the introduction of a new preposition at 12:25. They write that

> the harder reading principle is irrelevant in the case of unintentional scribal changes. It is worth pointing out that ὑποστρέφω εἰς occurs seventeen times in the NT, with sixteen of these being found in Luke-Acts. In contrast, ὑποστρέφω ἐκ occurs only once (2 Pet 2:21), while ὑποστρέφω ἀπό occurs only in Luke 4:1; 24:9; and Heb 7:1. It is possible that early scribes who encountered ὑπέστρεψαν ἀπό, an expression that does not occur elsewhere in Acts and is otherwise rare, or the even rarer ὑποστρέφω ἐκ, were so accustomed to writing ὑπέστρεψαν εἰς (see 1:12; 8:25; . . . and also 13:34; 14:21; 21:6; 22:17; 23:32) that they inadvertantly [sic] introduced the error. This error was later corrected to either ἐξ or ἀπό. That scribes were not always thinking about the content of what they were writing is readily obvious from the textual history of the NT.[102]

From this, it would be rash to imagine that the third reading can only represent a scribal change that was intentionally motivated. That reading might have simply arisen as an error of a scribe whose "ear" was attuned to the normal pattern of expression within the New Testament and, especially, the Lukan texts.

No doubt more could be said in this analysis of the implications of the text-critical difficulties of 12:25 in relation to the theory of Lukan structure advanced in §9.2. But four things have been shown:

---

[101] The third reading also makes it impossible to reconcile the testimony of Acts with that of Galatians, even for those who think that Galatians 2:1-10 equates with Acts 11:27-30. Even in that scenario, the letter to the Galatians would need to have been written prior to the time described in 12:25, which in fact preceded Paul's founding of the Galatian churches.

[102] Parsons and Culy, *Acts*, 242–43.

1. The theory of Luke's structural interest that was proposed in §9.2 remains intact no matter which of the three primary readings is to be preferred as the original.

2. The third reading is best attributed to scribal activity, with priority given to one of the first two readings when reconstructing the original.

3. Scribal intentionality may have contributed to the construction of the third reading. In this case, it would seem that Luke's rhetorical strategy (as proposed in §9.2) was not recognised by some of the early transmitters of his text.

4. Scribal intentionality may not, in fact, have contributed to the construction of the third reading. In this case, there are no implications with regard to the affective history of Luke's rhetorical strategy (as proposed in §9.2).

Appendix 2

§9.6   Acts 11:1–13:1 Unlinked (NRSV)

[11:1] Now the apostles and the believers who were in Judea heard that the Gentiles had also accepted the word of God. [2]So when Peter went up to Jerusalem, the circumcised believers criticised him, [3]saying, "Why did you go to uncircumcised men and eat with them?" [4]Then Peter began to explain it to them, step by step, saying, [5]"I was in the city of Joppa praying, and in a trance I saw a vision. There was something like a large sheet coming down from heaven, being lowered by its four corners; and it came close to me. [6]As I looked at it closely I saw four-footed animals, beasts of prey, reptiles, and birds of the air. [7]I also heard a voice saying to me, "Get up, Peter; kill and eat." [8]But I replied, "By no means, Lord; for nothing profane or unclean has ever entered my mouth." [9]But a second time the voice answered from heaven, "What God has made clean, you must not call profane." [10]This happened three times; then everything was pulled up again to heaven. [11]At that very moment three men, sent to me from Caesarea, arrived at the house where we were. [12]The Spirit told me to go with them and not to make a distinction between them and us. These six brothers also accompanied me, and we entered the man's house. [13]He told us how he had seen the angel standing in his house and saying, "Send to Joppa and bring Simon, who is called Peter; [14]he will give you a message by which you and your entire household will be saved." [15]And as I began to speak, the Holy Spirit fell upon them just as it had upon us at the beginning. [16]And I remembered the word of the Lord, how he had said, "John baptised with water, but you will be baptised with the Holy Spirit." [17]If then God gave them the same gift that he gave us when we believed in the Lord Jesus Christ, who was I that I could hinder God?" [18]When they heard this, they were silenced. And they praised God, saying, "Then God has given even to the Gentiles the repentance that leads to life."

[12:1]About that time King Herod laid violent hands upon some who belonged to the church. [2]He had James, the brother of John, killed with the sword. [3]After he saw that it pleased the Jews, he proceeded to arrest Peter also. (This was during the festival of Unleavened Bread.) [4]When he had seized him, he put him in prison and handed him over to four squads of soldiers to guard him, intending to bring him out to the people after the Passover. [5]While Peter was kept in prison, the church prayed fervently to God for him. [6]The very night before Herod was going to bring him out, Peter, bound with two chains, was sleeping between two soldiers, while guards in front of the door were keeping watch over the prison. [7]Suddenly an angel of the Lord appeared and a light shone in the cell. He tapped Peter on the side and woke him, saying, "Get up quickly." And the chains fell off his wrists. [8]The

angel said to him, "Fasten your belt and put on your sandals." He did
so. Then he said to him, "Wrap your cloak around you and follow
me." ⁹Peter went out and followed him; he did not realise that what
was happening with the angel's help was real; he thought he was seeing
a vision. ¹⁰After they had passed the first and the second guard, they
came before the iron gate leading into the city. It opened for them of
its own accord, and they went outside and walked along a lane, when
suddenly the angel left him. ¹¹Then Peter came to himself and said,
"Now I am sure that the Lord has sent his angel and rescued me from
the hands of Herod and from all that the Jewish people were expecting." ¹²As soon as he realized this, he went to the house of Mary, the
mother of John whose other name was Mark, where many had gathered and were praying. ¹³When he knocked at the outer gate, a maid
named Rhoda came to answer. ¹⁴On recognising Peter's voice, she was
so overjoyed that, instead of opening the gate, she ran in and
announced that Peter was standing at the gate. ¹⁵They said to her, "You
are out of your mind!" But she insisted that it was so. They said, "It is
his angel." ¹⁶Meanwhile Peter continued knocking; and when they
opened the gate, they saw him and were amazed. ¹⁷He motioned to
them with his hand to be silent, and described for them how the Lord
had brought him out of the prison. And he added, "Tell this to James
and to the believers." Then he left and went to another place. ¹⁸When
morning came, there was no small commotion among the soldiers
over what had become of Peter. ¹⁹When Herod had searched for him
and could not find him, he examined the guards and ordered them to
be put to death. Then he [i.e., Herod]¹⁰³ went down from Judea to
Caesarea and stayed there. ²⁰Now Herod was angry with the people of
Tyre and Sidon. So they came to him in a body; and after winning over
Blastus, the king's chamberlain, they asked for a reconciliation,
because their country depended on the king's country for food. ²¹On
an appointed day Herod put on his royal robes, took his seat on the
platform, and delivered a public address to them. ²²The people kept
shouting, "The voice of a god, and not of a mortal!" ²³And immediately, because he had not given the glory to God, an angel of the Lord
struck him down, and he was eaten by worms and died. ²⁴But the word
of God continued to advance and gain adherents.

¹¹:¹⁹Now those who were scattered because of the persecution that took
place over Stephen travelled as far as Phoenicia, Cyprus, and Antioch,
and they spoke the word to no one except Jews. ²⁰But among them
were some men of Cyprus and Cyrene who, on coming to Antioch,
spoke to the Hellenists also, proclaiming the Lord Jesus. ²¹The hand of
the Lord was with them, and a great number became believers and

---

¹⁰³ Here I have changed the NRSV reading "Peter" to "he," meaning
"Herod." The Greek is ambiguous and can be read either way. I consider it best
to see Herod as the ambiguous third-person singular referent. See n. 60 above.

turned to the Lord. ²²News of this came to the ears of the church in Jerusalem, and they sent Barnabas to Antioch. ²³When he came and saw the grace of God, he rejoiced, and he exhorted them all to remain faithful to the Lord with steadfast devotion; ²⁴for he was a good man, full of the Holy Spirit and of faith. And a great many people were brought to the Lord. ²⁵Then Barnabas went to Tarsus to look for Saul, ²⁶and when he had found him, he brought him to Antioch. So it was that for an entire year they met with the church and taught a great many people, and it was in Antioch that the disciples were first called "Christians." ²⁷At that time prophets came down from Jerusalem to Antioch. ²⁸One of them named Agabus stood up and predicted by the Spirit that there would be a severe famine over all the world; and this took place during the reign of Claudius. ²⁹The disciples determined that according to their ability, each would send relief to the believers living in Judea; ³⁰this they did, sending it to the elders by Barnabas and Saul. ¹²:²⁵Then after completing their mission in Jerusalem[104] Barnabas and Saul returned and brought with them John, whose other name was Mark.

¹³:¹Now in the church at Antioch there were prophets and teachers: Barnabas, Simeon who was called Niger, Lucius of Cyrene, Manaen a member of the court of Herod the ruler, and Saul. . . .

---

[104] Here I have changed the NRSV reading; see n. 26 above.

CHAPTER 10

Chain-Link Interlock and the Interpretation of Acts

§10.1 Chain-Link Interlock and the Unity of Luke-Acts

§10.2 Chain-Link Interlock and the Structure of Acts

§10.3 Chain-Link Interlock and the Theology of Acts

§10.4 Chain-Link Interlock and Pauline Chronology

As demonstrated in the previous chapter, the narrative of Acts is constructed at key points in conformity with the pattern of chain-link interlock. It is not enough, however, simply to observe the existence of chain-link interlock in the Lukan narrative. The Lukan use of chain-link interlock leads naturally to further consideration of certain literary, theological, and historical dimensions of Acts. These include the unity of Luke-Acts (§10.1), the structure of Acts (§10.2), the theology of Acts (§10.3), and the character of Acts 11:27-30 in relation to historical reconstructions of Paul's life (§10.4)

§10.1 Chain-Link Interlock and the Unity of Luke-Acts

There is no dispute that the one who authored the third Gospel also authored the Acts of the Apostles. Throughout the centuries since they were authored, these two texts have frequently been read as separate books, each one relatively self-contained and set off from the other. Within the Christian canon, the Lukan Gospel took its position between the Gospels attributed to Mark and John, while the Acts of the Apostles was placed in a position to introduce the apostolic letters of Paul and other leading figures of the early church. That each Lukan text *could* be read independently of each other has proven itself to be the case, not least in view of the reading experience of Christians throughout the centuries.

But if the needs for an "ordered" Christian canon have involved placing the two Lukan texts in two different canonical contexts, the need for an ordered interpretation of these texts within their historical context has led to them being considered two parts of a single volume. In 1927, Henry Cadbury argued strongly that the two were inseparable volumes of a single monograph,[1] and in his wake most Lukan scholars have found it appropriate to put a hyphen between the words "Luke" and "Acts." According to Charles Talbert, "[T]o have heard Acts read in its pre-canonical context would have involved hearing Acts as volume two of a narrative of which the Third Gospel was volume one."[2] When the forty-seventh "Colloquium Biblicum Lovaniense" considered the issue of the unity of Luke-Acts in 1998, J. Veryheyden summarised the colloquium's findings in this way: "These two impressive documents . . . should be read and studied as the one great work by the same great author and theologian they were meant to be."[3] According to this view, the best Lukan readings are articulated in relation to both Lukan texts.

But by definition, consensus views have dissidents. So the hyphen has come under attack by interpreters who see the two texts as self-contained and independent of each other. Although the two texts have come from the same hand and are closely related, even sharing similar outlooks and concerns at times, they are nonetheless two distinct literary enterprises.[4]

---

[1] H. J. Cadbury, *The Making of Luke-Acts* (New York: Macmillan, 1927).

[2] C. H. Talbert, *Reading Acts: A Literary and Theological Commentary on the Acts of the Apostles* (New York: Crossroad, 1997), 2.

[3] J. Verheyden, "The Unity of Luke-Acts," *Hervormde Teologiese Studies* 55 (1999): 979.

[4] See especially M. C. Parsons and R. I. Pervo, *Rethinking the Unity of Luke and Acts* (Minneapolis: Fortress, 1993); R. I. Pervo, "Israel's Heritage and Claims upon the Genre(s) of Luke and Acts: The Problems of a History," in *Jesus and the Heritage of Israel* (ed. D. P. Moessner; Harrisburg: Trinity, 1999), 127–43; H. Conzelmann, *The Theology of St Luke* (trans. G. Buswell; Philadelphia: Fortress Press, 1982), 7 n. 1; H. W. Bartsch, *Wachet aber zu jeder Zeit: Entwurf einer Auslegung des Lukasevangeliums* (Hamburg-Bergstedt: Evangelischer Verlag, 1963), 11–14; G. Bouwmann, *Das dritte Evangelium: Einübing in die formgeschichtliche Methode* (Düsseldorf: Patmos, 1968), 62–67; G. Schneider, *Die Apostelgeschichte* (Freiburg: Herder, 1982), 1:76–82; J. M. Dawsey, "The Literary

Issues of style, genre, and theological foci are, it is suggested, problematical for the unity of the two texts.

To this discussion, the evidence of chain-link interlock needs to be applied. In his study of Luke's use of chain-link construction, Jacques Dupont was convinced that the overlapping of material in Luke 24 and Acts 1 demonstrated the literary unity of these two texts: "Luc ne s'est pas contenté de juxtaposer l'un à l'autre ses deux livres *A Théophile*; il les a emboîtés l'un dans l'autre, faisant en sorte, comme le dit Lucien, 'qu'ils soient mêlés par leurs extrémités' [citing Lucian of Samosata]."[5] In §9.1, however, it was noted that this conclusion already assumes what it is meant to demonstrate: the literary unity of Luke-Acts. One cannot say that there is a chain-link interlock at the textual boundary of Luke and Acts unless one is already convinced that Luke and Acts are two parts of a literary unity. It is possible, for instance, that Luke 24:47-49 refers to events recounted in Acts and that Acts 1 refers to events recounted in the Lukan Gospel without these gestures serving as transitional markers between two volumes of a single monograph. Instead of a chain-link transition, the cross-referencing gestures at the start of Acts and end of Luke might function simply as intertextual reference markers between the two independent texts. In that case, Luke has simply incorporated intertextual signals to subsequent and earlier monographs without expecting those two monographs to be recognised as a single literary entity.[6]

Unity of Luke-Acts: Questions of Style—A Task for Literary Critics," *NTS* 35 (1989): 48–66; A. C. Clark, *The Acts of the Apostles* (Oxford: Clarendon Press, 1933), 393–408; A. W. Argyle, "The Greek of Luke and Acts," *NTS* 20 (1974): 441–45. Occasionally this view is advocated but poorly supported, as in J. Knight (*Luke's Gospel* [London: Routledge, 1998], 9): "They [Luke and Acts] are in fact quite independent of each other. Each has features which are not shared by the other." The second sentence is not in dispute, of course, but does not necessarily support the first sentence, which it is meant to do. One gets the impression that Knight's undefended stance is motivated by his commissioned task of reading Luke's Gospel narratively on its own in a self-contained fashion.

[5] J. Dupont, "La question du plan des Actes des Apôtres à la Lumière d'un Texte de Lucien de Samosate," in his *Nouvelles Études sur les Actes des Apôtres*, 24–36, esp. 30.

[6] Cf. D. W. Palmer ("Acts and the Ancient Historical Monograph," in *The Book of Acts in Its Ancient Literary Setting*, vol. 1 [ed. B. W. Winter and A. D. Clark; Grand Rapids: Eerdmans, 1993], 1–29, esp. 25): "The recapitulatory preface of Acts does not necessarily imply that Luke is writing the second volume of a single work." Palmer provides further examples of the same. The point is also made by Parsons and Pervo, *Rethinking the Unity of Luke and Acts*, 60. We have already noted in §3.7 above Josephus's use of *transitio* at the start of his *Against Apion* (1.1–5), in which Josephus first recalls the argument of his earlier work

Alternatively it might be argued that Luke initially had intended to write only the Lukan Gospel, with Acts being conceived of only at a later time. In this case, the "foreshadowing" of things to come at the end of Luke's Gospel would simply have served as a pointer to events that Luke assumed his Christian readers were generally cognisant of, or at least could speculate about. In this scenario, the transitional function of Luke 24:47-49 arose only when Luke, for whatever reason, wrote Acts as a supplementary volume, in which case the Luke-Acts interlock was created at a second stage of composition. (For examples of chain-link interlock having been constructed in the course of a text's compositional history, see §5.8 and §5.9 above; possibly also §5.6.) It might have been, then, that the writing of Luke's Gospel was carried out without any intention of it being the first of a two-part monograph; only later, when undertaking the writing of Acts, did Luke take steps to incorporate the first volume into a two-volume work. In this scenario of compositional history, textual features of Luke's Gospel that later were incorporated into a chain-link construction had not originally been intended to serve in that role. Nonetheless, by the time that Luke began the writing of Acts, a chain-link construction had transpired.

In view of these possible scenarios, the unity of Luke-Acts cannot be demonstrated on the basis of the chain-link construction at the apparent textual seam of the two Lukan narratives, at least not at the time when the Lukan Gospel was conceived. Neither can that unity be easily demonstrated on the basis of the compatibility of those volumes with regard to shared theological themes. Ben Witherington, for instance, highlights a number of thematic features that both texts share as evidence of their compositional unity. For instance, the expectation of gentile blessing in the Lukan Gospel (i.e., 2:32; 3:6; 4:24-27; 14:15-24) correlates to the obvious development of that blessing in the Acts narrative. Similarly, Gospel statements that Jesus' followers should expect to be persecuted (i.e., 21:12-13; 22:33) correlates to the fulfilment of that expectation throughout the Acts narrative. Or again, the favourable posture towards Samaritans in the Lukan Gospel (9:52-56; 17:11-19) correlates to the narrative of Acts 8. From thematic correlation of this kind, Witherington suggests that "there is indeed some sort of compositional unity to Luke-Acts."[7] But with this estimate Witherington oversteps the

---

Jewish Antiquities. The *transitio* functions to relate the two monographs "in essential connection" (Lucian), but falls short of making the two to be parts of a single monograph.

[7] B. Witherington, *The Acts of the Apostles: A Socio-Rhetorical Commentary* (Grand Rapids: Eerdmans, 1998), 8. See further parallels in C. H. Talbert, *Literary Patterns, Theological Themes and The Genre of Luke-Acts* (Missoula: Scholars Press, 1974). See also my "Moral Character and Divine Generosity:

bounds of his own methodological procedures, since he had already recognised that distinctions need to be made between various kinds of unity: "authorial or compositional or narrative or generic or theological or thematic."[8] By his own admission, then, thematic unity of the sort that he identifies does not necessitate the literary unity of the two texts.[9]

The thematic similarities within the two texts can be impressively documented, but it is not clear that the gap between thematic similarity and literary unity can be crossed simply by marshalling the thematic corollaries until, at some point, enough corollaries are in hand. The impressive thematic correlations within the two texts are well-suited to play a confirmatory role, lashing the two texts tightly together once it is demonstrated on other grounds that they were, in fact, intended as a literary unity. But by itself thematic correlation is not a sure foundation for demonstrating literary unity.

In fact, one of the arguments against the literary unity of the two texts involves an apparent narrative rupture precisely at the point of the proposed chain link at their textual seam. Despite a good degree of commonality between the two ascension narratives,[10] in the Lukan Gospel Jesus' ascension seems to occur on the same day as his resurrection, "the first day of the week" (24:1), whereas Acts 1:3 speaks of Jesus having remained with his disciples for "forty days."[11] Other differences between

---

Acts 13:13-52 and the Narrative Dynamics of Luke-Acts" (*New Testament Greek and Exegesis: A Festschrift for Gerald F. Hawthorne* [ed. A. M. Donaldson and T. B. Sailors. Grand Rapids: Eerdmans, 2003]), 141–64. I analysed the *material* concerns of the Lukan gospel with the *universal* interests of Acts, finding that "a common underlying theology of riches" is shared by the two texts: "The theology of possessions articulated in the gospel on the level of personal identity and responsibility finds its extension and application in Acts on the level of national religious identity and responsibility" (164).

[8] Witherington, *The Acts of the Apostles*, 5.

[9] The same approach is shared by many, including J. B. Green, *The Theology of the Gospel of Luke* (Cambridge: Cambridge University Press, 1995), 48: "the Gospel of Luke creates needs related to God's purpose that go unfulfilled in Luke, but are addressed directly in Acts. This draws attention to the unity of Luke and Acts at the narrative level." See further J. B. Green, "Internal Repetitions in Luke-Acts: Contemporary Narratology and Lukan Historiography," in *History, Literature and Society in the Book of Acts* (ed. B. Witherington; Cambridge: Cambridge University Press, 1996), 283–99.

[10] For instance, narrative consistency is found in the following features: the main characters (Jesus and disciples), the temporal location (last encounter between Jesus and disciples), Jesus' commissioning of the disciples, and even points of terminology (e.g., "promise of the Father").

[11] This analysis is based on the Alexandrian text of Luke and Acts, in which Jesus' ascension is specifically located in Bethany in Luke and in Jerusalem in Acts, some forty days later. These problems do not appear in the Western text.

the Gospel and Acts accounts are noticeable, but these are not conflicting differences, merely supplemental ones.[12] This is true even with regard to the geographical location of the ascension, as recounted in the two accounts. In Luke, it is said to have occurred near Bethany, while in Acts it occurred simply on the Mount of Olives. Since Luke has already informed the audience of his Gospel that Bethany is situated on the Mount of Olives (Luke 19:29), there is no narrative puzzle here for those who postulate the unity of Luke-Acts. Puzzlement would only arise for the person whose attention had lapsed in Luke 19, not for the "ideal audience."[13] But the discrepancy between the two Lukan texts with regard to the timing of the ascension nonetheless remains problematical when chronological matters are the focus of comparison.

In this regard, a variety of interpreters have demonstrated that the two ascension accounts in the two Lukan texts "are indispensable to their respective narrative contexts," with the temporal discrepancy between them being "readily explained on literary grounds."[14] Regardless of

---

See, for instance, E. J. Epp, "The Ascension in the Textual Tradition of Luke-Acts," in *New Testament Textual Criticism: Its Significance for Exegesis* (ed. E. J. Epp and G. D. Fee; Oxford: Clarendon Press, 1981), 131–45. Discussion of the priority of the Western and Alexandrian texts has become a debated issue in recent years. For my part, I follow the arguments favouring the priority of the Alexandrian text. Cf. C. Tuckett, "How Early is 'the' 'Western' Text of Acts?" in *The Book of Acts as Church History: Text, Textual Traditions and Ancient Interpretations* (ed. T. Nicklas and M. Tilly; Berlin: de Gruyter, 2003), 69–86; and J. Delobel, "The Nature of 'Western-Readings' in Acts: Test Cases," in *Recent Developments in Textual Criticism: New Testament, Other Christian Literature and Jewish Literature* (ed. W. Weren and D.-A. Koch; Assen: van Gorcum, 2003), 69–94.

[12] For example, a cloud and the heavenly messengers mentioned in Acts are not mentioned in Luke. Differences of this sort are of no real significance with regard to narrative unity. This is also probably the case in the details about the disciples after the ascension. In Luke they return "to Jerusalem" and were found "continually in the temple" (24:52-53), whereas in Acts they return "to Jerusalem" and go to "the room upstairs where they were staying" (1:12). There is no reason to think that these are mutually exclusive of each other, since Luke intended neither depiction to be exhaustive of the disciples' movements.

[13] Contrast the view of M. Hengel ("Luke the Historian and the Geography of Palestine in the Acts of the Apostles," in his *Between Jesus and Paul: Studies in the Earliest History of Christianity* [Minneapolis: Fortress, 1983], 97–128, esp. 107): "The best explanation for the difference is that Luke wrote the second book some time after the πρῶτος λόγος had already been produced."

[14] M. C. Parsons, *The Departure of Jesus: The Ascension Narratives in Context* (Sheffield: Sheffield Academic, 1987), 190, 194. Parsons counters the view, sometimes proposed, that Luke-Acts was originally a single narrative that was divided up within the canon for theological purposes, with a second ascension story being added as a consequence. (This view was advocated, for instance, by P.-H.

whether Luke knew of two ascension traditions and simply incorporated them both into his texts,[15] the two versions are well suited to the respective narratives in which they appear, and they might lose their effectiveness if their places were exchanged. As Mikael Parsons states, in his Gospel Luke is attempting "to educate his readers concerning the relationship between the crucifixion and exaltation" of Christ, and to this end Luke required a closely consecutive sequence of death-resurrection-ascension. To have a forty-day period at the close of the Gospel would "destroy the effect of the ending of Luke." But in Acts, it is critical to establish that the disciples are the "reliable and legitimate successors of Jesus." The extended postresurrection, preascension ministry of Jesus in the Acts account, then, "is important in establishing a positive identity for the disciples in the book of Acts." Within the forty-day period that Acts permits, the instruction of the disciples takes place, enabling them to be better prepared for their role in the narrative that follows.[16]

Although the temporal differences in the two ascension stories enable those stories to fit their respective contexts particularly well and would not be well suited in inverted sequence,[17] this observation does little to prove the narrative unity of Luke-Acts. It might go some way in explaining why, in a two-volume monograph, an apparently awkward narrative wrinkle appears right at the point of transition between the volumes, but that explanation is itself dependent on the demonstration of the literary unity of the two Lukan volumes. What does emerge from studies such as

---

Menoud, "Remarques sur les textes de l'ascension dans Luk-Acts," in *Neutestamentliche Studien für Rudolf Bultmann* (ed. W. Eltester. Berlin: Töpelmann, 1957), 148–56. That it has not been laid to rest is clear from M. P. Bonz's case in *The Past as Legacy: Luke-Acts and Ancient Epic* [Minneapolis: Fortress Press, 2000], 151–54.) According to Parsons (*The Departure of Jesus*, 190), "both ascension stories are thoroughly Lukan."

[15] See especially Talbert, *Literary Patterns*, 58–61, for a discussion of these and other issues.

[16] Parsons, *The Departure of Jesus*, 195. Similar explanations can be found in B. R. Gaventa, "The Archive of Excess: John 21 and the Problem of Narrative Closure," in *Exploring the Gospel of John: In Honor of D. Moody Smith* (ed. R. A. Culpepper and C. C. Black; Louisville: Westminster John Knox Press, 1996), 240–52, esp. 247; Gaventa, "The Eschatology of Luke-Acts Revisited," *Encounter* 43 (1982): 27–42; E. Franklin, *Christ the Lord: A Study of the Purpose and Theology of Luke-Acts* (Philadelphia: Westminster, 1975), 29–41; A. W. Zwiep, *The Ascension of the Messiah in Lukan Christianity* (Leiden: Brill, 1997), 116–17.

[17] Cf. also the way that the three accounts of Paul's conversion in Acts 9, 22, and 26 serve the narrative interests of their respective contexts. See D. Marguerat, *The First Christian Historian: Writing the "Acts of the Apostles"* (Cambridge: Cambridge University Press, 2002), 179–204.

Parsons, however, is that Luke's narrative is arranged according to literary and theological interests primarily.[18]

Consequently, there is scope for considering Robert Maddox's claim that "[T]he ascension is the major bridge from volume one to volume two."[19] While this estimate may be correct, its merit requires independent evidence regarding the compositional unity of the two volumes. If that evidence is not forthcoming, then the ascension narratives might not, in fact, function as one of the structural pivots from a volume one to a volume two, but might just as easily be said to associate two related but independent monographs.

To my mind, however, the Lukan Gospel and the Acts of the Apostles are more probably to be seen as a unity than as two separate and autonomous literary products. In this case, the ascension narratives are to be seen as significant unifying features of the two-volume work. So A. W. Zwiep aptly writes:

> Whatever one may say about traditions and sources of the ascension narratives, the way Luke has positioned the ascension texts at the key points of his two-volume work (at the centre and close of the first, in the opening chapter of the second book) suggests that the ascension of Jesus is of central significance to Luke. Given the Lukan tendency to pattern his narrative around the principle of symmetry, there can be little doubt that Luke's hand has been heavily at work in Lk 24 and Acts 1. In structuring the narrative symmetrically, Luke has effected a unified composition.[20]

But how can the claim that the Lukan Gospel and Acts are "a unified composition" be demonstrated? As Daniel Marguerat and James Dunn have argued, an estimate of this sort is reliably based on a few simple but

[18] This point was commendably made long ago by Paul Schubert especially in relation to Luke 24; "The Structure and Significance of Luke 24," in *Neutestamentliche Studien für Rudolph Bultmann* (ed. W. Eltester; Berlin: Töpelmann, 1957), 165–86, esp. 176–77. According to C. J. Hemer (*The Book of Acts in the Setting of Hellenistic History* [Tübingen: J. C. B. Mohr (Paul Siebeck), 1989], 32 n. 14), "the problems of sequence [in] the accounts of the Ascension . . . are to be seen in the context of the admitted overall unity [of Luke-Acts], and are not sufficient in themselves to challenge it." Cf. Schubert (165): "[P]rominent and unmistakeable is the obvious and close literary transition from volume I (Lk 24:50-53) to volume II (Acts 1:1-4), however obscure and puzzling, textually, grammatically and exegetically, its details have proved to be."

[19] R. Maddox, *The Purpose of Luke-Acts* (Göttingen: Vandenhoeck & Ruprecht, 1982), 10.

[20] Zwiep, *The Ascension of the Messiah*, 115. On p. 118, Zwiep helpfully illustrates the existence of seventeen motifs shared between Luke 24:36-53 and Acts 1:1-14.

significant source-critical observations. On at least three occasions Luke omits or minimises a narrative feature in the Lukan Gospel and includes that feature within the narrative of Acts in a manner that is best explained as intentional crafting, with Luke being concerned to place the narrative feature in the position where, in his view, it would be most effective. In these three instances (set out below), Luke demonstrates that his literary imagination spanned two volumes even before the first volume was authored.

First, the Lukan trial scene omits the accusation against Jesus, as reported in Mark 14:58, in which Jesus is said to have threatened to destroy the temple (cf. Matt 26:61). But the same accusation omitted in Luke's account of Jesus' trial reappears in Luke's account of Stephen's trial, with close lexical affinity:

> Mark 14:58:   We heard him say, "I will destroy this temple that is made with hands."
>
> ὅτι ἡμεῖς ἠκούσαμεν αὐτοῦ λέγοντος ὅτι ἐγὼ κατα–
> λύσω τὸν ναὸν τοῦτον τὸν χειροποίητον.
>
> Acts 6:14:   For we have heard him say that this Jesus of Nazareth will destroy this place.
>
> ἀκηκόαμεν γὰρ αὐτοῦ λέγοντος ὅτι Ἰησοῦς ὁ Ναζω–
> ραῖος οὗτος καταλύσει τὸν τόπον τοῦτον.

Evidently Luke saw fit to move the accusation from his Gospel to Acts, with the wording of Acts corresponding closely to that of Mark. As Marguerat suggests, Luke omits the accusation from the account of Jesus' trial since the narrative of Acts 1–5 emerges largely in the context of the temple precinct. The hint of a temple criticism at the end of the Lukan Gospel would form a poor basis for the beginning of the Acts narrative.[21] Similarly, Dunn estimates that Luke introduced the shift in the material in order "to reserve the confrontation and split over the Temple until the Stephen episode" in Acts 6–7.[22]

Second, with regard to the account in Mark 7:1-23 in which Jesus is said to have "declared all foods clean" (7:19), Matthew follows the Markan pericope without too much idiosyncrasy (the notable exception being the omission of the Markan punchline of Mark 7:19). Surprisingly, however, Luke omits the pericope altogether from its expected position in Luke 9. The omission of this episode from the Lukan Gospel is likely to have been motivated by the requirements of the Acts narrative. It is in Acts 10 that the demarcation between pure and impure foods is revealed

---

[21] Marguerat, *The First Christian Historian*, 47–48.

[22] J. D. G. Dunn, *The Acts of the Apostles* (Valley Forge: Trinity Press International, 1996), xv.

to Peter in a vision from God. There Peter declares that he had "never eaten anything that is common or unclean" (10:14). Moreover, he is shown to be greatly perplexed at having been told that "what God has made clean, you must not call profane" (10:15), as if this were the first time that the eradication of purity issues from the meal-table had ever been presented to him. All this would sit uneasily in a narrative in which Jesus had already declared that there is no such thing as common or unclean food. The dropping of the account from the Lukan Gospel is, then, best seen in relation to the narrative requirements of Acts.

Third, when following his Markan source fairly closely with regard to Jesus' purpose for speaking in parables (Mark 4:10-12), Luke truncates the quotation from Isaiah 6:9-10 significantly.[23]

Mark 4:12:   in order that "they may indeed look, but not perceive, and may indeed listen, but not understand; so that they may not turn again and be forgiven."

βλέποντες βλέπωσιν καὶ μὴ ἴδωσιν, καὶ ἀκούοντες ἀκούωσιν καὶ μὴ συνιῶσιν, μήποτε ἐπιστρέψωσιν καὶ ἀφεθῇ αὐτοῖς.

Luke 8:10:   so that "looking they may not perceive, and listening they may not understand."

βλέποντες μὴ βλέπωσιν καὶ ἀκούοντες μὴ συνιῶσιν.

But Luke evidently knows a fuller version of the Isaiah passage, one that appears five verses from the end of Acts:[24]

Acts 28:26-27:   You will indeed listen, but never understand, and you will indeed look, but never perceive. For this people's heart has grown dull, and their ears are hard of hearing, and they have shut their eyes; so that they might not look with their eyes, and listen with their ears, and understand with their heart and turn—and I would heal them.

ακοῇ ἀκούσετε καὶ οὐ μὴ συνῆτε καὶ βλέποντες βλέψ—
ετε καὶ οὐ μὴ ἴδητε· ἐπαχύνθη γὰρ ἡ καρδία τοῦ λαοῦ

---

[23] Although Luke truncates quotations from scripture also in 19:38 and 20:17 (cf. the slight truncation in 18:20), he seems generally to prefer not to truncate scriptural quotations. Compare the following with their Markan counterparts: Luke 3:22; 10:27-28, 20:42-43; 21:27. In 3:4-6 Luke truncates his Markan source by omitting the reference to Malachi 3:1, but then significantly extends Mark by quoting nine more lines of Isaiah 40.

[24] This version also corresponds perfectly with the expansion of Isaiah 6:9-10 in Matthew 13:14-15, a feature that might be of use to those who think that among Luke's sources was a copy of Matthew's Gospel (thus omitting the need for "Q").

τούτου καὶ τοῖς ὠσὶν βαρέως ἤκουσαν καὶ τοὺς
ὀφθαλμοὺς αὐτῶν ἐκάμμυσαν· μήποτε ἴδωσιν τοῖς
ὀφθαλμοῖς καὶ τοῖς ὠσὶν ἀκούσωσιν καὶ τῇ καρδίᾳ
συνῶσιν καὶ ἐπιστρέψωσιν, καὶ ἰάσομαι αὐτούς.

Following the pattern of the previous two examples, in this case Luke appears "to reserve the full version [of Isa 6:9-10], and therefore the full weight of the prophetic text, for his final verses" in Acts.[25]

These three observations are extremely telling instances of Luke's construction of his Gospel narrative with an eye on its effect on the Acts narrative.[26] The book of Acts is neither an afterthought nor an independent volume. The two Lukan books form "a major two-volume literary work that links a narrative of the activities of the churches to a story of Jesus."[27] Although the two Lukan volumes may be marked by certain differences in style and genre,[28] and although different kinds of sources may

[25] Marguerat, *The First Christian Historian*, 48; cf. Dunn, *The Acts of the Apostles*, xv.

[26] Dunn (*The Acts of the Apostles*, xv) compares Luke's technique in these three examples with "his holding back of the information in 22.17-20 for the more dramatic second telling of Paul's conversion-commission [in Acts 26]." While this is an intriguing comparison, Dunn's point would benefit from the acknowledgement that each telling of the story of Paul's narrative fits well within its own narrative context, a point he makes in his *Jesus Remembered* ([Grand Rapids: Eerdmans, 2003], 211–12). See esp. Marguerat, *The First Christian Historian*, 179–204.

[27] L. W. Hurtado, *Lord Jesus Christ: Devotion to Jesus in Earliest Christianity* (Grand Rapids: Eerdmans, 2003), 340.

[28] Discussion of the genre of Luke's two-volume work would take us too far afield, especially since chain-link construction at the Luke-Acts seam has nothing of substance to offer the debate. Proposals include: (1) the historical monograph (G. Schille, *Die Apostelgeschichte des Lukas* [Berlin: Evangelische Verlaganstalt, 1984], 66; D. E. Aune, *The New Testament in Its Literary Environment* [Philadelphia: Westminster, 1987], 77–115; Palmer, "Acts and the Ancient Historical Monograph"; D. D. Schmidt, "Rhetorical Influences and Genre: Luke's Preface and the Rhetoric of Hellenistic Historiography," in *Jesus and the Heritage of Israel: Luke's Narrative Claim upon Israel's Legacy* (ed. E. P. Moessner; Harrisburg: Trinity, 1999), 27–60); (2) the ancient biography (R. A. Burridge, *What are the Gospels? A Comparison with Graeco-Roman Biography* [Cambridge: Cambridge University Press, 1992]; idem, "About People, by People, for People: Gospel Genre and Audiences," in *The Gospels for All Christians: Rethinking the Gospel Audiences* [ed. R. J. Bauckham; Grand Rapids: Eerdmans, 1998], 113–46); (3) the succession narrative (Talbert, *Literary Patterns*); (4) apologetic historiography (G. E. Sterling, *Historiography and Self-Definition: Josephus, Luke-Acts and Apologetic Historiography* [Leiden: Brill, 1992]); (5) the ancient scientific treatise (L. Alexander, *The Preface to Luke's Gospel: Literary Convention and Social Context in Luke 1.1-4 and Acts 1.1* [Cambridge: Cambridge University Press, 1993]; and

underlie them, and although certain narrative interests and foci shift in the two volumes, Luke nonetheless seems to have conceived of one grand plot line running throughout the two volumes. Interpreters may want to question whether Luke's two-volume monograph was *successful* with regard to its literary unity, but that he *intended* it to be successful in this matter is most likely. The two Lukan volumes were not necessarily completed at the same time and made public simultaneously, of course. A gap of anywhere between a few months to perhaps a few years might have separated their initial distribution. But this is simply a footnote issue to the main issue of the underlying unity within the two volumes. The fact of the matter is that Luke can be seen to have made adjustments to the plot in volume one in view of the needs of the plot in volume two. With this evidence in place, the vast and oft-times impressive array of supplementary evidence (i.e., thematic and narrative correlation between the two volumes) can be marshalled to support this conclusion. Chain-link construction at (what really is) the Luke-Acts seam is precisely one type of supporting evidence.

§10.2 Chain-Link Interlock and the Structure of Acts

In his *Nouvelles Études sur Les Actes des Apôtres*, Jacques Dupont included a chapter outlining the existence of chain-links in Luke-Acts. Dupont's conclusions have converged with our own in three cases: the Luke-Acts seam; Acts 8:1-3; Acts 19:21-41.[29]

---

(6) the historical novel, epic, or apostolic romance (R. I. Pervo, *Profit with Delight: The Literary Genre of the Acts of the Apostles* [Philadelphia: Fortress, 1987]; Bonz, *The Past as Legacy*).

Aune makes the following point (*New Testament in its Literary Environment*, 77), which is apropos to the discussion of chain-link construction at the Luke-Acts seam: "By itself, Luke could (like Mark, Matthew and John) be classified as a type of ancient biography. But Luke, though it might have circulated separately, was subordinated to a larger literary structure. Luke does not belong to a type of ancient biography for it belongs with Acts, and Acts cannot be forced into a biographical mold." This approach is preferable to that of R. A. Burridge, who considers Luke to be a biography but Acts to be historiography ("The Gospels and Acts," in *Handbook of Classical Rhetoric in the Hellenistic Period (330 B.C–A.D. 400)* [ed. S. E. Porter; Leiden: Brill, 1997], 507–32, esp. 516): "Acts contains many biographical features . . . as well as some shared elements of romance, travelogue, and the early novel, but it is probably best seen as a historical monograph."

[29] Dupont ("La question du plan des Actes," 31) considers whether Acts 11–13 includes a chain link construction, but decides against it, considering it a poor transition: "On peut penser que, si Luc avait eu conscience de commencer quelque chose de vraiment nouveau, il aurait pris soin d'assurer une meilleure transition."

Two of Dupont's cases, however, are not compelling. In the first instance, he argues that Acts 14 and 15 incorporate a chain-link transition at 15:1-4. According to Dupont, Acts 15:1-2 connects with 15:5-6 in introducing the provocative issue that requires the solution prescribed by a leadership council, as described in 15:7-29. Similarly, Acts 15:3-4 is related to 14:27 since it continues the motif of Paul's travels, and consequently relates to the whole travel narrative of Acts 13-14.[30] In my view, Dupont's case is not convincing. The account of Paul's travels in Acts 15:3-4 is thoroughly at home in its own context and has no "backward" aspect to it. Consequently, the construction expected of a chain-link interlock makes no appearance in this case.

Dupont also claims that 15:36–16:5 functions according to the rules of chain-link construction.[31] But Dupont only manages to draw lines of connection from these verses to other passages in Acts. It is true that there is a transition of sorts in this section, since within these sections we see the rearrangement of Paul's colleagues—i.e. Paul's sudden and unexpected break with Barnabas concerning John Mark and Paul's newly formed association with Timothy. But there are no characterising marks of chain-link construction in this section. The Barnabas material appears early in the text unit (15:36-41), with Barnabas having been Paul's companion since Acts 11, and the Timothy material appears late in the text unit (16:1-5), with Timothy playing a role in the material that follows (17:14-15; 18:5; 19:22; and 20:4). So there is no overlap of material here, which is the hallmark of chain-link construction. What Acts 15:36–16:5 represents, then, is not a chain-link transition (contra Dupont) but a bridge paragraph—i.e., A/a+b/B (as discussed in §3.8).

It appears, then, that four chain-link interlocks are at work in the Acts narrative. The first one links Acts to the Lukan Gospel (Luke 24:47-53; Acts 1:1-12), and the others are evident at 8:1b-3, 11:27–12:25, and 19:21-41. At this point consideration must be given to the position of these interlocks within the overall structure of Acts. In particular, it needs to be asked whether Luke's chain links demarcate the major text units within the Acts narrative.

It is probable that more proposals have been suggested for the structure of Acts than for just about any other canonical New Testament narrative.[32] If one literary feature or narrative theme is prioritised, one text-unit demarcation emerges; if another is prioritised, another demar-

---

[30] Dupont, "La question du plan des Actes," 32.

[31] Dupont, "La question du plan des Actes," 32-33.

[32] Perhaps the problem is illustrated in Burridge, "The Gospels and Acts," where an outline of Luke's Gospel is offered (p. 516), along with outlines of the other canonical Gospels, but no attempt to outline Acts is evident.

cation follows suit. The result has been a plethora of suggestions as to the structure of Acts. So, for instance, the text has been said to consist of:[33]

- two parts (the midpoint being 11:27; or 13:1; or 15:36);[34]

- three parts (the second and third parts commencing at 6:1 and 11:19; or 8:4 and 13:1; or 8:4 and 21:18; or 9:32 and 15:36; or 6:1 and 15:36);[35]

- four parts (the final three commencing at 8:1, 13:1, and 21:16; or 8:4, 15:36 and 21:27; or 8:4, 15:36, and 22:30; or 9:1, 15:36, and 21:27; or 6:1, 9:32, and 12:25; or 5:1, 11:19, and 21:15);[36]

- five parts (the final four commencing at 6:1, 13:1, 15:36, and 19:21; or 6:1, 9:32, 15:36, and 19:21; or 8:4, 11:19, 15:36, and 19:21);[37]

[33] In this survey, the introduction of Acts has been omitted from consideration.

[34] So, for instance, respectively: C. Perrot, "Les Actes des Apôtres," in *Introduction critique au Nouveau Testament*, vol. 2 (ed. A. George and P. Grelot; Paris: Desclée, 1976), 253–55; J. Klausner, *From Jesus to Paul* (London: Allen and Unwin, 1946), 212; P.-H. Menoud, "Le plan des Actes des Apôtres," *NTS* 1 (1954-55): 44–51, and Trocmé, *Le "Livre des Actes" et l'histoire*. Like Trocmé, Bonz (*The Past as Legacy*, 164) divides Acts between Acts 15 and 16, labelling Acts 13–15 as the "Prelude to the Pauline Mission," and thereby undervaluing its significance.

[35] So, for instance, respectively: I. H. Marshall, *The Acts of the Apostles* (Sheffield: Sheffield Academic Press, 1992); H. Lindsell, "Introduction to the Acts of the Apostles," in the *Eyre & Spottiswoode Study Bible* (London: Eyre & Spottiswoode, 1964), 1624–25, esp. 1625. T. Bergholz's outline (*Der Aufbau des lukanischen Doppelwerkes* [Frankfurt am Main: Peter Lang, 1995], 55, 139) is virtually identical, except he identifies the start of the second text unit as 8:1a rather than 8:4; F. Ó Fearghail, *The Introduction to Luke-Acts: A Study of the Role of Lk 1,1–4,44 in the Composition of Luke's Two-Volume Work* (Rome: Editrice Pontificio Instituto Biblico, 1991), 67–84; A. Wikenhauser, *Die Apostelgeschichte* (Regensburg: Verlag Friedrich Pustut, 1938), 5–6; Schneider, *Die Apostelgeschichte*, 7–9.

[36] So, for instance, respectively: L. Alexander, "Acts," in *The Oxford Bible Commentary* (ed. J. Barton and J. Muddiman; Oxford: Oxford University Press, 2001), 1030; E. Haenchen, "The Book of Acts as Source Material for the History of Early Christianity," in *Studies in Luke-Acts* (ed. L. E. Keck and J. L. Martyn; Nashville: Abingdon, 1966), 259; L. T. Johnson, *The Acts of the Apostles* (Collegeville: Liturgical Press, 1992), v–vii; J. Jervell, *Die Apostelgeschichte* (Göttingen: Vandenhoeck & Ruprecht, 1998), 5–7; M. Goulder, *Type and History in Acts* (London: SPCK, 1964), 65, 98; D. L. Wiens, *Stephen's Sermon and the Structure of Luke-Acts* (N. Richland Hills: BIBAL Press, 1995).

[37] So, for instance, respectively: the Jerusalem Bible; J. Roloff, *Die Apostelgeschichte* (Göttengen: Vandenhoeck & Ruprecht, 1988), 13–14; J. C. O'Neill, *The Theology of Acts in Its Historical Setting* (rev. ed.; London: SPCK, 1970).

- six parts (the final five commencing at 6:8, 9:32, 12:25/13:1, 16:6, and 19:21; or 3:1, 6:1, 13:1, 21:37, and 28:16);[38]
- eight parts (the final seven commencing at 6:1, 9:1, 9:32, 11:19, 13:1, 15:36, and 19:21).[39]

And so on.[40]

If chain-link transitions are prioritised as structural indicators of main text units, then four such units emerge: 1:1–8:3; 8:4–12:25; 13:1–19:41; 20:1–28:31. Most of these text-unit boundaries have appeared frequently in proposed structural outlines of Acts. There is no novelty, for instance, in proposing that 8:4 or 13:1 is the start of a new text unit. What is novel, at least to my knowledge, is the proposal that 20:1 is the beginning of the final text unit of Acts. But this is a slightly exaggerated novelty since the demarcation of text-unit boundaries within chain-link transitions can at times be difficult to determine precisely because of the material overlap involved in those transitions. So, while there is some reason for us to think (along with a good number of scholars) that 19:21 is the start of the fourth and final text unit of Acts, four reasons (considered in §9.4) suggest that the text-unit boundary is to be moved to the other end of the chain-link transition, so that 20:1 is recognised as the true start of that final main text unit. With this shift in text-unit demarcation, each of the text-unit boundaries suggested here has already been advocated as such by a variety of interpreters.

Since none of the proposed text-unit boundaries suggested here is completely without precedent in scholarly outlines of Acts currently on offer, it is all the more intriguing that (to my knowledge) no other proposal for the structure of Acts matches in precise terms the four-fold structure suggested here. Allowing chain-link transitions to determine structural boundaries results in an altogether novel structural demarcation within the book. Certainly smaller text units fall within these larger blocks of material, and other literary features are well suited to mark them out. But text-unit divisions that are identified by features other

---

[38] So, for instance, respectively: J. P. Polhill, *The Acts of the Apostles* (Nashville: Broadman, 1992), 72–74 and R. N. Longenecker, "The Acts of the Apostles," in *The Expositor's Bible Commentary* (Grand Rapids: Zondervan, 1981), 9:234, both following C. H. Turner ("Chronology of the Bible." *A Dictionary of the Bible*, vol. 1. [ed. J. Hastings; Edinburgh: T&T Clark, 1898], 421), although Turner's approach has come under significant fire (so, e.g., O'Neill, *The Theology of Acts*, 64–65); F. S. Spencer, *Acts* (Sheffield: Sheffield Academic, 1997), 5.

[39] The NRSV follows this outline, according to the space dividers inserted into its text at these points.

[40] Witherington (*The Acts of the Apostles*, v–ix), for instance, outlines thirteen sections as well as the prologue.

than chain-link construction should best be seen as delineating units subordinate to the main ones identified by chain-link construction.

It is not self-evident that the position of a chain link indicates the boundaries of *main* text units, since chain-link interlock can appear at lesser structural levels as well. But in the case of Acts, eight observations give the suggestion a strong basis. In each of the following eight points, the structural demarcation suggested here coincides with significant features of the narrative's plot.

First, the main transition in the Lukan writings (i.e., the transition from the Gospel of Luke to Acts) proceeds on the basis of a chain-link interlock. Obviously Luke might have chosen a different structure to assist with the transition at that point. Either a simple anticipatory transition at the end of Luke's Gospel or a simple retrospective transition at the beginning of Acts might have been enough to lash the two texts together. Instead, it was a chain-link structure that Luke favoured to carry the weight of the transition between the two main text units.[41]

Second, as was demonstrated above (§9.2), the significant shift from Peter to Paul in the narrative's focus is matched by the appearance of a chain-link interlock at precisely that point (11:27–12:25). Again, then, the structural weight of a transition between main text units is borne by a chain-link construction.

Third, working backwards from Acts 13, it was seen (in §9.3) that Acts 12 is the culmination of a tightly knit text unit that begins at 8:4. The material running from 8:4 through to Acts 12 has been woven together through a complex chain-link construction. The bedrock for the complex chain-link is found at the beginning of Acts 8, so that a main text unit runs from 8:4 to 12:25. That the text unit does not begin earlier than 8:4 is suggested by the fact that the early chapters of Acts remain focussed on events affecting the Christian movement in Jerusalem up to 8:3, whereas in 8:4–12:25 the geographical focus begins to expand into further regions of the Mediterranean basin.[42]

---

[41] Although a full study of Luke's Gospel has not been carried out within the time frame of this project, I am unaware of the presence of chain-link interlock in that volume. This is not surprising, however, if Luke's use of chain-link interlock coincides with his view of temporal epochs and geographical boundaries in combination (as suggested below). An attempt to demarcate the structure of Luke's Gospel according to concentric figures is evident in the work of T. P. Osborne, "Deux grandes structures concentriques centrales et une nouvelle approche du plan global de l'Evangile de Luc (première partie)," *RevB* 110 (2003): 197–221.

[42] Throughout the whole of Acts, of course, Jerusalem remains a geographical (not to mention theological) grounding point for the expansion of the Christian movement. So, rightly, Johnson (*The Acts of the Apostles*, 11): "[T]he geographical movement in Acts . . . is not simply outward. Each movement of the Gospel away from Jerusalem also circles back to it (see 8:14; 11:1-18, 29-30;

Fourth, working forwards from Acts 13, placing a main text-unit boundary at the seam between Acts 19 and 20 results in the creation of a single text unit (13:1–19:41). At least three things need to be said of such a text unit: a) it encapsulates the whole of Paul's public ministry; b) it is bounded at both ends by stories of Paul's encounter with pagan magic (13:4-12; 19:11-20, 23-40);[43] and c) it depicts the whole of Paul's public ministry as commissioned by the church (13:3) and as the result of his having been "set apart" by the Spirit (13:2; cf. 19:21). Placing a main text unit boundary elsewhere in the narrative fails to have these notable attractions.

Fifth, expanding on the fourth point, the text unit of Acts 13–19 climaxes in Paul's ministry at Ephesus where "for the first time in the preaching of Paul there is an authentic universal dimension as the Word of God is preached to both Jews and Gentiles outside the synagogue context" (as in 19:10, Ἰουδαίους τε καὶ Ἕλληνας; cf. 19:17, and Paul's own summary of his Ephesian ministry in 20:21). In this way, the Ephesus material of Acts 19 "serves as *the continuation, culmination* and *climax* of the missionary journeys of Paul."[44] Moreover, as noted above, Demetrius' description of Paul's ministry easily serves as a Lukan summary of the significance of Paul's public ministry since Acts 13: "in almost the whole of Asia this Paul has persuaded and drawn away a considerable number of people" (19:26).[45]

Sixth, with Paul's missionary activity coming to an end in Acts 19, the final eight chapters comprise his journeys to Jerusalem and Rome as one "bound in the Spirit" (20:22; cf. 19:21 and the Spirit's role at the beginning of the third text unit, 13:2). With the narrative of Paul's public ministry coming to a close in the Ephesian accounts, the narrative of his progress to Jerusalem and ultimately to Rome is contained within a single text unit (20:1–28:31).

Seventh, Beverly Gaventa has observed that Luke's depiction of Paul with the gathered church in Acts 20 replicates the depiction of the

---

12:25; 15:2; 18:22; 19:21; 20:16; 21:13; 25:1). Luke is concerned to show that the expansion of Christianity into the wider world and among the Gentiles took place in continuity and communication with the original community in Jerusalem."

[43] On this, see esp. H.-J.Klauck, *Magic and Paganism in Early Christianity: The World of the Acts of the Apostles* (trans. B. McNeil; Edinburgh: T&T Clark, 2000).

[44] S. Cunningham, "Through Many Tribulations," *The Theology of Persecution in Luke-Acts* (Sheffield: Sheffield Academic Press, 1997), 264 and 263 respectively (emphasis added).

[45] Cf. Klauck (*Magic and Paganism in Early Christianity*, 110): "Artemis of Ephesus has her devotees in all the Mediterranean world but Christianity is speedily catching up with her. Even Demetrius, the foe of Christianity, bears witness that it has already filled all Asia Minor."

gathered church in Acts 2 and 4. So the gathered church is marked out by instruction (2:42; 4:31, 33; 20:20, 24-27, 31), the breaking of bread (2:42, 46; 20:7, 11), prayer (2:42; 4:24-31; 20:36), and the sharing of goods (2:44-45; 4:32, 34-37; 20:33-35).[46] In this way the beginning of the fourth main text unit of Acts touches base with the first text unit, reinforcing its depiction of the gathered church. The start of the final main unit:

a) testifies to the universal character of Christianity despite its various indigenous forms depicted in the intervening chapters;

b) demonstrates that the universal character of Christianity has not been compromised in the period since its founding; and

c) indicates, most importantly, that Paul himself has sought to replicate the universal character of Christianity in communities throughout the Mediterranean basin.

Significantly, then, the text unit in which Paul makes his final return to Jerusalem, is taken into custody, and is sent as a prisoner to Rome begins with an implicit affirmation that the Christian communities he has nurtured far beyond Jerusalem are nonetheless in complete harmony with the ethos, spirituality, practice, and faith of the Jerusalem Christian community. With this established at the start of the last text unit, the events that unfold in that text unit are given an added dimension of irony, intrigue, and dramatic effect.

Eighth, the Lukan structural divisions as indicated by chain-link interlock correspond with and elucidate Jesus' programmatic statement of 1:8 that his followers will be his "witnesses in Jerusalem, in all Judaea and Samaria, and to the ends of the earth." So the first text unit from 1:1–8:3 is unified by its singular focus on the Christian community in Jerusalem. And that of 8:4–12:25, while keeping one foot in Jerusalem and stepping out as far as Antioch, includes significant material regarding the spread of the Christian movement through Samaria (Acts 8:4-25) and the Judaean region and its borders (e.g., 8:26-40; 9:32-43; 10:1-48).[47] This coincides precisely with the signal given in the anticipatory gesture of 8:1b that introduces the second main text unit, which speaks of the Christians being "scattered throughout the region of Judaea and Samaria." And the third and fourth text units (13:1–19:41 and 20:1–28:31

---

[46] B. R. Gaventa, "Theology and Ecclesiology in the Miletus Speech: Reflections on Content and Context," *NTS* 50 (2004): 36–52.

[47] Further discussion of the internal arrangement and coherence of Acts 8:4–12:25 is too complex to be offered here.

respectively) are clearly interested in the spread of Christianity beyond Jerusalem, Judaea and Samaria—that is, "to the ends of the earth."[48]

These eight observations indicate the structural weight that Luke places on chain-link transitions. They suggest that when Luke required a transition to mark the main text-unit boundaries, it was chain link that he chose for this purpose on four occasions.

It is proposed here, then, that Acts is comprised of four main text units. Loveday Alexander also speaks of Acts as "a drama with four major acts," although she considers it important to stress "that this is a modern, not an ancient, division."[49] But in fact, while Acts does seem to be comprised of four main parts, this estimate is not simply a modern one. Instead, it is based on that fact that Luke, along with Graeco-Roman rhetoricians and others from the ancient world, marks off distinct text units by means of the careful placement of relatively noticeable transition markers at critical points in the narrative. Four of those critical points have presented themselves as marking off macro-level units by means of chain-link interlock, with four distinct macro text units being created accordingly. The four are delineated as follows, with suggested thematic descriptors beside them:

Acts 1:1–8:3   Early Christianity in Jerusalem

Acts 8:4–12:25   Persecution and the Consequent Spread of Christianity (with the transition beginning at 8:1b)

Acts 13:1–19:41   The Spread of Christianity through the Ministry of Paul (with the transition beginning at 11:27)

Acts 20:1–28:31   The Spread of Christianity through Events that Take Paul from Jerusalem to Rome (with the transition beginning at 19:21)

Among scholarly proposals for the structure of Acts, that of Daniel Marguerat comes closest to this proposal, itself being comprised of four parts:[50]

---

[48] So Bergholz (*Der Aufbau der lukanischen Doppelwerkes*, 136): "Mit Hinweis auf Apg 1,8 hatten wir aber die Zäsur der Hauptteile nach geographischen Gesichtspunkten bei Apg 13 gesetzt, was durch den Gliederungshinweis des Paulusteiles in Apg 9,15f bestätigt wurde." See also his argument on pp. 47–48 in support of his view (coinciding closely with my own) that Jesus' geographical overview of 1:8 corresponds with three parts of the Acts narrative, the first ending in 8:1a, the second ending in 12:25, and the third running throughout Acts 13–28. On p. 44, Bergholz lists other ways in which the structural significance has been interpreted in relation to the developments in the Acts narrative.

[49] Alexander, "Acts," 1030.

[50] Marguerat, *The First Christian Historian*, 111. Marguerat calls these structural divisions "non-original," but I have not managed to find a precedent, nor

Acts 1–7	The Golden Age of the Community of Jerusalem
Acts 8–12	The Peter Cycle
Acts 13–20	Paul's Mission
Acts 21–28	The Martyrdom of Paul

Disregarding Marguerat's descriptors, the main point of difference between our proposals is that Marguerat finds the last of the four main units to begin at Acts 21. While I have proposed that the final text unit begins at 20:1, I have also recognised that 19:21 has some merit in that regard. But there is virtually no case for placing the start of the final unit at 21:1. The first fourteen verses of Acts 21 continue the post-Ephesian journey that began in Acts 20 before the arrival in Jerusalem narrated in 21:15, and there are no major structural transition markers at the end of Acts 20 or the beginning of Acts 21. So while Marguerat's proposed structure falls closely in line with mine, our proposed structures go their own way at the point where Marguerat's position has little textual basis.

There is one final point to note. Acts 15:36 is frequently identified as the location of a new main text-unit. My analysis, however, offers no basis for this text-unit division. Perhaps on this matter much of Lukan scholarship is still following in the footsteps of those such as Hans Conzelmann who differentiated the two stages of ecclesiastical development within Acts: the law-oriented "Urkirche," followed by the more universal "'heutigen' Kirche." For Conzelmann, the line of ecclesiastical differentiation falls at Acts 15.[51] For some, the attraction of such a demarcation seems to be its intrinsic valuation of the early period as "primitive" Christianity, out of which later Christianity emerged. But the structural development of Acts, as demarcated by chain-link interlock, indicates that a main text-unit falls nowhere close to Acts 15. Consequently a differentiation between the early law-oriented church and the contemporary universal church along the lines made by Conzelmann has little structural merit.[52]

To say that a main text-unit does not begin anywhere near Luke's account of the Apostolic Council of Acts 15 is not, of course, to diminish

---

does he cite any. The closest I can find is the three-part outline of Lindsell ("Introduction to the Acts of the Apostles," 1625), comprising 1:1–8:3, 8:4–12:25; 13:1–28:31. See also the close four-part division of Alexander ("Acts," 1030), with the final three parts commencing at 8:1, 13:1, and 21:17.

[51] E.g., H. Conzelmann, *Die Mitte der Zeit: Studien zur Theologie des Lukas* (5th ed.; Tübingen: Mohr Siebeck, 1964), 8 n. 1. Conzelmann's scheme is plagued by a series of problems other than the one cited here.

[52] Similarly, as Ó Fearghail rightly notes (*The Introduction to Luke-Acts*, 77), "it is difficult to see why one should distinguish between [Paul's] missionary activity" on either side of 15:36.

the historical and theological significance of that council for Luke's narrative. Instead, it is simply to notice the placement of that event closer to the middle of a text-unit, just as Peter's critically important vision and experience with Cornelius in Acts 10–11 fall close to the middle of the previous text-unit. In a sense, just as the account of Peter's experiences in Acts 10–11 gives theological legitimacy to the narrative that falls on either side of it in the text unit of Acts 8:4–12:25, so the account of the Apostolic Council in Acts 15 gives theological legitimacy to the narrative that falls on either side of it in the text unit of Acts 13:1–19:41.[53]

§10.3   Chain-Link Interlock and the Theology of Acts

If structural priority is to be given to the chain-link transitions for determining the main text units of Acts, as I have suggested, and if those transitions appear in the places suggested above, then it might be asked whether any inferences can be drawn for understanding the theology of Acts. Three points suggest themselves.

First, as was shown in §10.2, Jesus' prophecy that his followers will be his "witnesses in Jerusalem, in all Judaea and Samaria, and to the ends of the earth" (1:8) corresponds closely to the structural arrangement of the narrative's four main text units. That the narrative ends in Rome rather than in some secluded outpost on the margins of the civilised world does not disqualify these final two sections as being the narrative fulfilment of Jesus' geographical prophecy concerning the "ends of the earth." This is especially true since the Lukan writings are not "Rome-centric" but "Jerusalem-centric." As Richard Bauckham notes, for most first-century Jews "Jerusalem lay at the centre of the inhabited world," and Luke himself reconstructs that "Jerusalem-centred perspective for readers of Acts."[54] What Luke narrates in Acts 13–28 is the activity of one particular Christian missionary progressively entering horizons far beyond Jerusalem. The audience is expected to imagine similar missions issuing out to other places and in other directions (just as there had already been a mission to Rome prior to Paul's arrival there). Luke does not think that his audience will be disappointed if his narrative fails to take them literally to the "ends of the earth"; his estimate of their historical imagination is far more charitable than that and is devoid of such a patronising component.

---

[53] On the relationship between Acts 10:1–11:18 and Acts 15, see esp. B. R. Gaventa, *The Acts of the Apostles* (Nashville: Abingdon, 2003), 211–12.

[54] R. J. Bauckham, "James and Jerusalem Church," in *The Book of Acts in Its Palestinian Setting* (ed. R. Bauckham; Grand Rapids: Eerdmans, 1995), 417, 422. See his fuller discussion on 417–27. Cf. also J. M. Scott, "Luke's Geographical Horizon," in *The Book of Acts in Its Graeco-Roman Setting* (ed. D. W. J. Gill and C. Gempf; Grand Rapids: Eerdmans, 1994), 483–544, esp. 495–99.

With Luke's structural divisions corresponding with and elucidating Jesus' programmatic statement of Acts 1:8, Luke depicts Jesus as one who foresees the future of the church and who has nothing but confidence in its universal expansion. Luke's Gospel has already depicted a Jesus whose words are reliable and sure.[55] The same applies to Acts, with Jesus' prophecy of 1:8 becoming embodied in the movement of the church from the salvation-historical "centre" of the earth in ever new configurations of ministry and worship. Throughout Acts 1–28, Luke demonstrates that Jesus' words are as reliable and trustworthy long after his earthly ministry as they were during that ministry. As Vernon Robbins well writes, with Jesus' words in 1:8 "[a] new program has emerged, and this program guides the ensuing narrative. In this way the program of Acts is authorized by Jesus himself, the founder and validator of the Christian movement."[56]

Second, the development of the church as envisaged by Jesus is itself shown to be a manifestation of the fulfilment of scripture. The chain-link interlock at the Luke-Acts seam not only enhances the unity of Luke-Acts but also contributes to the theological framework of those two volumes. It does this by highlighting the notion that the narrative recounted by Luke is itself the unfolding of a narrative preordained within scripture. So, in the chain link at the Luke-Acts seam, Jesus is said to open the minds of his disciples "to understand the scriptures" (24:45), an unveiling that takes effect in two distinct but related ways. First, scriptural fulfilment is claimed for the ministry of the Messiah who had to "suffer and on the third day rise from the dead" (24:46) in order to fulfil "everything written about me in the law of Moses and the prophets and the psalms" (24:44). These events are narrated in the Lukan Gospel. Secondly, scriptural fulfilment is claimed for the ministry of the church, whose task is to preach "repentance and forgiveness of sins . . . to all nations, beginning in Jerusalem" (24:47). These events are narrated in Acts according to the programme of Jesus' words in 1:8 and the literary structure outlined above. Consequently, for Luke, not only the events of Jesus' life and

---

[55] See, for instance, Jesus' four predictions about the fall of the temple in 13:32-35; 19:41-44; 21:20-24; 23:27-31. On the destruction of the temple within the Roman context of the late first century CE, see B. W. Longenecker, "Rome's Victory and God's Honour: The Jerusalem Temple and the Spirit of God in Lukan Theodicy," in *The Holy Spirit and Christian Origins: Essays in Honor of James D. G. Dunn* (ed. G. N. Stanton, B. W. Longenecker, and S. C. Barton; Grand Rapids: Eerdmans, 2004), 90–102.

[56] V. K. Robbins, "The Claims of the Prologues and Greco-Roman Rhetoric: The Prefaces to Luke and Acts in Light of Greco-Roman Rhetorical Strategies," in *Jesus and the Heritage of Israel: Luke's Narrative Claim upon Israel's Legacy* (ed. D. P. Moessner; Harrisburg: Trinity Press International, 1999), 81.

death (as narrated in Luke's first volume) but also the events of the early Christian movement (as narrated in Luke's second volume) fall under the legitimising authority of scripture.

These theological claims implicit within the chain-link interlock at the Luke-Acts seam elaborate a similar claim that appears at the start of Luke's Gospel (1:1), where Luke speaks of the events that he narrates as having been "fulfilled among us" (πεπληροφορημένων ἐν ἡμῖν). By this he does not mean simply that they "took place in our time." He is claiming that the history of the early Christian movement is the embodiment of what the scriptures of Israel have foreseen as the accomplishment of the divine will.[57] Standing at the start and finish of the Lukan Gospel, claims of this sort form an *inclusio* around the Gospel. But since the claim to scriptural legitimisation in 24:45 looks ahead into Acts, and since Luke seems to have conceived of the two books as a single two-volume monograph, we can reasonably conclude that Luke envisaged the events recounted in Acts to fall within the "fulfilled among us" clause in the opening sentence of his Gospel. For Luke, then, the fulfilment of scripture is evident not only in God's empowering of the life and ministry of Jesus (4:21; 24:27, 32) but also in the life and ministry of Jesus' followers.[58]

---

[57] Alexander (*The Preface to Luke's Gospel*, 113) writes: "The reader in the know, that is the Christian reader, might well see in this a covert allusion to the fulfilment of prophecy, but it is unlikely that anyone less privileged would have grasped the allusion." I take it that Luke is writing principally for "the reader in the know." In a later article ("Formal Elements and Genre: Which Greco-Roman Prologues Most Closely Parallel the Lukan Prologues?" in *Jesus and the Heritage of Israel: Luke's Narrative Claim upon Israel's Legacy* [ed. D. P. Moessner; Harrisburg: Trinity Press International, 1999], 9–26, esp. 26), Alexander nuances the matter along the lines of a "forward" (i.e., naïve) reading and a "backward" (i.e., informed) reading. W. Kurz "Promise and Fulfillment in Hellenistic Jewish Narratives and in Luke and Acts," in Moessner [ed.], *Jesus and the Heritage of Israel*, 147–70, esp. 148) speaks of Luke's πεπληροφορημένων as "a biblical allusion—granted, in nonbiblical Hellenistic idiom."

[58] According to R. I. Denova (*The Things Accomplished Among Us: Prophetic Tradition in the Structural Pattern of Luke-Acts* [Sheffield: Sheffield Academic Press, 1997], 17), "[F]or most scholars who accept the narrative unity of the two-books, the 'fulfillment of prophecy' (understood to be an apologetic device) is part of the substructure of the Third Gospel, but has little to do with the overall structure of the second book . . . [With a spattering of citations throughout the earlier chapters of Acts], [a] citation from scripture only resurfaces in the final chapter of Acts, in what is taken as an awkward attempt to tie the two books together." Such a view cannot be maintained once it is recognised that the theme of the fulfilment of scripture falls within the chain-link interlock that introduces Acts. As such, the theme establishes itself in prime structural and interpretative location.

The third theological point that can be drawn from the structure of Acts involves a particular theology of persecution. It has been shown that the second main text unit of Acts is characterised internally by a multiple chain-link system, with three text panels linked to the transition of 8:1-3 at 8:4, 9:1, and 11:19. The first and third of the chain-linked panels (i.e., 8:4-40 and 11:19-30/12:25 respectively) connect to 8:1-3 through the theme of "persecution promotes the spread of Christianity," with Christian witnesses being scattered as a result of persecution (8:4; 11:19). Even the second linked panel shares in this theme in an ironic fashion, with the arch-persecutor himself becoming the arch-witness, the first evidence of this being found in the second chain-linked panel of 9:1-31. And even the unlinked Petrine material plays a part in this, with the persecution account of 12:1-24 being followed by the appended summary: "But the word of God continued to advance and gain adherents" (12:24). Consequently, the second main text unit of Acts deserves to stand under a descriptor that does justice to the concern evident throughout virtually the whole of the text unit: persecution against Christianity results in the further dissemination of Christianity. (This is preferable, for instance, to Marguerat's simple descriptor, "The Peter Cycle" [see above].)

Furthermore, it is of no small significance that the third text panel of the second main text unit of Acts (i.e. 11:19-30) gives way to another chain-link construction at 11:27–12:25. What transpires structurally as a consequence of this is comparable to the structure of a wooden Russian doll, in which the first doll is lifted to reveal a second smaller doll under it, and a third under that, and so on. The pattern continues to replicate itself. In Luke's structural equivalent, the third major text unit (i.e. Acts 13:1–19:41) emerges specifically in connection with the third chain-linked text panel of the second major text unit (i.e. Acts 11:19-30), itself being headed by the motif of "persecution promotes Christianity" (see Chart 1 below). And since the second text unit emerged from the first at the point of Stephen's martyrdom (8:1-3), it is not surprising that Paul, who had passively participated in Stephen's martyrdom, later expected to face martyrdom as a Christian missionary (20:25, 38; cf. 21:11), which Luke's narrative implies was the actual outcome of Paul's time in Rome in Acts 28.

Perhaps Luke's point is much like that expressed by Paul in Philippians, where imprisonment and persecution are not seen as occasions of shame and defeat but of honour and victory: "I want you to know, brothers and sisters, that what has happened to me has really served to advance the gospel" (Phil 1:12; cf. 1:14, 28-30). In Luke's narrative, Paul's ministry that the chain-link of 11:27–12:25 introduces is presented as a preeminent example of the principle deeply embedded within the Lukan narrative: i.e., opposition to God is itself used by God to further God's own ways.[59] Through the chain-link interlock connecting the second and third main text units of Acts, Luke has "bought into essential connection" (Lucian's words) the "persecution-yet-spread" motif of the second text unit and the account of Paul in the third and fourth text units. In Luke's narrative of Paul, the persecutor *par excellence* is shown to become the witness *par excellence*, himself experiencing persecution of a kind that advances the gospel in surprising ways. And so, the narrative ends with Paul confidently preaching the gospel of "the empire of God" (τὴν βασιλείαν τοῦ θεοῦ) in the empire's capital city (28:31).[60] So persecution against a small group of unimpressive people in Jerusalem is shown by Luke to result in a series of unforeseen events that take the empire by storm. As Beverly Gaventa correctly notes:

> Both of these threads, the triumph of God who will not allow the gospel to be overcome *and* the rejection of the gospel and the persecution of its apostles, belong to the narrative Luke develops. To eliminate either of them is to miss something essential to the Lukan story. Certainly it is possible to say . . . that God's word will finally triumph. . . . That confidence, however, is not the same as triumphalism and does not negate the continued presence of persecution and rejection in the narrative of Acts.[61]

As theology in narrative form, Acts is not simply about the historical advancement of early Christianity, or about primary figures within that

[59] Marguerat (*The First Christian Historian*, 108) rightly notes, "[T]he irony of God consists in integrating even the actions of his enemies in order to make them contribute to the advancement of the Word 'to the ends of the earth.'" Cf. R. C. Tannehill (*The Narrative Unity of Luke-Acts: A Literary Interpretation* [2 vols.; Philadelphia: Fortress, 1986/1990], 1:30): Prominent in Luke is the "theme of human opposition which does not stop the mission but contributes to its spread." C. K. Barrett (*The Acts of the Apostles* [Edinburgh: T&T Clark, 1994], 709) notes that this pattern "occurs several times in Acts and represents the way in which Luke conceived the progress of Christianity": that is, "a difficulty is encountered; steps are taken to deal with it; not only is the problem solved but a notable advance takes place as a result." Cf. 6:1-7; 19:9-10; 15:1-35.

[60] Here I differ from R. C. Tannehill ("Rejection by Jews and Turning to Gentiles: The Pattern of Paul's Mission in Acts." in *Luke-Acts and the Jewish People: Eight Critical Perspectives* [ed. J. B. Tyson; Minneapolis: Augsburg, 1988], 83–101, esp. 98) who argues that "Acts ends on a tragic, not a triumphant note." Contrast R. Jewett (*Dating Paul's Life* [London: SCM Press, 1979], 45): "Luke intended to conclude his work on the most positive note he could find." See the optimistic treatment of the ending of Acts in O'Neill, *The Theology of Acts*, 60–65.

[61] B. R. Gaventa, "Towards a Theology of Acts: Reading and Rereading," *Int* 42 (1988): 146–57, esp. 157. The gist of the quotation from Gaventa, and of the paragraphs offered here, counters the view of Pervo (*Profit with Delight*, 28), that the theme of persecution in Acts offers "lots of excitement" but "little theology."

movement, such as Peter or Paul. Nor is it essentially Christologically or pneumatologically focussed. The narrative of Acts embodies "theology" in the true sense of that word, focussed on God and the way in which the sovereign and unrivalled God is working to achieve God's ends, despite opposition.[62] The God of this narrative is in the process of accomplishing an almighty and universal victory—not a victory along the lines of Rome's military victories in Jerusalem, Judaea, and throughout the Mediterranean basis, but a victory of an altogether different sort. Just as Rome aspired to rule the whole of the civilised world and to gather all peoples together in a single diverse-but-unified society of concord, so this God would be content with nothing short of a victory "to the ends of the earth," affecting the whole of the created order and unifying the diverse nations of the world.

Luke is convinced that this process, itself the fulfilment of scripture, cannot be stopped, despite whatever persecution might rise up against God's people in Christ. This Lukan conviction is briefly indicated in the Nazareth incident of Luke 4, when a mob of Jesus' fellow Nazarenes lead him out of the village to the brow of the hill in order to throw him down and stone him to death. Luke "under-narrates" the outcome of this scene: "But he passed through the midst of them and went on his way" (Luke 4:30). This rather surreal occurrence is played out time and time again in the narrative of Acts, in which obstacles to the progress of God's empire are shown to arise repeatedly but are overcome inevitably. Whether complications and adversities arise from within Christian communities or beyond them, and no matter their nature or severity, the empire of God progresses steadily and surely, ultimately surmounting all barriers and impediments, as ever-new permutations of Christian community become established throughout the world. This is a God whose empire has no geographical boundaries, no temporal end, and no limitation of resources. Gamaliel speaks the Lukan viewpoint when he notes that if the God who had overseen Jewish history supports the expansion of Christianity, it will not be possible to restrain that expansion, no matter what obstacles are put in front of it (Acts 5:39). Precisely the same point is reinforced through the structural composition of Acts, with chain-link interlocks guiding the forward motion of the narrative through terrain in which the "expansion despite persecution" motif is one of the main nutrients.

---

[62] See B. R. Gaventa, "Initiatives Divine and Human in the Lukan Story World," in Stanton, Longenecker, and Barton [eds.], *The Holy Spirit and Christian Origins*, 79–89.

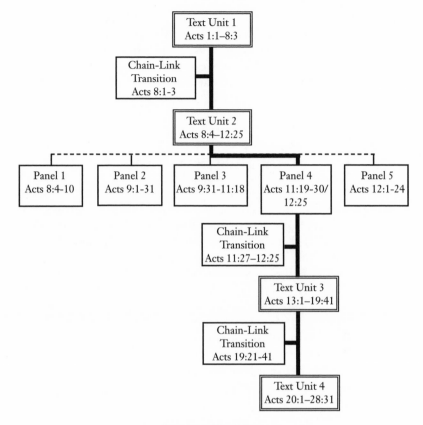

Text-Unit Flow Chart

§10.4 Chain-Link Interlock and Pauline Chronology

The final issue that must be considered in relation to Lukan chain-link interlock pertains to the link between the Petrine and Pauline sections of Acts (i.e., 11:27–12:25). This passage includes one of the most problematical passages for the reconstruction of Pauline chronology.[63] One of the major issues to be addressed in any chronological reconstruction of Paul's life is the relationship of Paul's visit to Jerusalem as recounted in Galatians 2:1-10 and the sequence of Paul's visits to Jerusalem as recounted in Acts 9, 11, (12, if εἰς is read at 12:25), 15, 18, and 21. For many interpreters, this framework of five (or six) journeys as recounted in

---

[63] For instance, Trocmé (*Le 'Livre des Actes' et l'histoire*, 87) articulates the position of many when speaking of "insolubles difficultés que pose la comparaison entre ces chapitres [Acts 11–15] et les chap. 1–2 de l'epître aux Galate.'"

Acts "is the most vulnerable point in Pauline chronology,"[64] with the result that one or two of the journeys are seen to be historically spurious. Of Paul's journeys to Jerusalem depicted in Acts, it is his participation in the delivery of the Antiochene collection that is most frequently cited as being "historically suspect," as Luke Johnson describes it.[65] For many interpreters, Paul's account in Galatians 2 corresponds to the events of Acts 15—Paul's third (or fourth) visit to Jerusalem in Acts but in Galatians only his second. If the first Jerusalem visit of Galatians 1:18-19 roughly equates to the first visit in Acts (9:26-29), and if the second Jerusalem visit of Galatians 2:1-10 roughly equates to the visit of Acts 15:1-21, then Paul's second visit described in Acts 11:27-30 has no corresponding equivalent in the primary source material (i.e., Paul's letters).

Conversely, some interpreters envisage the events of Galatians 2:1-10 to correspond to Paul's visit to Jerusalem as described in Acts 18:22 ("when he had landed at Caesarea, he went up and greeted the church"). In this view, not only Paul's visit of Acts 11 but also that of Acts 15 are suspect, or at least, in the latter case, placed too early in the narrative. For John Knox, Robert Jewett, and Gerd Lüdemann, for instance, the description of the Apostolic Council in Acts 15 belongs to the time of Acts 18:22, not that of Acts 15. Luke has made adjustments to the sequence of things in order to make it appear that Paul's independent missionary activity (without Barnabas) was "the direct consequence of the Apostolic Conference at Jerusalem."[66] In this way

> [n]ot only is Paul's independence thereby supported by the Jerusalem pillars, but also the specific goal of the second journey is pictured as related to the distribution of the Jerusalem decree [Acts 15:22-29]. By placing the Apostolic Conference before the second missionary journey, Luke can make Paul appear to be a faithful representative of the Jerusalem centered salvation-history.

In each of these two schemes (i.e., Gal 2:1-10 = Acts 15, or Gal 2:1-10 = Acts 18:22), the five-journey (or six-journey) motif of Acts is explained away, with one or two of Paul's visits of the Acts narrative shown to be

---

[64] J. Knox, *Chapters in a Life of Paul* (rev. ed.; London: SCM Press, 1989), 93. J. Murphy-O'Connor (*Paul: A Critical Life* [Oxford: Clarendon, 1996], 94 n. 116) writes: "According to the present text of Acts, Paul made six visits to Jerusalem (9:26-8; 11:29-30; 12:25; 15:1-2, 11; 18:22; 21:1, 5, 17). The first and the last can be equated with Gal. 1:18 and Rom. 15:25 respectively. Source criticism suggests that the other four are all to be equated with Gal. 2:1."

[65] Johnson, *The Acts of the Apostles*, 208.

[66] Jewett, *Dating Paul's Life*, 93, from which the following quotation is also taken. Cf. also Knox, *Chapters in a Life of Paul*; G. Lüdemann, *Paul, Apostle to the Gentiles: Studies in Chronology* (London: SCM Press, 1984).

historically implausible. In either scheme, Paul's visit to Jerusalem in Acts 11:27-30 is thought to be historically unreliable, whatever literary function it might perform. So in the 1987 revision of his influential *Chapters in a Life of Paul*, John Knox continues to claim that "virtually everyone agrees that it [i.e., Paul's visit to Jerusalem in Acts 11:27-30] could not have taken place."[67] Similarly, Georg Strecker claimed in 1962 that "Die Identifizierung der Reise von Act 15 mit der von Gal 2:1ff. ist denn auch eines der gesicherten Ergebnisse der Acta-Kritik."[68] These bold claims concerning the certainty of the consensus view are overstated, since a number of interpreters consider the Jerusalem trip of Acts 11:27-30 to correspond to Paul's second trip as described in Galatians 2:1-10, with the events recounted in Acts 15 involving a supplementary meeting (occurring after the writing of Galatians) to discuss matters subsequent to the meeting described in Acts 11/Galatians 2. This view has capable defenders today,[69] with even Knox recognising that it "should not be dismissed too lightly."[70]

The historical veracity of Paul's journey to Jerusalem in Acts 11 is not a matter that I intend to pronounce judgement on at this point. What interests me instead is the variety of explanations regarding Luke's motivation for depicting Paul as travelling to Jerusalem from Antioch at this point in the narrative. If Galatians 2:1-10 is Paul's version of the journey recounted by Luke in Acts 11, then Luke simply placed the journey at that point in the narrative since that was roughly the time when the event occurred. But if Paul's trip to Jerusalem as recounted in Acts 11 is in fact "historically suspect," as many think, what might have prompted Luke to include this Jerusalem journey at this point in the narrative? Unless Galatians 2:1-10 is to be identified with the Antiochene relief visit of Acts 11:27-30, some explanation for Luke's depiction of Paul's visit in Acts 11 is in order. This will be the focus of the following discussion, to which Luke's interest in text-unit interlock will be added.

---

[67] Knox, *Chapters in a Life of Paul*, 49.

[68] G. Strecker, "Die sogenannte zweite Jerusalemreise des Paulu,'" *ZNW* 53 (1962): 67–77, esp. 74.

[69] According to Hemer (*The Book of Acts in the Setting of Hellenistic History*, 247), it is a view that is "fairly widespread." See, for instance, Hemer, *The Book of Acts in the Setting of Hellenistic History*, 261–70; F. F. Bruce, *The Epistle of Paul to the Galatians* (Exeter: Paternoster, 1982), 43–56; R. N. Longenecker, *Galatians* (Waco: Word Books, 1990), lxxiii–lxxxiii; A. J. M. Wedderburn, "Some Recent Pauline Chronologies," *ET* 92 (1981): 103–8, esp. 107; idem, "Paul and Barnabas: The Anatomy and Chronology of a Parting of the Ways," in *Fair Play: Diversity and Conflicts in Early Christianity* (ed. Ismo Dunderberg et al.; Leiden: Brill, 2002), 291–310, esp. 305–6; Bauckham, "James and the Jerusalem Church," 468–70.

[70] Knox, *Chapters in a Life of Paul*, 44 n. 1.

On occasion it has been suggested that Luke simply fabricated the whole of Antiochene famine visit and Paul's position within it.[71] But while many are suspicious about the historical reliability of Paul's participation in the delivery of the Antiochene collection, those suspicions usually do not include the delivery of an Antiochene collection itself, nor Barnabas' participation in it.[72] Since an Antiochene tradition probably informs the narrative of 11:27-30, Paul's inclusion within the Antiochene delivery party alongside Barnabas is (in view of the evidence from Paul's letter to the Galatians) alone to be seen as historically suspect.[73] Does this

[71] E.g., Strecker ("Die sogenannte zweite Jerusalemreise des Paulus") argues that the central features of 11:27-30 can be attributed to Lukan interests and redaction, and concludes (p. 75): "Die sogenannte Zweite Reise des Paulus nach Jerusalem . . . hat nicht stattgefunden; sie ist vielmehr als lukanische Kombination aus dem Zusammenschluß verrschiedener Traditionselemente zu verstehen." For Strecker, this Lukan assemblage has been attached to a piece of Antiochene tradition in 11:19-26 (p. 76).

[72] M. Hengel and A. M. Schwemer (*Paul between Damascus and Antioch* [London: SCM Press, 1997], 242–43) write: "I [presumably Hengel] see no occasion to dismiss the whole report simply as a Lukan invention. The supportive journey will have taken place. Its seems natural that it was led by Barnabas, who came from Jerusalem."

[73] R. Riesner (*Paul's Early Period: Chronology, Mission Strategy, Theology* [Grand Rapids: Eerdmans, 1998], 321) calls Paul's inclusion in the delivery party historically "problematical." Roloff (*Die Apostelgeschichte*, 183) writes: "Er [Lukas] hat ferner . . . den Namen des Paulus neben den des Barnabas gestellt, und zwar wahrscheinlich ganz unreflecktiert: Für ihn galt es als ausgemacht, daß damals Paulus alle Aktivitäten des Barnabas geteilt haben muß."

Although Hengel and Schwemer think that Paul had nothing to do with the delivery of the Antiochene collection, they nonetheless envisage ways in which Paul might have been involved in some fashion, perhaps having been involved in its organisation, although not its delivery (*Paul between Damascus and Antioch*, 465 n. 1273). Or perhaps Paul "travelled with the delegation but kept out of Jerusalem himself because there his life was still in danger, or because the people there did not want to see him" (242). Alternatively, it is possible that "in Gal. 2.1 Paul simply passes over the collection visit of Acts 11.30 in silence" (242) because it was "unimportant in retrospect" (464 n. 1260). That is, on this trip Paul "had nothing to do with Peter and other authorities . . . as they had left Jerusalem because of the persecution by Agrippa . . . and the messengers [i.e., Barnabas, Paul, etc.] had to leave the city again quickly because of the danger." But any scenario that involves Paul travelling even to the vicinity of Jerusalem is somewhat problematic, since Paul's failure in Galatians 1–2 to mention even this would only need to have been pointed out in order to bring Paul's claims in that letter under extreme suspicion. Certainly he would not have left that eventuality open (cf. Barrett, *The Acts of the Apostles*, 559–60; Hemer, *The Book of Acts in the Setting of Hellenistic History*, 265). As Hengel and Schwemer (*Paul between Damascus and Antioch*, 242) argue: "It would remain inexplicable why Paul, who in Gal. 2.10

inclusion of Paul within the Antiochene delivery party arise simply because Luke's competency as a historian is deficient on this occasion? Martin Hengel and Anna Maria Schwemer consider the account of Paul's visit to Jerusalem in 11:27-30/12:25 to be "one of those inaccuracies which often creep into Luke's account—as into the accounts of any historian, ancient or modern."[74] Here Luke's supposed historical slip is explained simply as an understandable blunder, just as Knox speaks of Luke having been "clearly mistaken in placing a visit of Paul to Jerusalem between the acquaintance and conference visits."[75]

For some, this blunder arose inadvertently from Luke's cognisance of two different traditions dealing with Paul's visit to Jerusalem at the time of the "Apostolic Council," as reported in Acts 15. According to Joachim Jeremias, for instance, Paul undertook a single journey to discuss matters with the apostles, but this single journey had a double purpose: (1) to discuss the issue of gentile Christian identity and (2) to deliver famine relief from Antiochene Christian communities. The first purpose was preserved in a tradition recounted in Acts 15, while the second purpose was preserved in a tradition recounted in Acts 11.[76] In this view, Acts 11:27-30 is a tradition that has strayed from its temporal moorings, Luke having inserted it ahead of time in order to try to do justice to the two accounts that had come to him but which he incorrectly understood as representing different journeys.

This view has not gained many adherents. It is often criticised on the basis that Paul mentions nothing about a dual purpose of the visit in Galatians 2:1-10. Paul would not have missed the opportunity (so the argument goes) to mention the relief aspect of the collection when the Jerusalem apostles requested that he encourage his gentile converts to "remember the poor" (Gal 2:10).[77] Consequently, Paul's visit to Jerusalem

---

mentions in detail the obligation to support the poor imposed on him at Jerusalem, should have kept quiet about aid to the Jerusalem poor which had been given earlier."

[74] Hengel and Schwemer, *Paul between Damascus and Antioch*, 245–46.

[75] Knox, *Chapters in a Life of Paul*, 49. Luke draws sharper criticism for this "blunder" from A. Loisy, *Les Actes des Apôtres* (Paris: Minerva, 1920), 475; Schille, *Die Apostelgeschichte des Lukas*, 267–68.

[76] J. Jeremias, "Sabbathjahr und neutestamentliche Chronologie," *ZNW* 27 (1928): 98–103.

[77] Jewett (*Dating Paul's Life*, 34) notes that when Paul wrote his Galatian letter "one would think that a reference to the relief project would be a natural opportunity for him to demonstrate both [his] good will and independence" in relation to the Jerusalem church. Cf. Hengel and Schwemer, *Paul between Damascus and Antioch*, 242. But the force of this observation is weakened since the aorist ἐσπούδασα of Galatians 2:10 can be interpreted as signalling that Paul had already adopted an attitude of "remembering the poor," as illustrated in the

as recounted in Galatians 2:1-10 probably had no relief aspect to it, making the "double tradition" explanation unsuitable as an explanation for
Luke's depiction of Paul visiting Jerusalem in Acts 11.

Other explanations by-pass the "blunder" theory, attributing Paul's
inclusion in the Antiochene delivery more directly to Luke's own narrative intentions. For Robert Funk, for instance,[78] Luke's description of
Paul delivering the Antiochene collection to aid the Jerusalem community corresponds to the collection referred to in 1 Corinthians 16, 2
Corinthians 8–9, and Romans 15. This collection was initiated by Paul
among his communities and brought to Jerusalem in approximately 57
CE, so that it's "historical" placement is properly in Acts 21, when Paul
arrives in Jerusalem just prior to his arrest. Funk rightly notes that, since
Luke knows of Paul's collection for Jerusalem (cf. Acts 24:17: "After
some years I came to bring my nation alms and offerings"), it is curious
that he fails to narrate it within Acts. Equally curious is the fact that Luke
nowhere offers his audience any clue as to Paul's motivation for travelling
across the Mediterranean basin to get to Jerusalem, although from 19:21
onwards we hear of Paul's unrestrained resolve to go there. On three
occasions Luke reveals that Paul knows that he will be in great danger
upon arriving in Jerusalem, and yet Paul is depicted as being utterly
determined to get to Jerusalem nonetheless (in Ephesus, 20:22-24, 37-
38; in Tyre, 21:4; and in Caesarea, 21:11-14). Of course, those familiar
with Paul's late letters will know why he is so resolved to arrive in
Jerusalem: he has committed himself to delivering the collection of support from his predominantly gentile communities for the benefit of the
"poor among the saints" in Jerusalem (Rom 15:26). This effort lay at the
heart of Paul's energies and theology throughout the mid-50s. But the
audience of Acts knows virtually nothing of this enterprise, at least from
Luke's own writings.[79] According to Funk, Luke has shifted that collection from the end of Paul's public ministry to the beginning. This shift
might have been motivated by Luke's concern not to recount an embar-
rassing episode in the life of his main protagonist, since Paul's collection
was probably not well received in Jerusalem (as he himself feared; cf.
Rom 15:30-31). Or it might have been motivated by Luke's concern not
to raise the profile of the continuing controversy over gentile member-

---

delivery of the Antiochene collection. On this, see Bruce, *The Epistle of Paul to the
Galatians*, 126; R. Y. K. Fung, *The Epistle to the Galatians* (Grand Rapids:
Eerdmans, 1988), 103–4; Longenecker, *Galatians*, 61.

[78] R. Funk, "The Enigma of the Famine Visit," *JBL* 75 (1956): 130–36.

[79] The closest Luke gets is to use the a participial form of διακονεῖν to
describe Paul's coworkers ("those ministering with him"), the same verb that
Paul uses to describe his collection (Rom 15:31; 2 Cor 8:4; 9:1), and that Luke
used of the Antiochene collection in Acts 11:29 and 12:25.

ship within Christian communities, an issue that he depicted as having been resolved in Acts 15. Either way, Paul's efforts to deliver a collection from his gentile communities to Jerusalem were the consequent victim in Luke's narrative.[80]

This is an intriguing explanation, but may not be wholly compelling. It does not necessarily follow, for instance, that Luke simply included Paul within the Antiochene collection party of Acts 11 in order to compensate for undernarrating Paul's own collection later in the narrative. There is little to suggest that "compensatory historiography" was Luke's normal *modus operandi* or that he sought to preserve traditions in whatever manner possible. His handling of Gospel sources indicates that he is not averse to allowing traditions to disappear from view altogether.[81]

---

[80] Cf. L. E. Keck ("The Poor among the Saints in the New Testament," *ZNW* 56 [1965]: 100–29, esp. 107): "Either the author of Acts was ignorant of the offering brought to Jerusalem by Paul and of its importance to him, or he deliberately transformed his information for the sake of his portrait of Paul. In view of the terminology of 24:17, the latter alternative is to be preferred. Perhaps he treated the offering this way because he knew that it failed to do what Paul hoped it would; at the same time, his concern to show the unity of Paul and the Jerusalem church would prevent him from saying so." B. Holmberg (*Paul and Power: The Structure of Authority in the Primitive Church as Reflected in the Pauline Epistles* [Philadelphia: Fortress, 1980], 43) speaks of Paul's collection having been "something of a missionary and diplomatic catastrophe," which Luke deemed it best "to pass over it in merciful silence." Cf. also Knox, *Chapters in a Life of Paul*, 51.

Barrett (*The Acts of the Apostles*, 559) cites with approval the argument of K. F. Nickle (*The Collection: A Study in Paul's Strategy* [London: SCM Press, 1966], 148–51) in explaining why Luke downplays Paul's own collection efforts. According to Nickle, at the time that Luke wrote, Judaism and Christianity had become separate religions in the eyes of Rome, and Paul's collection "would therefore have been regarded by the Roman authorities as an illegal operation" (150). Unlike Barrett, I see no force in the argument. Similarly, I am not quite convinced by Bauckham's explanation ("James and the Jerusalem Church," 479–80), that Paul's collection for the Jerusalem community goes virtually unmentioned since, in Luke's view, "Jerusalem was central as the centre from which the centrifugal movement of the gospel went out to the ends of the earth, but not as the centre to which, in a corresponding centripetal movement, the eschatological people of God must constantly look back." That is only one interpretation of the significance of Pauline collection, which Luke could have avoided while still narrating the collection, giving it significance in terms of intercommunal harmony, not least between Jewish and gentile constituencies—a feature that would have played well within Luke's narrative. Precedent for that interpretation of the Pauline collection is evident already in the Antiochene collection of Acts 11:27-30, which Luke did not consider illegitimately centripetal.

[81] Cf. Talbert (*Literary Patterns*, 60), on another matter: "Nor is it likely that the author of Luke-Acts can be thought of as the type of historian who would

Consequently, if Funk's explanation carries weight, it has at best identified only a secondary motivation for Luke's inclusion of Paul within the Antiochene party.

Robert Jewett has also offered an explanation for the supposed historical inaccuracy of Acts 11 in a manner that also avoids attributing it to a historical blunder. In this explanation, Luke's depiction of Paul visiting Jerusalem in Acts 11 was the result of Luke's concern to legitimate Paul's "first missionary journey" of Acts 13–14. As Jewett states, "This early Jerusalem journey is an integral part of Luke's theological framework. The author of Acts pictures Paul as closely tied with the Jerusalem church so as to maintain the continuity of the salvation-history."[82] Prior to each of Paul's three "missionary journeys" in Acts Paul spends time in Jerusalem. Luke needed to ensure the ubiquity of the pattern for each of the three missionary journeys, necessitating that Paul proceed to Jerusalem prior to Acts 13.

But while Luke wants to link Paul and Jerusalem as closely as possible, this explanation oversteps the bounds of evidence. Of Paul's three missionary journeys in Acts, only the second is narrated in such a way as to suggest that it arises directly out of and as a consequence of the Jerusalem visit (cf. 15:22-31).[83] With regard to the third missionary journey, it is true that Paul is said to have gone to Jerusalem in 18:22 (he "went up," ἀναβάς), and his missionary activity takes place subsequent to that event in 18:23. But the narrative indicates that a significant period of time intervened between these two points and offers no suggestion of a causal link between Paul's Jerusalem visit and his missionary journey. After Paul's departure from Jerusalem, Luke states that Paul "spent some

---

include all traditions known to him in order to be fair. This was certainly not the way he treated Mark, for example."

[82] Jewett, *Dating Paul's Life*, 91. Knox (*Chapters in a Life of Paul*, 26) notes that "the missionary journey scheme suits perfectly the conception of the author of Acts, that Paul throughout his career works closely with the older communities of Syria and Palestine and more or less under the authority of the Twelve," adding that "this way of visualizing and representing the career of Paul is based entirely upon Acts, with no support from the letters whatsoever" (25).

[83] Jewett (*Dating Paul's Life*, 93) suspects that the Jerusalem council of Acts 15 has been moved forward from its natural position at Acts 18:22 (cf. Knox, Lüdemann), with "a specific theological motivation" involved, "that of making the independent missionary activity of the second expedition, when Barnabas was absent, appear to be the direct consequence of the Apostolic Conference at Jerusalem. Not only is Paul's independence thereby supported by the Jerusalem pillars, but also the specific goal of the second journey is pictured as related to the distribution of the Jerusalem decree. By placing the Apostolic Conference before the second missionary journey, Luke can make Paul appear to be a faithful representative of the Jerusalem centered salvation-history."

time" in Antioch (ποιήσας χρόνον τινά, 18:23). Evidently Luke felt no urgency to root the third missionary journey of 18:23ff in an authenticating visit to Jerusalem in 18:22. Had that been necessary, he would have wanted to elaborate the meaning of Paul's "going up" more distinctly in terms of both its geographical referent (would all Graeco-Roman readers have understood the allusion to Jerusalem?) and its specifics (did Paul meet with James and the elders?).

The same situation applies with respect to the first of Paul's missionary journeys in Acts 13–14. The visit to Jerusalem in 11:27-30 has no strong causal connection with the missionary journey of Acts 13–14. The legitimacy of the journey of Barnabas and Saul in Acts 13–14 is rooted in the faithful worship of the Antiochene community, the calling of the Spirit, and the commissioning of the Antiochene Christians (13:2-3). Luke makes no attempt to trace direct lines of causality and legitimacy from the first missionary journey back to Barnabas and Paul's visit to Jerusalem in Acts 11–12. And Acts 14:26-27 suggests that Paul and Barnabas reported back to Antiochene communities at the end of the first missionary journey, where they stayed "for some time" without any hint that they considered Jerusalem to be the ultimate base of their missionary work.

Jewett himself notes that the first missionary journey does not follow his expected pattern of legitimisation. He explains this as owing to the fact that the theology of an underlying Antiochene (and anti-Jerusalem) source is showing through the Lukan pages. So he writes:

> Luke's interest was to show the missionary work of Paul as centering in Jerusalem. Yet Acts 13–14 pictures the first epoch-making expedition as originating at and returning to Antioch rather than Jerusalem. If Acts 15:1-34 is an insertion by the redactor, as many commentators assume, the narrative of 14:28 would have originally continued in 15:35ff., thus stating explicitly that Paul and Barnabas did not visit Jerusalem or anywhere else upon returning from the first missionary journey. The best explanation of these details seems to be that Acts 13–14 was part of the preLukan material originating in Antioch, designed to emphasize the independent role of the Antioch congregation. . . . The polemic is clearly aimed against Jerusalem, as indicated by the lack of any reference to Peter, by the commencement of the account with the report of unfairness on the part of Jerusalem leaders to the Hellenistic widows (Acts 6:1ff.), and by the emphasis on the successful western mission as resulting from the obedience to the Spirit by the Antioch leaders.[84]

Disregarding some of the (questionable) details of this argument, the primary issue remains: The narrative of Acts offers only a sequential

[84] Jewett, *Dating Paul's Life*, 11–12.

rather than causal or legitimating relationship between the Jerusalem visit of Acts 11–12 and the first missionary journey of Acts 13–14. An appeal to the disruptive effect of an underlying source does not succeed in forging the causal link that Jewett's case requires.

Of course it would be right to say with Knox that Paul's "missionary career is supported directly by Antioch but indirectly by Jerusalem" even with regard to the first missionary journey.[85] But the basis for the Jerusalem community's indirect support of Paul comes primarily through (1) its previous encounter with him in 9:26–29,[86] and (2) the person of Barnabas, a member of the Jerusalem community (4:36–37) and an envoy of that community to the Antiochene community to ensure its stability (11:22). The most that can be argued with regard to Paul's inclusion within the Antiochene delegation is that there is nothing in the Lukan account to suggest that the Jerusalem community queried the partnership of Paul and Barnabas when they delivered the Antiochene collection. Consequently, Stephen Wilson's estimate of the matter hits the target squarely, with only a slight tendency for exaggeration:

> The rather tortuous attempt to show that the mission in 13.1f. is, by a series of connections, legitimised by Jerusalem is highly improbable. Nothing in 11.27–13.4 suggests that this is the case; the only legitimiser is the Spirit, not the Jerusalem Church.[87]

In my estimate, none of the explanations surveyed above regarding Luke's "problematical" depiction of Paul visiting Jerusalem in 11:27–30 is wholly satisfactory, for reasons noted. Assuming for the moment that Paul's visit to Jerusalem in Acts 11 is not historically accurate, an adequate explanation for Luke's inclusion of Paul in the Antiochene collection must follow a different course. That course, it is proposed, takes full account of Luke's structural and rhetorical interests. Simply put, if it can be shown that Paul was unlikely to have travelled to Jerusalem in the time-frame suggested by Acts 11–12, then his appearance at that point in

---

[85] Knox, *Chapters in a Life of Paul*, 14. Knox notes that each of the three journeys "had its beginning and its end in Antioch or Jerusalem" (25). Or compare M. D. Hooker's careful manner of phrasing the matter (*Paul: A Short Introduction* [Oxford: Oneworld, 2003], 12): Luke depicts Paul "as commissioned by Antioch, and as answerable to Jerusalem."

[86] See esp. Haenchen, *Die Apostelgeschichte*, 323–24. On 324 Haenchen writes: From this point on "haben die Zwölf Paulus . . . akzeptiert. Er ist nun nicht nur von Christus berufen, sondern auch von den Aposteln anerkannt, und damit in jeder hinsicht 'rite vocatus.'"

[87] S. G. Wilson, *The Gentiles and the Gentile Mission in Luke-Acts* (Cambridge: Cambridge University Press, 1973), 182; cited with apparent approval by Barrett, *Acts*, 601. See also Gaventa, "Initiatives Divine and Human in the Lukan Story World."

the narrative is due solely (or at least primarily) to Luke's interest in chain-link interlock. The tradition about the delivery of an Antiochene collection to Jerusalem was superbly suited to facilitate this interest, since it already included the two geographical centres prominent in the transitional material—Jerusalem and Antioch. All that was needed was a balancing of the key figures Peter and Paul on either side of the transition material (i.e., 11:27-30/12:25 and 12:1-24).[88] With the simple insertion of Paul as a figure into the tradition regarding the Antiochene collection, a chain-link interlock was created, serving the rhetorical purpose of signalling a major text-unit transition. This is the foremost factor motivating Luke's placement of Paul within delivery of the Antiochene collection to Jerusalem. If other factors played a part in Luke's interests, they are of auxiliary significance to this one.

Consequently, without an interest in the rhetorical function of Acts 11:27–12:25 in its larger narrative context, expectations about Luke's historical veracity might become easily skewed. The passage serves a rhetorical function first and foremost, and needs to be appreciated in that light. Of course, it is arguable that the passage serves a rhetorical function while also being historically reliable, which is no doubt what Luke would maintain regarding the traditions linking Luke and Acts at their textual seam, for instance. But if there is enough reason to question the historical reliability of Luke's account of the Pauline visit to Jerusalem in Acts 11–12, it is preferable to appreciate that story for its rhetorical utility within a text-unit interlock than to chastise Luke for historical ineptness or to devise some rather spurious motivation in order to explain his narrative historically or theologically. Like all historians, Luke was more than a collector of historical traditions. He sought to persuade his audience of certain things, and to that end the historical traditions that he gathered both informed his rhetorical goals and were subservient to them.[89] As Knox rightly notes, Luke "arranged his materials in the order

---

[88] In this way, the Antiochene collection tradition is better suited to the chain-link transition than Luke's mention in 11:25-26 of Paul's participation in Antiochene Christianity.

[89] In this regard, the same can be said of Luke that S. Cohen (*Josephus in Galilee and Rome: His Vita and Development as a Historian* [Leiden: Brill, 1979], 233) says of Josephus: "When analyzing Josephan chronology we must always keep in mind the possibility that Josephus deliberately departed from the historical sequence for literary reason." Cf. L. Alexander ("Chronology of Paul," in *Dictionary of Paul and His Letters* [ed. G. F. Hawthorne and R. P. Martin; Downers Grove: InterVarsity Press, 1993], 115–23, esp. 122): "Exactly the same problem [i.e., Luke's historical sequence] occurs in the ancient historians (Josephus, Suetonius), whose vagueness or lack of information about sequence means that first-century chronology can rarely attain a high degree of precision."

that best suited the purpose of the book,"[90] and that purpose includes the placement of material for rhetorical force.

In short, if Luke "got it wrong" historically, he "got it right" rhetorically. Luke has constructed the narrative of Acts to correspond with the canons of rhetorical effectiveness primarily. Paul's participation in the Antiochene delegation has structural and rhetorical significance first and foremost, whether or not it has a historical corollary. For Luke, Paul's journey to Jerusalem was a structural and rhetorical necessity, despite any other merits that it might have had.

---

[90] Knox, *Chapters in a Life of Paul*, 11. For a full discussion, see Cadbury, *The Making of Luke-Acts*, chs. 12 and 13.

CHAPTER II

Conclusions

In the previous chapters of this project, the study of chain-link interlock has been carried out in relatively self-contained chapters. Three points of triangulation have provided the focus of this study: (1) evidence from first- and second-century Graeco-Roman rhetoricians (two references); (2) evidence from sources antecedent to or roughly contemporary with the New Testament (eleven examples); and (3) evidence from the New Testament itself (fifteen examples). This triangulation of evidence is not insignificant. It provides chain-link interlock with a stronger evidential base than chiasm, for instance, for which evidence from rhetoricians is lacking until the fourth century CE. Similarly, the fairly widespread stylistic technique of diatribe is nowhere mentioned in the Graeco-Roman rhetorical handbooks. But chain-link construction has been shown to have a foothold in an assortment of evidential databases, each of them reinforcing the others, and all of them "interlocking" to illustrate the utility of chain-link interlock in the ancient world—not least in New Testament texts.

The following chart offers an overview of the fifteen New Testament examples of chain-link interlock studied in this project, demonstrating the A-b-a-B pattern that characterises the transition technique. The examples are here placed in their canonical order rather than the order in which they have been discussed. (The chain link at the end of the Lukan Gospel appears in relation to the Book of Acts in this table.)

TEXT-UNIT "A"	INTERLOCKED "b" (anticipatory)	INTERLOCKED "a" (retrospective)	TEXT-UNIT "B"
John 1:1–12:50	John 12:20-36	John 12:37-50	John 13:1 to end
John 13:1–14:31	John 14:30-31	John 18:1, 6	John 18:1ff.
Luke 1:1–24:53	Luke 24:47-49 (52-53)	Luke 24:50– Acts 1:12	Acts 1:1-8:3 (28:31)
Acts 1:1–8:3	Acts 8:1b, 3	Acts 8:2	Acts 8:4–12:25
Acts 8:4–12:25	Acts 11:27-30/12:25	Acts 12:1-24	Acts 13:1–19:41
Acts 13:1–19:41	Acts 19:21-22	Acts 19:23-41	Acts 20:1–28:31
Rom 7:7-25	Rom 7:25a	Rom 7:25b	Rom 8:1-39
Rom 10:14-17	Rom 10:16	Rom 10:17	Rom 10:18-21(ff.)
Rom 12:9–13/16	Rom 12:14(15?)	Rom 12:(15?)16	Rom 12:14/17-21
Rom 13:11-14	Rom 13:13	Rom 13:14	Rom 14:1–15:6
1 Cor 8:4-6/8	1 Cor 8:7	1 Cor 8:8	1 Cor 8:7/9-13
Rev 2:1–3:22	Rev 3:21	Rev 3:22	Rev 4:1ff.
Rev 6:1–8:5	Rev 8:2	Rev 8:3-5	Rev 8:6ff.
to Rev 15:4	Rev 15:1	Rev 15:2-4	Rev 15:5ff.
Rev 21:9–22:5/9	Rev 22:6-7a	Rev 22:7b-9	Rev 22:6/10-21

Each chapter of this project has contained its own set of conclusions, and no attempt will be made to reiterate them here point by point. But some of the more significant conclusions will be collated here, grouped in relation to their structural, theological, and historical significance.

The *structural significance* of chain-link interlock has been evident in every chapter of this project. In particular, cognisance of the utility of chain-link construction in the ancient world has permitted us to bypass the view that a number of the texts studied are structurally second-rate—a view either explicitly suggested or implicitly intimated in scholarly literature. Consequently, we have also been able to bypass the kinds of explanations that follow on from this—either that the text's author is himself a second-rate rhetor or that a later scribe has introduced structural deficiencies into the text. So, for instance, the structural deficiencies noted by many interpreters at various points in Paul's letter to the

Romans have been shown not to be deficiencies at all; instead, they are cases of laudable transitions, conforming exactly to the structure of chain-link interlock recommended by Quintilian and Lucian of Samosata. Those cases that have troubled modern interpreters are precisely the cases that Paul's original audience would have appreciated as being structurally transparent and stylistically commendable. Similarly, a structural "deficiency" noted by many interpreters of Revelation has in fact been shown to be an extremely "studied" example of chain-link interlock, attributable to the main author of Revelation rather than to a later second-rate, "shallow-brained," and "profoundly stupid" redactor.[1]

The structural significance of chain-link interlock has also been readily evident in relation to the Acts of the Apostles, with its four interlocks indicating the boundaries of its main text-units. When cognisance of chain-link interlock is brought to the narrative of Acts, the structure of that text emerges with clarity and force in a relatively unprecedented fashion. So, too, Revelation has been seen to place chain-link interlocks at strategic places in order to fuse together a variety of its episodes in its narrative of God's eschatological action vis-à-vis a world out of joint.

The *theological significance* of chain-link interlock has also been evident in this project in every chapter dealing with a New Testament text. So, by means of chain-link interlock the author of Revelation was seen to lash together two previously independent literary genres (epistle and apocalypse), thereby creating a new generic hybrid. That hybrid is itself a testimony to the author's theological commitments, indicating his conviction that the apocalyptic mysteries of God are to be disseminated to the whole of God's people.[2] This is in contrast to the sentiment occasionally expressed in apocalyptic texts in which apocalyptic mysteries are to be made available only to those initiated into the group of the elite few who alone are worthy to receive them and live their lives in accordance with them.

Similarly, in the Johannine Gospel, key themes are clustered together and incorporated into the main chain-link interlock in such a way as to provide a highly condensed mini-version of that Gospel at the central structural junction. Moreover, the recognition of this fact was seen to support certain literary and theological readings of the Johannine Gospel and to exclude others. A similar association of structure and meaning

---

[1] So R. H. Charles described his envisaged redactor of Revelation; cf. his *A Critical and Exegetical Commentary on the Revelation of St. John* (2 vols.; Edinburgh: T&T Clark, 1920), 1:l and 1:xviii respectively.

[2] For the author of Revelation, God's people was comprised of "the worthy and the unworthy" (as the author of 4 Ezra would have identified them) of Revelation 2–3, and no doubt of audiences beyond those mentioned there.

emerges from the structure of the Acts of the Apostles. In that text, chain-link interlock is the structural basis on which a Lukan theodicy is built, defending God's reputation and enhancing confidence in God as the one who ultimately ensures the advance of the Christian movement. It also supported Luke's theology of scriptural fulfilment and his conviction concerning the trustworthiness of Jesus throughout the church's history. And in relation to Paul's letter to the Romans, chain-link interlock plays an important role in deciphering the identity of the "I" who speaks in Romans 7.

The *historical significance* of chain-link interlock has been evident especially in relation to Johannine, Lukan, and Pauline texts. For instance, the compositional history of the Johannine Gospel has been shown to have affected that Gospel's two main chain-link interlocks in contrasting ways, with one chain link being developed and the other being dismantled in successive versions of that Gospel. As a corollary of these adjustments to the chain-link interlocks at successive stages of the Johannine Gospel's development, it is possible to recognise a subtle shift in the narrative's theology in the course of maturation towards its final form.

The historical relevance of chain-link interlock has also been suggested in relation to the enterprise of reconstructing a chronology of Paul's life. If it is the case that, historically speaking, the narrative of Acts and the narrative of Galatians 1–2 are out of sync, as many interpreters believe, the recognition of the placement and function of chain-link interlock within the Acts narrative offers a novel explanation as to why the synchronisation may, in fact, be skewed.

All in all, the fifteen New Testament examples of chain-link interlock studied in this project illustrate the way in which Christian authors regularly infused the simple technique of chain-link interlock with significant interpretative import. An awareness of the form, character, and function of chain-link interlock in the ancient world has permitted us to reexamine a number of complex issues in prominent New Testament texts and to shed new light on those issues from structural, theological, and historical angles.

While this project is complete within the parameters I have set for it, it has not completed the task of studying instances of chain-link interlock in the ancient world. I suspect, in fact, that it has only scratched the surface of pertinent study. In the early chapters of this project I attempted to establish a methodological basis from which the study of chain-link interlock can proceed further (chs. 1–4), and in later chapters I analysed selected texts from the ancient world (ch. 5) and from the New Testament in particular (chs. 6–10). But a significant amount of work no doubt remains in "uncovering" and analysing chain-link interlock in a variety of other texts, both within the New Testament itself[3] and in the vast Jewish and Graeco-Roman literature that lies beyond the New Testament.

---

[3] I have made no attempt, for instance, to analyse the following texts in order to discover whether, where, and in what fashion they are animated by chain-link interlock: the synoptic Gospels, the majority of the letters in the Pauline corpus, Hebrews, the Petrine corpus, the Johannine epistles, and Jude. Nor can I claim to have discovered all the chain-link interlocks of the texts that have been studied here.

Works Cited

Achtemeier, P. J. "Omne Verbum Sonat: The New Testament and the Oral Environment of Late Western Antiquity." *JBL* 109 (1990): 3–27.

Alexander, L. *The Preface to Luke's Gospel: Literary Convention and Social Context in Luke 1.1-4 and Acts 1.1.* Cambridge: Cambridge University Press, 1993.

———. "Chronology of Paul." Pages 115–23 in *Dictionary of Paul and His Letters.* Edited by Gerald F. Hawthorne and Ralph P. Martin. Downers Grove: InterVarsity Press, 1993.

———. "Formal Elements and Genre: Which Greco-Roman Prologues Most Closely Parallel the Lukan Prologues?" Pages 9–26 in *Jesus and the Heritage of Israel: Luke's Narrative Claim upon Israel's Legacy.* Edited by D. P. Moessner. Harrisburg: Trinity Press International, 1999.

———. "Acts." Pages 1028–61 in *The Oxford Bible Commentary.* Edited by J. Barton and J. Muddiman. Oxford: Oxford University Press, 2001.

Allen, O. W., Jr, *The Death of Herod: The Narrative and Theological Function of Retribution in Luke-Acts.* Atlanta: Society of Biblical Literature, 1997.

Argyle, A. W. "The Greek of Luke and Acts." *NTS* 20 (1974): 441–45.

Ashton, J. *Understanding the Fourth Gospel.* Oxford: Clarendon Press, 1991.

————. *Studying John: Approaches to the Fourth Gospel*. Oxford: Clarendon Press, 1994.

————. *The Religion of Paul the Apostle*. New Haven: Yale University Press, 2000.

Aune, D. E. *The New Testament in Its Literary Environment*. Philadelphia: Westminster, 1987.

————. *Revelation 1–5*. Dallas: Word Books, 1997.

————. *Revelation 17–22*. Nashville: Thomas Nelson, 1998.

————. *The Westminster Dictionary of New Testament and Early Christian Literature and Rhetoric*. Louisville: Westminster John Knox Press, 2003.

Babbitt, F. C., trans. *Plutarch's* Moralia. Loeb Classical Library. London: William Heinemann; Cambridge, MA: Harvard University Press, 1969.

Bar-Ilan, M. "Illiteracy in the Land of Israel in the First Centuries C.E." Pages 46–61 in *Essays in the Social Scientific Study of Judaism and Jewish Society*. Vol. 2. Edited by S. Fishbane and S. Schonfeld. Hoboken: KTAV, 1992.

Barker, M. *The Revelation of Jesus Christ*. Edinburgh: T&T Clark, 2000.

Barr, D. *Tales of the End: A Narrative Commentary on the Book of Revelation*. Santa Rosa: Polebridge Press, 1998.

Barrett, C. K. *Luke the Historian in Recent Study*. Philadelphia: Fortress Press, 1970.

————. *A Commentary on the Epistle to the Romans*. 2d ed. London: Adam & Charles Black, 1971.

————. *The Gospel according to St John*. 2d ed.; London: SPCK, 1978.

————. *Essays on John*. London: SPCK, 1982.

————. *The Acts of the Apostles*. Edinburgh: T&T Clark, 1994.

Bartsch, H. W. *Wachet aber zu jeder Zeit: Entwurf einer Auslegung des Lukasevangeliums*. Hamburg-Bergstedt: Evangelischer Verlag, 1963.

Bauckham, R. J. *The Climax of Prophecy: Studies on the Book of Revelation*. Edinburgh: T&T Clark, 1993.

————. *James*. London: Routledge, 1999.

————. "James and Jerusalem Church." Pages 415–80 in *The Book of Acts in Its Palestinian Setting*. Edited by R. J. Bauckham. Grand Rapids: Eerdmans, 1995.

————. *God Crucified: Monotheism and Christology in the New Testament*. Carlisle: Paternoster, 1998.

———. "The Audience of the Fourth Gospel." Pages 101–11 in *Jesus in Johannine Tradition*. Edited by R. T. Fortna and T. Thatcher. Louisville: Westminster John Knox Press, 2001.

Beale, G. K. *The Book of Revelation*. Grand Rapids: Eerdmans, 1999.

Beard, M., ed. *Literacy in the Roman World*. Ann Arbor: Journal of Roman Archaeology, 1991.

Beasley-Murray, G. R. *John*. Waco: Word Books, 1987.

———. *Gospel of Life: Theology in the Fourth Gospel*. Peabody: Hendrickson Publishers, 1991.

Becker, J. "Die Abschiedsreden Jesu im Johannesevangelium." *ZNW* 61 (1970): 215–46.

Beckwith, I. T. *The Apocalypse of John*. New York: Macmillan, 1919.

Bergholz, T. *Der Augbau des lukanischen Doppelwerkes*. Frankfurt am Main: Peter Lang, 1995.

Berlin, A. "Shared Rhetorical Features in Biblical and Sumerian Literature." *Journal of the Ancient Near Eastern Society of Columbia University* 10 (1978): 35–42.

Bernheim, P.-A. *James, Brother of Jesus*. London: SCM Press, 1997.

Bernard, J. H. *The Gospel according to St John*. Edinburgh: T&T Clark, 1928.

Best, E. *The Letter of Paul to the Romans*. Cambridge: Cambridge University Press, 1967.

Betori, G. "Luke 24:47: Jerusalem and the Beginning of the Preaching to the Pagans in the Acts of the Apostles." Pages 103–20 in *Luke and Acts*. Edited by G. O'Collins and G. Marconi. New York: Paulist Press, 1993.

Betz, H. D. *Lukian von Samosata und das neue Testament: religions-gechichtliche und paränetische Parallellen*. Berlin: Akademie-Verlag, 1961.

Beutler, J., S.J. "Die Heilsbedeutung des Todes Jesu im Johannesevangelium nach Joh 13,1-20." Pages 188–204 in *Der Tod Jesu: Deutungen im Neuen Testament*. Edited by K. Kertelge. Freiburg im Breisgau: Herder, 1976.

———. *Habt keine Angst: Die erste johanneische Aschiedsrede (Joh 14)*. Stuttgart: Katholisches Bibelwerk, 1984.

———. "Synoptic Jesus Tradition in the Johannine Farewell Discourse." Pages 165–73 in *Jesus in Johannine Tradition*. Edited by R. T. Fortna and T. Thatcher. Louisville: Westminster John Knox Press, 2001.

Black, D. A. "The Pauline Love Command: Structure, Style, and Ethics in Romans 12:9-21." *Filologia Neotestamentaria* 1 (1989): 3–21.

Boismard, M.-E. (and A. Lamouille). *L'Evangile de Jean*. Paris: Éditions du Cerf, 1977.

Bonz, M. P. *The Past as Legacy: Luke-Acts and Ancient Epic*. Minneapolis: Fortress Press, 2000.

Boomershine, T. E. "Jesus of Nazareth and the Watershed of Ancient Orality and Literacy." *Semeia* 65 (1995): 7–36.

Bouwmann, G. *Das dritte Evangelium: Einübing in die formgeschichtliche Methode*. Düsseldorf: Patmos, 1968.

Bowman, J. W. "The Revelation to John: Its Dramatic Structure and Message." *Interpretation* 9 (1955): 436–53.

Brodie, T. L. *The Gospel according to John: A Literary and Theological Commentary*. Oxford: Oxford University Press, 1993.

Bronznick, N. M. "'Metathetic Parallelism'—An Unrecognized Subtype of Synonymous Parallelism." *Hebrew Annual Review* 3 (1979): 25–39.

Brouwer, W. *The Literary Development of John 13–17: A Chiastic Reading*. Atlanta: Society of Biblical Literature, 2000.

Brown, R. E. *The Community of the Beloved Disciple: The Life, Loves, and Hates of an Individual Church in New Testament Times*. New York: Paulist Press, 1979.

———. *The Gospel according to John*. 2 vols. New York/London: Doubleday, 1966, 1970.

Broyles, C. C. *The Conflict of Faith and Experience in the Psalms: A Form-Critical and Theological Study*. Sheffield: JSOT Press, 1989.

Bruce, F. F. *The Book of Acts*. Grand Rapids: Eerdmans, 1988.

———. *The Epistle of Paul to the Galatians*. Exeter: Paternoster, 1982.

Brueggemann, W. *The Psalms and The Life of Faith*. Minneapolis: Augsburg Fortress, 1995.

Bryan, C. *A Preface to Mark: Notes on the Gospel in Its Literary and Cultural Settings*. Oxford: Oxford University Press, 1997.

———. *A Preface to Romans: Notes on the Epistle in Its Literary and Cultural Setting*. Oxford: Oxford University Press, 2000.

Bultmann, R. *Das Evangelium des Johannes*. Göttingen: Vandenhoeck & Ruprecht, 1957.

———. "Glossen im Römerbrief." Pages 278–84 in his *Exegetica: Aufsätze zur Erforschung des Neuen Testaments*. Edited by E. Dinkler. Tübingen: Mohr Siebeck, 1967.

———. *Theology of the New Testament*. Vol. 2. New York: Scribner, 1955.

Burchard, C. "Fußnoten zum neutestamentlichen Griechisch." *ZNT* 61 (1970): 157–71.

Burge, G. M. "Situating John's Gospel in History." Pages 3–46 in *Jesus in Johannine Tradition*. Edited by R. T. Fortna and T. Thatcher. Louisville: Westminster John Knox Press, 2001.

Burridge, R. A. *What are the Gospels? A Comparison with Graeco-Roman Biography*. Cambridge: Cambridge University Press, 1992.

———. "The Gospels and Acts." Pages 507–32 in *Handbook of Classical Rhetoric in the Hellenistic Period (330 B.C–A.D. 400)*. Edited by S. E. Porter. Leiden: Brill, 1997.

———. "About People, by People, for People: Gospel Genre and Audiences." Pages 113–46 in *The Gospels for All Christians: Rethinking the Gospel Audiences*. Edited by R. Bauckman. Grand Rapids: Eerdmans, 1998.

Butler, H. E., trans. *Quintilian*. Loeb Classical Library. Cambridge, MA: Harvard University Press, 1986.

Byrne, B., S. J. *Romans*. Collegeville: Liturgical, 1996.

Cadbury, H. J. *The Making of Luke-Acts*. New York: Macmillan, 1927.

———. "The Summaries in Acts." Pages 392–402 in *The Beginnings of Christianity*. Vol. 5. Edited by F. J. Foakes-Jackson and K. Lake. London: Macmillan, 1933.

Carson, D. A. *The Gospel according to John*. Grand Rapids: Eerdmans, 1991.

Charles, R. H. *A Critical and Exegetical Commentary on the Revelation of St. John*. 2 vols. Edinburgh: T&T Clark, 1920.

Childs, B. S. *Isaiah*. Louisville: Westminster John Knox Press, 2001.

Clark, A. C. *The Acts of the Apostles*. Oxford: Clarendon Press, 1933.

Clark, D. J. "Criteria for Identifying Chiasm." *Linguistica Biblica* 5 (1975): 63–72.

Classen, C. J. "St Paul's Epistles and Ancient Greek and Roman Rhetoric." Pages 265–91 in *Rhetoric and the New Testament: Essays from the 1992 Heidelberg Conference*. Edited by S. E. Porter and T. H. Olbricht. Sheffield: Sheffield Academic Press, 1993.

Cohen, S. *Josephus in Galilee and Rome. His Vita and Development as a Historian*. Leiden: Brill, 1979.

Collins, J. J. *Daniel*. Minneapolis: Augsburg Fortress, 1993.

Colson, F. H., trans. *Philo of Alexandria*. Loeb Classical Library. London: Heinemann; Cambridge, MA: Harvard University Press, 1934.

Conzelmann, H. *Die Mitte der Zeit: Studien zur Theologie des Lukas*. 5th ed. Tübingen: Mohr Siebeck, 1964. Translated by Geoffrey Buswell as *The Theology of St Luke*. Philadelphia: Fortress Press, 1982.

Cope, E. M. *An Introduction to Aristotle's Rhetoric*. New York: Georg Olms Verlag, 1970.

Cornford, F. M. *The Origin of Attic Comedy*. London: Arnold, 1914.

Cotterell, P., and M. Turner. *Linguistics and Biblical Interpretation*. London: SPCK, 1989.

Cranfield, C. E. B. *The Epistle to the Romans*. Edinburgh: T&T Clark, 1975.

Cunningham, S. *"Through Many Tribulations": The Theology of Persecution in Luke-Acts*. Sheffield: Sheffield Academic Press, 1997.

Dahl, N. A. "Missionary Theology in the Epistle to the Romans," in his *Studies in Paul: Theology for the Early Christian Mission*. Minneapolis: Ausburg Press, 1977).

Dahood, M. J. "Chiasmus." Page 145 in *International Dictionary of the Bible Supplement*. Edited by K. Crim. Nashville: Abingdon, 1976.

Davies, P. R. *Daniel*. Sheffield: JSOT Press, 1985.

Dawsey, J. M. "The Literary Unity of Luke-Acts: Questions of Style—A Task for Literary Critics." *NTS* 35 (1989): 48–66.

de Boer, M. C. *Johannine Perspectives on the Death of Jesus*. Kampen: Pharos Publishing House, 1996.

Delitzsch, F. *The Prophecies of Isaiah*. Translated by J. Martin. Edinburgh: T&T Clark, 1867.

Delobel, J. "The Nature of 'Western-Readings' in Acts: Test Cases." Pages 69–94 in *Recent Developments in Textual Criticism: New Testament, Other Christian Literature and Jewish Literature*. Edited by W. Weren and D.-A. Koch. Assen: van Gorcum, 2003.

Denova, R. I. *The Things Accomplished Among Us: Prophetic Tradition in the Structural Pattern of Luke-Acts*. Sheffield: Sheffield Academic Press, 1997.

Dewey, J. *Markan Public Debate: Literary Technique, Concentric Structure, and Theology in Mark 2:1–3:6*. Chico: Scholars Press, 1980.

———. "Oral Methods of Structuring Narrative in Mark." *Interpretation* 53 (1989): 32–44.

———. "Textuality in an Oral Culture: A Survey of the Pauline Traditions." *Semeia* 65 (1995): 37–65.

————. "The Gospel of John in Its Oral-Written Media World." Pages 239–52 in *Jesus in Johannine Tradition*. Edited by R. T. Fortna and T. Thatcher. Louisville: Westminster John Knox Press, 2001.

Dibelius, M. *James*. Philadelphia: Fortress, 1976.

Dillon, R. J. "The Spirit as Taskmaster and Troublemaker in Romans 8." *CBQ* 60 (1999): 682–702.

Dodd, C. H. *The Epistle of Paul to the Romans*. London: Hodder & Stoughton, 1947.

————. *Historical Tradition in the Fourth Gospel*. Cambridge: Cambridge University Press, 1965.

Dunn, J. D. G. *Romans*. Dallas: Word Books, 1988.

————. *The Acts of the Apostles*. Valley Forge: Trinity Press International, 1996.

————. *The Theology of Paul the Apostle*. Grand Rapids: Eerdmans, 1998.

————. *Jesus Remembered*. Grand Rapids: Eerdmans, 2003.

————. "Altering the Default Setting: Re-envisaging the Early Transmission of the Jesus Tradition." *NTS* 49 (2003): 139–75.

Dupont, J. "La question du plan des Actes des Apôtres à la Lumière d'un Texte de Lucien de Samosate." Pages 24–36 in his *Nouvelles Études sur les Actes des Apôtres*. Paris: Éditions du Cerf, 1984. Repr. from *NTS* 21 (1974–75): 220–31.

Epp, E. J. "The Ascension in the Textual Tradition of Luke–Acts." Pages 131–45 in *New Testament Textual Criticism: Its Significance for Exegesis*. Edited by E. J. Epp and G. D. Fee. Oxford: Clarendon Press, 1981.

Filho, J. A. "The Apocalypse of John as an Account of a Visionary Experience: Notes on the Book's Structure." *JSNT* 25 (2002): 213–34.

Fiorenza, E. "The Eschatology and Composition of the Apocalypse." *CBQ* 30 (1968): 537–69, 561–63.

Fiorenza, E. Schüssler "Composition and Structure of the Revelation of John." *CBQ* 39 (1977): 344–66.

————. *The Book of Revelation: Justice and Judgement*. Philadelphia: Fortress, 1985.

Fitzmyer, J. A. Romans: *A New Translation with Introduction and Commentary*. New York: Doubleday, 1993.

————. *The Acts of the Apostles*. New York: Doubleday, 1998.

Ford, J. M. *The Revelation of John*. Garden City: Doubleday, 1975.

Fowler, H. W. and F. G. Fowler, trans. *The Works of Lucian.* Oxford: Oxford University Press, 1905.

Franklin, E. *Christ the Lord: A Study of the Purpose and Theology of Luke-Acts.* Philadelphia: Westminster, 1975.

Frey, J. *Die johanneische Eschatologie.* Vol. 3. Tübingen: Mohr Siebeck, 2000.

Freyne, S. *Galilee from Alexander the Great to Hadrian, 323 BCE to 135 CE: A Study of Second Temple Judaism.* Notre Dame: University of Notre Dame Press, 1980.

Fung, R. Y. K. *The Epistle to the Galatians.* Grand Rapids: Eerdmans, 1988.

Funk, R. "The Enigma of the Famine Visit." *JBL* 75 (1956): 130–36.

Gaisser, J. H. "A Structural Analysis of the Digressions in the Iliad and the Odyssey." *HSCP* 73 (1969): 1–43.

García Martínez, F. *The Dead Sea Scrolls Translated: The Qumran Texts in English.* 2d ed. Grand Rapids: Eerdmans, 1996.

Garrow, A. *Revelation.* London/New York: Routledge, 1997.

Gathercole, S. J. *Where is Boasting? Early Jewish Soteriology and Paul's Response in Romans 1–5.* Grand Rapids: Eerdmans, 2002.

Gaventa, B. R. *From Darkness to Light: Aspects of Conversion in the New Testament.* Philadelphia: Fortress, 1986.

———. "The Archive of Excess: John 21 and the Problem of Narrative Closure." Pages 240–52 in *Exploring the Gospel of John: In Honor of D. Moody Smith.* Edited by R. A. Culpepper and C. C. Black. Louisville: Westminster John Knox, 1996.

———. "The Eschatology of Luke-Acts Revisited." *Encounter* 43 (1982): 27–42.

———. "Towards a Theology of Acts: Reading and Rereading." *Int* 42 (1988): 146–57.

———. *The Acts of the Apostles.* Nashville: Abingdon, 2003.

———. "Initiatives Divine and Human in the Lukan Story World." Pages 79–89 in *The Holy Spirit and Christian Origins: Essays in Honour of James D.G. Dunn.* Edited by G. N. Stanton, B. W. Longenecker, and S. C. Barton. Grand Rapids: Eerdmans, 2004.

———. "Theology and Ecclesiology in the Miletus Speech: Reflections on Content and Context." *NTS* 50 (2004): 36–52.

George, A. "Les récits d'apparitions aux Onze à partir de Luc 24,36–53." Pages 75–94 in *La résurrection du Christ et l'exégèse moderne.* Edited by P. deSurgy et al. Paris: Éditions du Cerf, 1969.

Giblin, C. H. "Structural and Thematic Correlations in the Theology of Revelation 16–22." *Biblica* 55 (1974): 487–504.

———. "The Tripartite Narrative Structure of John's Gospel." *Biblica* 71 (1990): 449–67.

Goulder, M. *Type and History in Acts.* London: SPCK, 1964.

Green, J. B. *The Theology of the Gospel of Luke.* Cambridge: Cambridge University Press, 1995.

———. "Internal Repetitions in Luke-Acts: Contemporary Narratology and Lukan Historiography." Pages 283–99 in *History, Literature and Society in the Book of Acts.* Edited by B. Witherington. Cambridge: Cambridge University Press, 1996.

Greenstein, E. L. "How Does Parallelism Mean?" In his *A Sense of Text: The Art of Language in the Study of Biblical Literature.* Winona Lake: Eisenbrauns, 1983.

Guthrie, G. H. *The Structure of Hebrews: A Text Linguistic Analysis.* Leiden: Brill, 1994.

———. *Hebrews.* Grand Rapids: Zondervan, 1998.

Haenchen, E. "The Book of Acts as Source Material for the History of Early Christianity." Pages 258–78 in *Studies in Luke-Acts.* Edited by L. E. Keck and J. L. Martyn. Nashville: Abingdon, 1966.

———. *Die Apostelgeschichte.* Göttingen: Vandenhoeck & Ruprecht, 1977.

———. *Die Johannesevangelium: Ein Kommentar.* Tübingen: Mohr, 1980.

Harris, W. *Ancient Literacy.* Cambridge, MA: Harvard University Press, 1989.

Hartman, L. F., and A. A. di Lella. *The Book of Daniel.* Garden City: Doubleday, 1978.

Harvey, J. D. *Listening to the Text: Oral Patterning in Paul's Letters.* Grand Rapids: Baker, 1998.

Havelock, E. A. "The Alphabetization of Homer." Pages 3–21 in *Communication Arts in the Ancient World.* Edited by E. A. Havelock and J. P. Herschbel. New York: Hastings House, 1978.

Heinze, A. *Johannesapocalypse und johanneische Schriften.* Stuttgart: Kohlhammer, 1998.

Hemer, C. J. *The Book of Acts in the Setting of Hellenistic History.* Tübingen: J. C. B. Mohr (Paul Siebeck), 1989.

Hendriksen, W. *The New Testament Commentary: Exposition of the Gospel according to John.* Grand Rapids: Baker Books, 1953.

Hengel, M. "Luke the Historian and the Geography of Palestine in the Acts of the Apostles." Pages 97–128 in his *Between Jesus and Paul: Studies in the Earliest History of Christianity*. Minneapolis: Fortress, 1983.

———. *The Johannine Question*. London: SCM Press, 1989.

Hengel, M., and A. M. Schwemer. *Paul between Damascus and Antioch*. London: SCM Press, 1997.

Hezser, C. *Jewish Literacy in Roman Palestine*. Tübingen: Mohr Siebeck, 2001.

Hijmans, B.L., Jr. Inlaboratus et Facilis: *Aspects of Structure in Some Letters of Seneca*. Leiden: Brill, 1976.

R. F. Hock, and E. N. O'Neill, eds. *The Progymnasmata*. Vol. 1 of *The Chreia and Ancient Rhetoric*. Atlanta: Scholars Press, 1986.

———. *Classroom Exercises*. Vol. 2 of *The Chreia and Ancient Rhetoric*. Atlanta: Society of Biblical Literature, 2002.

Hoffmann, G. *Das Johannesevangelium ein Alterswerk: Eine psychologische Studie*. Gütersloh: Kaiser, 1933.

Holladay, W. "The Recovery of Poetic Passages of Jeremiah." *JBL* 85 (1966): 401–35.

Holmberg, B. *Paul and Power: The Structure of Authority in the Primitive Church as Reflected in the Pauline Epistles*. Philadelphia: Fortress, 1980.

Hooker, M. D. *Paul: A Short Introduction*. Oxford: Oneworld, 2003.

Horsley, R. A. *Hearing the Whole Story: The Politics of Plot in Mark's Gospel*. Louisville: Westminster John Knox, 2001.

Hurtado, L. W. *Lord Jesus Christ: Devotion to Jesus in Earliest Christianity*. Grand Rapids: Eerdmans, 2003.

Jeremias, J. "Sabbathjahr und neutestamentliche Chronologie." *ZNW* 27 (1928): 98–103.

Jervell, J. *Die Apostelgeschichte*. Göttingen: Vandenhoeck & Ruprecht, 1998.

Jewett, R. *Dating Paul's Life*. London: SCM Press, 1979.

Johnson, L.T. *The Acts of the Apostles*. Collegeville: Liturgical Press, 1992.

Juel, D. *Luke-Acts*. London: SCM, 1983.

Käsemann, E. *Jesu Letzter Wille nach Johannes 17*. Tübingen: J. C. B. Mohr (Paul Siebeck), 1966.

———. *An die Römer*. 4th ed. Tübingen: Mohr Siebeck, 1980. Translated by Geoffrey W. Bromiley as *Commentary on Romans*. Grand Rapids: Eerdmans, 1980.

Keck, L. E. "The Poor among the Saints in the New Testament." *ZNW* 56 (1965): 100–29.

Kelber, W. H. *The Oral and Written Gospel: The Hermeneutics of Speaking and Writing in the Synoptic Tradition, Mark, Paul and Q.* Philadelphia: Fortress Press, 1983.

Kennedy, G. A. *New Testament Interpretation through Rhetorical Criticism.* Chapel Hill: University of North Carolina Press, 1984.

———. *Progymnasmata: Greek Textbooks of Prose Composition and Rhetoric.* Leiden: Brill, 2003.

Kikawada, I. M. "The Shape of Genesis 11.1-9." Pages 18–32 in *Rhetorical Criticism: Essays in Honor of James Muilenberg.* Edited by J. J. Jackson and M. Kessler. Pittsburgh: Pickwick, 1974.

Kilallen, J. J. "Persecution in the Acts of the Apostles." Pages 143–60 in *Luke and Acts.* Edited by G. O'Collins and G. Marconi. New York: Paulist Press, 1993.

Kilburn, K., trans. *Lucian.* Loeb Classical Library. Cambridge, MA: Harvard University Press, 1968.

Klauck, H.-J. *Magic and Paganism in Early Christianity: The World of the Acts of the Apostles.* Translated by B. McNeil; Edinburgh: T&T Clark, 2000.

Klausner, J. *From Jesus to Paul.* London: Allen and Unwin, 1946.

Knight, J. *Luke's Gospel.* London: Routledge, 1998.

Knox, J. *Chapters in a Life of Paul.* Rev. ed. London: SCM Press, 1989.

Kovacs, J. L. "'Now shall the ruler of this world be driven out': Jesus' Death as Cosmic Battle in John 12:20–36." *JBL* 114 (1995): 227–47.

Kraft, H. *Die Offenbarung des Johannes.* Tübingen: Mohr Siebeck, 1974.

Kraus, H.-J. *Psalmen.* Neukirchen-Vluyn: Keukirchener Verlag, 1978.

Kümmel, W. G. *Introduction to the New Testament.* Translated by Howard Clark Kee. London: SCM, 1975.

Kurz, W. "Promise and Fulfillment in Hellenistic Jewish Narratives and in Luke and Acts." Pages 147–70 in *Jesus and the Heritage of Israel: Luke's Narrative Claim upon Israel's Legacy.* Edited by D. P. Moessner. Harrisburg: Trinity Press International, 1999.

Kuss, O. *Der Römerbrief.* Regensburg: Verlag Friedrich Pustet, 1963.

Lagrange, M.-J. *Saint Paul Épitre aux Romains.* 6th ed. Paris: Gabalda, 1950.

Lambrecht, J. "A Structuration of Rev 4.1–22.5." Pages 77–104 in *L'Apocalypse johannique et l'Apocalyptique dans le Nouveau Testament.* Edited by J. Lambrecht. Leuven: Leuven University, 1980.

―――. "The Caesura between Romans 9:30-3 and 10:1-4." *NTS* 45 (1999): 141–47.

Leenhardt, Franz J. *The Epistles to the Romans*. Translated by Harold Knight; London: Lutterworth Press, 1961.

Levinsohn, S. H. "Review of G. H. Guthrie, The Structure of Hebrews: A Text Linguistic Analysis." *NovT* 43 (2001): 182–88.

Lietzmann, D. H. *Einführung in die Textgeschichte des Paulusbriefe an die Römer*. 5th ed.; Tübingen: J. C. B. Mohr, 1971.

Lincoln, A. T. *Truth on Trial: The Lawsuit Motif in the Fourth Gospel*. Peabody: Hendrickson, 2000.

Lindars, B. *The Gospel of John*. London: Oliphants, 1972.

―――. "The Passion in the Fourth Gospel." Pages 67–85 in his *Essays on John*. Leuven: Leuven University Press, 1992.

Lindsell, H. "Introduction to the Acts of the Apostles." Pages 1624–25 in the *Eyre & Spottiswoode Study Bible*. London: Eyre & Spottiswoode, 1964.

Loisy, A. *Les Actes des Apôtres*. Paris: Minerva, 1920.

Longenecker, B. W. *Eschatology and the Covenant: A Comparison of 4 Ezra and Romans 1–11*. Sheffield: Sheffield Academic Press, 1991.

―――. *2 Esdras*. Sheffield: Sheffield Academic Press, 1995.

―――. "Revelation 19,10: One Verse in Search of an Author." *ZNW* 91 (2000): 230–37.

―――. "Moral Character and Divine Generosity: Acts 13:13-52 and the Narrative Dynamics of Luke-Acts." Pages 141–64 in *New Testament Greek and Exegesis: A Festschrift for Gerald F. Hawthorne*. Edited by A. M. Donaldson & T. B. Sailors. Grand Rapids: Eerdmans, 2003.

―――. "Rome, Provincial Cities and the Seven Churches of Revelation 2–3." Pages 281–91 in *The New Testament in Its First Century Setting*. Edited by P. J. Williams, Andrew D. Clarke, Peter M. Head, and David Instone-Brewer. Grand Rapids: Eerdmans, 2004.

―――. "Rome's Victory and God's Honour: The Jerusalem Temple and the Spirit of God in Lukan Theodicy." Pages 90–102 in *The Holy Spirit and Christian Origins: Essays in Honor of James D. G. Dunn*. Edited by G. N. Stanton, B. W. Longenecker, and S. C. Barton. Grand Rapids: Eerdmans, 2004.

Longenecker, R. N. "The Acts of the Apostles." Pages 205–573 in Vol. 9 of *The Expositor's Bible Commentary*. Grand Rapids: Zondervan, 1981.

―――. *Galatians*. Waco: Word Books, 1990.

Löning, K. *Die Saulustradition in der Apostelgeschichte.* Münster: Aschendorff, 1973.

Lord, A. B. *The Singer of Tales.* Cambridge, MA: Harvard University Press, 1960.

———. "The Gospels and Oral Traditional Literature." Pages 33–91 in *The Relationships Among the Gospels.* Edited by W. O. Walker. San Antonio: Trinity University Press, 1978.

———. "Words Heard and Words Seen." Pages 1–17 in *Oral Tradition and Literacy: Changing Visions of the World.* Edited by R. A. Whitaker and E. R. Sienart. Durhab: Natal University, 1986.

Louw, L. P. "Discourse Analysis and the Greek New Testament." *Bible Translator* 24 (1973): 108–18.

Lucian. Translated by H. W. Fowler and F. G. Fowler. Oxford: Oxford University Press, 1905.

Lucian. Translated by K. Kilburn. Loeb Classical Library. London: William Heinemann; Cambridge, MA: Harvard University Press, 1968.

Luciani Samosatensis Opera. Translated by C. Jacobita. Leipzig: Teubner, 1887.

Lüdemann, G. *Paul, Apostle to the Gentiles: Studies in Chronology.* London: SCM Press, 1984.

———. *Das frühe Christentum nach den Traditionen der Apostelgeschichte.* Göttingen: Vandenhoeck & Ruprecht, 1987.

Lund, N. W. *Chiasmus in the New Testament: A Study in the Form and Function of Chiastic Structures.* Chapel Hill: University of North Carolina, 1942; Repr. Peabody: Hendrickson, 1992.

Luz, U. *Das Geschichtsverständnis des Paulus.* Munich: Kaiser Verlag, 1968.

Maddox, R. *The Purpose of Luke-Acts.* Göttingen: Vandenhoeck & Ruprecht, 1982.

Marguerat, D. *The First Christian Historian: Writing the "Acts of the Apostles."* Cambridge: Cambridge University Press, 2002.

Marrou, H. I. *A History of Education in Antiquity.* New York: Sheed & Ward, 1956.

Marshall, I. H. *The Acts of the Apostles.* Sheffield: Sheffield Academic Press, 1992.

Martyn, J. L. *History and Theology in the Fourth Gospel.* Nashville: Abingdon, 1968.

Mason, S. *Josephus and the New Testament.* Peabody: Hendrickson, 1992; 2d ed. Peabody: Hendrickson, 2003.

Mathewson, D. *A New Heaven and a New Earth: The Meaning and Function of the Old Testament in Revelation 21.1–22.5*. London: Sheffield Academic Press, 2003.

Meeks, W. A. "The Man from Heaven in Johannine Sectarianism." Pages 169–205 in *The Interpretation of John*. 2nd ed. Edited by J. Ashton. Edinburgh: T&T Clark, 1997.

Mekkattukunnel, A. G. *The Priestly Blessing of the Risen Christ: An Exigetico-Theological Analysis of Luke 24, 50–53*. Bern: Peter Lang, 2001.

Menoud, P.-H. "Remarques sur les textes de l'ascension dans Luk-Acts." Pages 148–56 in *Neutestamentliche Studien für Rudolf Bultmann*. Edited by W. Eltester. Berlin: Töpelmann, 1957.

———. "Le plan des Actes des Apôtres." *NTS* 1 (1954–55): 44–51.

———. "During Forty Days." Pages 167–79 in his *Jesus Christ and the Faith: A Collection of Studies by Philippe Menoud*. Pittsburgh: Pickwick, 1978.

Meye Thompson, M. *The Humanity of Jesus in the Fourth Gospel*. Philadelphia: Fortress Press, 1988.

Michel, O. *Der Brief an die Römer*. 5th ed.; Göttingen: Vandenhoeck & Ruprecht, 1978.

Millard, A. *Reading and Writing in the Time of Jesus*. Sheffield: Sheffield Academic Press, 2000.

Minear, P. "The Original Function of John 21." *JBL* 102 (1983): 85–98.

Mlakuzhyil, G. *The Christocentric Literary Structure of the Fourth Gospel*. Rome: Editrice Pontificio Instituto Biblico, 1987.

Moberly, R. W. L. "Proclaiming Christ Crucified: Some Reflections on the Use and Abuse of the Gospels." Pages 83–104 in his *From Eden to Golgotha: Essays in Biblical Theology*. Atlanta: Scholars Press, 1992.

Moiser, J. "Rethinking Romans 12–15." *NTS* 36 (1990): 571–82.

Moloney, F. J. *The Johannine Son of Man*. 2nd ed. Rome: Bibliotea di Scienze Religiose, 1978.

———. *Signs and Shadows: Reading John 5–12*. Minneapolis: Fortress, 1996.

———. "The Function of John 13–17 within the Johannine Narrative." Pages 43–66 in *Literary and Social Readings of the Fourth Gospel*. Vol. 2 of *"What is John?" Readers and Readings of the Fourth Gospel*. Edited by F. F. Segovia. Atlanta: Scholars Press, 1998.

———. *Glory Not Dishonour: Reading John 13–21*. Minneapolis: Fortress, 1998.

———. "Raymond Brown's New Introduction to the Gospel of John: A Presentation—And Some Questions." *CBQ* 65 (2003): 1–21.

Moo, D. *The Epistle to the Romans.* Grand Rapids: Eerdmans, 1996.

Morgenstern, J. "Psalm 121." *JBL* 58 (1939): 311–23.

Morgenthaler, R. *Lukas und Quintilian: Rhetorik als Erzählkunst.* Zürich: Gotthelf, 1993.

Morris, L. L. *The Gospel according to John.* Grand Rapids: Eerdmans, 1971.

———. *The Epistle to the Romans.* Grand Rapids: Eerdmans, 1988.

Morton, A. Q., and G. H. C. MacGregor. *The Structure of Luke and Acts.* London: Hodder & Stoughton, 1964.

Most, G. W. *The Measures of Praise: Structure and Function in Pindar's Second Pythian and Seventh Nemean Odes* (Göttingen: Vandenhoeck & Ruprecht, 1985).

Motyer, J. A. *The Prophecy of Isaiah.* Leicester: InterVarsity, 1993.

Mounce, R. H. *The Book of Revelation.* Grand Rapids: Eerdmans, 1977.

Müller, F. "Zwei Marginalien im Brief des Paulus an die Römer." *ZNW* 40 (1941): 249–54.

Murphy-O'Connor, J. *Paul: A Critical Life.* Oxford: Clarendon, 1996.

Neeley, L. L. "A Discourse Analysis of Hebrews." *Occasional Papers in Translation and Textlinguistics* 3–4 (1987): 1–146.

Nicholson, G. *Death as Departure: The Johannine Descent-Ascent Schema.* Chico: Scholars Press, 1983.

Nickle, K. F. *The Collection: A Study in Paul's Strategy.* London: SCM Press, 1966.

Nida, E. A. *Componential Analysis of Meaning.* The Hague: Mouton, 1975.

Nock, A. D. *St. Paul.* London: Oxford University Press, 1938.

North, C. R. *The Second Isaiah.* Oxford: Clarendon Press, 1964.

O'Day, G. R. "Johannine Theology as Sectarian Theology." Pages 199–203 in *Readers and Readings of the Fourth Gospel.* Vol. 1 of "What is John?" Edited by F. F. Segovia. Atlanta: Scholars Press, 1996.

———. "The Gospel of John: Reading the Incarnate Words." Pages 25–32 in *Jesus in Johannine Tradition.* Edited by R. T. Fortna and T. Thatcher. Louisville: Westminster John Knox Press, 2001.

Ó Fearghail, F. *The Introduction to Luke-Acts: A Study of the Role of Lk 1,1–4,44 in the Composition of Luke's Two-Volume Work.* Rome: Editrice Pontificio Instituto Biblico, 1991.

Ogg, G. *The Chronology of the Life of Paul.* London: Epworth, 1968.

Omerzu, H. "Das Schweigen des Lukas: Überlegungen zum offenen Ende der Apostelgeschichte." Pages 127–44 in *Das Ende des Paulus: Historische, theologische und literaturegeschichtliche Aspekte*. Edited by F. W. Horn. Berlin: de Gruyter, 2001.

Ong, W. J. *The Presence of the Word*. New Haven: Yale University Press, 1967.

———. *Interfaces of the Word: Studies in the Evolution of Consciousness and Culture*. Ithaca: Cornell University Press, 1977.

———. *Orality and Literacy: The Technologizing of the Word*. London: Routledge, 1988.

O'Neill, J. C. *The Theology of Acts in Its Historical Setting*. Rev. ed. London: SPCK, 1970.

———. *Paul's Letter to the Romans*. Harmondsworth: Penguin Books, 1975.

Osborne, T. P. "Deux grandes structures concentriques centrales et une nouvelle approche du plan global de l'Evangile de Luc (première partie)." *RevB* 110 (2003): 197–221.

Painter, J. *The Quest for the Messiah: The History, Literature and Theology of the Johannine Community*. Edinburgh: T&T Clark, 1991.

———. *Just James: The Brother of Jesus in History and Tradition*. Columbia: University of South Carolina Press, 1997.

Palmer, D. W. "Acts and the Ancient Historical Monograph." Pages 1–29 in *Ancient Literary Setting*. Vol. 1 of *The Book of Acts in its First-Century Setting*. Edited by B. W. Winter and A. D. Clark. Grand Rapids: Eerdmans, 1993.

———. "The Literary Background of Acts 1.1-14." *NTS* 33 (1987): 427–38.

Parker, D. C. "A New Oxyrhynchus Papyrus of Revelation: P115 (P. Oxy. 4499)." *NTS* 46 (2000): 159–74.

Parker, P. "Three Variant Readings in Luke-Acts." *JBL* 83 (1964): 165–70.

Parry, D. T. N. "Release of the Captives: Reflections on Acts 12." Pages 156–64 in *Luke's Literary Achievement: Collected Essays*. Edited by C. M. Tuckett. Sheffield: Sheffield Academic, 1995.

Parsons, M. C. *The Departure of Jesus: The Ascension Narratives in Context*. Sheffield: Sheffield Academic, 1987.

Parsons, M. C., and R. I. Pervo. *Rethinking the Unity of Luke and Acts*. Minneapolis: Fortress, 1993.

Parsons, M. C., and M. M. Culy. *Acts: A Handbook on the Greek Text.* Waco: Baylor University Press, 2003.

Parunak, H. van Dyke "Transitional Techniques in the Bible." *JBL* 102 (1983): 525–48.

Peng, K.-W. "[The] Structure of Romans 12.1–15.13." Ph.D. diss., University of Sheffield, 1997.

Perrot, C. "Les Actes des Apôtres." Pages 239–99 in *Introduction critique au Nouveau Testament.* Vol. 2. Edited by A. George and P. Grelot. Paris: Desclée, 1976.

Pervo, R. I. *Profit with Delight: The Literary Genre of the Acts of the Apostles.* Philadelphia: Fortress, 1987.

———. "Israel's Heritage and Claims upon the Genre(s) of Luke and Acts: The Problems of a History." Pages 127–43 in *Jesus and the Heritage of Israel: Luke's Narrative Claim upon Israel's Legacy.* Edited by D. P. Moessner. Harrisburg: Trinity, 1999.

Pesch, R. *Die Apostelgeschichte.* Neukirchen-Vluyn: Neukirchener Verlag, 1986.

Philo of Alexandria. Vol. 6. Translated by F. H. Colson. Loeb Classical Library. London: Heinemann, 1934; Cambridge, MA: Harvard University Press.

Piper, R. A. "Satan, Demons and the Absence of Exorcisms in the Fourth Gospel." Pages 253–78 in *Christology, Controversy and Community: New Testament Essays in Honour of David R. Catchpole.* Edited by D. G. Horrell and C. M. Tuckett. Leiden: Brill, 2000.

Polhill, J. P. *The Acts of the Apostles.* Nashville: Broadman, 1992.

Polzin, R. "The Framework of the Book of Job." *Interpretation* 28 (1974): 182–200.

Porter, S. E. "The Theoretical Justification for Application of Rhetorical Categories to Pauline Epistolary Literature." Pages 100–122 in *Rhetorica and the New Testament.* Edited by S. E. Porter and T. H. Olbricht. Sheffield: Sheffield Academic Press, 1993.

Plutarch. *Moralia.* Translated by F. C. Babbitt. Loeb Classical Library. London: William Heinemann; Cambridge, MA: Harvard University Press, 1969.

Pratscher, W. *Der Herrenbruder Jakobus und die Jacobustradition.* Göttingen: Vandenhoeck & Ruprecht, 1987.

Prigent, P. *Commentary on the Apocalypse of St. John.* Translated by W. Pradels. Tübingen: Mohr Siebeck, 2001.

Pryor, J. W. *John: Evangelist of the Covenant People*. London: Darton, Longman & Todd, 1992.

Quintilian. *Institutio oratorio*. Translated by H. E. Butler. Loeb Classical Library. London: William Heinemann; Cambridge, MA: Harvard University Press, 1986.

Reasoner, M. *The Strong and the Weak: Romans 14.1–15.13 in Context*. Cambridge: Cambridge University Press, 1999.

Reed, J. T. "Using Ancient Rhetorical Categories to Interpret Paul's Letters: A Question of Genre." Pages 292–324 in *Rhetoric and the New Testament: Essays from the 1992 Heidelberg Conference*. Edited by S. E. Porter and T. H. Olbricht. Sheffield: Sheffield Academic Press, 1993.

Renan, E. *Les Origines du Christianisme, v. Les Évangiles; vi. L'Église chrétienne*. Paris: Calmann Lévy, 1877/79.

Rensberger, D. "The Messiah Who Has Come into the World: The Message of the Gospel of John." Pages 15–23 in *Jesus in Johannine Tradition*. Edited by R. T. Fortna and T. Thatcher. Louisville: Westminster John Knox, 2001.

Rhoads, D. "Performing the Gospel of Mark." In *Body and Bible: Interpreting and Experiencing Biblical Narratives*. Edited by B. Krondorfer. Philadelphia: Trinity Press International, 1992.

Richard, E. *Acts 6:1–8:4: The Author's Method of Composition*. Missoula: Scholars Press, 1978.

Riesner, R. *Paul's Early Period: Chronology, Mission Strategy, Theology*. Grand Rapids: Eerdmans, 1998.

Rissi, M. "Der Aufbau des vierten Evangliums." *NTS* 29 (1983): 48–53.

Robbins, V. K. *The Tapestry of Early Christian Discourse: Rhetoric, Society and Ideology*. London: Routledge, 1996.

———. "The Claims of the Prologues and Greco-Roman Rhetoric: The Prefaces to Luke and Acts in Light of Greco-Roman Rhetorical Strategies." Pages 63–83 in *Jesus and the Heritage of Israel: Luke's Narrative Claim upon Israel's Legacy*. Edited by D. P. Moessner. Harrisburg: Trinity Press International, 1999.

Rohrbaugh, R. L. "The Social Location of the Marcan Audience." *BTB* 23 (1993): 114–27.

Roloff, J. *Die Apostelgeschichte*. Göttingen: Vandenhoeck & Ruprecht, 1988.

Rosseau, F. *L'Apocalypse et le milieu prophétique du Nouveau Testament: Structure et préhistoire du texte*. Montreal: Bellarmin, 1971.

Rowe, G. O. "Style." Pages 121–57 in *Handbook of Classical Rhetoric in the Hellenistic Period (330 B.C.–A.D. 400)*. Edited by S. E. Porter. Leiden: Brill, 1997.

Rowley, H. H. "The Unity of the Book of Daniel." Pages 249–60 in his *The Servant of the Lord and Other Essays on the Old Testament*. 2nd ed. Oxford: Blackwell, 1965.

Rubinkiewicz, R. "Apocalypse of Abraham." Pages 681–705 in *Old Testament Pseudepigrapha*. Vol. 1. Edited by J. H. Charlesworth. Garden City: Doubleday, 1983.

———. "La vision de l'homme dans l'Apocalypse d'Abraham." Pages 139–44 in *ANRW* 2.19.1. Edited by W. Hasse. Berlin: de Gruyter, 1979.

Russell, D. A., trans. *Quintilian, The Orator's Education*. Vol. 2, Books 3–5. Loeb Classical Library: London: Harvard University Press, 2001.

Sanders, J .A. "Intertextuality and Canon." Pages 316–33 in *On the Way to Nineveh: Studies in Honor of George M. Landes*. Edited by S. L. Cook and S. C. Winter. Atlanta: Scholars Press, 1999.

Sanders, J. T. *Ethics in the New Testament*. Philadelphia: Fortress, 1975.

Schille, G. *Die Apostelgeschichte des Lukas*. Berlin: Evangelische Verlag-anstalt, 1984.

Schmidt, D. D. "Rhetorical Influences and Genre: Luke's Preface and the Rhetoric of Hellenistic Historiography." Pages 27–60 in *Jesus and the Heritage of Israel: Luke's Narrative Claim upon Israel's Legacy*. Edited by D. P. Moessner. Harrisburg: Trinity, 1999.

Schmithals, W. *Die Apostelgeschichte des Lukas*. Zürich: Theologischer Verlag, 1982.

———. *Der Römerbrief*. Gütersloh: Gütersloher Verlag, 1988.

Schnackenburg, R. *Das Johannesevangelium*. Freiburg: Herder, 1976.

Schneider, G. *Die Apostelgeschichte*. Vol. 2. Freiburg: Herder, 1982.

Schnelle, U. "Die Abschiedsreden im Johannesevangelium." *ZNW* 80 (1989): 64–79.

Schreiner, T. R. *Romans*. Grand Rapids: Baker Books, 1998.

Schubert, P. "The Structure and Significance of Luke 24." Pages 165–86 in *Neutestamentliche Studien für Rudolph Bultmann*. Edited by W. Eltester. Berlin: Töpelmann, 1957.

Scott, J. M. "Luke's Geographical Horizon." Pages 483–544 in *The Book of Acts in Its Graeco-Roman Setting*. Edited by D. W. J. Gill and C. Gempf. Grand Rapids: Eerdmans, 1994.

Segovia, F. F. *The Farewell of the Word.* Minneapolis: Fortress Press, 1991.

———. "The Journey(s) of the Word of God: A Reading of the Plot of the Fourth Gospel." *Semeia* 53 (1991): 23–54.

Seitz, C. R. "How is the Prophet Isaiah Present in the Latter Half of the Book? The Logic of Chapters 40–66 within the Book of Isaiah." *JBL* 115 (1996): 219–40.

———. "The Book of Isaiah 40–66: Introduction, Commentary and Reflections." Pages 307–52 in *The New Interpreter's Bible.* Edited by L. E. Keck et al. Nashville: Abingdon Press, 2001.

Shiner, W. *Proclaiming the Gospel: First-Century Performance of Mark.* Harrisburg: Trinity Press International, 2003.

Siegert, F. *Argumentation bei Paulus gezeigt an Röm 9–11.* Tübingen: Mohr Siebeck, 1985.

Snyman, A. H. "Style and Meaning in Romans 8:31-39." *Neot* 18 (1984): 94–103.

Smith, D. Moody. *The Composition and Order of the Fourth Gospel.* New Haven: Yale University Press, 1965.

———. *The Theology of the Gospel of John.* Cambridge: Cambridge University Press, 1995.

Spencer, F. S. *The Portrait of Philip in Acts: A Study of Roles and Relations.* Sheffield: Sheffield Academic, 1992.

———. *Acts.* Sheffield: Sheffield Academic, 1997.

Spilsbury, P. "*Contra Apionem* and *Antiquitates Judaicae*: Points of Contact." Pages 348–68 in *Josephus' Contra Apionem: Studies in its Character and Context.* Edited by L. H. Feldman and J. R. Levison. Leiden: Brill, 1996.

Staley, J. L. *The Print's First Kiss: A Rhetorical Investigation of the Implied Reader in the Fourth Gospel.* Atlanta: Scholars Press, 1988.

Stamps, D. L. "The Johannine Writings." Pages 609–32 in *Handbook of Classical Rhetoric in the Hellenistic Period (330 B.C–A.D. 400).* Edited by S. E. Porter. Leiden: Brill, 1997.

Stanley, K. *The Shield of Homer: Narrative Structure in the* Iliad. Princeton: Princeton University Press, 1993.

Stanton, G. N. *Jesus and the Gospels.* Oxford: Oxford University Press, 1989.

Sterling, G. E. *Historiography and Self-Definition: Josephus, Luke-Acts and Apologetic Historiography.* Leiden: Brill, 1992.

Stewart, A. "Stesichoros and the Françoise Vase." Pages 53–74 in *Ancient Greek Art and Iconography*. Edited by W. G. Moon. Madison: University of Wisconsin Press, 1983.

Stibbe, M. *John*. Sheffield: Sheffield Academic Press, 1993.

———. *John as Storyteller: Narrative Criticism and the Fourth Gospel*. Cambridge: Cambridge University Press, 1992.

Stock, A. "Chiastic Awareness and Education in Antiquity." *Biblical Theology Bulletin* 14 (1984): 23–27.

Stone, M. E. "A Reconsideration of Apocalyptic Visions." *HTR* 96 (2003): 167–80.

Strauss, D. F. *Das Leben Jesu*. Tübingen: C. F. Osiander, 1837.

Strecker, G. "Die sogenannte zweite Jerusalemreise des Paulus." *ZNW* 52 (1962): 67–77.

Streeter, B. H. *The Four Gospels: A Study in Origins*. 5th ed. London: Macmillan, 1936.

Stuhlmacher, P. *Paul's Letter to the Romans: A Commentary*. Louisville: Westminster John Knox; Edinburgh: T&T Clark, 1994.

Sweet, J. *Revelation*. London: SCM Press, 1979.

Talbert, C. H. *Literary Patterns, Theological Themes and The Genre of Luke-Acts*. Missoula: Scholars Press, 1974.

———. *Acts*. Atlanta: John Knox Press, 1984.

———. *Reading John: A Literary and Theological Commentary on the Fourth Gospel and the Johannine Epistles*. New York: Crossroad, 1992.

———. *Reading Acts: A Literary and Theological Commentary on the Acts of the Apostles*. New York: Crossroad, 1997.

Tannehill, R. C. *The Narrative Unity of Luke-Acts: A Literary Interpretation*. 2 vols. Philadelphia: Fortress, 1986/1990.

———. "Rejection by Jews and Turning to Gentiles: The Pattern of Paul's Mission in Acts." Pages 83–101 in *Luke-Acts and the Jewish People: Eight Critical Perspectives*. Edited J. B. Tyson. Minneapolis: Augsburg, 1988.

Terrien, S. *The Elusive Presence: Toward a New Biblical Theology*. New York: Harper & Row, 1978.

Thatcher, T. *The Riddles of Jesus in John: A Study in Tradition and Folklore*. Atlanta: Society of Biblical Literature, 2000.

———. "Introduction." Pages 1–9 in *Jesus in Johannine Tradition*. Edited by R. T. Fortna and T. Thatcher. Louisville: Westminster John Knox, 2001.

Thomson, I. H. *Chiasmus in the Pauline Letters*. Sheffield: Sheffield Academic Press, 1995.

Thüsing, W. *Die Erhöhung und Verherrlichung Jesu im Johannesevangelium*. Münster: Aschendorff, 1970.

Thyen, H. "Aus der Literatur zum Johannesevangelium." *Theologische Rundshau* 42 (1977): 211–70.

Tite, P. L. *Compositional Transitions in 1 Peter: An Analysis of the Letter-Opening*. London: International Scholars, 1997.

Torrey, C. C. *The Second Isaiah*. Edinburgh: T&T Clark, 1928.

Trocmé, E. *Le "Livre des Actes" et l'histoire*. Paris: Presses Universitaires de France, 1957.

Tuckett, C. "How Early is 'the' 'Western' Text of Acts?" Pages 69–86 in *The Book of Acts as Church History: Text, Textual Traditions and Ancient Interpretations*. Edited by T. Nicklas and M. Tilly. Berlin: de Gruyter, 2003.

Turner, C. H. "Chronology of the Bible." Pages 403–25 in *A Dictionary of the Bible*. Vol. 1. Edited by in J. Hastings. Edinburgh: T&T Clark, 1898.

Twelftree, G. H. "Exorcisms in the Fourth Gospel and the Synoptics." Pages 135–43 in *Jesus in Johannine Tradition*. Edited by R. T. Fortna and T. Thatcher. Louisville: Westminster John Knox, 2001.

Vanni, U. *La Struttura Letteraria dell'Apocalisse*. Rome: Herder, 1971.

Verheyden, J. "The Unity of Luke-Acts." *Hervormde Teologiese Studies* 55 (1999): 964–79.

Volkmann, R. *Die Rhetorik der Griechen und Römer in systematischer Übersicht*. 1885. Repr. Hildesheim: Georg Olms, 1963.

Wade, G. W. *The Book of the Prophet Isaiah*. London: Methuen, 1911.

Walaskay, P. W. *Acts*. Louisville: Westminster John Knox Press, 1998.

Wall, R. W. "Successors to 'the Twelve' according to Acts 12:1-17." *CBQ* 53 (1991): 628–43.

Watson, D. F. *Invention, Arrangement and Style: Rhetorical Criticism of Jude and 2 Peter*. Atlanta: Scholars Press, 1988.

Watson, W. G. E. *Traditional Techniques in Classical Hebrew Verse*. Sheffield: Sheffield Academic Press, 1994.

Wedderburn, A. J. M. "Some Recent Pauline Chronologies." *ET* 92 (1981): 103–8.

———. "Paul and Barnabas: The Anatomy and Chronology of a Parting of the Ways." Pages 291–310 in *Fair Play: Diversity and Conflicts in*

Early Christianity. Edited by Ismo Dunderberg, Christopher Tuckett and Kari Syreeni. Leiden: Brill, 2002.

Wendt, H. H. *Die Apostelgeschichte*. Göttingen: Vandenhoeck & Ruprecht, 1899.

Wenham, G. J. *Genesis 1–15*. Waco: Word Books, 1987.

Westcott, B. F. *The Gospel according to St. John*. Grand Rapids: Eerdmans, 1954.

Westermann, C. *Isaiah 40–66: A Commentary*. Translated by David M. G. Stalker: London: SCM, 1969 [German original 1966].

White, J. L. *The Form and Function of the Body of the Greek Letter: A Study of the Letter-Body in the Non-Literary Papyri and in Paul the Apostle*. Missoula: University of Montana Press, 1972.

———. *The Apostle of God: Paul and the Promise of Abraham*. Peabody: Hendrickson, 1999.

Wiens, D. L. *Stephen's Sermon and the Structure of Luke-Acts*. N. Richland Hills: BIBAL Press, 1995.

Wikenhauser, A. *Die Apostelgeschichte*. Regensburg: Verlag Friedrich Pustut, 1938.

Wilckens, U. *Der Brief an die Römer*. 3 vols. Zürich: Benziger Verlag, 1980; Neukirchen-Vluyn: Neukirchener Verlag, 1978–1982.

Wilcox, P., and D. Paton-Williams. "The Servant Songs in Second Isaiah." *JSOT* 42 (1988): 79–102.

Williams, C. H. *I am He: The Interpretation of "Anî Hû" in Jewish and Early Christian Literature*. Tübingen: Mohr Siebeck, 2000.

Willis, J. T. "Alternating (ABA'B') Parallelism in the Old Testament Psalms and Prophetic Literature." Pages 49–76 in *Directions in Biblical Hebrew Poetry*. Edited by E. R. Follis. Sheffield: JSOT Press, 1987.

Wilson, S. G. *The Gentiles and the Gentile Mission in Luke-Acts*. Cambridge: Cambridge University Press, 1973.

Winter, B. W. "Acts and Food Shortages." Pages 59–78 in *The Book of Acts in Its Graeco-Roman Setting*. Edited by D. W. J. Gill and C. Gempf. Grand Rapids: Eerdmans, 1994.

Witherington, B. *The Acts of the Apostles: A Socio-Rhetorical Commentary*. Grand Rapids: Eerdmans, 1998.

Wood, H. *The Histories of Herodotus: An Analysis of Formal Structure*. The Hague: Mouton & Co., 1972.

Yarbro Collins, A. *The Combat Myth in the Book of Revelation*. Missoula: Scholars Press, 1976.

Young, E. J. *The Book of Isaiah*. Vol. 3. Grand Rapids: Eerdmans, 1972.

Ziesler, J. *Paul's Letter to the Romans*. London: SCM Press, 1989.

Zwiep, A. W. *The Ascension of the Messiah in Lukan Christology*. Leiden: Brill, 1997.

Index of Biblical and Ancient Sources

Index of Modern Authors